Where to Watch Bi

East Midlands

D0476660

THE *WHERE TO WATCH BIRDS* SERIES

Where to watch birds in Africa

Where to watch birds in Bedfordshire, Berkshire, Buckinghamshire, Hertfordshire and Oxfordshire

Where to watch birds in Cumbria, Lancashire and Cheshire

Where to watch birds in Devon and Cornwall

Where to watch birds in Dorset, Hampshire and the Isle of Wight

Where to watch birds in East Anglia

Where to watch birds in the East Midlands

Where to watch birds in France

Where to watch birds in Ireland

Where to watch birds in Italy

Where to watch birds in Kent, Surrey and Sussex

Where to watch birds in Northeast England

Where to watch birds in Scotland

Where to watch birds in Somerset, Avon, Gloucestershire and Wiltshire

Where to watch birds in South America

Where to watch birds in Southern Spain

Where to watch birds in Wales

Where to watch birds in the West Midlands

Where to watch birds in Yorkshire and North Humberside

Where to watch birds in the

East Midlands

Lincolnshire, Northamptonshire, Derbyshire, Leicestershire and Nottinghamshire

Graham P Catley

Christopher Helm

A & C Black · London

Christopher Helm (Publishers) Ltd, a subsidiary of
A & C Black, 35 Bedford Row, London WC1R 4JH

0-7136-4460-5

A CIP catalogue record for this book
´is available from the British Library

Printed and bound by Biddles Limited, Guildford, Surrey
in Great Britain

CONTENTS

Contents

ACKNOWLEDGEMENTS

The production of this guide to the best birdwatching sites in the East Midlands region would not have been possible without the generous assistance of a number of local experts, who have provided information, maps, written sections of the text and checked through the various initial drafts to ensure that the information is as accurate as possible based on their local expertise. This publication is in many ways a tribute to the continuing cooperation within the birdwatching community.

In particular, I owe a debt of thanks to John Wright whose excellent sketches enliven the text and show some of the bird species characteristic of various sites within this guide. John is a very talented artist from Leicestershire whose work I am sure is set to receive national recognition in the near future.

For assistance with the sites mentioned I wish to thank in particular Bob Bullock, who single-handed provided all of the information on Northamptonshire, and Andrew Harrop and Andrew Mackay who similarly covered all the sites in Leicestershire. The following local experts have also provided texts and information on the localities listed: in Derbyshire, Roy Frost for the East Moors and Ogston Reservoir, Neil Topliss for Staunton Harold and Foremark Reservoirs, Philip Shooter for Padley Gorge, the Dales and Cromford Canal, Martin Roome for Willington Pits, and John Bradley for Carsington Reservoir; in Nottinghamshire, Bernie Ellis for Hoveringham, Mark Dennis for Colwick, Netherfield and Holme Pierrepont, Chris Mills for Attenborough, and Andy Sims and Dave Atkinson for Girton, Besthorpe and South Muskham. For further useful comments on Gibraltar Point and Rutland Water I thank Kevin Wilson and Tim Appleton, the respective wardens of these two first-class reserves.

In addition, I owe a great debt to David Hursthouse, who not only provided numerous contacts and introductions but also provided invaluable assistance with the accounts on the Upper Derwent, Derbyshire, and the Sherwood Forest Region, Lound and the Idle Valley, all within Nottinghamshire.

I also extend thanks to the large number of birders in whose company I have spent the past 27 years enjoying watching birds in Lincolnshire and elsewhere. It is hoped that this guide will assist many people to gain similar enjoyment form the birds of the East Midlands in the coming years.

And finally, I have to thank my wife Julia for her never-ending patience with my obsessive behaviour and for giving me a good kick/pep talk when the book was not going well.

INTRODUCTION

The five counties which comprise the East Midlands region covered by this guide provide some excellent and varied habitats, which in turn attract a wide range of bird species. The diverse range of habitats encompasses such different areas as the major estuaries of the Humber and Wash, with their teeming populations of waders and wildfowl, the major rivers of the Trent, Nene, Welland and Witham with their extensive sand and gravel workings and flooded pits, to the historic ancient woodland and its modern coniferous counterpart in Sherwood Forest, to old parkland like that at Bradgate and Fawsley, and to the limestone dales and the wild gritstone moorlands of Derbyshire. Inland reservoirs include Britain's largest man-made lake at Rutland Water, and it and other such bodies of water act as magnets for birds and birdwatchers alike. Small areas of lowland heath and ancient woodland still survive, mainly as reserves or as precarious remnants of previously more extensive areas. For the most part, however, the area is dominated by arable farmland, with more pastoral areas to the west of the region. Most of the land lies at low altitudes only rising to any notable height in north Derbyshire. Large population centres occur inland especially around Derby, Nottingham, Leicester and Northampton, while Lincolnshire remains sparsely populated.

The region is well noted for migration, with a vast array and huge numbers of migratory birds passing through the area every year. The 40 miles (64 km) of Lincolnshire coast are a prime site for watching coastal migration and even seabirds, in addition to which there are major cross-country migration corridors which follow the course of the Rivers Trent, Welland and Nene and east–west along the Humber estuary. It is these movements which add to the variety of birds found at inland reservoirs, gravel pits and other suitable migration spots, and which in turn attract birdwatchers in search of terns, waders, gulls and a variety of passerine migrants.

Some of the areas dealt with in this guide are fairly well known, while others are poorly watched and recorded and offer potential for new discoveries. Above all else, however, it is hoped that this guide will help more people to appreciate the birds of the region and the excellent reserves and sites which exist, which will in turn help to ensure the survival of these localities and maybe even the development of new ones, ensuring the future of the birds which entrance us all. All birdwatchers are encouraged to follow the Country Code and always put the welfare of birds first.

HOW TO USE THIS BOOK

THE REGION

This book covers the five counties of Derbyshire, Leicestershire, Lincolnshire, Northamptonshire and Nottinghamshire, with the sites mentioned being for the most part split into county sections. Some sites, however, obviously span county boundaries, and where this occurs, it is made clear in the individual accounts.

Each locality within the book has a major heading, the area or site itself, in some cases further split down into smaller units, with a reference number which relates to the species index at the back of the book. The relevant 1:50,000 Ordnance Survey map sheet reference number is also given alongside the name of the main site. Localities are then discussed under the headings habitat, species, timing and calendar. For each county there are a number of major locations which attempt to cover in total a good cross-section of the species and habitats to be found within the county. Finally, a short list of additional sites offers brief details, under the same headings, related to what are, in the most part, less extensive sites.

Habitat

This section gives a general idea of the physical make up of the locality including, where relevant, geology, geography, vegetation, size, status, ownership and whether there is open access or a permit is needed. It is intended to give readers a picture in words of the site and to enable them to ascertain what common species will be found, in connection with the habitat, in addition to those mentioned in the next section.

It is important to bear in mind that some localities, particularly working gravel-pit complexes, are undergoing continual alteration, which may make profound changes to physical features described within the book, even in a relatively short period of time. The details given were, however, correct at the time of writing in 1995.

Species

This section does not attempt to include every species of bird which occurs or has occurred at each locality. It is assumed that certain very widespread and common species such as Blackbird, Robin, Wren, Dunnock, Woodpigeon, Collared Dove, Rook, Magpie and the like will occur in most of the non-urban areas throughout the region. Some of these species may, however, be mentioned in connection with large coastal arrivals of wintering birds during October and November, Blackbird, for example, or with species such as Swallow and Sand Martin or even Woodpigeon where spectacular numbers gather at roost sites.

The species included for each locality therefore fall into two categories: those where a site has a good selection of say deciduous or coniferous woodland species, which can all be seen quite easily, and the less widespread more specialist and scarcer species. The commonest species should be encountered, given that any constraints on the time of year and weather are applicable, on a routine walk around the locality. Some species may be restricted to one area of a described site, however, so a thorough exploration of the site may be needed to find all the relevant species, and of course there are always days when even the most obvious species will, for some reason, remain uncooperative! Such details are described in the species section, which should be consulted in conjunction with the list of species in the calendar section.

The species section progresses through the year from the winter period to autumn detailing which species occur at which season and also showing the particular type of weather or conditions of the local habitat which may lead to the arrival of unusual or infrequently recorded species. In general, the coastal localities are best known for the appearance of migrating birds, whether on passage, on visible migration, as displaced vagrants or as scarce wintering species. The scarce migrants are limited in their occurrence by the prevailing weather conditions, as is the occurrence of seabirds, and details of the best weather conditions are included to maximise the chances of connecting with the arrival or passage of these birds. Similarly, passage migrants are mentioned for inland localities, where they will be scarce and again affected by the prevailing weather, as their occurrence is a source of attraction for birdwatchers, especially at inland gravel pits and reservoirs.

There seems to be an ever-growing fascination with rare birds and their patterns of occurrence and thus records of rarities at the localities included have been mentioned in passing, although it should be appreciated that such birds may only have occurred on a few occasions or even just once. These species should not be expected on a routine visit, they are the rewards for frequent visits over several years, but they do demonstrate the potential of the locality for attracting rarer species.

The vast majority of the species names used in this guide are those to be found in all the popular field guides. For a number of years there has, however, been a long running debate over standardisation of English bird names which has led to a great deal of debate and controversy. Most journals still use the English names, in common usage, but there are a few species for which slight alterations to the general field guide English name have become generally accepted. These mostly refer to a species where an adjective is used to qualify a family name, which could, in practice, refer to one of several species, for example Wheatear, where there are numerous species. The bird which occurs commonly in Britain is thus now known as Northern Wheatear. The other such name change used in this book is *Common* Buzzard. One other species or subspecies is also affected, as the 'Herring' Gulls with yellow legs, which are becoming more frequent visitors to this country and to sites within the region, are now recognised as being much more closely related to the Lesser Black-backed Gull than to the Herring Gull and thus they are treated here under the proposed new name of Yellow-legged Gull.

Timing

Obviously some birdwatching sites are better for a variety of species, or for a specific range of species, at different times of year and at different times of the day or during specific weather conditions. Where this applies to a certain locality this is mentioned in this section. For example, to see or hear crepuscular species such as owls, Nightjars and singing Grasshopper Warbler will entail an evening or very early morning visit. In general, spring and summer birding is at its best in the early mornings when birds are at their most active and most likely to be singing. In other cases a locality may have certain disadvantages, heavy pressure from dog walkers, its use as bombing range!, or may be closed at certain times, and thus these points are mentioned to help people avoid a wasted journey. If little information is included here, then the locality is worthy of a visit at any time of year.

Access

For all localities the relevant Ordnance Survey 1:50,000 map sheet reference number is given in the heading. It is recommended that people visiting the localities included in this book should use the OS maps in conjunction with the details in the access section and the relevant maps. As some localities are approached via a series of unclassified minor roads, the OS maps will be particularly useful. Where such things as car parks may not be marked on the OS map, or may not have a title/name on the map, then the appropriate six-figure grid reference is given next to the car park details in this section. Details on how to read grid reference figures are given in the key to each OS sheet.

For all localities listed, access is described from the nearest large town, village or major classified road. Distances are given in miles, with the equivalent in kilometres in parentheses, or where the distances are less than a mile in yards and metres.

Larger scale maps of some reserves, woodlands, country parks etc. are sometimes displayed in car parks, advisory literature and visitor centres.

Details of permits, where necessary, opening times of reserves, hides and marked trails are given where the information was available. Details are correct as of 1995, but information for future years should be checked against local information sources.

Calendar

This is a fairly self explanatory section, which details the species to be expected at certain times of year. The list is of course qualified, as explained in the species section, with regard to weather-dependent species and passage migrants. Even for 'resident' species, however, it should be noted that the birds concerned may be found in different areas of a larger locality at differing times of the year such as when breeding and in winter.

In general, spring migration starts in mid March, usually earlier further south and inland, peaking in volume in late April to early May and then tailing off into early June when most breeding birds will be engaged in nesting activities. The later spring, late May to mid June is often the best time for the appearance of rarer birds. By late July, many adult waders are already returning south from their northern breeding grounds. Autumn migration then builds to a peak in late August as most of our summer visitors slip away southwards. September and October can produce spectacular coastal migration in the right weather conditions, but throughout there will be migration taking place amongst waders, hirundines, finches, Skylarks, pipits and buntings. Even inland waders, terns and such regular migrants as Starlings, thrushes, Skylarks, Meadow Pipits and hirundines will be in good numbers. Most migration is completed by mid November when winter visitors will have settled into their chosen wintering areas, but gales in the North Sea or even on the west coast, and hard weather on the continent, may still lead to movements of seabirds, arrivals of wildfowl and even late arrivals of flocks of Fieldfares and, in some years, Waxwings.

Key to the Maps

	Open water
	A and B roads
	Motorways
	Other minor roads
	Rivers/canals
	Small streams
	Tracks
	Footpaths
	Railway lines
	Embankments/dams
	Built-up areas
	Hides
	Car parks
	Deciduous woodland and scrub
	Coniferous woodland
	Coniferous woodland with clear fells
	Mixed woodland
	Rough grassland
	Marsh
	Parkland
	Sand and mud flats
	Moorland
	Reedbeds

LINCOLNSHIRE

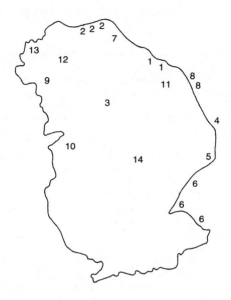

1 THE NORTHEAST LINCOLNSHIRE COAST OS Map 113

CLEETHORPES–HUMBERSTON FITTIES

Habitat

As busy seaside resorts, Cleethorpes and Humberston would appear to have little to offer the birdwatcher, but a combination of large, important intertidal mud flats, some attractive salt-marsh and easily worked areas of migrant cover make it worthy of exploration, especially during migration periods and in the winter months. To the north of the pier low tide reveals large areas of sandy shore, with extensive areas of rock and beds of cockles attractive to waders and gulls alike. Further south, the mud flats are more open and widen into a broad sandy expanse south of the leisure centre. Salt-marsh is found around the Buck Beck outfall, which itself provides a bathing area for gulls and waders roosting there during high tides. A sewage outfall off Buck Beck, known as the A frame, due to its obvious construction, is a magnet for feeding gulls, while the sewage works just inland of the seawall has an interesting selection of young trees and bushes which can attract migrants. The same can be said of the ornamental plantings around the boating lake, which also attract a wealth of gulls, the tame wildfowl collection sometimes bringing in wild relatives in the winter.

Humberston Fitties is mainly occupied by extensive caravan sites, but many of the semi-permanent chalets have sycamores and sallows in the gardens, and a belt of young pines along the sea defences also offers some cover for migrants.

Species

One of the main attractions of this site is the exceptional views which it offers of birds which in other localities are usually wild and unapproachable. Owing to the regular presence of large numbers of people walking along the beach and seafront, the waders and gulls feeding on the rich intertidal mud flats become very tame. In addition to this there is an easily viewed high-tide roost, off Buck Beck outfall, which means that close study of most birds is possible with a minimum of effort. The high-tide wader roost is worthy of attention throughout the year, with the exception of high summer (late June to mid July). The beach at Cleethorpes is at its best in the winter when it is an excellent spot for close range study of the more regular gulls, making the finding of rarer species easier.

Large flocks of Knot, Bar-tailed Godwit, Dunlin, Sanderling, Ringed Plover and Turnstone, with lesser numbers of Grey Plover and Curlew, feed north of Cleethorpes Leisure Centre towards Grimsby Docks, allowing detailed study as they feed close to the seawalls. One or two Purple Sandpipers are also regular on the shore to the north of Cleethorpes, opposite Fuller Street railway bridge. The most numerous gulls are Common and Black-headed, in that order, with variable numbers of Herring and Great Black-backed Gulls. The larger gulls often gather on sand bars farther offshore at low tide, and in the late evening can be seen on the beach at Buck Beck outfall. Both Glaucous and Mediterranean

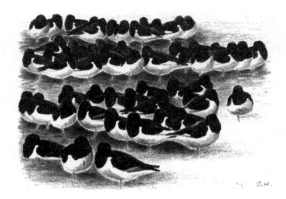

Oystercatchers

Gulls are regularly found amongst the commoner species, but there may be up to 10,000 of both Black-headed and Common Gulls and 500 Herrings to sort through.

En route to the Buck Beck outfall it is worth a quick look at the boating lake where an ornamental wildfowl collection includes such species as Lesser White-fronted Goose, Blue-winged Teal and Red-crested Pochard! Occasionally wild birds join them, however, and such species as Long-tailed Duck and Eider have appeared. The trees and shrubs around the lake and the adjacent pumping station may hold a few migrants in spring and autumn including Willow Warbler, Chiffchaff, Lesser Whitethroat, Spotted or even Pied Flycatcher, and have in the past produced Yellow-browed and Icterine Warblers and Serin. On winter afternoons, as high tide approaches, the waders and gulls feeding further up the estuary gather to bathe in the freshwater creek and roost on the sand bar at Buck Beck outfall. A narrow strip of salt-marsh here is badly disturbed by dog walkers but a few Brent Geese have recently taken to feeding there and a Little Egret spent a few days on the pools in October 1993.

In winter the wader roost is dominated by Knot (up to 10,000), Oystercatcher (2,000), Bar-tailed Godwit (1,000), and Dunlin (5,000), but also with a reasonable flock of Ringed Plover (2–300), Sanderling (400) and Turnstone (3–400). Redshank are quite common, feeding in the creeks, and a single Spotted Redshank wintered at this site for over ten years. Huge numbers of Lapwing (3,000), and Golden Plover (2,000) feed and rest in the area from November to January, often flighting out onto the beach to bathe. A similar species composition occurs in spring and autumn but May counts include higher totals of Ringed Plover, up to 700, and Sanderling, with 1,075 of the latter being counted on 31 May 1992. During the autumn (July–September) a few Curlew Sandpiper and Little Stints can usually be found amongst the other waders, and small numbers of terns, which fish in the mouth of the estuary, come in to roost at high tide.

Common, Arctic and Sandwich Terns all occur and the gathering of gulls has twice played host to stunning Sabine's Gulls. Kingfishers are frequent winter visitors to the Beck, and Rock Pipits to the saltings, where flocks of Meadow Pipits and Skylarks also feed along with a flock of Twite. Small parties of Snow Buntings make irregular appearances,

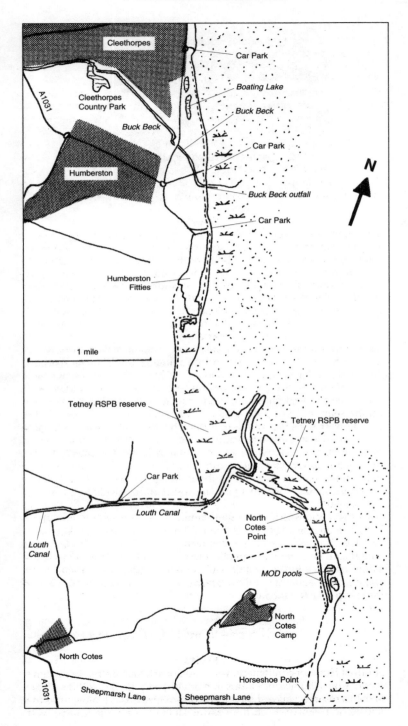

and Stonechats, mainly passage birds between September and November and in March, may winter.

The narrow belt of Scots pines along the edge of the Fitties holiday camp is badly disturbed, but even so, its coastal location, immediately across the Humber from Spurn Point, means it does receive a few passage migrants and it is always worthy of a look in the early mornings during spring and autumn. The same can be said of the gardens of the chalets in the caravan park where stunted sycamores and shrubs offer some cover. Black Redstarts, Northern Wheatears and Long-eared Owls are almost annual between March and April, and October and November, and the location has also had three Parrot Crossbills, Arctic Warbler, Firecrest and two Richard's Pipits. During the autumn a few Arctic Skuas may be seen offshore harassing the feeding terns and occasionally a few Gannets and odd seabirds may pass up the Humber.

Timing

The period two hours before and around high tide is the best time to visit the wader roost; a late afternoon or evening tide is best in the autumn when the sun will be behind the observation point. Early morning can produce a few migrants, which may be disturbed later in the day. Midsummer, when the site is inundated with holidaymakers, is best avoided. Sunday markets in midwinter may make parking difficult along Cleethorpes seafront but Saturdays are less disturbed.

Access

Cleethorpes foreshore is easily viewed from the seafront car parks (TA 303 098 to 319 071) which run north and south from the pier and railway station, both signposted in the town. The railway, connected to the whole of the country through services to Doncaster and Newark, offers convenient access via public transport, the station being situated right on the seafront. The boating lake, A frame and foreshore are reached by following the seafront road south to the Leisure Centre and then the minor road signposted to Humberston Fitties. There are several car parks along this stretch of road, from where it is a short walk through the boating lake area to the foreshore. Continue on this minor road for half a mile (0.8 km) to a roundabout and continue straight ahead for Humberston Fitties where a car park is situated adjacent to the seawall (TA 332 061).

Access to the Fitties is along the dune ridge to the south through the belt of small pines to the yacht club. There is open access to the beach and foreshore but frequent signs warn of the dangers of tidal creeks which can fill remarkably quickly on a rising tide and have led to occasional fatalities in the past. If walking out towards the A frame or the water's edge it is best to follow a falling tide and be constantly aware of the dangers of the location.

TETNEY–NORTH COTES

Habitat

South of Humberston Fitties a wide area of salt-marsh stretches south to North Cotes Point and forms the major part of the RSPB's Tetney Marshes reserve. Criss-crossed with tidal creeks, this is a dangerous area and is best viewed from the seawall. Inland, arable fields are worth checking in spring for passage waders including Dotterel, and in winter for hunting raptors. The sea-bank path at Tetney follows the outside edge of a large reclaimed area of former salt-marsh, which has now been mostly turned over to arable farmland, with the grassy banks still being grazed by cattle. A series of large hawthorn bushes and a hawthorn hedge form the principal migrant habitat at North Cotes, where there are also two large brackish pools, the MOD pools, which can prove useful in spring and summer but often dry out in hot summers before autumn passage commences. The disused airfield inland of North Cotes Point was, until recently, all pasture but recent work has converted an increasing amount to unattractive arable.

Species

The walk around the new reclamation embankments and on the foreshore adjacent to the old RAF camp, offers views over a large area of salt-marsh, tidal creeks, the new reclamation fields and the open shoreline and mud flats. In the winter months, Redshanks and Grey Plovers feed in the creeks and borrow pits with a few Dunlin. Out on the mud flats large flocks of Oystercatcher, Grey and Golden Plover, Lapwing, Knot, Dunlin and Bar-tailed Godwit feed at low tide with Shelduck and a flock of Brent Geese. The latter may also be found feeding on inland winter wheat fields but regularly return to the shore to rest and bathe. A few Lapland Buntings are usually to be found around the sea banks, with occasional flocks of Snow Buntings and more regular parties of Linnet and Twite. Rock Pipits are common in the creeks and salt-marsh. Raptors include 2–3 regular Merlins, Hen Harrier and the increasingly reliable Peregrine. Marsh Harriers are frequent on migration and other large raptors are occasionally seen flying over, sometimes having previously flown south at Spurn Point. Red Kite, Honey Buzzard, Montagu's Harrier, Osprey, Common and Rough-legged Buzzards have all been noted as has Common Crane.

The main summer interest is provided by the breeding colony of Little Terns, which nest on a stony part of the shore north of the MOD pools. Up to 80 pairs have nested, but as with the species' fortune everywhere, numbers and breeding success vary from year to year as the species suffers nesting losses from high tides and predation by foxes, Kestrels and Merlins. Yellow Wagtails breed around the grass banks of the reclamation, which also attract migrants such as Northern Wheatear and Whinchat in spring and autumn. The MOD pools dry out with regularity in late spring but are flooded again by late summer spring tides. Being shallow they attract passage waders such as Greenshank, Green and odd Wood Sandpipers and over the years have also had a number of visits from Little Egrets, Spoonbill, a Black-winged Stilt and a roosting Greater Sand Plover. Passage periods bring good numbers of Golden Plover, Ringed Plover, Dunlin, Knot, Turnstone and Sanderling to the foreshore where they are best observed from the bank by Horseshoe Point car park. Regular searching produces records of Curlew Sandpiper, Little Stint and Black-tailed Godwit and rarities have included Broad-billed Sandpiper. The salt-marsh and creeks at Tetney hold good numbers of Whimbrel in April, May, July and August, and the same creek held a unique combination of Pacific and American Golden Plover in July 1986.

This is not a good spot for seawatching as birds mostly pass well offshore, cutting across the estuary mouth to Spurn, but there is usually a good resting flock of Sandwich and Common Terns on the beach during late July and August (may number 200+ of each species). The highest numbers of terns roost during evening spring tides in this period.

Available habitat for passage migrants is strictly limited, with just a few hawthorn bushes on the sea embankment and one hawthorn hedge, but the usual range of common and scarce east coast species appear infrequently. There are, however, much better sites for looking for these species farther south along the coast. Even so, recent records of Marsh, Dusky, Yellow-browed, Dartford, Subalpine and Arctic Warblers, Rustic Bunting and several Richard's Pipits show the area still has potential. It is also worth noting that in the late 1800s and early part of this century Greenish and Radde's Warbler and Red-flanked Bluetail were added to the British list at this locality, and a Lanceolated Warbler was shot!

Timing

A good area to visit at any time of year. Timing visits to coincide with high spring tides in the early morning or late evening produces the best viewing conditions for waders and terns. As with any east coast locality the appearance of passage migrants depends on the prevailing weather conditions, with easterly winds needed to produce falls of irregular species.

Access

It is possible to walk along the grass-covered seawall from Humberston Fitties as far as the Tetney reserve, a walk of about 2 miles (3.2 km), checking the scattered hawthorn bushes *en route*, the salt-marsh to the east and the fields on the inland side for roosting waders at high tide and in spring for passage Dotterel.

The main entrance to the RSPB reserve at Tetney is from the A1031 at Tetney village or North Cotes, following the minor road to Tetney Lock where another minor road runs east down the side of the Louth Canal. About 400 yds/m farther on the road turns sharp left. There is limited parking here on the roadside (TA 345 025), from where a path heads northeast along the bank of the canal for 1.25 miles (2 km) out to the seasonal warden's caravan. It is then possible to take a circular walk around the new reclamation embankments, viewing the salt-marsh and creeks to the north, the reclaimed fields, the borrow pits on the southern side, and paying attention to birds feeding on the banks themselves. At the northeastern extremity of the new reclamation a wooden gate gives access to the old sea bank, which runs alongside the old airfield fence, right down to Horseshoe Point. From this path a sandy track leads off east across the salt-marsh, between the two larger MOD pools, to the shore. Breeding Little Terns can be seen from the point where this track passes through the dunes.

To approach from the opposite end of this section leave the A1031 just north of Marshchapel and east of North Cotes and turn east down Sheepmarsh Lane, the minor road signposted to Horseshoe Point. A further 2.5 miles (3 km) down the road it reaches the seawall where there is a car park (TA 382 018). To reach North Cotes Point and Tetney, simply walk north along the sea embankment or the beach.

Calendar

Resident: Little Grebe, Sparrowhawk, Barn Owl, Meadow Pipit, Reed Bunting.

December–February: Red-throated Diver, Cormorant, Brent Goose, Shelduck, Wigeon, Scaup, Eider, Common Scoter, Red-breasted Merganser, Hen Harrier, Merlin, Peregrine, Ringed Plover, Golden Plover, Grey Plover, Lapwing, Knot, Sanderling, Purple Sandpiper (scarce), Dunlin, Ruff, Jack Snipe, Snipe, Bar-tailed Godwit, Curlew, Redshank, Turnstone, Mediterranean Gull, Glaucous Gull, Short-eared Owl, Kingfisher, Rock Pipit, Stonechat, Twite, Lapland Bunting, Snow Bunting.

March–June: Red-throated Diver, Common Scoter, Marsh Harrier, Hen Harrier, Osprey (passage), Merlin, Hobby, Peregrine, Ringed Plover, Dotterel (scarce April–May), Grey Plover, Knot, Sanderling, Dunlin, Ruff, Jack Snipe, Bar-tailed Godwit, Whimbrel, Curlew, Redshank, Greenshank, Green Sandpiper, Common Sandpiper, Turnstone, Little Gull, Glaucous Gull, Sandwich Tern, Common Tern, Arctic Tern, Little Tern, Turtle Dove, Cuckoo, Short-eared Owl, Yellow Wagtail, Black Redstart, Redstart, Whinchat, Stonechat, Northern Wheatear, Ring Ouzel, Grasshopper Warbler, Reed Warbler, Sedge Warbler, Firecrest.

July–November: Red-throated Diver, Brent Goose, Eider, Common Scoter, Velvet Scoter, Red-breasted Merganser, Marsh Harrier, Hen Harrier, Merlin, Hobby, Golden Plover, Knot, Sanderling, Ruff, Black-tailed Godwit, Green Sandpiper, Wood Sandpiper, Arctic Skua, Great Skua, Mediterranean Gull, Little Gull, Sandwich Tern, Common Tern, Arctic Tern, Little Tern, Long-eared Owl, Short-eared Owl, Kingfisher, Wryneck (scarce), Rock Pipit, Black Redstart, Redstart, Whinchat, Stonechat, Northern Wheatear, Ring Ouzel, Icterine, Barred and Yellow-browed Warblers (all scarce), Firecrest, Pied Flycatcher, Red-breasted Flycatcher (scarce) Red-backed Shrike, Great Grey Shrike, Twite, Lapland Bunting, Snow Bunting.

2 THE INNER HUMBER   OS Maps 112 and 113

Habitat

There is a pronounced change in character in the Humber from the largely sandy and gentle shelving open mud flats of the outer estuary, southeast of Grimsby, and the less extensive but richer silt laden intertidal shoreline of the upper reaches west of Skitter Ness. Areas of saltings are restricted in width but some interesting short grass still exists in places where cattle are present to graze the sward. The sea defences are a mixture of natural, grass-covered, clay banks and man-made stone and tar constructions, with extensive tracks along the bank tops, offering the best viewpoints for birding in several localities. The areas of intertidal mud are in a constant state of flux within a dynamic estuary where the currents frequently change, moving vast amounts of silt and materials in short periods of time and quickly changing the local geography. The richest feeding areas for waders and wildfowl are found where the tides are depositing the rich silt brought down by the Rivers Trent and Ouse from their confluence at Alkborough. As the nature of estuary changes upriver from Grimsby so does the variety of birds which predominate, and to see the maximum number of species it is necessary to visit one of the outer estuary sites in addition to the Inner Humber.

Differences in substrate even on a very localised level have effects on the bird communities which make use of them, with more stony inter-tidal areas and extensive beds of seaweed attracting different species to the open, soft, silt areas, which again differ from the drier upper shore-line mud and tidal creeks.

GOXHILL HAVEN–EAST HALTON SKITTER

Habitat

From East Halton Skitter to Skitter Ness, a formerly grazed area of fore-shore has been allowed to revert to rough grassland. Being above the reach of even the highest tides it is largely dry, with some wet borrow pits against the sea defence banks, with ribbons of *Phragmites*. The areas adjacent to East Halton Skitter are the wettest and are covered in sea aster, which in the autumn attracts large numbers of butterflies and produces a good crop of seeds, in turn attracting feeding flocks of finch-es and buntings in the later autumn and winter months. On the inland side of the seawall is a series of old clay extraction workings with some open water and reedbeds. Those at Skitter Ness are managed as a reserve by the Lincolnshire Trust (LTNC), with a grass meadow sur-rounding the pits and an extensive area of hawthorn scrub.

Species

Wintering Short-eared Owls are a speciality of this section, with up to eight birds in good winters but more usually 1–4 hunting the rough grass foreshore. Flocks of Reed Buntings, Yellowhammers, Chaffinches and Tree Sparrows forage on the foreshore and roost in the tall hawthorn hedgerows. Owing to the essentially brackish nature of the foreshore here, the area in some years attracts a few Lapland and Snow Buntings with irregular Twite and the local Skylarks. Rock Pipits are a common sight feeding on the rocky shoreline and amongst the flooded sea aster. They reach peak numbers in late October and early November when up to 40 birds may be present but through the winter up to ten are more usual. Kestrels, Sparrowhawks and the odd Merlin also hunt the area. Waders on the foreshore include Dunlin, Redshank, odd Grey Plover, Turnstone, sometimes a flock of Knot and a few Ringed Plover. The main flock of wintering Curlew, about 200, is more usually to be found on the inland fields along with a large flock of Golden Plover (up to 2,000) and Lapwing. A walk across the rough fore-shore may well flush a few Snipe and the odd Jack Snipe, which are also regular at the Dawson City reserve. The close-grazed grues at the Goxhill end of the section provide winter feeding for a flock of Wigeon and a roost site for Curlew and other waders at high tide.

Offshore at Goxhill Skitter, a huge sandbank appears at low tide and attracts vast numbers of feeding Common (most numerous) and Black-headed Gulls, with lesser numbers of Great Black-backed Gulls. Spring and summer brings a large breeding population of Meadow Pipits and attendant Cuckoos, which also prey on the Reed Warblers nesting in the reedbeds of the borrow pits and adjacent claypits. Short-eared Owls sometimes linger well into May and may be seen displaying, whilst Marsh Harriers have become increasingly regular passage birds from

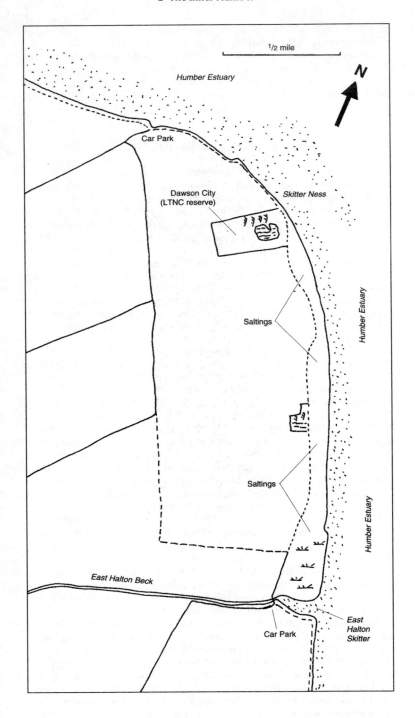

mid April through May. A few pairs of Redshank still breed on the fore-shore and odd pairs of Lapwing and Oystercatcher on the inland fields, with flocks of non-breeding Curlew present throughout the summer increasing during June with arrivals of continental birds. Displaying Shoveler and Teal are regular in April and Dawson City produced a Nearctic Green-winged Teal (standing next to a feeding Spoonbill) one April day. Passage flocks of northern small dark Ringed Plovers, Grey Plovers, breeding plumaged Dunlin, Sanderling and Turnstone all occur along the shore from April to early June.

During the autumn the mud exposed on the edges of the borrow pits attracts Green Sandpipers, Greenshank and irregular Spotted Redshank, Ruffs, Curlew Sandpiper and Little Stints. In late July and August a notable total of juvenile Kestrels are attracted to feast on the myriad small tortoiseshell butterflies which adorn the flowering sea aster. Hirundines roost in the reedbeds and the usual mix of Dunlin, Ringed Plover, Redshank, Curlew and Bar-tailed Godwit is found on the shore.

Access

East Halton Skitter lies 6 miles (10 km) northeast of Immingham. Minor roads from South Killingholme and Barrow-on-Humber lead to East Halton village. In the centre of the village the main road makes a right angle turn near the Black Bull public house and a post office. Take the minor road to the east past a telephone box, which then turns sharp left; after 4–500 yds/m it turns right then left again before going over an old railway bridge and then runs straight for 1.5 miles (2.4 km) before again bending sharp right and coming to an end half a mile (0.8 km) farther on. (TA 145 229). Park here and walk along the grass seawall which runs north, with the 'grues', a local name for the tidal grasslands, on your right, and watch for Short-eared Owls, pipits, finches and buntings on the salt-marsh.

The village of Goxhill, situated 5 miles (8 km) east of Barton-on-Humber, is approached via minor roads from Barrow-on-Humber. Upon entering the village follow signs to North End and continue north on a minor road to the Haven a further 2 miles (3.2 km) to the north. (TA 119 253). Park on the roadsides and walk right along the stone seawall for 1 mile (1.6 km) to view the Lincolnshire Trust reserve of Dawson City on the right. Access is by permit only but most of the reserve can be seen from the seawall. The grass sea defence bank continues through to East Halton Skitter, a further 2 miles (3.2 km), with salt-marsh to the left, grass and arable fields, a small oak copse and borrow pits to the right.

GOXHILL HAVEN–NEW HOLLAND

Habitat

The seawall between Goxhill Haven and New Holland pier is a barren stone construction, and the intertidal zone is quite restricted on all but spring tides, but the presence of a grain and animal feed import and export terminal at New Holland Pier inadvertently, through spillage, provides an important winter feeding resource for large flocks of wild-fowl. A flooded claypit just west of the pier, owned by the NRA, is man-aged by the Lincolnshire Trust (LTNC). During the late summer the water level often falls and produces a series of muddy islands attractive to waders and wildfowl.

2 The Inner Humber

Species

The winter period offers some exceptional birding along this section of the Humber, with the diving-duck flock being of most interest. Wildfowl gather to feed on the grain and animal feeds spilt from the old pier (during shipping operations), which washes down river towards Goxhill Haven.

A herd of Mute Swans, up to 150 birds, with the odd Whooper, feed near the pier and resort to Fairfield's Pit during rough weather and at high tide. The diving-duck flock increases in numbers from November, generally reaching a peak in January or February, depending on the severity of the weather. Pochard predominate, with recent counts of over 2,000, followed by Tufted Duck (500–1,000), Goldeneye (up to 450) and Scaup, which vary from about ten to over 260 in good influx years. November usually produces a flock of Common Scoter (50–250), with a few Velvet Scoter and odd Long-tailed Duck and Eider, but all of these species depart by the end of December. The fields immediately inland hold vast flocks of Golden Plover (up to 4,000) and Lapwing (2–4,000), with roosting waders at high tide, and when the fields are flooded, including Turnstone, Redshank, Dunlin and Ringed Plover. The Turnstone flock has increased to over 100 birds, and another interesting feature here is the flock of over 70 Carrion Crows which feed on the foreshore at low tide. A Merlin is regular, along with the ubiquitous Sparrowhawks, and there are odd sighting of Hen Harrier and Peregrine. A large flock of 4–600 Collared Doves frequents the grain terminal along with the House Sparrows and flocks of Greenfinches. Flocks of Skylark are a feature of frosty weather, feeding on the winter cereal fields and, especially in November, small flocks of Snow Buntings may be found along the seawall. Fairfield's Pit reserve has a good number of Little Grebes, up to 30, with a variety of other duck present in the winter.

Spring and summer offer fewer rewards. Little Grebes and Ruddy Ducks breed on the two claypits, with Reed, Sedge and Grasshopper Warblers around Fairfield's Pit, where the non-breeding Mute Swan herd also summers and a pair of Oystercatcher usually attempt to breed. It is worth looking out for summer-plumaged Scandinavian Rock Pipits on the stony shore during March and early April. From July, if the water level falls in Fairfield's Pit, there may be passage waders, Ruff, Greenshank, Common Sandpiper, Black-tailed Godwit and odd Little Stint and Curlew Sandpiper, while on the fields and shore to the east the flock of Golden Plovers increases to about 1,000 by late August, with a similar number of Lapwing, up to 100 Redshank, 80 Turnstone, 200 Dunlin, Ringed Plovers and, in good arrival years, up to 30 Curlew Sandpipers. Sand Martins gather in force (1–4,000) to feed over the fields.

Access

For New Holland, leave the A1077 Barton to Immingham road, at Barrow-upon-Humber, take the B1206 to New Holland. Turn left at the roundabout at the village outskirts and follow the new by-pass to a railway crossing. Immediately over the crossing turn left down a track between the railway and a warehouse, round a sharp right bend with a flooded claypit to the left, and park at the end of the track (TA 080 244). To view the duck flock in the winter walk back along the track to the railway crossing and then turn left then right between a series of ware-

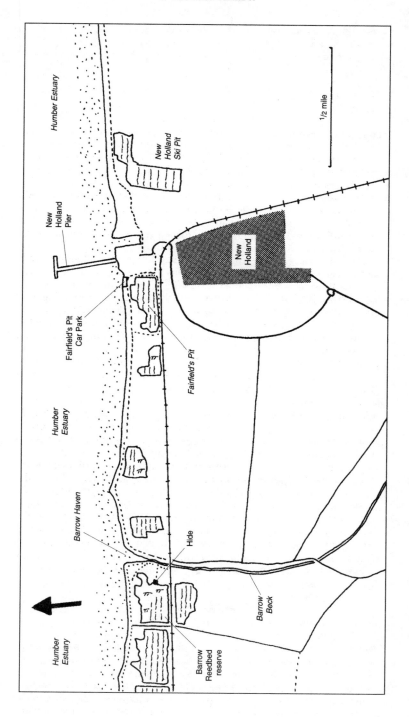

houses with a dock to the left. After about 200 yds/m rejoin the sea-bank footpath, signed on the right, and walk around an old scrap yard on the left to the stone sea defences from where the Humber becomes visible.

BARROW HAVEN–BARTON CLAYPITS

Habitat

Inland from the estuary banks, between Barrow Haven and Chowder Ness, Barton-on-Humber, are a series of abandoned clay-extraction pits. All these were dug in the heyday of the local brick and tile industry when there were several yards using the local clay. Most have long since disappeared but two traditional working clay-tile yards still exist at Barton, and small areas are still being excavated and forming new pits with extensive early colonisation by greater reedmace. The pits, which lie mostly between the Humber bank and the Cleethorpes–Barton railway line, form a complex of deep water areas interspersed with shallower sections, extensive reedbeds and surrounding areas of mainly hawthorn and blackthorn scrub with invading willow and sallows in some of the drier reedbeds. Many of the pits are used for fishing and some for watersports but a significant proportion are nature reserves owned by the Lincolnshire Trust (LTNC), which has a visitor centre at Far Ings where there is a series of four hides overlooking open water, reedbeds, scrub and a small scrape. The intertidal zone here is a rich mixture of silt and stony sections, which holds a good feeding population of waders.

Species

The wealth of birdlife in this complex of habitats can be gauged from attainable day totals of 90+ species in May and 70–80 during the autumn. The foreshore has in recent years become more important for feeding waders and, except in June, there are good numbers of several species to be seen at low tide. Dunlin are the most numerous throughout, with a peak of 2,000 in midwinter, but significant numbers of Redshank (150) winter, Ringed Plover (up to 100) some winters and on passage in May, Turnstone (a peak of 140 winter and 120 on spring passage), and a good variety of Grey Plover, Lapwing, Curlew, Greenshank and Bar-tailed Godwit also occur, with Curlew Sandpiper and Little Stints occasional in May and July–October.

The flooded claypits attract wildfowl, with recent peaks of 1,500 Pochard, 400 Tufted Duck and as many as 50 Scaup, mostly in rough weather and in February, after the close of the shooting season. In severe winters, Smew, Goosander and odd Slavonian, Black-necked or Red-necked Grebes may appear, as do odd Red-throated, Black-throated and Great Northern Divers. Gadwall and Shoveler are present all year, with a few pairs breeding, while the local Ruddy Duck population carries on growing. Single pairs of Garganey appear each spring and breed irregularly.

The extensive reedbeds hold a significant population of breeding Reed Warblers (over 300 pairs), Sedge Warblers (130+ pairs) and Bearded Tits (4–6 pairs). A few Bearded Tits stay the winter but most leave during the autumn and return in March. Water Rails can be heard singing from March to June, with winter totals inflated by winter visitors. On cold calm evenings the squealing chorus combined with the whinnying of Little Grebes produces an eerie atmosphere. Odd pairs of Kingfisher breed, with much higher numbers in autumn. The Bittern is something of a speciality bird, being present every winter (1–3 birds), but being rarely seen, often only at dusk as they fly to roost. Management of the local reserves is attempting to create suitable breeding conditions for the Bittern, and one summered during 1994, so booming Bitterns may yet reappear in reedbeds where they bred from the 1940s to 1980. Good totals of Great Crested and Little Grebes nest, and a pair of Common Terns have recently bred successfully on special rafts at Far Ings.

Bittern

The scrub which surrounds the pits, mainly hawthorn and blackthorn, occasionally hides roosting Long-eared Owls in winter when the berry crop sustains varying sized flocks of Fieldfare, Redwing and Blackbirds for a few weeks. At such times there may be small parties of the exquisite Waxwing with the thrushes but they can be surprisingly elusive in the large areas of scrub. Abundant breeding Willow Warbler, Lesser Whitethroat and Blackcap are joined by a few Chiffchaffs and Whitethroats, with Grasshopper Warblers reeling from the edges of some of the reedbeds in April and May but few staying to breed.

The spring and autumn migration periods always produce a good variety of birds, with notable numbers of Sand Martin, Swallow, House Martin and Swift using the pits for feeding, and in the case of the first three species, roosting. Marsh Harriers pass through during April to May in increasing numbers and Hobbies have become more regular, but Ospreys remain a scarce transient, possibly due to the lack of dead trees for perching. Common, Arctic and Black Terns plus Little Gulls are all regular in spring and autumn, often being seen on the Humber in preference to the pits.

Strong north to southeasterly winds in the autumn can bring a variety of seabirds as far as the Humber Bridge, where most turn back east, but with a significant proportion passing on westwards. Gannets are most regular, along with Arctic Skuas, but Great, Pomarine, and Long-tailed Skuas have all occurred. Fulmar and Manx Shearwater are almost annual and parties of Kittiwake may appear as often in May and June as in the autumn. Flocks of sea-duck, Common and Velvet Scoters, Eiders, and Red-breasted Mergansers are more regular from mid October, and

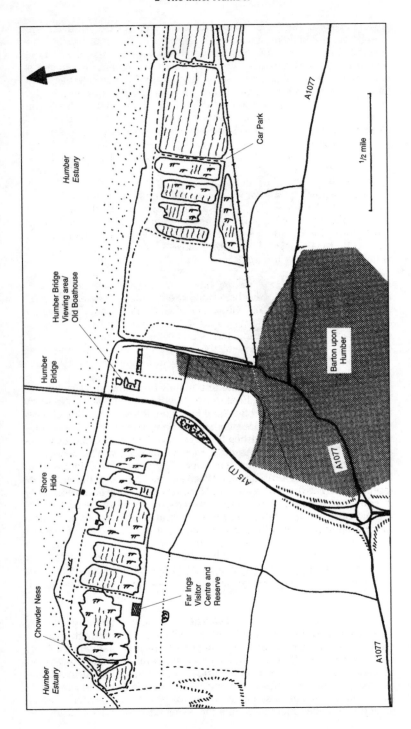

1/2 mile

Humber Estuary

Car Park

A1077

Humber Bridge Viewing area/ Old Boathouse

Humber Bridge

Barton upon Humber

A1077

A15 (T)

Shore Hide

Chowder Ness

Humber Estuary

Far Ings Visitor Centre and Reserve

A1077

November gales may well bring scuttling parties of Little Auks up the Humber.

As the estuary acts as an east–west guiding line for migrants there is often a good visible passage to be seen from the old boathouse area on early mornings in spring and autumn, involving such species as Skylark, Meadow Pipits, finches, corvids, Woodpigeons, wagtails and hirundines.

Access

Barrow Haven: A minor road is signposted from Barrow-upon-Humber to Barrow Haven. This crosses a hump-backed bridge and turns right after a further 400 yds/m. Go straight ahead here to a railway crossing, park in a designated car park on the right immediately over the crossing (TA 062 236). Walk across the bridge over the Haven and through the gate to the right onto the sea bank to view the pits to the west. A set of wooden steps just through the gate to the left leads through the hawthorn scrub to a hide overlooking the Lincolnshire Trust reserve pit of Barrow Reedbed. The grass sea-bank path continues west to Barton-upon-Humber, with flooded claypits to the left and the Humber foreshore to the right.

Barton-upon-Humber: The claypits to the east of the town have numerous tracks and footpaths around them which allow easy exploration. From the town, take the A1077 towards Barrow-upon-Humber and turn left down Falkland Way. One mile (1.6 km) farther on the road passes over a railway crossing and becomes narrow. There is a public car park, at the eastern end of this road 100 yds/m from where it becomes a rough track (TA 042 229). The Old Boathouse and Humber Bridge viewing area are signposted from the town. A large car park (TA 028 235) gives access to the Humber bank. River watching, for seabirds, is carried out from the Old Boathouse shelter immediately to the west of the Haven mouth, and by walking west along the riverbank it is possible to view all the west-side pits. The Far Ings reserve and visitor centre is 1 mile (1.6 km) west along Far Ings road. Turn left off the viewing area approach road just north of the railway station at the Sloop public house and follow the minor road to the visitor centre on the right where there is a car park (TA 012 229) and then access to the four hides on the reserve. Alternatively, from the A1077 Barton to Scunthorpe road, take the minor road north, signposted to the Clay Pits, and at the bottom of the hill turn left; the visitor centre is another 200 yds/m on the right beyond the turn to Westfield Lakes Hotel.

SOUTH FERRIBY, READ'S ISLAND AND WINTERINGHAM HAVEN

Habitat

The remnants of Read's Island and the rich mudflats of South Ferriby basin form one of the richest feeding areas for waders and wildfowl on the upper estuary. Read's Island supposedly formed around the wreck of a sunken ship in the sixteenth century and gradually grew in size to a maximum of 500 acres. For many years there was a house on the island with a resident stock man and, latterly, gamekeeper. It was grazed with cattle and sheep until the 1970s when it was stocked with fallow deer, a few of which remain today. An obviously rich area for wintering wildfowl it was used as a shooting preserve by the owners until recently. Erosion has accelerated in the last ten years, and now only about 80 acres (32 ha) remain, the house and building being lost into the estuary a few years ago. It is now mainly dominated by rough grass and hemlock with some short sward, grazed by Canada Geese, which provides a high-tide roost site for waders.

Two hides are situated at South Ferriby and Winteringham Haven, both overlooking extensive areas of mud flats at low tide, and the area to the east of Winteringham Haven has a quite extensive salt-marsh with invading blocks of tall reed.

Species

Pink-footed Geese, formerly abundant winter visitors, have been undergoing a slight revival of fortunes, with over a thousand present in the 1993–94 winter. Unfortunately the birds roost site on sand bars off Winteringham Haven has been eroded and they are now less predictable in occurrence, although flocks can still be seen flighting to feed on inland fields from October through to February, when most depart again for Iceland. The whole of the upper estuary is a nationally important area for wintering Golden Plover (up to 20,000) and Lapwing (up to 10,000), with additionally significant numbers of Wigeon, Teal, Curlew, Redshank and Dunlin around Read's Island and good sized flocks of Pintail and Wigeon off Winteringham/Whitton. Small parties of wild swans, Bewick's and Whoopers appear from October to November, sometimes staying the winter.

The best areas for observing the waders at all seasons are the muddy basin to the east of South Ferriby sluice and the mud on the front edge of Read's Island, which is visible from the main road. Cormorants (up to 40) are often to be seen loafing on the eastern end of Read's Island but the major gull roost off Winteringham Haven, which holds tens of thousands of Black-headed, Common and Great Black backed Gulls, along with up to 1,500 Herring Gulls in midwinter, is too far offshore to be properly visible in the failing light of winter afternoons. Even so, odd Glaucous and Iceland Gulls, which feed on local rubbish tips, may accompany the other large gulls to the roost and can sometimes be seen on the sand banks off Winteringham before flying to roost.

The winter months invariably produce a few Short-eared Owls, hunting the island or the sea banks, and occasional Hen Harriers, with Merlins being regular and Peregrines increasingly so. A walk along the foreshore may well flush Snipe and Jack Snipe, and parties of Bearded Tits sometimes frequent the foreshore reedbeds in winter and during September to October when irrupting flocks may be 'pinging' along the Humber banks. Most of the interesting breeding birds are confined to inacessible Read's Island, where Curlew, Oystercatcher, Redshank and Lapwing all nest along with increasing numbers of Canada Geese (50 pairs in 1994), a pair of Kestrels and Stock Doves in special nest boxes, and the locally important Shelduck population. The number of Shelduck on the mud flats often reaches 700 in May but the number of young in creches in July rarely exceeds 150, showing that breeding success is rather limited. A few pairs of Ringed Plover and Oystercatcher breed on stony parts of the sea defences.

It is to be hoped that more frequent summering by Marsh Harriers on the estuary will be consolidated into a local breeding population. They

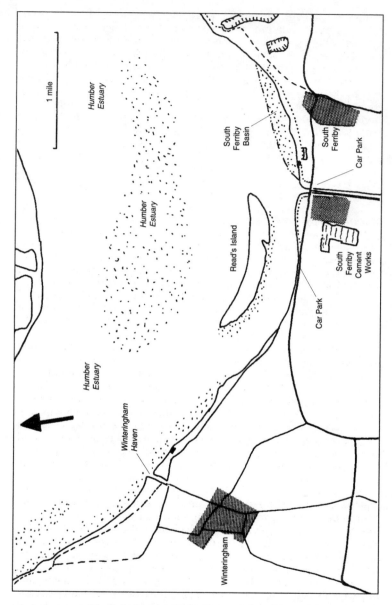

are now a regular sight from mid April onwards, with peak numbers of adults and young in late August and September. Hobbies are also being seen more regularly along the Humber and even Peregrines have occurred in July when the first Merlins return. The small areas of salt-marsh have breeding Meadow Pipits, Reed Buntings and a few pairs of Redshank, while Yellow Wagtails that breed on the inland fields often come to the seawalls to feed, especially in early autumn when the myriad insects attract large feeding flocks of pipits and Pied as well as

Yellow Wagtails, and several Common Sandpipers.

The spring and autumn passage periods bring an increasing variety of waders, with regular appearances by small parties of Black and Bar-tailed Godwit, Avocets, Curlew Sandpipers, Little Stints, Knot, Whimbrel, Ruff, Greenshank, Grey Plover, Common Sandpipers and Turnstone. Breeding-plumaged Dunlin (up to 2,500) and Ringed Plover (up to 600) are a feature of April and May, with autumn peaks for Ringed Plover again reaching 600 in August. Rarities inevitably occur, and both Pacific and American Golden Plovers have been found along with White-rumped and Broad-billed Sandpipers.

'Spring' tides, from July to September, can produce some spectacular movements of waders searching out high-tide roosts, and on calm, warm days, thousands of Sand Martins feed over the beds of sea aster, on occasions pulling in a hunting Hobby.

Access

South Ferriby, Read's Island: The A1077 Barton to Scunthorpe road passes through South Ferriby village and alongside the Humber oppo-site Read's Island where two lay-bys (TA 968 212) provide a convenient parking spot for viewing the island. A small, recently constructed car park is located just south of the road opposite the Hope and Anchor public house. From there cross the road, cross a bridge over a drain to the right and then bear left over a stile onto the grass bank. Follow this to view the mud flats and gain access to the hide which overlooks the best areas for waders in the basin.

Winteringham Haven: Heading west on the A1077 take a right turn to Winteringham. In the village centre turn right, down a gentle hill, to where the road crosses a drainage channel on a sharp left-hand bend. Park here (TA 935 228) and climb the stile on the right to follow the grass sea-bank path to a hide which overlooks the salt-marsh and mud flats. Alternatively, go over the bridge and bear right down the track to the Yawl club where the riverbank footpath continues west, with salt-ings and reedbeds to the right, or go through the kissing gate, on the right, and down the track between the high hawthorn hedges to a view-point over the estuary.

Timing

The principal consideration on an estuary is the time of the tides and their relative heights. The highest 'spring' and lowest 'neap' tides coin-cide and occur every four weeks in relation to lunar cycles, with the highest of all the annual tides in April, May and August, September and October. A set of tide tables is thus essential before planning a visit. For waders on extensive mud flats, like those at South Ferriby and Read's Island, a visit commencing two to three hours before high tide will pro-duce the closest views of birds as they are forced closer to the shore by the rising tide. On the highest tides, however, most birds will be forced off the shore and into inaccessible high-tide roosts, on Read's Island, up to two hours before high tide. Seabirds and sea-duck on the Humber are most reliable with northerly to southeasterly winds and on a rising tide. With the tide drifting birds westwards towards the Humber Bridge they often give repeated views as they fly back east to avoid passing under the bridge and are then again drifted back by the flowing tide.

The New Holland diving-duck flock is best watched on a fairly calm day, the Humber can become quite choppy quickly due to the combined effects of wind and tide, in the two to three hours around high tide when the birds are most settled and often drift in closer to the shore. As the tide falls the parties of duck drift off east towards Goxhill Haven, eventually flying back to the feeding area to join the diving frenzy. As with all reedbeds, to fully appreciate the volume of birdsong during the spring, a warm, calm day is needed with an early start, the earlier the better, to pick up the crepuscular Water Rails and Grasshopper Warblers.

Calendar

Resident: Little Grebe, Great Crested Grebe, Cormorant, Shelduck, Gadwall, Shoveler, Pochard, Tufted Duck, Ruddy Duck, Sparrowhawk, Water Rail, Ringed Plover, Lapwing, Curlew, Redshank, Barn Owl, Kingfisher, Meadow Pipit, Bearded Tit, Willow Tit, Tree Sparrow, Reed Bunting.

November–March: Red-throated and Black-throated Divers (scarce), Red-necked, Slavonian and Black-necked Grebes (all scarce), Bittern, Mute Swan (large herd), Bewick's Swan, Whooper Swan, Pink-footed Goose, Wigeon, Teal, Pintail, Scaup, Common Scoter, Goldeneye, Smew, Red-breasted Merganser, Goosander, Hen Harrier, Merlin, Peregrine, Golden Plover, Grey Plover, Dunlin, Jack Snipe, Turnstone, Little Auk (November gales), Short-eared Owl, Rock Pipit, Stonechat, Redwing, Fieldfare, Carrion Crow (flocks), Snow Bunting, Corn Bunting.

April–June: Garganey, Marsh Harrier, Hobby, Oystercatcher, Avocet, Sanderling, Little Stint, Curlew Sandpiper, Dunlin, Ruff, Black-tailed Godwit, Bar-tailed Godwit, Whimbrel, Greenshank, Common Sandpiper, Turnstone, Little Gull, Common Tern, Arctic Tern, Black Tern, Turtle Dove, Cuckoo, Short-eared Owl, Yellow Wagtail, Whinchat, Northern Wheatear, Ring Ouzel (April–May), Grasshopper Warbler, Sedge Warbler, Reed Warbler, Lesser Whitethroat.

July–October: Gannet, Bittern, Wigeon, Common Scoter, Marsh Harrier, Merlin, Hobby, Avocet, Golden Plover, Grey Plover, Little Stint, Curlew Sandpiper, Dunlin, Ruff, Black-tailed Godwit, Bar-tailed Godwit, Whimbrel, Greenshank, Green Sandpiper, Common Sandpiper, Turnstone, Arctic Skua, Little Gull, Common Tern, Arctic Tern, Black Tern, Short-eared Owl, Sand Martin and Swallow (large roost), Yellow Wagtail, Whinchat, Stonechat.

3 MARKET RASEN AREA

Habitat

Market Rasen is situated on an area of blown sands, in the valley of the River Race, which rises from the scarp slope of the Wolds, above Tealby, to the west, and flows down to join the River Ancholme at Bishopbridge. The principal sites of interest are the woodlands and remnants of the old heathland along with the western scarp of the Wolds and the small but interesting Toft Newton Reservoir.

LINWOOD WARREN/ WILLINGHAM AND WALESBY FORESTS

Habitat

Few spots could be said to be typical of the old heathland which covered much of this district in the nineteenth century, when Hen Harriers bred in numbers, but the small Lincolnshire Trust (LTNC) reserve at Linwood Warren is a good example. Although subject to increasing encroachment by birch and pine scrub, recent management work has opened up extensive areas and rejuvenated the heather and acidic-bog vegetation which characterises the reserve. Adjacent to the reserve is a golf course, with the typical variety of short-turf fairways and rough patches of grass, birch and pine scrub.

The most extensive tracts of the old sandy warrens were converted to coniferous woodland, the present day Willingham and Walesby Forests, now increasingly reaching maturity and becoming subject to a system of clear-felling, which is opening up large areas of the forest. Replanting with more consideration for the wildlife potential of the district is a welcome development and looks set to enhance the value of the site. Within the forest, which consists mainly of Scots and Corsican pine varieties, there are areas of larch and some stands of alders and poplars along the watercourses which dissect the woodland.

Species

While such species as Coal Tit and Treecreeper are fairly widespread through the forest areas during the winter months, contact with a large roving mixed-passerine flock dominated by Coal, Long-tailed, Blue and Great Tits and, depending on the severity of the winter, variable numbers of Goldcrests and Treecreepers, the odd Lesser or Great Spotted Woodpecker, may produce an exciting encounter as the flock moves swiftly through the forest, their imminent arrival being announced by a constant battery of contact calls. The interface between conifer and deciduous woodland, even pockets of birch scrub, can often be a good spot to bump into these flocks. Fruiting birch and alders attract feeding flocks of Redpolls and Siskins. A small field in the centre of Willingham Forest, planted with brassicas and with an abundant growth of seed-bearing weeds, proves a magnet for Chaffinches, Brambling, Greenfinches, Dunnocks, Redpolls and, in the 1992–93 winter, played host to a rare nearctic White-throated Sparrow for several weeks.

Stands of larch are the best place to look for feeding Common Crossbills, which can be extremely quiet and elusive when feeding, often being given away by their distinctive call notes and the sound of falling cones. The Scots pines by the picnic site held a flock of Parrot Crossbills in the 1990–91 winter, and two Arctic Redpolls joined a flock of Mealy and Lesser Redpolls at Linwood. Bullfinches are quite numerous and favour the blocks of blackthorn scrub, moving to growths of hazel in the spring to feed on catkins. Sparrowhawks are a constant sight soaring over the woodland on sunny days or dashing down the rides at breakneck speed.

By March the Sparrowhawks will be displaying over the woodlands, Mistle Thrushes singing at full volume and all three woodpeckers will be drumming or calling, in the case of the Green, as they establish breeding territories. Look for Lesser Spotted in boggy patches of old birch with rotten and broken trees. Summers are enriched with the song of a plentiful population of Willow Warbler, Chiffchaff, Blackcap and Garden Warbler, while the clear-fells echo to the distinctive descending lilt of Tree Pipits and the purring of Turtle Doves. Spotted Flycatchers are common around the forest edges, and occasional singing Wood Warblers pause for a few days in May in the older deciduous areas of the woodland. Siskins are sometimes present through the summer and Common Crossbills may breed in small numbers, but the best time to look for this species is from June onwards during irruption years, when vibrant flocks are to be seen and heard chipping over the tree-tops. Roding Woodcocks can be heard on late spring evenings as they drift over the tree-tops, and the increasing area of clear-fells will hopefully soon make the churring song of the Nightjar once again a regular feature of the forest during the summer.

Timing

Winter walks are best on fine, sunny calm days, a rare commodity, when locating calling flocks of birds is made easier. Although the Willingham Forest walks are popular with the general public, disturbance is not usually a problem, except in the area immediately adjacent to the main car park. To make the most of the birdsong in spring an early start is recommended on a warm morning. Warm calm evenings, the hour before dark, are the time to listen for Nightjars and roding Woodcock.

Access

Linwood Warren reserve is restricted to Lincolnshire Trust permit holders only. Leave the A631 in Market Rasen on a minor road signposted to Linwood and the race course and the reserve entrance is on the right after 1.5 miles (2.4 km) (TF 129 879). A marked trail leads around the reserve taking in the different habitats.

Willingham Forest is well served with a series of waymarked forest trails of varying lengths, which pass through the most interesting parts of the forest. The main car park and picnic area is located just off the A631, 2 miles (3.2 km) west of Market Rasen (TF 138 884). From here the trails are signed with different coloured posts, marking trails of differing lengths. This forest has retained shooting rights and on some Saturdays during the shooting season, 1 September to 1 February, the trails are closed or restricted. Notice of the closure or restrictions are posted in the car park picnic site.

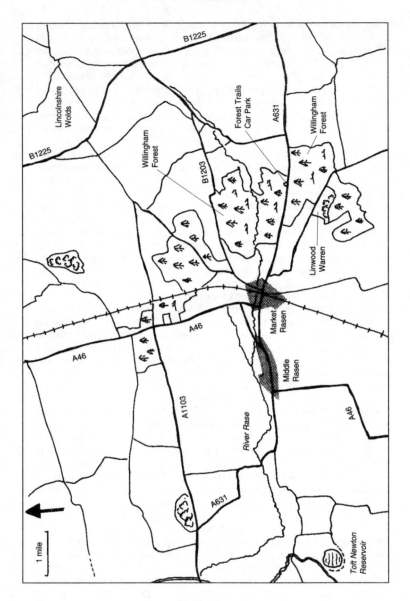

Calendar

Resident: Sparrowhawk, Kestrel, Woodcock, Stock Dove, Tawny Owl, Green Woodpecker, Great Spotted Woodpecker, Lesser Spotted Woodpecker, Mistle Thrush, Goldcrest, Long-tailed Tit, Willow Tit, Coal Tit, Treecreeper, Jay, Bullfinch, Yellowhammer.

October–March: Fieldfare, Redwing, Brambling, Siskin, Redpoll, Common Crossbill, Reed Bunting,

April–September. Woodcock, Turtle Dove, Cuckoo, Nightjar (scarce), Tree Pipit, Garden Warbler, Wood Warbler (scarce), Chiffchaff, Spotted Flycatcher, Common Crossbill (irregular).

THE WOLD SCARP

Habitat

Increasingly large tracts of land between the eastern side of the forest and the Wolds are being put down to long-term set aside, which combines with the rough grassland slopes of the Wold scarp to produce an impressive and extensive area of wild habitat. The fields, bordered by short hawthorn hedgerows, are large, whereas the Wold edge is often a mosaic of cattle- and sheep-grazed pasture and rougher grassland on the steeper slopes, with odd small deciduous copses around the isolated farms. Much of the steeper slope is wet, with *Juncus* and rough grasses dominating the vegetation, patches of gorse and broom most in evidence in the spring when their yellow flowers dot the green hillsides. The cultivated fields on the Wold summits are mostly put down to cereals, sugar beet and oilseed rape.

Species

The Wolds and adjacent fields are probably at their best for birds in the winter, but even then with wide open fields and large areas of suitable habitat the good birds are few and far between and take some finding. Woodpigeons are incredibly numerous, with vast flocks feeding on the fields of oilseed rape and brassicas. They regularly take to the air when disturbed and may move between feeding areas during the day, roosting at night in Willingham Forest and other plantations on the Wold tops. Their abundance attracts wintering Peregrines but a chance encounter with one on the wing marks a lucky day. Skylarks also form good sized flocks and sometimes become mixed in with the flocks of Meadow Pipits feeding in the rougher grass fields on the scarps.

The set-aside fields and stubbles provide winter feeding for flocks of Yellowhammer, Reed Bunting and some reasonable sized flocks of Corn Buntings. Grey Partridge are still quite common and coveys are easily seen in the bare winter fields. Stock Doves also tend to form feeding flocks in the winter months and are a regular sight on the scarps where they will often mingle in with large feeding flocks of Rooks, Jackdaws, Carrion Crows and Magpies. Raptors are probably the key interest group in this habitat. Barn Owls, still fairly common in Lincolnshire as a a whole, take advantage of the rough set asides and the wold scarps and can often be seen hunting in daylight in midwinter. They are joined by varying numbers of Short-eared Owls from September to April. In the winter, Merlins roam the tops and valleys and Common Buzzards are fairly regular if elusive, while odd Rough-legged Buzzards are found on some part of the Wolds in most winters, with even a few recent reports of visits by the odd wandering Red Kite during the 1990s.

Good numbers of Skylark and Meadow Pipit breed, with a few pairs of Lapwing still holding their own. Scrubby areas have breeding Linnets, Yellowhammers, Whitethroats, Turtle Doves and, in some of the damper spots, Grasshopper Warblers. A few pairs of Corn Buntings are present in cereal fields on the Wold tops and the short grass slopes often have a few pairs of Yellow Wagtail and may play host to a few migrant Northern Wheatears in the spring. Local breeding Kestrels hover over the scarp slopes and the inland valleys where Sparrowhawks can reach quite high densities, breeding in the small copses and hunting over the open fields and hedgerows. In addition to these two common species there are increasing summer reports of Hobbies, which may well be breeding in the area. Set asides have also recently proved attractive to calling Quail in the spring and summer.

Timing

For raptors and owls the months from October to March are the best period for this area, with the additional interest of wintering passerine flocks. March is a good month for seeing local Sparrowhawks and any other lingering raptors in display. Summer months are quieter but the area is not looked at much at this time of year and could repay further investigation.

Access

The western scarp of the Wolds is really quite impressive and good views are possible from several localities, but the best vantage points are along a minor road which runs north–south from the A631 Market Rasen to Louth road, to the village of Walesby. A minor road, signpost- ed to Tealby, runs north from the A631, 2.75 miles (4.2 km) west of Market Rasen. The scarp and valley of North Willingham are visible on the right. On reaching Tealby village, the forded road via Tealby Thorpe is usually too deep for cars in the winter months, turn left onto the B1203 for 250 yds/m then right again onto a minor road signed to Walesby. This again offers views up the Wold scarp to the right, with a nice plantation in the valley by Castle Farm, and also views over the set- aside fields to the left. At the T junction in Walesby turn left to return to Market Rasen through another block of Willingham Forest or turn right and then left onto another minor road which runs west towards Usselby.

From Walesby three public footpaths lead north across the valley of the youthful Kingerby Beck up the Wold scarp towards Normanby le Wold. The views over the forest and surrounding area are magnificent, on a clear day. Further north, another excellent walk follows the Viking Way through Nettleton Valley, rich pasture grazed by cattle and sheep on the sandstone outcrop. From the A46, 1 mile (1.6 km) south of Caistor, turn left into Nettleton village and follow the road to an obvious right-hand bend (TF 113 997). Here a track leads off to the left and is well signed. It is 2.5 miles (4 km) up the valley to a minor road, which runs along the wold top, and by turning right and following this road down the hill a circular route brings you back to the starting point.

Calendar

Resident: Sparrowhawk, Kestrel, Stock Dove, Barn Owl, Green Woodpecker, Skylark, Meadow Pipit, Mistle Thrush, Yellowhammer.

October–March: Hen Harrier, Common Buzzard, Rough-legged Buzzard (scarce), Merlin, Peregrine, Golden Plover, Lapwing, Short-eared Owl, Fieldfare, Redwing, Great Grey Shrike (rare), Tree Sparrow, Brambling, Reed Bunting, Corn Bunting.

April–September: Hobby, Quail, Turtle Dove, Cuckoo, Short-eared Owl, Northern Wheatear, Grasshopper Warbler,

TOFT NEWTON RESERVOIR

Habitat

Out to the west of West Rasen lies the small circular concrete-sided Toft Newton Reservoir, which is owned by the NRA and managed as a trout fishery. The outer banks and periphery are all sheep-grazed short pasture, while the surrounding land is mostly uninspiring arable. As the only sizeable water area for many miles around and lying at the upper end of the Ancholme valley, which runs north–south from the Humber estuary, obviously makes the reservoir an attractive and essential stop-over location for a variety of passage species.

Species

In spite of considerable disturbance, Toft Newton holds a good range of wintering wildfowl. If disturbance becomes too severe, however, the birds will fly onto the upper stretches of the River Ancholme, north of Bishopbridge. A mixed flock of Pochard and Tufted Duck is the staple fare, with a few Gadwall, small numbers of Goldeneye and occasional records of Goosander, Common Scoter, Velvet Scoter and even Eider and Long-tailed Duck. A drake Smew has been a regular winter visitor for the last few years. Cormorants are always present but not welcomed by the bailiff. Small parties of Bewick's Swans have occurred in some winters, feeding on the valley fields and flying to the reservoir to bathe and rest. A varying sized flock of Great Crested Grebes, often in excess of 30, is present and the reservoir seems to have an unusual ability for attracting Slavonian and Red-necked Grebes in spite of its inland location.

A winter gull roost is composed mainly of Black-headed and Common Gulls but inevitably there have been records of the increasing Mediterranean Gull. A flock of Yellowhammers feeds around the grassy perimeter and large flocks of Rooks and Jackdaws are a feature of the surrounding farmland. The spring and autumn migration periods produce a good variety of species but many birds do not linger for long due to the constant disturbance. Black-necked and Slavonian Grebes occur on passage, and that ace fish-eater, the Osprey, has become an annual visitor in spring at least. The birds make regular forays to take trout from the reservoir, taking them to eat in dead trees or on the nearby fields, in full view of the fishermen. Up to three birds were together in May 1994.

The insect-rich concrete walls attract passage White and Yellow Wagtails, a few pairs of the latter staying to breed nearby, and Common Sandpipers. Black, Common and Arctic Terns are rare transients, but immature Little Gulls will sometimes stay for a few days. A few waders appear each autumn, feeding on the algae and weed washed up on the concrete banks. Most are juvenile birds which quickly adapt to the disturbance from fishermen and thus often become very tame, giving good views. Numbers are low but usually include a few Dunlin, Ruff, Common Sandpiper and, in good autumns, maybe a Curlew Sandpiper or Little Stint.

Timing

The principal problem at this location is the extensive use of the reservoir for trout fishing. Anglers walk all around the inside of the reservoir walls, and boats are scattered over the water. Whilst disturbance to birdlife is obviously not intentional it is considerable, but it is also surprising how adaptable some species will become. There is no real way around the problem as even early mornings and late evenings are busy, but the site is possibly quieter in the winter months. Spring and autumn offer the best chance of a scarce passage migrant but winter has a good show of wildfowl and a good chance of a scarce grebe.

Access

Toft Newton Reservoir is 5 miles (8 km) west of Market Rasen. Follow the A631 through Middle Rasen to West Rasen where the road takes a sharp right-hand bend. Go straight on here, signposted to Newton by Toft, onto a minor road and turn right, in Newton by Toft, to the reservoir (TF 033 875). Drive round to the back of the reservoir on arrival and ask permission from the water bailiff before going onto the reservoir banks.

Calendar

Resident: Sparrowhawk, Kestrel, Stock Dove, Barn Owl, Skylark, Meadow Pipit, Mistle Thrush, Yellowhammer.

October–March: Great Crested Grebe, Red-necked Grebe, Slavonian Grebe, Cormorant, Pochard, Tufted Duck, Scaup, Goldeneye, Smew, Golden Plover, Lapwing, gull roost, Fieldfare, Redwing, Tree Sparrow.

April–September: Osprey (annual April, May), Hobby, Little Stint, Curlew Sandpiper, Dunlin, Ruff, Little Gull, Common Tern, Arctic Tern, Black Tern, Turtle Dove, Cuckoo, Yellow Wagtail, White Wagtail (April, May), Northern Wheatear.

4 SUTTON ON SEA TO CHAPEL ST LEONARDS   OS Map 122

Habitat

The coastline south of Mablethorpe sprang to fame during the east coast floods of 1953, when large sections of the sea defences were destroyed and huge areas of countryside flooded. Since then much of this section of the coast has been protected with man-made sea defences of clay, stone and, more recently, concrete, with large areas being rebuilt and strengthened during the 1990s. Some natural dunes still exist south of Huttoft Car Terrace to Chapel St Leonards, where the seawall is again concrete. It is ironic that the destruction of the natural coastline also led in turn to the creation of some of the valuable bird-rich claypits lying inland of the sea defences along this stretch of coastline. The sea-bank claypits at Chapel, Anderby Creek, Wolla Bank,

Huttoft and Sandilands were all excavated to provide clay to rebuild the sea defences following the 1953 floods. Most of these pits, consisting of areas of deep water with reedbeds and willow/sallow scrub, are now managed as reserves by the Lincolnshire Trust (LTNC).

Four main types of habitat of interest to the birdwatcher are to be found along this stretch: the strip of sea defences and its attendant vegetation being of value at times of migration; the open beach and sea; the low-lying rich arable fields just inland, which, during the winter months, can be attractive to wildfowl and some waders; and the claypits themselves.

The remaining sand dunes are mostly covered in sea buckthorn scrub between Huttoft Car Terrace and Anderby Creek and are, in general, rather unattractive. The best areas of habitat for migrants are found immediately north and south of Anderby Creek, where much of the area of interest is found in small gardens with sycamores, willows and small hedgerows and lawns, but there is also an extensive area of young sycamores to the north of the creek behind the new sports complex.

Farther south there are extensive areas of sallows and willows at Chapel Six Marshes, where some open, grazed dune and longer grass occurs adjacent to Chapel Pit. A car park at Chapel coastguard lookout has some scrub surrounding it and provides a good vantage point for seawatching as the coast turns slightly southwest at this point and the raised concrete seawall provides a degree of elevation useful along this low-lying coastline. Other areas of sallows, willows and sycamores are found around the outfall at Chapel St Leonards, again often in gardens, which have proved to be attractive to migrants.

Inland of the sea defences the arable fields between Anderby Creek and Huttoft Bank often hold wintering wildfowl and can be checked from the coast road. Between Huttoft Bank and Sandilands some small areas of permanent pasture still remain, although the acreage has been greatly reduced in recent years. Alongside the seawall south of Sandilands a golf course provides a large area of short-mown grass with rougher patches of longer grasses, and the recent work on the sea defences has left areas of short grass with open sandy areas adjacent to the concrete seawall. A large concrete car terrace at Huttoft provides a convenient seawatching point, having some slight elevation, and also allowing watching to be carried out from a vehicle in bad weather.

Species

The sea is rather unpredictable with regard to the birds it holds along the Lincolnshire coast but in winter there will always be some species to be relied upon, albeit in variable numbers. Red-throated Divers are usually present, often, however, well out, but numbers vary from fewer than ten to hundreds during good feeding movements when up to 500 may be seen in a couple of hours, flying north or south offshore. Other divers are real rarities and if they do occur are just as likely to be seen on the claypits. Flocks of Common Scoter and a few Eider are regular, but the best variety of species is found during or after periods of strong northerly oriented winds. Scaup, Red-breasted Mergansers, Long-tailed Duck and Velvet Scoters become likely, and auks, mainly Guillemots, may be numerous but usually only offer flight views.

Periods of northerlies, especially in November, usually produce movements of Little Auks, birds flying north on days after the strongest winds. Northerlies in midwinter also often give rise to southerly movements of large gulls, mainly Herring and Great Black-backs, but good movements usually include a few Glaucous and odd Iceland Gulls as well. Small feeding flocks of Little Gulls are often a feature of the sea off Huttoft Bank in midwinter.

The claypits often attract a vagrant grebe, such as a Red-necked or Slavonian, the odd Long-tailed Duck or Scaup and fairly regular Smew. Bitterns are seen most winters but as everywhere are elusive, the hide overlooking Huttoft Pit being the best bet for locating one. The arable fields either side of the coast road along this stretch of the coast hold large flocks of Lapwing and Golden Plover, often with a few Ruff. In years with influxes of geese from the continent, often in January or February, the same fields may attract flocks of White-fronted, Barnacle, Bean and Pink-footed Geese, with small parties of Bewick's and Whooper Swans also occasionally present. Waders are few, but parties of Sanderling winter with a few Ringed Plover, and a few Purple Sandpipers are usually present somewhere between Trusthorpe to the north and Chapel. Rock Pipits are widespread along the sea embankments, and small numbers of Snow Buntings are often present but rather mobile. The inland fields may have odd Short-eared Owl, Hen Harrier and Merlins, with increasingly regular Peregrines.

Spring migration often sees a marked passage of Short-eared Owls returning to their breeding areas in Scandinavia and beyond. Northern Wheatears appear along the sea embankments with a few Stonechats and Black Redstarts joining them from late March when odd Firecrests are regularly encountered at Anderby Creek and Chapel. The reedbeds of the claypits are enlivened with singing Reed and Sedge Warblers, while Grasshopper Warblers can be relied upon along the stretch from Anderby Creek south to Chapel Six Marshes. Later, from April, the sea buckthorn scrub resounds to the songs of a multitude of Whitethroats. Scarce migrants such as Redstart, Whinchat and Ring Ouzel may be more numerous during periods of easterly winds and older stands of trees often attract a few passage Spotted and Pied Flycatchers and the occasional Wood Warbler.

Marsh Harriers are frequent but transient visitors to the claypits, and the coastal location of the reedbeds has produced a good number of rarities over the years from Great Reed and Marsh Warblers to Purple Herons, Little Egrets and Spoonbills. Similarly the coastal scrub can be productive, and Subalpine Warbler and Great Spotted Cuckoo are the two major rarities to have been found. The golf course at Sandilands usually holds passage Yellow Wagtails and occasionally waders such as Whimbrel, Ruff and Black-tailed Godwit, with Dotterel putting in an appearance on a few occasions. Breeding birds are fairly limited, with Reed, Sedge and Grasshopper Warblers present along with Whitethroats and Willow Warblers in the scrub and a few breeding duck on the pits, where Bearded Tits sometimes summer along with Water Rails.

By July, Sandwich, Common and Little Terns and Arctic Skuas are regularly present offshore, and the gull roost, off Huttoft Bank, often contains one or more Mediterranean Gull. A good autumn seawatch is possible anytime from August to November but the key factor, as usual, is the weather. A good strong blow, lasting a day or more, two or more days being better, from the north, northeast or east, will bring a marked passage of several species of seabirds, which can be observed from any of the locations mentioned along this stretch of coast. Most species usually move south in the strongest winds and return north as the wind abates, when they are best observed as they are generally moving slower and closer to the shore.

Gannets are usually the most numerous species in the early autumn (August–September), with lesser numbers of Kittiwake, Fulmar, Common, Arctic, Sandwich and Black Terns, Little Gulls, Arctic (most numerous), Great, Pomarine and Long-tailed Skuas. Numbers of the latter two species are connected with breeding sucess in the Arctic, with few in most years but larger numbers occurring generally about every fourth autumn. Strong northerlies also bring small numbers of Manx and Sooty Shearwaters and, especially in September, Leach's Petrels. The later autumn (October–November) has a changed species composition with more sea-duck, Common and Velvet Scoters, Red-breasted Mergansers, Long-tailed Duck, Guillemots, Little Auks, Kittiwakes and greater numbers of Great and Pomarine Skuas.

Pallas's Warbler

If water levels are low in Huttoft Pit it attracts the usual variety of migrant freshwater waders: Greenshank, Spotted Redshank, Green, Wood and Common Sandpipers, with a few Curlew Sandpiper and Little Stint. Black-tailed Godwits are a regular feature of the autumn, along with flocks of juvenile Ruffs, both species feeding extensively on the Sandilands golf course, where flocks of Whimbrel and odd Dotterel also drop in from time to time. Large flocks of Whimbrel can often be heard calling as they pass south overhead or offshore through the autumn.

Visible migration is often quite pronounced along this stretch of the coastline as the dune system is narrow and the stream of birds more concentrated. The August passage of Swifts, Swallows, Sand and House Martins and Yellow Wagtails is joined in September by flocks of Meadow Pipits, a few Grey Wagtails and, towards the month end and through October, by Skylarks, Chaffinches, Goldfinches and Linnets. Amongst falls of migrant Willow Warblers, Whitethroats, Lesser Whitethroats, Whinchat, Northern Wheatears, Redstarts, Spotted and Pied Flycatchers, with an easterly element to the wind, there is always the chance of a Wryneck, Icterine or Barred Warbler or Red-backed Shrike from early August onwards. Anywhere along the coast is suitable but the sycamore trees at Anderby Creek and Chapel St Leonards are favoured by Icterine Warblers, and from late September through October by those sprites the Firecrest and Yellow-browed Warbler and the exquisite Red-breasted Flycatcher. Black Redstarts frequent the more stony areas of the banks in late October and early November, when incoming flocks of thrushes, Woodcocks, Long-eared and Short-eared Owls can be found in any of the localities mentioned. The grassy areas south of Anderby Creek and also Sandilands golf course have proved attractive to vagrant Richard's Pipits.

This section of the coastal strip is not extensively watched but records of Greenish, Pallas's and Dusky Warblers and Isabelline Shrike show the potential of the area to attract eastern vagrants.

Timing

There is a limited intertidal area along this section of the coast and so the times of high and low tide are not important for seawatching. For winter visits a calm clear day will offer the best views of divers and sea-duck but onshore gales bring more chance of a passage of ducks, auks, gulls and divers. Spring and autumn visits will be most profitable with regard to migrants during or after spells of east or southeast winds, while the heaviest visible migration usually occurs in periods of light southwesterly winds when the birds move into the wind. For seabirds a day or two days of strong to gale force north to northeasterly winds, preferably with rain or reduced visibility, followed by a day of lighter winds is the ideal scenario but there will be some birds to see at most times during the autumn.

As you are looking east, the sun can be a problem in the early morning on clear days. In fine, settled conditions skuas and terns may move south in the late evening when the light is at its best, being behind the observer. Midsummer sees the usual influx of sunseeking holidaymakers at all the coastal car parks, which can become congested on warm weekend days, although midweek is still fairly quiet.

Access

All the sites mentioned in this section are accessed from the minor coastal road from Chapel St Leonards to the southern end of Sutton on Sea. Leave the main A52 just south of Sutton on Sea onto a minor road signposted to Sandilands. This road passes a large hotel on the right and then turns a sharp right-hand bend before running alongside the sea-wall, topped with chalets, to the entrance to the golf course. About 0.75 miles (1.2 km) farther on a small pull-in on the right (TF 533 793) is the car park for Huttoft Pits, a Lincolnshire Trust (LTNC) reserve. A path leads down the side of the field on the right to a hide overlooking the largest pit. After another 0.5 miles (0.8 km) a crossroads is signed right to Huttoft and left to the sea. The left turn offers access to the large concrete car terrace (parking fees are levied in the summer months only), where it is possible to park right next to the sea at high tide (TF 542 787). Even on low tides, however, the coast here is fairly steeply shelved and the tide edge is never far out, unlike further up the coast.

Travelling south again on the minor road, tracks lead off left to car parks adjacent to the dunes at Moggs Eye and Marsh Yard, borrow pits are present on the right of the road and the extensive wide open fields on either side of the road should be scanned for wildfowl and waders in the winter. Three miles (4.8 km) south of Sandilands is Anderby

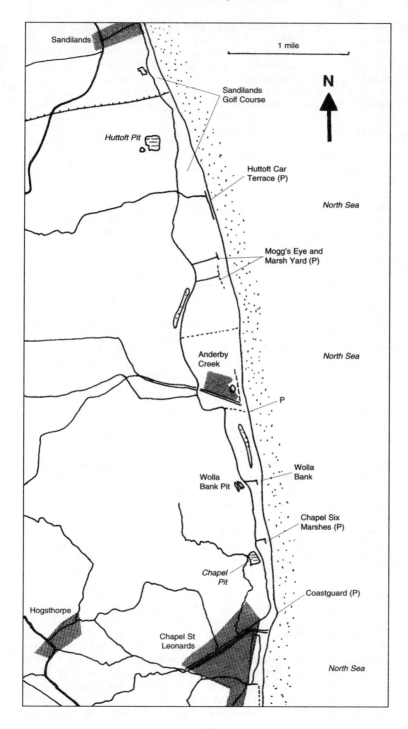

Sandilands

Sandilands
Golf Course

Huttoft Pit

1 mile

N

Huttoft Car
Terrace (P)

North Sea

Mogg's Eye and
Marsh Yard (P)

Anderby
Creek

North Sea

P

Wolla
Bank

Wolla
Bank Pit

Chapel Six
Marshes (P)

Chapel
Pit

Coastguard (P)

Hogsthorpe

Chapel St
Leonards

North Sea

Creek. Turn left here into the village where there is a car park at the end of the road adjacent to the dunes (TF 552 761). Walk up the sand track over the dunes and a small shelter is useful for seawatching in bad weather but unfortunately has a somewhat restricted perspective. Again from the car park, a track runs away northwards along the edge of some small gardens and eventually passes an open-air sports complex backed with young sycamores. An obvious pathway leads into the trees while the main path continues north through another small copse. By walking south from the car park and crossing the creek at its mouth another area of scrub with some odd sycamores and elders is reached.

Continue south on the coastal road and tracks off to the left lead to car parks at Wolla Bank (TF 557 749) and Chapel Six Marshes (TF 559 742). Both car parks are set adjacent to the dunes, with some extensive but largely impenetrable areas of marshland, willows, sallows and bramble, and at Chapel Six Marsh a small conifer plantation. The dunes in between the two car parks are grazed by donkeys, which forms a nice open area of short grassland. Chapel Pit, a Lincolnshire Trust (LTNC) reserve, is across the road from Chapel Six Marshes (TF 558 739).

As the coast road reaches the northern outskirts of Chapel St Leonards there is an obvious car park on the left of the road, with an area of willow and sallows across the road on the right (TF 562 732). This is the coastguard lookout car park at Chapel Point. There is some scrub around the car park and across the road. Otherwise, walk to the right on the seawall past a row of holiday chalets to the mouth of a fairly wide drainage channel, the Willoughby High Drain, and then walk down the side of the drain and turn left onto a narrow residential road, which runs south parrallel with the dunes. The gardens and scrub around the channel mouth and farther south are good for migrants.

Calendar

Resident: Sparrowhawk, Barn Owl, Bearded Tit, Reed Bunting.

December–February: Red-throated Diver, Bittern, Bewick's Swan, Whooper Swan, Pink-footed Goose, White-fronted Goose, Wigeon, Shoveler, Common Scoter, Hen Harrier, Merlin, Water Rail, Ringed Plover, Golden Plover, Lapwing, Sanderling, Purple Sandpiper (scarce), Snipe, Ruff, Little Gull, Glaucous Gull, Guillemot, Short-eared Owl, Rock Pipit, Stonechat, Twite, Snow Bunting.

March–May: Shoveler, Marsh Harrier, Merlin, Water Rail, Ruff, Short-eared Owl, Yellow Wagtail, Black Redstart, Redstart, Whinchat, Stonechat, Northern Wheatear, Ring Ouzel, Grasshopper Warbler, Reed Warbler, Sedge Warbler, Firecrest.

July–November: Red-throated Diver, Sooty Shearwater, Manx Shearwater, Leach's Petrel, Brent Goose (September–November), Eider, Common Scoter, Velvet Scoter, Red-breasted Merganser, Marsh Harrier (to October), Hen Harrier (September on), Merlin, Hobby, Water Rail, Golden Plover, Sanderling, Ruff, Black-tailed Godwit, Green Sandpiper, Wood Sandpiper, Pomarine Skua, Arctic Skua, Long-tailed Skua, Great Skua, Mediterranean Gull, Little Gull, Sandwich Tern, Common Tern, Arctic Tern, Little Tern, Guillemot, Long-eared Owl, Short-eared Owl, Wryneck (scarce), Rock Pipit (September on), Black Redstart, Redstart, Whinchat, Stonechat, Northern Wheatear, Ring

Ouzel, Icterine Warbler (scarce), Barred Warbler (scarce), Yellow-browed Warbler (scarce September–November), Pallas's Warbler (scarce October–November), Firecrest, Pied Flycatcher, Red-breasted Flycatcher (scarce September–November), Red-backed Shrike, Great Grey Shrike, Twite (September on), Snow Bunting (September on).

5 GIBRALTAR POINT   OS Map 122

Habitat

Situated at the southeastern extremity of Lincolnshire, with the North Sea to the east and the expanse of the Wash to the southwest, Gibraltar Point has long been recognised as an extremely important locality for watching migratory birds, a fact which led to it gaining reserve status, with management run by the Lincolnshire Trust, from 1949, when a Bird Observatory was also founded. The area presently has SSSI and National Nature Reserve status and has recently been designated as a Ramsar site and SPA.

Situated as it is on the east coast of Britain with a north–south leading line off into the Wash, it acts as a natural funnel for birds migrating down the east coast and also as a migrant trap for incoming birds from the continent. In spring it also acts as a last point of departure for large numbers of winter visitors originating in Scandinavia and further east. It is not just, however, a migration spot as the extensive sand bar at the southern tip of the reserve acts as an important high-tide roost for vast numbers of waders which feed in the Wash. In the winter months the saltings hold flocks of wintering passerines and the foreshore and salt-marsh attract large numbers of wildfowl including impressive flocks of Brent Geese.

Accommodation is provided in a modern field studies centre on the reserve, often booked well in advance for courses, and there is a well equipped visitor centre with displays and a variety of sale items from pens to a reasonable selection of books and local Bird Reports. The centre is manned by Lincolnshire Trust members and is open daily from May to October and at weekends in the winter. The reserve has an extensive system of pathways, the main ones being well surfaced (suit-able for wheelchairs), which lead visitors through a variety of habitats and to features of interest like the Mill Hill lookout point, the Wash view-point and the Mere and Fenland Lagoons. Visitors are encouraged not to venture off the marked paths, except on the outer foreshore where general access is allowed (except during the breeding season when tern nesting colonies are fenced off).

A walk from east to west, from the sea, leads through the variety of habitats which make up the bulk of the reserve. A gentle shelving sandy beach leads into a series of low developing dunes, with marram grass cover, intersected by wet to fairly dry dune slacks with some open muddy creeks and large expanses of short-grazed haliphytes and grass-es, especially at the northern end of the reserve. The older developing dunes at the north end of the beach have sea buckthorn and elder scrub, which also dominates the east dune ridges rising up from the beach slacks. Management of some of the east dunes has involved the clearance of invasive sea buckthorn and rosebay willowherb to restore grassland and dune-slack habitat. A small mostly reed-fringed pool with surrounding willow scrub, Shovelers Pool, lies at the northern end of the east dunes and can be a good spot for migrants. Behind the seawall then lies a large strip of old salt-marsh, holding many characteristic and colourful plants. Inland from here opens up a broad expanse of fresh-water marsh, which drains into a series of borrow pits with open water and beds of sedge and *Juncus*, attractive to dragonflies and *Acrocephalus* warblers in the autumn. At the northern end of this marsh there are two purpose made wader scrapes, the Mere with a single hide, and the Fenland Lagoon with two hides at the eastern and western end.

The west dunes are the oldest part of the complex and are covered in a mixture of buckthorn and elder scrub with a small stand of mature sycamores. Some areas are kept clear of scrub and are mown or sheep-grazed and further maintained by rabbits, forming areas of open sandy grassland. Further inland lies Syke's Farm an area which has access restricted to Lincolnshire Trust members only. It has a diverse canopy of trees including ash, sallow, beech, elm, sycamores and pines, most-ly planted in the 1960s, as well as an orchard of quite old fruit trees. This is a particularly attractive spot for migrant birds as it offers food, shelter from the elements under all conditions, and also a safe roosting place. To the south of the visitor centre stretches the salt-marsh of the Wash, with its tidal creeks, which is overlooked by a special hide, the Wash Viewpoint.

Species

Midwinter is an excellent time at Gibraltar Point, which has the advan-tage of offering the birds of the Wash, the North Sea and of the coastal salt-marsh, all within a compact area. High tides bring waders from their feeding grounds on the Wash to roost on the sand bar by the tern hut. Grey Plover, Bar-tailed Godwit, Curlew, Oystercatcher, Redshank, Knot and Dunlin feature with lesser numbers of Sanderling and Ringed Plover. Large flocks of Brent Geese are visible over the Wash salt-marsh, flighting onto inland fields to feed and out to the mouth of the River Steeping to bathe, while there are regular appearances from flocks of Pink-footed Geese flying to and from North Norfolk or between their favoured feeding areas. The salt-marsh and tidal creeks have even in some winters played host to a Spoonbill and, more recently, Little Egrets.

Offshore, Red-throated Divers are always present in varying numbers and occasional parties of sea-ducks, Common and Velvet Scoters, Eider, Red-breasted Mergansers and Goldeneye are to be seen bobbing on the water or flying by. Raptors are well represented with Hen Harrier, sometimes up to five roost nearby, Sparrowhawks, Merlin and Peregrine all regular, with Short-eared Owls usual and odd sightings of Barn Owl.

The saltings north of the tern hut right up towards Seacroft are a mag-net for feeding flocks of finches and buntings. Of principal interest are flocks of Snow Buntings and Twite, the latter often mixed in with Linnet, Redpoll and Goldfinch, and on one occasion an Arctic Redpoll. Lapland Buntings are sometimes present on the salt-marsh, but are less visible and often only located by their characteristic calls as they over-fly the area. Shorelarks, formerly regular, have become increasingly erratic visitors, mainly on autumn migration. Rock Pipits are everywhere around the saltings and salt-marsh, with upwards of 60 birds present. Depending on the quantity of the crop of sea buckthorn berries, large flocks of Fieldfare, Redwing, Blackbirds and Starlings are present from November to January. Both Blackcap and Chiffchaff are increasingly regular wintering birds, being found in the buckthorn and the favoured Syke's Farm area.

It is the spring and autumn migration periods which produce the greatest interest for most birdwatchers, however, with the variety of species seen on good days in May and from September to October rivalling any east coast watchpoint. Visible migration is particularly obvious at Gibraltar Point, with tens of thousands of birds moving south over the reserve at both seasons. Somewhat surprisingly, birds move south in spring as well as autumn, even arriving summer migrants such as Swallows, House Martins and Yellow Wagtails. The best spot at which to watch this spectacle is Mill Hill. Perched on top of the east dunes a special platform allows a good panoramic view of the flocks of birds as they pass south, concentrated by the lie of the land, and out over the Wash towards north Norfolk, which is easily visible on clear days. In March, departing flocks of Chaffinches, Brambling, Greenfinches, Siskins, Redpolls and thrushes can be seen heading off east. During April, movements of Linnets, Goldfinches, and Meadow Pipits dominate, with Swallows, House Martins, Sand Martins, Swifts and Turtle Doves gaining pace in May. Marsh Harriers are increasingly common passage birds in spring and the odd Osprey passes over each year, with Hobbies regular from mid May and increasing sightings of Montagu's Harrier.

The variety of species recorded on visible migration watches can be quite phenomenal, from pipits, wagtails, finches, thrushes, buntings and tits through geese, raptors, waders, gulls and terns, to pigeons and owls.

Something of a regular speciality here in recent early springs has been the Woodlark, with up to six birds in some years, present anytime from late February to late March, usually feeding on the close grazed dune ridges of the east or west dunes. The first spring migrants occur in March, Northern Wheatear, Stonechat, Black Redstart, Chiffchaff and that little jewel the Firecrest, all being reliable with the first flush of warm air. As with many east coast localities, however, cold weather often dominates in early spring and many migrants appear at inland localities before coastal ones. It is usually mid to late April before large falls of birds arrive, with the best variety of species present in early May. Whitethroats, particularly common breeding birds, arrive early to set up territories as good numbers of Willow Warblers and hirundines are passing through. A few pairs of Little Terns arrive to breed on the sand spit and Common, Arctic, Sandwich and Black Terns are seen on passage. The variety of waders present is enhanced by flocks of Whimbrel, usually just flying north, Little Ringed Plover, Ruff, Jack Snipe, Black-tailed Godwits, Spotted Redshank, Greenshank, Wood, Green and Common Sandpipers, with odd rarer species like Little and Temminck's Stints.

Drift migrants like Redstart, Wood Warbler and Ring Ouzel are present in early May in small numbers, given the right weather conditions, and with an element of east in the wind later in the month the odd Bluethroat, Red-backed Shrike, Wryneck, Common Rosefinch, Pied Flycatcher or something rarer, such as the 1993 Rustic Bunting, may well occur. Birding in the spring is always less predictable than autumn, however, and birds seldom linger long on the coast, even following a good arrival. Rare birds are a feature of coastal migration localities and although they cannot be relied upon to occur there is always the possibility of something out of the ordinary when birdwatching at Gibraltar Point in spring. Fly-over raptors have included several Honey Buzzards, Red Kites, four Black Kites and some long-staying Red-footed Falcons. Other exotic spring transients vary from regular Spoonbills, the almost annual Hoopoe, to the much rarer Night Heron, Crane, Tawny and Red-throated Pipit, Alpine Swift, Red-rumped Swallow and Bee-eater, to the most recent Penduline Tit. The Gibraltar Point list is indeed a long one and testifies to the reserve's ability to attract a wide range of vagrants as well as high totals of commoner migrant species.

Bluethroat

Breeding species of note include a few pairs of Little Tern, which can be watched from the vicinity of the tern warden's hut, or fishing out over the tidal rips and in the creeks, Ringed Plovers, Oystercatcher and high densities of Meadow Pipit and Whitethroat. The local Long-eared Owls often provide good views as they hunt over the freshwater marsh in the early evenings from mid May through June, with the odd summering Short-eared Owl sometimes also present for comparison. Marsh Harriers are increasingly seen throughout the summer, with large numbers present in the Wash, and even Montagu's Harriers are being seen more frequently during this season.

Summer and early autumn gatherings of gulls on the beach and the Mere often hold one or more Mediterranean Gull. Autumn wader passage is underway by early July with the first Wood and Green Sandpipers often on the Mere in late June. The Mere and Fenland lagoon, along with the shallow brackish pools on the shore, attract a wide range of species during the autumn, with Dunlin, Ruff, Snipe, Redshank, Greenshank, Green and Common Sandpipers all being regular, while less frequent visitors include Avocet, Little Stint, Curlew Sandpiper, Jack Snipe, Black-tailed Godwit, Spotted Redshank and Wood Sandpipers. The freshwater Mere has developed something of a reputation for attracting rarer waders, with Lesser Yellowlegs, Broad-billed and Pectoral Sandpipers, Red-necked and Wilson's Phalaropes to its credit. Being an isolated area of fresh water it also acts as something of a magnet for migrant Water Rails and other vagrants such as Spotted Crakes, Citrine Wagtail in 1983, and Great White Egret in 1993.

From mid July one of the great attractions of Gibraltar Point is the spectacle of the high-tide wader roost. Huge flocks of waders, which feed at low tide in the Wash, gather to pass the high-tide period on the sand spit which juts out southwards from the point itself, or on the beach further to the north. The first returning Sanderling, Knot and Bar-tailed Godwit are often still in brilliant full breeding plumage and make a marvellous sight bedecked in orange and greys. The number of birds involved is sometimes quite staggering, with peak counts of up to 20,000 Oystercatcher, 4,500 Grey Plover, 2,500 Sanderling, 35,000 Knot, 6,000 Dunlin and 10,000 Bar-tailed Godwit, and lesser numbers of Ringed Plover and Redshank. Flocks of Whimbrel regularly pass southward, calling continually.

July and August sees a build up of flocks of post-breeding Sandwich and Common Terns, with additional regular southerly passage by both species, especially in the last week of August and early September. Other species appear in smaller numbers, with Arctic and Black Terns fairly regular. The fishing terns attract marauding Arctic Skuas but the occurence of the other three species of skua, although annual, is much more weather dependent, with northerly gales in the North Sea needed to bring most seabirds into visible range. As the shoreline is so gently sloping here seawatching can be frustrating as birds are often distant and can be easily lost in wave troughs in rough weather. Good move-ments do occur, however, and close views can be obtained during moderate northeasterly winds. Some of the best conditions occur fol-lowing strong northerly winds when birds trapped in the Wash will be moving back northwards past the point, into the North Sea. Northerly gales in November will often bring parties of scuttling Little Auks and the larger Guillemots.

Visible migration brings a wide range of species south through the reserve in autumn, from the huge movements of Swifts in July through hirundines and wagtails in August to Meadow Pipits and finches in September, with thrushes, finches and buntings in October and November.

Although species of departing summer visitors such as Willow Warbler, Spotted Flycatchers, Whitethroats, Lesser Whitethroats and odd Northern Wheatears and Whinchats will be present throughout the autumn period, several species of drift migrants are more weather dependent and only appear in numbers during or soon after periods of easterly winds. August and September falls include good numbers of Redstart, Whinchat, Northern Wheatear, Garden Warbler and Pied Flycatcher, with regular records of Red-backed Shrike and Wryneck along with the rare but annual Icterine and Barred Warblers. From late September, falls take on a more easterly flavour, with incoming thrush-es including Ring Ouzels, Goldcrests, Robins, Dunnocks, Stonechats, Chiffchaffs and the recently more regular Yellow-browed Warbler, along with odd Red-breasted Flycatchers.

By late October and into early November easterlies bring in Long-eared and Short-eared Owls, Woodcocks and a few Firecrests. This has now become the best time to look for the recently rather rare Great Grey Shrike, while in an influx year a few parties of Waxwing can be expected. In some years Richard's Pipits may appear from late

September, often, however, only being seen or heard flying over to the south, as are most of the Lapland Buntings. Raptors are always unpredictable, but whatever is arriving on the east coast, be it Honey Buzzard or Rough-legged Buzzard then Gibraltar Point gets its share.

A long list of autumn rarities must surely be headed by that dazzling nearctic passerine, the American Redstart, which, on one November day, during its four-week stay in 1982, was seen in the same bush as an Isabelline Shrike from Asia. Other rarities have ranged from fly-by Alpine Swifts, Bee-eaters, Crane and Serin, to the likes of Short-toed Lark, Olive-backed Pipit, Greenish, Arctic and Pallas's Warbler, to Parrot Crossbill and Northern Waterthrush!

Timing

A visit at anytime of year will be productive. To watch visible migration anytime during the months of March to May and August to mid November will produce some birds, with the best movements on days with light to moderate northwesterly winds in spring, and south to southwesterlies in autumn. Drift migrants appear following periods of easterly winds during the same periods, and for seabirds a strong to gale force northeast to easterly wind is required.

To see the high-tide wader roost at its best it is necessary to time your visit to coincide with one of the peak 'spring' tides, which only occur over a four-day period once a month and usually in the early morning and evening. A check of the relevant tide tables will show the appropriate dates. Otherwise arrive early and stay late to make the most of this superb reserve, where the main problem is which part of the extensive area to cover before the day draws to a close.

Access

Situated 3 miles (4.8 km) south of Skegness the reserve is approached via a minor road, signposted to Gibraltar Point, from the town centre. There are two pay-and-display car parks. The first, from the north, at the Mere which gives access to the northern end of the reserve, the freshwater Mere and new Fenland Lagoon, as well as the Mill Hill Viewpoint. The main car park lies at the end of the road, beware the road makes a sharp left-hand turn over a blind hump just before the car park. The visitor centre, offices and field studies accommodation are all situated here at the site of the old coastguard lookout.

A series of well marked tarmac and chalk tracks and mown-grass pathways cover all the the principal habitats within the reserve and visitors are asked to keep to the marked footpaths. Access to the east dunes, foreshore and beach is via a tarmac track across the freshwater marsh. The Wash Viewpoint, south of the visitor centre, offers panoramic views over the vast expanses of salt-marsh and mud and sand flats of the Wash to the southwest. Syke's Farm plantation, is obvious on the right of the approach road just before the hump, a very good spot for holding migrants and for roosting raptors but access is restricted to permit holders only. The outside of the plantation can, however, be viewed adequately from the road.

Calendar

Resident: Little Grebe, Cormorant, Shelduck, Sparrowhawk, Oystercatcher, Redshank, Meadow Pipit, Reed Bunting.

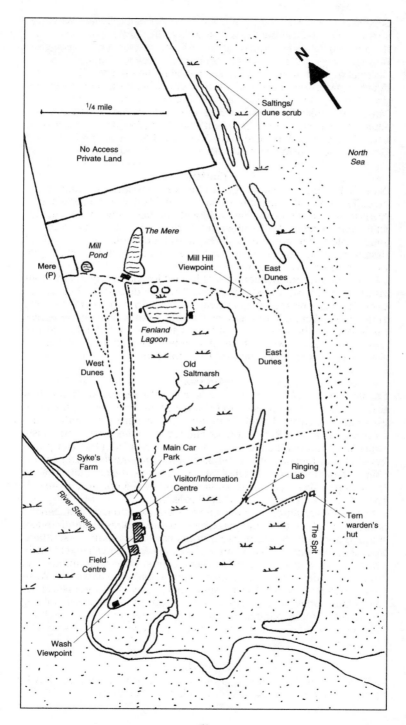

December–February: Red-throated Diver, Bewick's Swan, Whooper Swan, Pink-footed Goose, Brent Goose, Wigeon, Eider, Common Scoter, Goldeneye, Red-breasted Merganser, Hen Harrier, Merlin, Peregrine, Water Rail, Grey Plover, Knot, Sanderling, Dunlin, Snipe, Bar-tailed Godwit, Curlew, Turnstone, Guillemot, Short-eared Owl, Rock Pipit, Fieldfare, Redwing, Stonechat, Twite, Snow Bunting, Corn Bunting.

March–May: Red-throated Diver, Spoonbill (scarce), Brent Goose, Marsh Harrier, Hen Harrier, Montagu's Harrier (rare), Osprey (passage), Merlin, Hobby, Peregrine, Little Ringed Plover, Ringed Plover, Grey Plover, Knot, Sanderling, Dunlin, Ruff, Jack Snipe, Black-tailed Godwit, Bar-tailed Godwit, Whimbrel, Curlew, Spotted Redshank, Greenshank, Green Sandpiper, Wood Sandpiper, Common Sandpiper, Turnstone, Little Gull, Sandwich Tern, Common Tern, Arctic Tern, Little Tern, Turtle Dove, Cuckoo, Long-eared Owl, Short-eared Owl, Hoopoe (rare), Woodlark (rare), Yellow Wagtail, Black Redstart, Redstart, Whinchat, Stonechat, Northern Wheatear, Ring Ouzel, Grasshopper Warbler, Sedge Warbler, Reed Warbler, Wood Warbler (scarce), Firecrest, Brambling, Siskin, Common Crossbill (irregular).

June–July: Manx Shearwater, Gannet, Common Scoter, Marsh Harrier, Montagu's Harrier, Knot, Sanderling, Bar-tailed Godwit, Green Sandpiper, Wood Sandpiper, Arctic Skua, Sandwich Tern, Common Tern, Little Tern, Turtle Dove, Cuckoo, Swift (heavy passage), Grasshopper Warbler.

August–November: Red-throated Diver, Sooty Shearwater (rare), Manx Shearwater, Leach's Petrel (rare), Bewick's and Whooper Swan (October–November), Pink-footed Goose, Brent Goose, Wigeon, Gadwall, Teal, Eider, Common Scoter, Velvet Scoter, Goldeneye, Red-breasted Merganser, Honey Buzzard (rare), Marsh Harrier (to October), Hen Harrier (September on), Merlin, Hobby, Peregrine, Water Rail, Little Ringed Plover, Ringed Plover, Grey Plover, Knot, Sanderling, Little Stint, Curlew Sandpiper, Dunlin, Ruff, Jack Snipe, Woodcock, Black-tailed Godwit, Bar-tailed Godwit, Green Sandpiper, Wood Sandpiper, Common Sandpiper, Pomarine Skua, Arctic Skua, Long-tailed Skua (rare), Great Skua, Mediterranean Gull, Little Gull, Kittiwake, Sandwich Tern, Common Tern, Arctic Tern, Little Tern, Guillemot, Little Auk (November), Long-eared Owl, Short-eared Owl, Wryneck (scarce), Shorelark (rare), Rock Pipit (September on), Black Redstart, Redstart, Whinchat, Stonechat, Northern Wheatear, Ring Ouzel, Fieldfare, Redwing, Icterine Warbler (rare), Barred Warbler (rare), Yellow-browed Warbler (scarce September–November), Wood Warbler (scarce), Firecrest, Pied Flycatcher, Red-breasted Flycatcher (rare September–November), Red-backed Shrike, Great Grey Shrike (rare), Brambling, Siskin, Twite (September on), Lapland Bunting (September on), Snow Bunting (September on).

Habitat

The Wash is the largest and numerically most important estuary in the British Isles for combined wader and wildfowl totals. Lying half in Norfolk and half in Lincolnshire it presents an exceptional area for watching huge numbers of birds within the East Midlands region. Stretching from Gibraltar Point in the northeast to Terrington, east of the mouth of the River Nene, the Wash drains three major rivers in the Lincolnshire section, the Witham, Welland and Nene.

The surrounding farmland is all privately owned but some large sections of salt-marsh are managed by the RSPB and English Nature. There are numerous points of public access to the estuary embankments, outlined later, and the whole area is best explored from these banks by scanning out over the surrounding salt-marsh, mud flats and inland fields.

Huge areas of intertidal mud and sand flats provide ideal feeding and roosting areas for a large variety of waders and wildfowl, while salt-marshes and reclaimed arable fields just inland of the sea defences attract different waders, wintering passerines and hunting owls and raptors.

The geography of the Wash differs little around its perimeter, with subtle differences in substrate and vegetation accounting for the differing proportions of species using different areas. Typically, a raised sea bank, constructed of local clays, gives way abruptly to a wide expanse of salt-marsh vegetation, dominated by the likes of sea aster and various rough grasses, which then fades into an open expanse of mud, silt and sand, intersected by numerous tidal creeks which drain these flats at low tide. Spring tides usually inundate the salt-marsh, with the highest of the year lapping up to the base of the sea defences, especially if backed by a strong northerly wind down the North Sea, but neap tides rarely reach as high as the outer edge of the salt-marsh and it is always important to know the times and heights of local tides to make the most of birding in this vast area.

The Wash has been subjected over the years to fairly regular reclamation around its edges, which has resulted in a gradual loss of areas of salt-marsh and an extension of the rich arable farmland around its periphery. In their early stages reclamation schemes usually involve throwing up a clay bank around an area of salt-marsh, which is then seeded with grass for a few years to help dry out the salts before it is turned over to cultivation. In such periods these new seeded banks and grass enclosures can be beneficial to a variety of species of birds, but in the long term the loss of valuable natural habitat is of far greater consequence.

In such an extensive, generally flat and barren landscape there are few trees or hedgerows so where these do occur, as shelter-belts or isolated hedges, they can be of interest as spots to look out for migrant passerines and even as roost sites for raptors such as Sparrowhawks, Merlins, Long-eared Owls and Short-eared Owls. One famous Long-eared Owl roost is located at Nunn's Bridge, on the banks of the Hobhole drain, which runs into the River Witham.

The construction of the large clay sea defence embankments has also created a string of borrow pits, inland of the defences, which are to a lesser or greater degree flooded, with typically small linear reedbeds soon becoming established. More recent excavations may be shallow and, during dry spells, can provide useful feeding habitat for migrant waders which prefer the smaller pools to the open expanses of the Wash proper. Drainage ditches dissecting the agricultural fields inland may also have reedbeds and rough grass banks and as such may provide hunting grounds for raptors and owls throughout the year.

The mouths of the three major rivers, where the essentially fresh water meets the brackish water of the estuary, prove particularly attractive to diving duck, and are also recognised spots for watching seabirds during the right weather conditions in the autumn. A hide at the mouth of the River Witham provides shelter from the worst of the weather, in this open and windswept locality, which is welcome during cold winter days and in the gales which produce good numbers of seabirds.

Species

In some birdwatching locations the dramatic scenery combines with the presence of certain special birds to provide a rich birding experience. The scenery of the Wash could hardly be described as dramatic, but the flat, open (to some desolate) vistas have an enchantment of their own and it is the spectacle of the vast flocks of waders and wildfowl using the estuary which produce the magic of the birding experience. There is a good excuse for quoting figures from the regular monthly estuary counts to demonstate just how many birds are present and why the area presents such a magnificent birdwatching opportunity. All counts given are from the 1992 census.

One of the great success stories of the winter months has been the dramatic increase in the population of the dark-bellied Brent Goose, flocks of which are found right around the estuary. Their frequent movements between different feeding, bathing and roosting areas, and almost constant calling, make the flocks easy to locate. The peak January count in 1992 was an incredible 25,508. There is a steady decline in numbers through to the spring but a notable gathering of birds occurs in the area around Frampton Marsh into May when 6,390 birds were still present in 1992. A regular flock of Pink-footed Geese winters in the Holbeach

Brent Geese

Marsh area and other flocks fly over *en route* to and from their north Norfolk wintering areas. The totals of other wildfowl are dominated by Shelduck (8,674), Wigeon (2,821) and Mallard (2,299) (all January). A large flock of Pintail winters on the eastern side of the Nene Mouth, mostly on the Norfolk side of the county boundary at Terrington but with sometimes considerable numbers by the Nene Mouth itself.

Of the sea-duck, Eider are present all year but reach their highest totals from January to March, 692 being present in January 1992, with a past record count of 900 on 8 March 1986. The best locations for seeing Eider are to the northwest of the Witham Mouth, towards Freiston and Friskney. Other sea-duck occur in smaller numbers, with Red-breasted Merganser, Long-tailed Duck, Common and Velvet Scoters and Scaup all being annual in midwinter. Most records come from the favoured Witham and Welland Mouths but Holbeach Marsh produces records at high tide. A flock of Goldeneye winters off the Witham Mouth, where up to 150 birds have been recorded, and this locality is a favoured site for turning up odd Red- and Black-throated Divers and the three rarer grebes, Red-necked, Black-necked and Slavonian.

At low tide the vast flocks of Oystercatcher (17,155, February; 18,779, November), Grey Plover (4,361, January; 10,000, March), Knot (15,811, January; 43,002, November), Bar-tailed Godwit (5,054, February; 9,574, November), Curlew (1,667, January; 3,527, September), and Dunlin (11,629, January; 24,000, March and November), feed way out on the open mud flats and are often only visible as the flocks wheel and turn in flight or as massed blobs feeding on the shining mud and silt. As high tide approaches, the flocks move to safe high-tide roosts either on the upper shore during neap tides or on the fields immediately inland of the sea defences during higher tides. Their massed movements and constant contact calling makes an impressive spectacle and the roosts on the fields usually offer good views of the birds during the high-tide period. Do not attempt to get too close and disturb the roosting birds, however, as energy is precious during the winter and each flight uses up some of this vital commodity.

The Redshanks (2,648, April; 2,298, August) tend to feed closer to the estuary walls in the higher salt-marsh and tidal creeks along with the flock of Black-tailed Godwits, which is found during most of the year at Holbeach Marsh. The latter flock usually reaches a peak between September and January (400, September; 853, December) but then declines slowly through the winter until March when breeding birds depart. Returning migrants, many still in fine breeding plumage, are back by July/August when Greenshank and Spotted Redshank can also be numerous on passage with up to 100 of both species in some July and August counts. Ringed Plovers reach their peak during the spring and autumn migration peak periods, with up to 1,000 in May and August.

Recent mild winters have seen an incredible build up in the number of wintering Lapwing (50,616, December) and Golden Plover (4,593, December), which are usually to be found on the fields adjacent to the estuary, although both flight to feed on the outer flats on lower tides. The Golden Plover peak counts, however, occur in the late summer (8,329, August) as returning migrants flood into the east coast estuaries to moult. Two American Golden Plovers have recently been found amongst these flocks. In addition to the above species of wader, up to 350 Turnstone are recorded during the winter, with a pronounced spring passage peak (631, April) when most birds are present around the Witham Mouth. Other species occur on migration, notably Whimbrel (April–September) and small numbers of Curlew Sandpiper, Little Stint, Green, Wood and Common Sandpiper, but locating them in amongst the hordes of the commoner species can be difficult. Borrow pits around the estuary banks may dry out to reveal muddy margins in the late summer and autumn. These are the best places to look for the scarce species like Little Stint and Curlew, Green and Wood Sandpipers. The strip of borrow pits at Holbeach Marsh has turned up no fewer than three star rarities, White-rumped and Sharp-tailed Sandpipers and Long-billed Dowitcher.

It is no surprise that the Wash holds a good population of raptors at all seasons with the amount of available prey on offer. In winter, Merlins and Hen Harriers are relatively common, their true numbers usually only revealed by coordinated counts of roosting birds. Such counts have revealed that up to 17 to 20 Hen Harriers may be using the area in midwinter, but the exact number of Merlins is more obscure, although at least 10–15 birds are recorded most years. Single birds may be seen anywhere over the salt-marsh and adjacent fields during the day time, but the areas between the Witham Mouth and Gedney is the best site to look for roosting birds. Merlins will often use small copses or shelter-belts near the estuary banks, sometimes sharing their roosts with Sparrowhawks, which are a regular sight over the Wash throughout the year. Winter also brings small numbers of Peregrines every year but they are seldom tied to a particular locality and tend to roam widely. Kestrels are resident, reaching their most impressive numbers in August when recently fledged juveniles join adults hunting butterflies over the sea aster on the salt-marsh.

From April to September a visit to the Wash is unlikely to fail to locate a Marsh Harrier as a number of pairs now breed in the area and several immature non-breeding birds are present through the summer months. Males can be seen in display from early April when their appearance overlaps with that of the departing Hen Harriers. A small population of Montagu's Harriers continues to struggle to establish itself around the Wash, with the result that there are sporadic sightings of a few birds, often first summer individuals, from late April through to August. Other large raptors pass by occasionally as the northwestern banking of the Wash is a natural leading line for migrants passing through Gibraltar Point and not wishing to move over the open water. Red Kites have appeared a few times in spring and autumn and there are also records of Black Kite, White-tailed Eagle and Honey Buzzard.

Short-eared Owls winter in variable numbers, and in odd years a pair or two may stay to breed on the saltings. Their communal roosts may be situated in long grass areas on the banks or the edges of the salt-marsh. Birds can often be seen hunting the embankments or rough dyke edges around the inland fields during the day time in midwinter, where Barn Owls may also be seen hunting at dusk during the winter months. The same habitat, between Wainfleet and Friskney, played host to a memorable Snowy Owl, during the 1990–91 winter, which attracted hundreds of admiring birdwatchers during its stay. A few Long-eared Owls return each winter to their favoured roost in the hawthorns on the bank of the Hobhole drain near Nunn's Bridge. They can be viewed from the metal track which runs along the opposite bank of the drain towards its outfall by the Pilgrim Fathers monument. Huge numbers of gulls roost in the Wash but they are seldom in suitable locations to offer good views. Large gulls, which feed inland, can be seen as they fly down the Witham to roost in the late afternoon. The Herrings and Great Black-backs sometimes being joined by the odd Glaucous or Iceland Gull in the early part of the year.

Passerines do not figure high on the Wash species list but there are some interesting wintering birds and the extensive lengths of grass embankments with odd bushes, all within easy reach of the east coast, attract a few passage migrants. Rock Pipits are particularly numerous in winter, although making any sensible estimate of their total population is far from easy. There could well be hundreds of birds on the extensive salt-marshes and tidal creeks. During the early spring, examples of the Scandinavian race, *Anthus p. littoralis*, may be seen in their distinctive breeding plumage. Twite flocks are scattered in their distribution, often being found with Lapland Buntings where any work has disturbed the banks and given rise to a growth of seeding plants. Lapland Buntings may be common in some winters but maximum numbers (200+) occurred at Butterwick when a new reclamation project led to the con-struction and seeding of some new banking. Stubble fields adjacent to the banks remain a good bet for this species and large flocks of Skylarks. In the fens inland, Corn Buntings remain fairly common and winter feeding flocks may be encountered around the Wash embank-ments along with small parties of Snow Buntings, anywhere where seed-ing weeds or spilt grain are to be found.

During the spring and autumn migration periods, March to May and August to October, a scattering of migrants, Northern Wheatears, Whinchats, Stonechats and flocks of thrushes with a few Ring Ouzels frequent the grassy banks, with occasional records of other species in any patches of scrub, small copses or hedgerows running down to the Wash embankments. Species such as Willow Warbler, Chiffchaff, Redstart, Pied and Spotted Flycatchers all occur infrequently and such rarities (normally coastal) as Barred Warbler, Red-breasted Flycatcher, Red-backed, Woodchat and Lesser Grey Shrikes have all been found by persistent observers.

Looking for seabirds can be profitable under the correct weather con-ditions when northerly gales force birds down the North Sea and into the Wash to take shelter. At such times the birds fly around the edges of the Wash, returning out to sea again at Gibraltar Point. Skuas, however, may not return out to sea but head off high inland down the River Nene in particular, but also the Welland, and on an overland migration route. Although Common Terns are regular throughout the summer, there is a pronounced passage of birds from August when small numbers of Little and Black Terns and Little Gulls also appear. The best locations for see-ing all these birds seem to be at the Witham Mouth, where a purpose built hide offers shelter from the weather, and along the shore at Holbeach Marsh. The period of two hours either side of high tide is obviously best; at other times the birds may be too far offshore to iden-tify. The principal seabirds involved are Gannet, Fulmar, Arctic and Great Skua, with lesser numbers of Pomarine and Long-tailed Skuas, Manx Shearwaters and Leach's Petrels, but rarities such as Sabine's Gull have been noted on a few occasions, and in the late autumn Little Auks and Guillemots can be pushed into the Wash by gales. A Black Guillemot, a very rare bird for Lincolnshire, spent a few days at the Witham Mouth in the 1977/78 winter.

Timing

To make the most of a visit to the Wash, at least part of the time there should coincide with high tide and the period either side of this to see sea-duck and seabirds and the spectacular wader roosts. In the spring and autumn early morning and late evening high tides will be the higher ones and are the best as most of the birds present will be affected. In winter, with restricted hours of daylight, a late morning high tide will offer the best opportunity for seeing wintering wildfowl and waders. Details of obtaining tide times are given in the introduction. Remember in winter that walking along the exposed embankments can be very cold so it is best to wear too much rather than too little clothing, and *be prepared* for bad weather.

On weekdays the RAF bombing range at Holbeach St Matthew may be in use, and at such times noise from the aeroplanes can be considerable, but disturbance to the birds seems minimal. Obviously avoid days with fog and reduced visiblity, and in summer on hot days remember that during the middle of the day heat haze will make observations difficult if not impossible over the salt-marsh and mud flats.

Access

Because the reclaimed land adjacent to the Wash has a system of minor roads often resembling a spiders web, it is strongly recommended that the relevant Ordnance Survey map is consulted when making visits to the specific sites mentioned here. Access in all cases is limited to walking along the sea defences, grass-covered earth banks, and watching over the surrounding inland fields, the salt-marsh and mud flats.

The Nene Mouth: Simple to find. Take the minor road off the A17(T) immediately east of the river bridge at Hubbert's Bridge, and continue down this road for 3 miles (4.8 km) to a car park by the old lighthouse. From here access to the sea bank leads out to the edge of the salt-marsh and the mouth of the river.

Gedney Drove End: Signposted from the A17(T), onto the B1359. The village of Gedney Drove End is 5 miles (8 km) down the B1359, from where the road turns right, and after 1.25 miles (2 km) there is a car park by the sea bank (TF 478 283), with footpaths to the left and right onto the sea bank.

Holbeach Marsh car park: Found by following a series of minor roads from the A17(T) to Holbeach St Matthew, which is signposted. When in the village a minor road by a telephone box leads to a car park adjacent to the sea wall (TF 408 338).

Kirton Marsh: Leave the A16 at Kirton 3 miles (4.8 km) south of Boston (TF 305 386) onto a minor road which runs southeast for 3.5 miles (5.6 km) to a small car park by the sea wall.

Frampton Marsh: From the A16 in Kirton take the minor road to Frampton village and continue along this road to Road's Farm, bear right and follow this track to a car park from where a public footpath leads onto the seawall.

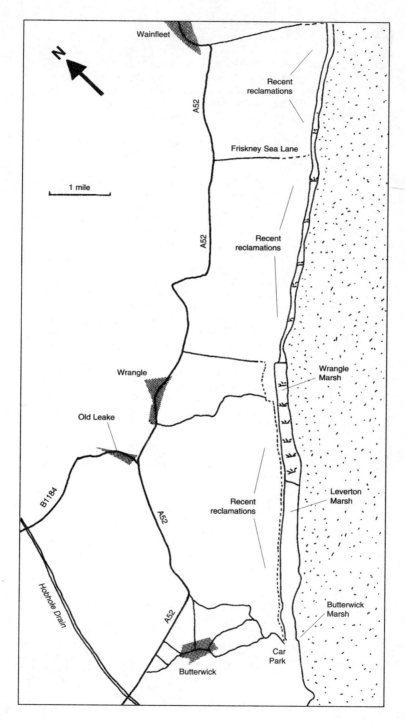

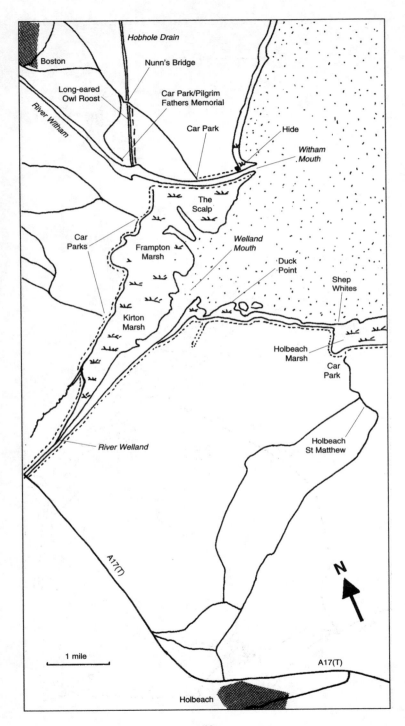

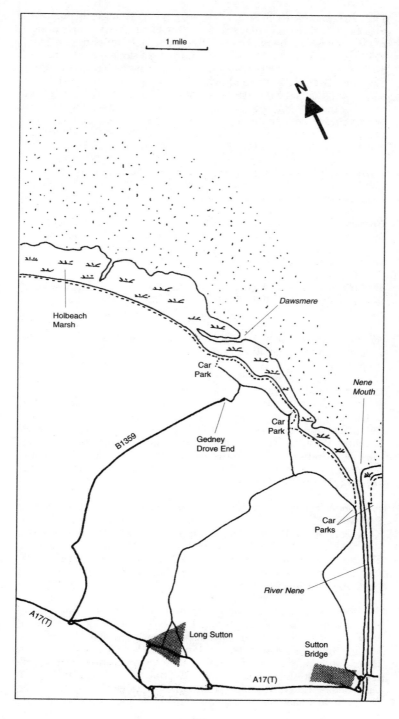

The Witham Mouth: In Boston follow signs to the docks and then signs to Fishtoft. In the centre of the small village turn right to Nunn's Bridge. At the point where the road crosses the bridge, at Nunn's Bridge (TF 367 415), take a sharp right just over the bridge, up a slope onto the bank of the Hobhole drain. The Long-eared Owl roost is in the hawthorns across the drain. Continue to the end of this track, the mouth of the Hobhole and the Pilgrim Fathers monument is to be found to the right of the out-flow. For the Witham Mouth car park continue along the minor road at Nunn's Bridge, without turning right for the above, until the road ends, and park on the roadside. The actual river mouth, with a hide for sea-watching, is another 2 miles (3.2 km) east along the riverbank.

Butterwick Marsh: Leave Boston on the A52 Skegness road and turn right into Butterwick village. From the village follow one of the minor roads which leads to a small parking area (TF 408 437).

Friskney: Leave the A52 5 miles (8 km) north of Wrangle village and turn right onto a minor road which leads down to a RAF observation tower. Continue to the next raised bank, a small copse is half a mile (0.8 km) to the north along this bank.

Wainfleet: From the A52 at Wainfleet St Mary a road runs southeast from a sharp bend on the A52, 2 miles (3.2 km) to the sea bank.

Calendar

All year: Cormorant, Shelduck, Eider, Lapwing, Curlew, Redshank, Skylark, Meadow Pipit, Reed Bunting.

November–March: Red-throated Diver, Red-necked Grebe, Slavonian Grebe, Bewick's Swan, Whooper Swan, Pink-footed Goose, Brent Goose, Wigeon, Pintail, Scaup, Long-tailed Duck, Common Scoter, Velvet Scoter, Goldeneye, Red-breasted Merganser, Hen Harrier, Merlin, Peregrine, Oystercatcher, Ringed Plover, Golden Plover, Grey Plover, Lapwing, Knot, Sanderling, Dunlin, Ruff, Snipe, Black-tailed Godwit, Bar-tailed Godwit, Curlew, Turnstone, Glaucous Gull, Guillemot, Long-eared Owl, Short-eared Owl, Rock Pipit, Stonechat, Tree Sparrow, Twite, Lapland Bunting, Snow Bunting, Corn Bunting.

April–June: Brent Goose, Marsh Harrier, Montagu's Harrier, Hobby, Peregrine, Ringed Plover, Dotterel (scarce April–May), Grey Plover, Knot, Sanderling, Dunlin, Ruff, Black-tailed Godwit, Bar-tailed Godwit, Whimbrel, Spotted Redshank, Greenshank, Common Sandpiper, Turnstone, Little Gull, Common Tern, Arctic Tern, Little Tern, Turtle Dove, Cuckoo, Short-eared Owl, Yellow Wagtail, Whinchat, Stonechat, Northern Wheatear, Ring Ouzel.

July–October: Fulmar, Manx Shearwater, Leach's Petrel, Gannet, Brent Goose, Wigeon, Teal, Pintail, Scaup, Long-tailed Duck, Common Scoter, Velvet Scoter, Red-breasted Merganser, Marsh Harrier, Hen Harrier, Merlin, Hobby, Peregrine, Ringed Plover, Golden Plover, Grey Plover, Knot, Sanderling, Little Stint, Curlew Sandpiper, Dunlin, Ruff, Black-tailed Godwit, Bar-tailed Godwit, Whimbrel, Spotted Redshank, Greenshank, Green Sandpiper, Common Sandpiper, Turnstone, Arctic Skua, Great Skua, Mediterranean Gull, Little Gull, Sandwich Tern,

Common Tern, Arctic Tern, Little Tern, Black Tern, Long-eared Owl, Short-eared Owl, Rock Pipit, Whinchat, Stonechat, Northern Wheatear, Twite, Lapland Bunting, Snow Bunting, Corn Bunting.

7 NORTH KILLINGHOLME HAVEN WADER PITS

OS Sheet 113

Habitat

This relatively small site has proved over the last 25 years to be one of the best spots for watching waders in Lincolnshire, offering easy watching and often unrivalled views of a large variety of waders and wildfowl. The site has an enviable list of rare species to its credit.

Composed of three flooded clay-extraction pits, owned by National Power, but at present managed by the Lincolnshire Trust, the pits are adjacent to the southern bank of the Humber estuary, to the east, with industrial areas to the north and south and agricultural fields to the west. The largest pits have a mix of shallow water, open mud, islands and beds of *Phragmites* and *Juncus* bordered with tall hawthorn hedgerows. The smaller pits have mainly deep water with a reed fringe and a larger area of invading hawthorn and blackthorn scrub. The larger pit, adjacent to the Humber bank, is brackish, while the pit inland of the railway line is mainly freshwater as are the smaller of the pits. The adjacent Humber shore has a narrow stony fringe, with open mud flats at low tide. The concrete seawall offers a vantage point overlooking the pits and the open estuary, which can be of interest during rough weather when odd seabirds and wildfowl may be seen.

The main attraction of the pits lies in the fact that the water is only shallow and the levels can be controlled to provide suitable conditions for feeding and roosting waders during spring and autumn. Their location along the Humber estuary attracts waders, which feed on the open mud flats at low tide and gather to roost and feed in the pits during the high-tide period. Although during recent years expanding industrial installations on the adjacent foreshore have brought an increase in disturbance and have led to a decrease in the number of waders using the pits, the importance of the site became very obvious during August 1995 when record totals of Black-tailed Godwit and Redshank occurred.

Species

In general the water levels are kept at their highest during the midwinter period so birding interest centres on odd wildfowl and occasional vagrant grebes. During bad weather there are occasional records of Red-necked and Slavonian Grebes and Red-throated Diver and in the past a wintering herd of Mute Swans and occasional small parties of Bewick's and Whooper Swans occurred. Gulls often drop in to bathe on the way to their roost on the Humber, with Black-headed and Common Gulls being most numerous, but small numbers of large gulls also appear from time to time with Glaucous Gull in some winters. The more shallow area near the Humber bank holds Snipe (up to 100), and a few Jack Snipe are annual with a maximum of seven birds in some years, while Water Rails are seen quite frequently around the reed-fringed edges of the islands. A larger reedbed has developed in the most westerly pit in recent years and for several winters one or two Bitterns have been seen. As they feed in the narrow reed fringes around the islands and pit edges they often give reasonable views to patient observers. Long-eared Owls roost in the hawthorn scrub and Short-eared Owls are often seen over nearby rough grass fields. Even species such as Snow Bunting have sometimes wintered along the seawall, where weed seeds prove attractive and Bearded Tits are occasional in the reedbeds.

Breeding species include a good population of Reed and Sedge Warblers in the *Phragmites* and sedges around the pits, with Grasshopper Warblers regular in rough grass areas amongst the industrial sites and odd birds often singing from the stunted roadside hawthorns. Water Rails have bred in recent years and an odd pair of Oystercatcher usually attempt to do so, with Canada and Greylag Geese and Mute Swans also breeding. A good variety of warblers occur in the hawthorns, with Lesser Whitethroats being numerous. During mid to late May, hunting Long-eared Owls may be seen over adjacent rough grass fields from as early as 7 pm, when they offer exceptional views.

Waders occur in their greatest numbers and variety during the spring and autumn migration periods, which may in effect melt together with the last northbound waders passing in early June and the first Green Sandpipers and Ruff appearing back from mid June. A total of 38 species of wader has been recorded at the pits since 1970, an exceptional total for such a relatively small site. Dunlin and Redshank are present in winter, with Dunlin peaking in October at over 1,000 birds, while in 1995 Redshank peaked at 900 during August on spring tides. Spotted Redshanks and Ruffs, once regular with up to 16 birds between June and August and up to 140 in September respectively, have both declined markedly of late. Regular passage species include Greenshank, Black and Bar-tailed Godwits, Curlew Sandpiper, Little Stint, Green, Wood and Common Sandpipers. A new wintering population of Black-tailed Godwits, which has become established on the outer Humber in recent winters, often arrives at Killingholme during August and stays there for a few weeks. During 1995 this flock reached a record total of 178 birds in the pits in late August.

The list of vagrants is a long one, with species from Europe and Scandinavia such as Red-necked Phalarope, Kentish Plover and Temminck's Stint matched by birds with more distant origins, from Sharp-tailed Sandpiper (eastern Siberia) to Grey Phalarope (from the Arctic) to five species of nearctic wader: American Golden Plover, Pectoral, White-rumped and Baird's Sandpipers and Lesser Yellowlegs. Spoonbills were also regular visitors during the late 1970s but none has been seen of late, maybe due to increased disturbance. The adjacent shore attracts feeding Whimbrel, Turnstone and Ringed Plovers, some of the latter breeding on a large area of tipped chalk to the south of the pits. Wildfowl also gather in the early autumn, before the start of the shooting season, with Shoveler, Teal and Wigeon all regular and Pintail and Garganey being almost annual.

Being on the side of the Humber with grazing marshes farther to the northwest and southeast, there are regular records of Short-eared Owls from the autumn through to April–May, and Marsh Harriers, which are

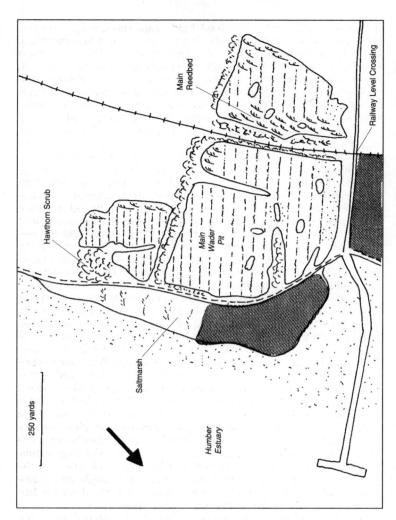

increasing on the Humber, are seen several times during the spring.

The concrete seawall also offers a place from which to watch the estuary on rough and windy days, when with north to easterly winds and bad weather seabirds may be forced up the Humber. The range of species observed varies from terns of five species, Arctic and Great Skuas to Guillemots, Kittiwakes and sea-duck, which may all occur in reasonable numbers. The concrete walls swarm with spiders and small flies during hot weather when flocks of Yellow and Pied Wagtails and a few Northern Wheatears gather to harvest the rich pickings. Even odd Black Redstarts and Stonechats occur during the later autumn, particularly along the concrete seawall to the north of the pits.

Being a regularly watched site, over the years there have been records of other vagrants, from Wryneck to White-winged Black Tern, Little Egret and Red-footed Falcon.

Timing

Something of interest may be found at anytime of year but the spring and autumn passage periods are the most interesting. With the highest tides being early morning and early evening these are the best times to see the highest numbers of waders. As the light is best in the evening, with the early morning sun making it difficult to see the larger pits on early morning tides, it is best to visit in the evening. There is also less disturbance from the industrial areas in the evening and on Sundays.

Access

North Killingholme pits are 3 miles (4.8 km) north of Immingham. Travelling east on the A160 Ulceby to Immingham road turn left at a roundabout 2 miles (3.2 km) east of South Killingholme village, beyond where the road runs between oil refineries on either side; after the roundabout the road passes under a railway bridge. Turn left after 100 yds/m onto Rosper road and follow it northwest for 2 miles (3.2 km) to where the road swings left, and take a right turn onto an unclassified road signed to North Killingholme Haven. The pits are on the right after a further three-quarters of a mile (1.2 km), with the two larger pits either side of the disused railway line. These two pits are best viewed from a car parked on the roadside, which will act as a hide and offer exceptional views of the roosting waders. It should be noted that during working hours this road is very busy with heavy lorry traffic and at such times it is not advisable to park on the road. The smaller pits lie south of the second pit and are reached by walking or driving along the concrete seawall, which then offers views over the pits. In bad weather it is possible to park in places on the seawall and watch the Humber from the car.

Calendar

October–March: Bittern, Water Rail, Dunlin, Redshank, Snipe, gulls, Long-eared Owl, Stonechat, Bearded Tit, vagrant grebes and sea-duck.

April–September: Wigeon, Teal, Shoveler, Garganey (scarce), Water Rail, Oystercatcher, Ringed Plover, Dunlin, Curlew Sandpiper, Little Stint, Ruff, Black-tailed Godwit, Bar-tailed Godwit, Redshank, Greenshank, Curlew, Whimbrel, Green Sandpiper, Common Sandpiper, Turnstone, Common Tern, Long-eared Owl, Cuckoo, Yellow Wagtail, Grasshopper Warbler, Reed and Sedge Warbler, Lesser Whitethroat, Whitethroat.

8 THE EAST LINCOLNSHIRE COAST: MABLETHORPE TO DONNA NOOK

Habitat

This area of the Lincolnshire coast has a well preserved natural sand-dune system, with high vegetated dunes, dune slacks, and extensive areas of open sand and mud flats beyond an ever expanding salt-marsh, all of which make the area one of national importance. Most of the area is made up of the Saltfleetby, Theddlethorpe National Nature Reserve and the 2425-acre Lincolnshire Trust (LTNC) reserve of Donna Nook, which stretches from Pyes Hall (Somercotes Haven) in the north to Saltfleet Haven in the south. There are thus 5 miles (8 km) of coastline, with generally open access*, which have become well known through the occurrence of rare migrants, in particular, and also through the presence of a wealth of wintering species. (* There is restricted access to the beach and foreshore areas from Pyes Hall south to Howden's Pullover on weekdays when the RAF are using the bombing ranges. A series of marker boards are situated at all public access points, with red flags flying to indicate that the shore is in use and these boards should not be passed.)

From the centre of Mablethorpe a line of dunes runs north and has pockets of elder scrub amongst the sea buckthorn, all of which can hold migrants, especially in autumn. A concrete shelter adjacent to the tourist information centre offers protection from bad weather for sea-watching and also looks out over the outfall which runs down the centre of the beach. The Saltfleetby–Theddlethorpe reserve consists mainly of a string of high old sand dunes, the principal vegetation being sea buckthorn with large areas of elder scrub and open areas of marram and long rough grasses, grazed into short turf over large areas by the abundant rabbit population.

From Churchill Road north to Sea View Farm the area is more varied, with higher dunes on the landward side, intervening freshwater dune slacks, a strip of younger dunes then an extensive salt-marsh, with a further line of developing dune ridges out towards the sea. Sea buckthorn again dominates the younger dunes along with some elder, but clumps of sallows and willows occur in the freshwater areas, which are covered in marsh orchids during the summer. Management involves the creation of permanent freshwater pools for the important natterjack toad population and for an important variety of dragonflies, clearance of invading buckthorn scrub from developing dunes, and mowing of the freshwater marsh to encourage flowers. Attractive pockets of older, mainly sycamore, trees are found at Sea View Farm and 'Paradise'.

North of Saltfleet Haven the foreshore has an extensive area of salt-marsh vegetation stretching right up to Pyes Hall. The dune system varies in width but is generally narrower and less vegetated than that further south, with little apart from clumps of sea buckthorn and patches of elders. Management work in the centre of the Donna Nook reserve has created some shallow freshwater pools, and some willows and sallows have been planted. The borrow pits on the seaward side of the man-made clay sea defences, which run from Howdens Pullover northwards, often provide muddy margins during the spring and autumn which may be attractive to waders. An obvious group of mature sycamore trees, to the south of Stonebridge car park at Donna Nook, is part of the Donna Nook RAF base and therefore out of bounds. North of Stonebridge car park the dunes lead to the site of the old Pyes Hall where a small group of sycamores and a large block of elders are a magnet for migrants.

Species

Over the last 30-year period this part of the Lincolnshire coast has received the the most frequent attention from birdwatchers and thus it has a creditable list of migrant and vagrant species. Its prime east coast location ensures a good supply of migrants but the often extensive areas of habitat and low numbers of birdwatchers make the discovery of rarer species infrequent. The area, however, probably offers some of the greatest potential for finding your own rare birds within the region. The extensive cover of sea buckthorn on the dune systems provides a source of food for large flocks of Fieldfare, Redwing and Blackbird from November through to early January, but the winter scene in the dunes can be a rather barren one, with just a few Woodcock, odd Blackcaps and a few Yellowhammers present. Formerly regular wintering Great Grey Shrikes now seem reduced to just passage birds, mainly in September–November but occasionally in March and April. Flocks of Carrion Crows, often containing 100 birds, feed on the foreshore at Theddlethorpe and Donna Nook and gather in the scrub in the dunes and on inland fields to roost. The ubiquitous Magpie also reaches high densities, with over 100 birds in winter at Theddlethorpe and Saltfleetby.

The salt-marsh areas at Saltfleetby, Saltfleet and Donna Nook provide some exceptional winter birding. Flocks of Rock Pipits, as many as 30–60 together at favoured sites like Rimac and Skidbrooke, mingle with Meadow Pipits and large flocks of Skylarks, Linnets, Twite and a few Lapland Buntings in the areas of rough wet grass. Twite flocks are also often found in association with the two key wintering passerines, Snow Bunting and Shorelark. Flocks of Snow Buntings vary in size through the winter months, and although they may occur anywhere, often feeding along the tide wrack, they are most regular on the saltings at Rimac and from Pyes Hall south to Donna Nook or on the shingle ridges by the mouth of Saltfleet Haven. Shorelarks, formerly a much more frequent visitor, with records of flocks of up to 120 birds at Donna Nook in the 1960s, are now rather scarce, but a small flock usually winters on the saltings at Rimac and others may well occur amongst the samphire beds further north from Saltfleet Haven to Donna Nook. The foreshore at Rimac usually has a few wintering Jack Snipe, and more on passage, and occasionally Water Pipit may winter on the freshwater pools adjacent to the car park. The outer foreshore from Rimac northwards is the haunt of large flocks of Lapwing, Golden Plover, Knot, Redshank, Mallard, Wigeon, Shelduck and dark-bellied Brent Geese. The latter peaking at around 1,500–2,000 birds in January, are best seen from Sea Lane Saltfleet, Howden's Pullover or the Rimac and Sea View car parks.

With such an abundance of flying food there are inevitable concentrations of raptors. Merlins (up to seven), Hen Harriers (5–6), Sparrowhawks and odd Peregrines all winter along this stretch of coast, and sudden dreads by huge clouds of waders and wildfowl usually mean a raptor is in the area. Cormorants gather to rest at the mouth of Saltfleet Haven along with large flocks of large gulls, mainly Herring and Great Black-backs but with regular records of Glaucous Gull from January onwards, and frequent Kittiwakes. The sea is often rather quiet in midwinter but there are always Red-throated Divers offshore with a few Guillemots and small wintering flocks of Common Scoter. One of the best places for watching these birds is the higher dunes just to the north of Mablethorpe, where a sunken forest offshore seems to attract feeding birds and the outfall pulls in feeding gulls.

Shorelarks

The usual scatter of scarce early spring migrants can be expected any-where with suitable habitat. Finding Firecrests in the sea buckthorn scrub is mainly a matter of luck and good hearing, but Stonechats, Black Redstarts and Northern Wheatears favour close-grazed grassy and sandy areas and manure hills. The distinctive Scandinavian race of Rock Pipit is a regular early spring migrant on the foreshore and should not be confused with Water Pipit. Short-eared Owls on their return jour-ney often concentrate on the coastal dunes and foreshore in March and April. Visible migration along the dunes involves Meadow Pipits, Skylarks, Swallows, Sand and House Martins, Linnets, Goldfinches, Turtle Doves and small numbers of raptors, notably Marsh Harriers and Hobbies during May.

Spring falls of migrants are infrequent but a few species, such as Ring Ouzels, may stay off passage for longer periods than is usual. Whitethroats are easily the most numerous breeding warbler, with less-er numbers of Sedge Warbler, Willow Warbler, Blackcap and a few pairs of Grasshopper Warbler at Rimac. Territory-holding Nightingales have been fairly regular in recent years, with passage birds in April and May often joining them in song. Scarce migrants in the later spring, mainly May, are mostly drifted in on east or northeast winds with mist or rain. Falls are dominated by Northern Wheatear, Whinchat, Redstart, Willow Warbler (often of the race *acredula*), Spotted Flycatcher and smaller numbers of Pied Flycatcher, Wood Warbler and perhaps a Golden Oriole, Wryneck, Red-backed Shrike or the increasingly rare Ortolan Bunting. The numbers of birds, however, are never as impres-sive as in autumn and many falls will involve only a few birds of a lim-ited number of species.

Easterlies, with rain, from mid May, are the best conditions for bringing in the delightful Red-spotted Bluethroats, males of which have been recorded singing and briefly holding territory, or maybe a Common Rosefinch, with a good chance of a singing Marsh Warbler from late May to mid June. Overshooting spring migrants from the south have included Spoonbill, Little Egret, Purple Heron and Night Heron, all at Rimac on the freshwater pools and at Donna Nook on the 'flashes'. The sandy foreshore plays host to significant flocks of summer-plumaged northern Ringed Plovers, Dunlin and Sanderling, the latter numbering 600+ in most years. The sandy fields on the inland side of the sea bank at Donna Nook are a regular spring stop-over for trips of Dotterel, the best fields varying with the stage of cultivation from year to year. Breeding Little Terns hang on precariously on the outer ridges, suffering from disturbance by human visitors, flooding by spring tides and predation from foxes, Kestrels and early autumn Merlins. Feeding birds are best seen at the mouth of Saltfleet Haven, where they also rest on the beach. Keep well away from designated, fenced, breeding areas where a few pairs of Oystercatcher and Ringed Plover also nest.

From July onwards the terns and gulls which feed offshore gather to rest and roost on the sand bars around the mouth of Saltfleet Haven, where they give good views. Sandwich Terns, with attendant fledged young, many colour-ringed birds originate from the Farne Islands colonies, build up to a few hundred birds by mid August. Smaller numbers of Common Terns with a few Arctics and Kittiwakes are also present and the gathering of birds attracts odd vagrants such as the 1993 Lesser Crested and White-winged Black Terns and over the years a number of Sabine's Gulls. The fishing terns also pull in feeding Arctic Skuas, which loaf offshore and frequently fly right up the beach chasing food-carrying adult terns. Later in the autumn, skuas may rest on the beach here and offer unrivalled opportunities for study. Up to 20 Pomarine Skuas were seen on the beach here daily in September 1987.

This stretch of the coast in general is not good for seawatching in bad weather as the shore is so exposed and rough seas make seeing birds in the swell often impossible. The best vantage points are the dunes and shelters at Mablethorpe, which offer a little height and shelter. Passage waders include the usual species, Greenshank, Spotted Redshank (regular in Grainthorpe Haven), Green and Wood Sandpipers and a few Little Stints and Curlew Sandpipers on the saltings. Large flocks of Whimbrel move south during July–August.

Most of the passerine interest of the autumn is related to falls of Scandinavian and eastern species, which arrive in easterly winds anytime from early August onwards, but with most frequency from the third week of August through to the first week of November. Species such as Redstart, Whinchat, Northern Wheatear, Willow Warbler and Whitethroat may be widespread but specialised feeders such as Pied, Spotted and Red-breasted Flycatchers and the rarer *Phylloscopus* warblers become concentrated in favoured stands of sycamores, willows and sallows. Good sycamore copses are found at Pyes Hall, Saltfleet village, Sea View Farm and Theddlethorpe village, with extensive patches of willows and sallows in the freshwater marsh at Rimac where a long willow hedge runs the length of the inland side of the reserve. Icterine and Barred Warblers, both very scarce even in good conditions, are best searched for in berry-laden elders.

Wrynecks are often on open sandy areas amongst the dunes; larks, pipits, wagtails and buntings on the stubble or worked fields just inland of the coastal strip and Red-backed Shrikes are often associated with hawthorn and elder bushes. Late September and October offer the best chance of eastern vagrants; amongst the migrant Stonechats may be a Siberian Stonechat, a Firecrest, Yellow-browed or Pallas's Warbler with the Chiffchaffs and Goldcrests in the sycamores, or a Richard's Pipit in the long grass of the dunes. This area of the coast is particularly noted for Richard's Pipits, up to ten birds occur in some years, with the dunes to the north of Rimac car park and the freshwater marsh, dunes and fields north from Howden's Pullover to Pyes Hall being regularly frequented spots.

There is a prominent passage of Rock and Meadow Pipits and Reed Buntings during October with variable numbers of Lapland Buntings, often just heard and seen flying through but also frequenting the inland stubble fields with flocks of Skylarks. Grounded flocks of Fieldfares, Redwing and Blackbirds are accompanied by small numbers of Ring Ouzels and later arrivals in October and November usually bring a few Black Redstarts, Firecrests and Long-eared Owls with the Woodcock. Regular ringing at Theddlethorpe dunes in recent years gives an indication of what vagrants may be skulking in the sea buckthorn scrub, with records of Thrush Nightingale, Red-flanked Bluetail, Cetti's, Blyth's Reed, Subalpine, Arctic and Radde's Warblers.

Observations at Donna Nook and Saltfleetby give an even better hint of what is there to be found by the diligent observer with an enviable list which includes Red-breasted Goose (with Brents), White-tailed Eagle, Red-footed Falcons, Spotted Crake, Corncrake, Common Crane, American Golden Plover, Pectoral, Buff-breasted and Broad-billed Sandpipers, Great Snipe, Laughing Gull, Great Spotted Cuckoo, Scops Owl, Bee-eaters, Tawny and Olive-backed Pipits, Thrush Nightingale, Red-flanked Bluetail, Desert Wheatear, Savi's, Marsh, Greenish, Radde's and Dusky Warblers, Woodchat, Lesser Grey and Isabelline Shrikes, Arctic Redpolls, Parrot Crossbills, Ortolan and Rustic Buntings and the most recent and most unlikely yet, the Alpine Accentor in November 1994.

Timing

This area offers something of interest throughout the winter, and spring and autumn migration periods. As with other coastal localities, seabirds are best looked for after or during northerly gales, and drift migrants following periods of easterly to southeasterly winds. Within these general confines the foreshore at Saltfleet village is best looked at early in the morning before holiday makers and dog walkers cause disturbance. The foreshore at Donna Nook is an RAF bombing range with access only possible to the shore at weekends and when the red warning flags are not flying.

The stretch of dunes north from Stonebridge car park to Pyes Hall is best looked at on weekdays before bombing starts at about 0800 hours, as the incoming planes fly low over the dunes and cause real noise problems. At weekends there are usually no problems, except the widespread ones of disturbance by dog walkers. An added attraction at Donna Nook in the late autumn is provided by the grey seals, which pup on the upper reaches of the beach near the Stonebridge car park. Please heed the instructions relating to reducing disturbance to these mammals.

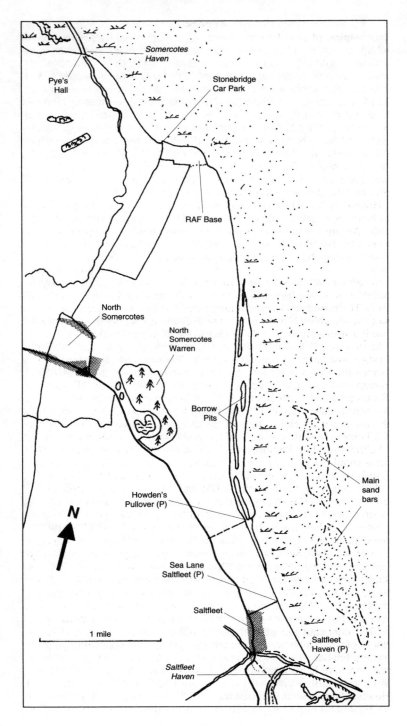

Access

This section of coastline has plenty of available public access points which are detailed here. Other tracks and roads are usually private and visitors should only use the well signed official access points. All of the area is accessed from the main A1031 Cleethorpes to Mablethorpe coast road. For Donna Nook and Pyes Hall follow the signs to Donna Nook and the sea, in North Somercotes village. Once through the village the road runs straight for 2 miles (3.2 km) to the car park at Stonebridge (TF 422 998). Access to the beach and foreshore is usually restricted on weekdays, when the red flags are flying, but is unrestricted at weekends. Pyes Hall is a 1-mile (1.6 km) walk north along the dunes or beach. The Donna Nook reserve proper can be reached by walking south for about 1.5 miles (2.4 km) along the beach before entering the dunes south of the coastguard tower.

Howden's Pullover is signed from the A1031, 1.5 miles (2.4 km), south of North Somercotes village, 0.75 miles (1.2 km), south of the Lakeside Lido. An uneven track leads down to the sea bank where there is a car park (TF 449 952). It is then possible to walk north to Donna Nook reserve along the sea bank, dunes or foreshore, or south to Saltfleet village.

In Saltfleet village take the turn down Sea Lane where a car park with toilets and a cafe, open in summer, is found after 400 yds/m (TF 457 944). The raised sea defences here offer good views over the extensive salt-marsh, which is particularly interesting in the winter. Tracks lead off north towards Howden's Pullover and south to Saltfleet Haven.

Moving south through Saltfleet the road turns sharp right over two bridges just after a garage on the right. Take the left turn immediately before the sharp bend and an uneven track follows the bank of the Haven itself to a small car park adjacent to a line of dunes (TF 464 934). Footpaths head north on either side of the dune ridge, offering views of the scrub, salt-marsh and inland fields. It is also possible to walk out to the mouth of the Haven to look for seabirds, gulls and waders but the tidal creeks hereabouts are very dangerous and vigilance is necessary.

Saltfleetby–Theddlethorpe NNR has six access points, all of which have small car parks and offer immediate access to the dune system, foreshore and beach, which forms the reserve as a whole. In Saltfleet village, travelling south on the A1031, the road bends sharp right over a bridge over the Haven, here a track leads straight on to Paradise at the northern end of the reserve. Moving further south along the A1031, successive metalled tracks lead off left to Sea View Farm (TF 465 924) opposite the B1200 turning to Louth. This small car park is set adjacent to a group of old sycamore trees, which prove attractive to passage flycatchers and warblers. About 800 yds/m further south the A1031 turns sharp right, a track leads off sharp left to the Rimac car park (TF 468 916), reached via the rough track over a wooden bridge which spans the Great Eau. A salt-marsh viewpoint (with access for the disabled) has recently been constructed straight out from this car park. Following the A1031, checking the grass fields on either side of the road for large flocks of Golden Plover and sometimes grey geese in the winter, it takes a sharp left-hand bend, then after 1.5 miles (2.4 km) again turns right. A left turn here leads down Churchill Road to another car park (TF 478 901). Two further car parks can be accessed from Theddlethorpe St Helen village. After the church the A1031 has been improved into a gentle right-hand curve. A left turn on this bend splits into two metalled

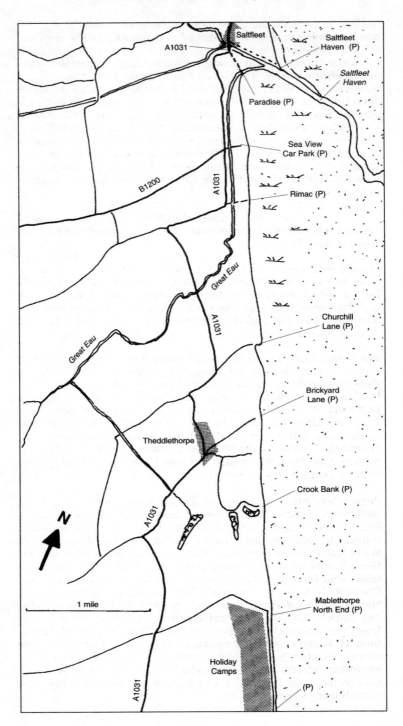

tracks, the northern one going down to Brickyard Lane (TF 485 888) and the southern one winding about 1 mile (1.6 km) to Journey's End (TF 489 884), down Sea Lane.

A number of car parks are found at Mablethorpe, with the most useful being at North End (TF 498 870) and on the dune top, 1 mile (1.6 km) further south. From the A1031, 1.5 miles (2.4 km) south of Theddlethorpe, take the minor road east, signposted to Mablethorpe North End, and where the road turns at right angles to the right there is a car park immediately in front and to the right with access to the dunes and beach. Continuing on this road, which runs south at the base of the dune system, after 800 yds/m the entrance to a car park on the left is marked by an overhead height restriction bar. From this car park the seawatching shelter is a further 200 yds/m farther south along the dunes or beach.

Calendar

Resident: Little Grebe, Sparrowhawk, Barn Owl, Meadow Pipit, Tree Sparrow, Reed Bunting.

December–February: Red-throated Diver, Bewick's Swan, Whooper Swan, Brent Goose, Shelduck, Wigeon, Shoveler, Common Scoter, Hen Harrier, Merlin, Peregrine, Water Rail, Ringed Plover, Golden Plover, Lapwing, Sanderling, Snipe, Glaucous Gull, Guillemot, Short-eared Owl, Shorelark, Rock Pipit, Water Pipit (rare), Stonechat, Twite, Lapland Bunting, Snow Bunting.

March–May: Red-throated Diver, Common Scoter, Marsh Harrier, Hen Harrier, Osprey (passage), Merlin, Hobby, Peregrine, Quail, Ringed Plover, Dotterel (scarce, April–May), Grey Plover, Knot, Sanderling, Dunlin, Ruff, Jack Snipe, Bar-tailed Godwit, Whimbrel, Curlew, Redshank, Greenshank, Green Sandpiper, Common Sandpiper, Turnstone, Little Gull, Glaucous Gull, Sandwich Tern, Common Tern, Arctic Tern, Little Tern, Turtle Dove, Cuckoo, Short-eared Owl, Shorelark, Yellow Wagtail, Black Redstart, Redstart, Whinchat, Stonechat, Northern Wheatear, Ring Ouzel, Grasshopper Warbler, Reed Warbler, Sedge Warbler, Firecrest.

August–November: Red-throated Diver, Sooty Shearwater, Manx Shearwater, Leach's Petrel, Brent Goose (September–November), Eider, Common Scoter, Velvet Scoter, Red-breasted Merganser, Marsh Harrier (to October), Hen Harrier (September on), Merlin, Hobby, Water Rail, Golden Plover, Knot, Sanderling, Ruff, Black-tailed Godwit, Green Sandpiper, Wood Sandpiper, Pomarine Skua, Arctic Skua, Long-tailed Skua, Great Skua, Mediterranean Gull, Little Gull, Sandwich Tern, Common Tern, Arctic Tern, Little Tern, Guillemot, Long-eared Owl, Short-eared Owl, Kingfisher, Wryneck (scarce), Rock Pipit (September on), Black Redstart, Redstart, Whinchat, Stonechat, Northern Wheatear, Ring Ouzel, Icterine Warbler (scarce), Barred Warbler (scarce), Yellow-browed Warbler (scarce, September–November), Pallas's Warbler (scarce, October–November), Firecrest, Pied Flycatcher, Red-breasted Flycatcher (scarce, September–November), Red-backed Shrike, Great Grey Shrike, Twite (September on), Lapland Bunting (September on), Snow Bunting (September on).

9 LAUGHTON FOREST, SCOTTON COMMON

Habitat

Laughton Forest is the modern title for the extensive, mainly coniferous, woodland planted by the Forestry Commission on what was the open sandy heathland known as Scotton Common. The area forms part of the extensive blown-sand region of northwest Lincolnshire, which overlies the ironstone bearing sandstone that gave rise to the steel industry of Scunthorpe and led to the destruction of most of the natural heathland of the area which supported a wide variety of heathland species until into the nineteenth century. The former Scotton Common was composed of dry sandy heath with some pockets of wet acidic scrub and areas of open acid bogs, some of which remain within the forest as SSSIs. Planting with conifers began in the 1920s, and the vast majority of the common was under blanket conifers by 1935 when the last Black Grouse was recorded. These early plantings reached maturity from 1980, and extensive clear-felling and replanting has taken place on a rotational basis from then onwards. The vast majority of the forest is under private ownership but is leased to the Forest Enterprise, which means that there is a rather limited degree of access to some of the area. Tracks constructed of Scunthorpe slag and chalk dissect the blocks of conifers and serve to break up the monotony of parts of the forest.

Most of the forest is composed of Corsican and Scots pine, with a few small plantations of larch and small areas of birch, willow, hawthorn and blackthorn scrub, and even stands of poplars. The acid bogs left as SSSIs within the forest consist of open water, often with a reed fringe, and surrounding willow and birch scrub with odd standard Scots pines. There are, in addition, areas of birch woodland and some older oak woodland to the south of the forest proper, with some fairly extensive areas of rough grazing towards Morton, while to the west the open rich peaty soils of the Trent floodplain are intensively cultivated. The most recent developments in the forest concern the proposed creation of an 198-acre (80 ha) area of heathland in the east of the forest, which will replace the coniferous woodland there as it is felled. This Forest Enterprise management plan is an exciting development in what is a naturally important remnant of the old Lincolnshire heathlands.

To the east of the main forestry block lies the Lincolnshire Trust (LTNC) reserve of Scotton Common. Extensive areas of invading birch and pine have been cleared recently to create a more open heathland habitat and present management involves grazing by Hebridean sheep to keep the ground vegetation short. Recent reserve extensions onto a large open area of short-grazed fields with pockets of gorse and birch scrub to the northeast have added to the value of the reserve. This area as a whole offers extensive potential for a variety of specialist bird species and yet remains largely underwatched.

The whole area is surrounded by mainly arable farmland but there are further pockets of heathland to the north around Scotton village, some of which have recently been converted to golf courses. The River Trent is a short distance to the west and flood management 'washes' exist at Susworth and Scotterthorpe, which can prove attractive especially during the winter and spring, when they hold flocks of Wigeon and Teal and often attract hunting Short-eared Owls.

Species

Most blocks of conifer forest are at their least impressive in the winter months when they can appear very sterile birding haunts unless the birder is lucky enough to bump into one of the many roving flocks of small birds, dominated by the tits, which make up a sizeable proportion of the resident bird population. Coal, Blue and Great Tits dominate the Laughton flocks but there are good numbers of Treecreeper, Long-tailed Tit and Goldcrest in most years. Parties of Siskin, Redpoll and Common Crossbill are more erratic, with several in some winters and hardly any in others. These three species are most reliable in late March and April when returning winter visitors stop off to feed on the ripening pine cones, often feeding in their greatest numbers in the old trees by the main car park. At such times they are joined by Greenfinches, Goldfinches, Chaffinches and a few Brambling, which during the winter form large flocks (up to 500 Chaffinches) around the edges of the forest, often feeding on the disturbed ground of free range pig units, which have increased in the sandy fields around the forest notably to the southwest around the cricket ground and on the road out towards Morton.

Rarer species have occurred and a party of Parrot Crossbills favoured the car park trees in the 1990–91 winter, when an Arctic Redpoll was found in a large flock of Redpolls feeding in the birch scrub. More recently up to seven Arctic Redpolls have been present in flocks of up to 450 Mealy Redpolls during the 1995–6 winter. The locally high concentrations of Mistle Thrushes are resident and often in song by December, while visiting flocks of Redwing and Fieldfare are found in surrounding fields, roosting in the forest, again often in greatest numbers in April. There is a huge winter Woodpigeon roost. Raptors always include several Sparrowhawks, often in display by February, the odd Common Buzzard is seen occasionally and Rough-legged Buzzards have wintered.

Spring and summer offer the best birding with the speciality species being relatively common and easy to see. Great Spotted and Green Woodpeckers are both common but heard more than seen, Treecreepers reach high densities along with Coal Tits and the beautiful song of the Mistle Thrush is always in the air. Several pairs of Sparrowhawks can be seen skydiving in display on warm spring mornings when the local Grey Herons are already sitting on their nests.

Summer visitors include impressive numbers of Chiffchaff, Willow Warbler and Garden Warbler with the clear-fells resounding to the songs of newly arrived Tree Pipits, which perform their parachute displays from mid April right through the summer. Woodlarks have also been found in the area for some years but their numbers remain low. The best chance of seeing this species is to listen for the singing males in March and early April when they perform their song flight high over suitable territories. Common Crossbills may linger in some years and there is often a further arrival of birds in June and July along with Siskins. Warm summer evenings from late May are most productive, with the singing Tree Pipits and warblers gradually replaced in the late evening by roding Woodcocks and that most characteristic heathland sound the churring of the Nightjar. In recent years up to 30 churring

Nightjar

males have been censused here. By standing on the tracks adjacent to the clear-fells exceptional views can be had of the males' wing-clapping display flight, and the birds will often come close to investigate human intruders. On no account, however, should tape recordings be used to attract birds, which are easily seen without resorting to this behaviour. The sqeaky-gate call of young Long-eared Owls is usually evident as dusk approaches and adults are often out hunting early during late May and June when they can often be seen drifting over the clear-fells or perched up in trees around the edges of the open areas.

Timing
As with most woodland sites the greatest bird activity is in the early morning and to a lesser extent the late evening. In winter, calm days make locating the feeding passerine flocks easier, as they can be heard and seen more easily. During the spring and summer, early mornings, from dawn, provide the greatest volume of birdsong but several species can be seen throughout the day, while an evening visit on a warm calm day from late May to late August is the time to hear and see Woodcock and Nightjars.

Access
There are at present only two designated car parks in Laughton Forest, which are both accessed from the minor road which effectively encircles the forest running from the A159, Gainsborough to Scunthorpe road, through Laughton village and from Scotter village. From the A159 take the road to Laughton village, and after passing through the village turn right, just before the cricket ground on the right. This minor road runs for 3 miles (4.8 km) to the northwestern tip of the forest at Tuetoes Hills where there is a car park on the left (SE 845 015). The main car parking area for the forest walks is found by turning right up a rough track, opposite a signed road to Hardwick Grange Farms, 1.5 miles (2.4 km), from Laughton village (SK 842 999).

Access to the southern end of the forest, south of the main through-track which passes the car park, is prohibited, but the northern section has relatively open access. By following the rough track eastwards from the car park some open clear-felled areas are found on either side of the track. The old pines by the car park are a favourite feeding site for Common Crossbills. Access to the Lincolnshire Trust reserve at Scotton Common is by permit only. Turn off the A159, 2.5 miles (4 km) south of

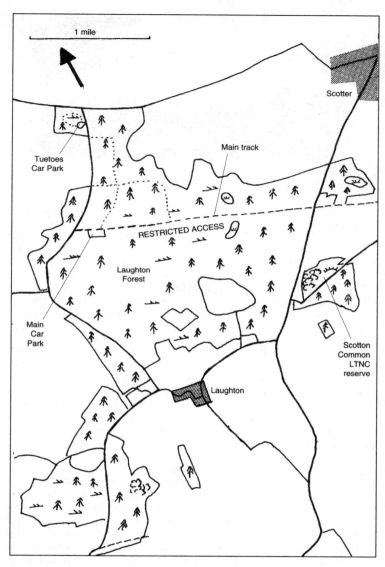

Scotter, or north of Blyton, down a road signposted to Scotton. The reserve is on the left after just over half a mile (0.8 km) and is signposted.

Calendar

Resident: Sparrowhawk, Woodcock, Tawny Owl, Green Woodpecker, Great Spotted Woodpecker, Mistle Thrush, Goldcrest, Long-tailed Tit, Coal Tit, Treecreeper, Chaffinch, Bullfinch, Yellowhammer.

April–September: Grey Heron, Hobby (rare), Stock Dove, Turtle Dove, Cuckoo, Long-eared Owl, Nightjar, Tree Pipit, Garden Warbler, Chiffchaff, Willow Warbler, Spotted Flycatcher, Jay, Siskin, Common Crossbill.

October–March: Common Buzzard (rare), Woodpigeon (large roost), tit flocks, Brambling, Chaffinch (large flocks), Siskin, Redpoll, Common Crossbill.

10 THE LINCOLN AREA   OS Map 121

The wider area around the city of Lincoln offers an attractive range of birdwatching localities, all within easy reach of each other. The city lies in a gap cut through the ridge of the limestone heights by the River Witham on its course down to the Wash. Extensive sand and gravel deposits lie to the west and south of the city, while the broad valley of the Witham to the east forms an important habitat.

HARTSHOLME PARK/SWANHOLME LAKES

Habitat
On the southern outskirts of the city are Hartsholme Country Park and Swanholme Lakes, a series of artificial lakes and gravel pits amongst a setting of ornamental woodlands, with some large areas of wet natural birch, Scots pine, sallow, willow and blackthorn combined with planted understorey of rhododendron and bramble. Open areas of rough grassland increase the diversity of vegetation. The Country Park is managed by the local council, and being so close to the city is very popular with the general public.

Species
This locality offers a good range of woodland species within a fairly easily worked area, which is of easy access from the city centre. The winter months bring varying flocks of Siskin and Redpoll to the alders, and wandering tit flocks often contain Treecreepers and Goldcrests, with the odd Firecrest noted in a recent winter. Indeed Firecrests may be more regular in what is prime wintering habitat, with a good growth of evergreens amongst the deciduous trees. Both Great and Lesser Spotted Woodpeckers are present, with the latter at their most obvious from March through April when the males are drumming and displaying. The damper areas of the park have a few Woodcock and odd Water Rails are fairly regular and may be easy to see with a little patience.

Summer produces a good range of breeding warblers, Chiffchaff, Willow and Garden Warbler, Blackcap, Whitethroat and Lesser Whitethroat with several pairs of Spotted Flycatcher. Wood Warblers make occasional brief singing visits in early May and local Hobbies can sometimes be seen hawking dragonflies from late May onwards through to early September.

Timing
Early morning visits are recommended to avoid the crowds, especially at weekends, but even when a lot of people are present most keep to the footpaths and the woodland species are often still visible later in the

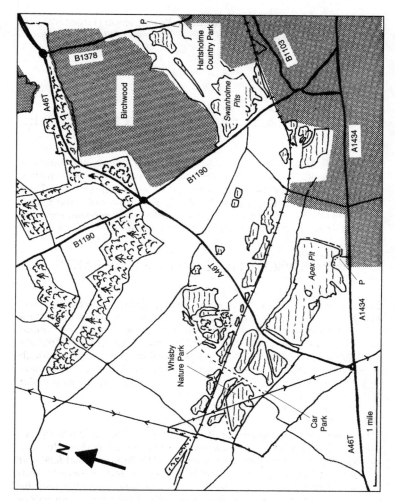

day. Autumn is probably the quietest period, although parties of young
warblers and tits will enliven the day.

Access

The entrance to Hartsholme Country Park is off Skellingthorpe road
(the B1378), one of the city artery routes, signed to Birchwood from a
roundabout on the A46 Lincoln by-pass (at SK 934 710). The park is
obvious on the right after 1 mile (1.6 km), where there is a car park. A
footpath leads through the woodland down the side of a linear channel
to Swanpool Lakes.

Calendar

Resident: Sparrowhawk, Kestrel, Tawny Owl, Green Woodpecker, Great
Spotted Woodpecker, Lesser Spotted Woodpecker, Mistle Thrush,
Goldcrest, Long-tailed Tit, Willow Tit, Coal Tit, Treecreeper, Jay,
Redpoll, Bullfinch, Yellowhammer.

October–March: Water Rail, Woodcock, Fieldfare, Redwing, tit flocks, Brambling, Siskin.

April–September: Hobby, Turtle Dove, Cuckoo, Garden Warbler, Wood Warbler (scarce May), Spotted Flycatcher.

WHISBY NATURE PARK/APEX PIT

Habitat

To the south and west of the city are extensive gravel and sand deposits between North Hykeham, Thorpe-on-the-Hill and Whisby, which have given rise to a large scale aggregate extraction industry, which in turn has left abandoned workings as flooded sand and gravel pits, now forming a bird-rich environment. The pit complex at Whisby has now been turned into a nature park managed and run jointly by the local councils and the Lincolnshire Trust (LTNC), with open public access and a visitor centre. In spite of the numbers of visitors the site maintains its importance for a wide and varied number of species of birds.

Habitat ranges from shallow open, fairly recently flooded workings, with islands for breeding gulls and terns, through deeper more established waters, to boggy marshland sites with *Juncus* and reedmace, to sallow and willow scrub, and to birch with some old standard oaks. More open areas of grassland are found interspersed amongst the trees. The main pit at Whisby has four hides along the banks. Nearby Apex Pit, an older pit with an extensive acreage of deep water, is an important spot for wildfowl and also plays host to a huge gull roost.

Species

Wildfowl numbers vary with the weather conditions and the state of flooding in adjacent wetland sites but this area usually has a good variety of species from the ubiquitous Mallard through Wigeon, Teal, a few Shoveler, good totals of Gadwall, Pochard and Tufted Duck to a few Ruddy Ducks. A large flock of feral Greylag Geese is usually present along with large numbers of Canada Geese in summer.

Whisby Pits are the best site for dabbling duck, while Apex draws in good numbers of Great Crested Grebe (up to 50), small numbers of Goldeneye and Goosander, again as many as 50 of the latter occurring in midwinter. The Goosander, however, move between other local feeding sites during the day, and the best times to see them are early morning and evening. Cormorants, which feed locally, rest and roost in dead trees at the northern side of Apex Pit and also on electricity wires/pylons which cross the pits at Thorpe-on-the-Hill, visible from Whisby. The marshy areas amongst the pits attract a few Snipe with odd Jack Snipe and a few wintering Green Sandpiper. A Bittern has been recorded in several recent winters but as is always the case with this species, sightings are rare.

The gull roost on Apex Pit reaches its peak in midwinter but there are sizeable totals of birds using it throughout the year. The principal species is Black-headed Gull (10–20,000 in winter), with smaller numbers of Common Gulls and in winter up to 500 Herring and Great Black-backed Gulls, feeding on the local tips during the day. Mediterranean Gulls have become a regular feature of winter evenings, with up to four birds on good nights and as many as 7–8 different birds during the winter. The larger species pull in the odd Glaucous and Iceland Gull, some of which appear regularly over a period of days or even weeks. A Kumlien's Gull was present for one evening in December 1992. Whisby is probably at its best in the spring and summer when the pits attract a good range of breeding birds and also prove a good spot for passage migrants. A breeding colony of Black-headed Gulls and Common Terns (35 pairs in 1994) tends to be situated where the appropriate conditions exist, that is where there are islands exposed in the spring. Work to regulate the levels in the main pit at Whisby should, however, make this a more permanent breeding site, and in 1994 the Common Terns nested close to the main footpath, giving superb views to visitors. Regular checking of the gull colony, and attendant non-breeding gulls, has in the past produced spring records of two Ring-billed Gulls, Laughing Gull and Caspian Tern. Other species of tern occur in spring, with Arctic and Black the most regular along with a few Little Gulls in April–May.

The shingle islands also support a few pairs of Little Ringed and Ringed Plovers, and other passage waders sometimes make brief visits, but the sandy substrate is obviously not very rich in food and most species of wader are transient visitors. Green Sandpipers are regular though, and species such as Redshank, Greenshank and Common Sandpiper frequent, while there are records of Little and Temminck's Stint and Curlew Sandpiper. Breeding-plumaged Black-necked and Slavonian Grebes have graced the pits in spring and good numbers of both Little and Great Crested Grebe nest. The scrub areas are a local stronghold of the Nightingale, with up to 4–5 males in song here each year. Garden Warblers are also numerous, and there is the usual good range of breeding summer warblers plus Cuckoo, Turtle Dove and 1–2 pairs of Kingfisher.

There are breeding colonies of Sand Martins in the pits, which are still being excavated, and the constant presence of these birds plus Swallows, House Martins and Swifts, which feed on the abundance of flying insects, no doubt account for the frequent visits by Hobbies during the summer. During July and August large flocks of Lesser Black-backed Gulls frequent the tips and roost on Apex Pit, often loafing at Whisby during the day. Several hundred birds occur at their peak and regular scrutiny is now leading to the discovery of Yellow-legged Gulls amongst the flocks in the summer. The Lesser Black-backs peak again in September and October when up to 800 birds have been counted in the Apex roost. Autumn brings more regular sightings of passage waders, peak counts of Green and Common Sandpipers, and Black Terns and the young Common Terns are on the wing. Such a well watched productive birding locality has naturally had its share of rare birds in recent years. In addition to the above gulls and terns, a drake American Wigeon with Wigeon in October, a Woodlark on recently cleared scrub in March, Wryneck in September and, best of all, a singing male White-spotted Bluethroat, which held territory in some sallow scrub for several days in June 1987.

Timing

Although Whisby is very popular with the general public, a good series of footpaths keep disturbance to a minimum, and while early mornings may be best a visit at any time of day will pay dividends, weekends of course being the busiest times for visitors. To view the gull roost arrive at least an hour before dark, and preferably two hours in the winter months.

Access

Whisby Nature Park is signposted from the A46 Lincoln bypass (at SK 923 679) down a minor road, with a car park and visitor centre on the right after a further 700 yds/m. A number of well signed trails lead around differing areas of the reserve. A number of hides overlook the most productive pit. Apex Pit can best be viewed from the south side where a rough access track leads to a boating club. From the A1434 in North Hykeham take a left turn adjacent to the Wagon and Horses public house (at SK 932 662) onto the access track and park where the track turns sharp right with the pit immediately in front. Walk down a track to the left to view the gull roost and waterfowl.

Calendar

Resident: Little Grebe, Great Crested Grebe, Greylag Goose, Gadwall, Pochard, Tufted Duck, Ruddy Duck, Sparrowhawk, Kestrel, Kingfisher, Green Woodpecker, Great Spotted Woodpecker, Lesser Spotted Woodpecker, Meadow Pipit, Mistle Thrush, Long-tailed Tit, Willow Tit, Yellowhammer, Reed Bunting.

October–March: Cormorant, Wigeon, Teal, Pochard, Tufted Duck, Goldeneye, Goosander, Snipe, Green Sandpiper, Mediterranean Gull, Lesser Black-backed Gull, Iceland and Glaucous Gulls (scarce), Fieldfare, Redwing, Tree Sparrow, Brambling, Siskin.

April–September: Garganey (scarce), Ruddy Duck, Hobby, Little Ringed Plover, Ringed Plover, Lapwing, Dunlin, Ruff, Green Sandpiper, Common Sandpiper, Mediterranean Gull (rare), Little Gull, Black-headed Gull (colony), Lesser Black-backed Gull, Yellow-legged Gull, Common Tern (breeding), Black Tern, Turtle Dove, Cuckoo, Sand Martin (colony), Yellow Wagtail, Nightingale, Sedge Warbler, Reed Warbler, Garden Warbler, Spotted Flycatcher.

THE NORTH WITHAM FENS

Habitat

To the east of Lincoln the broad open valley of the River Witham, once regularly subject to flooding and with a rich population of typical fenland birds, has now been transformed, through drainage, into a rich mainly arable landscape of huge open fields intersected with wide drainage dykes and dotted with odd scattered old willow trees. Wide drainage channels cross the fens at regular intervals, their grass banks sometimes grazed by herds of sheep, with some having small reedbeds along the inner sides. These former fens named after the villages on their edges, Branston, Potterhanworth, Nocton, Dunston, Blankney and Martin still attract large numbers of wildfowl and a good selection of raptors and so are worthy of scrutiny. On the bank of the Witham at Bardney, the settling ponds of the sugar-beet factory have long been of interest to local birdwatchers for the passage waders and wildfowl they attract, but access is generally prohibited.

Species

At first glance the fens may appear a bleak and desolate landscape in midwinter and indeed birds may be thin on the ground. Scanning the fields from different point along the roads which cross the area should produce good flocks of Stock Doves and Red-legged and Grey Partridge. Nocton Fen, has in several winters, held a wintering herd of wild swans, mainly Bewick's, which feed on the open fields and fly to Bardney to bathe on the pits. In spite of being white on a brown and green landscape the swans can be difficult to see at times due to subtle

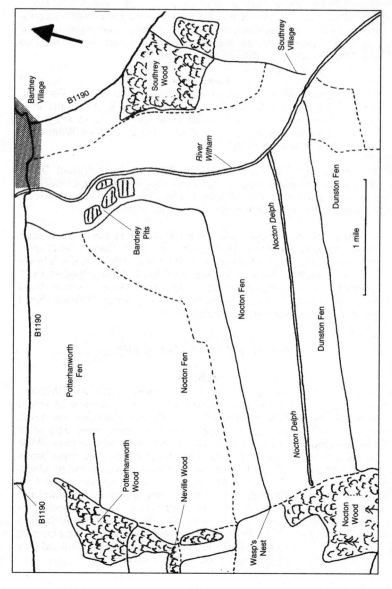

topographical differences across the fens and the distances involved. Odd parties of Pink-footed Geese also appear occasionally and a flock of Greylags is usually present at Bardney. Raptors are one of the high-lights of the winter here though, with regular sightings of Kestrel, Sparrowhawk, Merlin, Peregrine and Hen Harrier and less frequent Common Buzzard and even Rough-legged Buzzard in 1994. Barn Owls are a relatively common breeding bird and up to 4–5 may be seen on the wing in late afternoons in winter. Summer is less productive, but Marsh Harriers are regularly seen and Barn Owls often hunt in the day-time when feeding young.

By autumn, large flocks of Golden Plover and Lapwing are found on the harvested fields, and migrant Ruff and Dotterel have been found in August. The most notable feature of the autumn, however, is the roost of Marsh Harriers, which at its peak in late August or September may number 15+ birds. They seem to prefer sugar-beet fields for their roost site. Hobbies are also seen fairly frequently along the woodland edges during the autumn period.

Timing

Winter visits for wildfowl and raptors and Barn Owls, with autumn being best for the Marsh Harrier roost and flocks of Golden Plovers.

Access

The fens to the east of Lincoln are best viewed by taking the B1190 to Washingborough and Potterhanworth Booths towards Bardney. Three miles (4.8 km) from Potterhanworth Booths a right turn is signposted to Wasp's Nest. This uneven minor road runs right around Potterhanworth and Nocton Fens and allows the area to be viewed from the car. At Wasp's Nest the road bends sharp right then left and right and sharp left again at Neville Wood. A bridleway leads off to the right and joins a public footpath running along the eastern edge of Potterhanworth Wood, which gives views over the fens and into the edge of the wood-lands, which are, however, strictly private and closely monitored. Another footpath runs south from Wasps Nest alongside Nocton Wood and past the end of Nocton Delph, again allowing views of woodland birds and over the Fens. Other minor unclassified roads cross Blankney and Martin Fens, leaving the B1189 Branston–Billinghay road; the main B1191 road crosses the fens from Martin to Martin Dales leading into Woodall Spa (see Kirkby-on-Bain area).

Calendar

Resident: Kestrel, Sparrowhawk, Stock Dove, Barn Owl, Skylark,

October–March: Bewick's Swan, Whooper Swan, Pink-footed Goose, Wigeon, Goosander, Hen Harrier, Common Buzzard, Merlin, Peregrine, Golden Plover, Lapwing, Short-eared Owl, Brambling.

April–September: Marsh Harrier, Hobby, Golden Plover, Lapwing, Turtle Dove.

Habitat

Constructed in 1969, this 200-acre (81 ha), concrete-sided reservoir is owned by Anglian Water and is used for a variety of water sports, with a relatively small section in the southeastern corner being maintained as a disturbance-free area.

As the reservoir banks were raised high above the surrounding low-lying farmland it now stands as a landmark visible from several miles away on a clear day. Being higher than the surrounding farmland, the wide path around the top of the banks provides a good vantage position from which to scan the surrounding fields, which are largely arable with intersecting dykes and occasional hawthorn hedgerows.

The reservoir itself has steeply sloping inner banks of concrete with a low protecting concrete wall, the open water being dotted with buoys, used for water sports, which in turn provide perches for terns. The outer banks, again steep sided, are grassed and in places close-grazed by sheep, with some small plantations of mainly deciduous trees, which are now becoming well established. Older plantations exist around the bottom of the banks where an open flat area is also grazed. A small linear shelter-belt on the southern edge of the reservoir is composed mainly of old ash trees.

Species

Winter interest is split between wildfowl and other marine species on the reservoir, the gull roost and the species which frequent the surrounding farmland and drainage dykes. Being so close to the east coast, Covenham is in a good position for attracting vagrant sea-duck, grebes and divers. Typical wintering species include Great Crested Grebe, Cormorant, increasing numbers at their peak in the early mornings, Mallard, Tufted Duck, Pochard and Goldeneye, the latter sometimes peaking at over 100 birds. Added to these are regular but not constant appearances by small numbers of Pintail, Shoveler, Teal, Scaup, Common Scoter, Smew and Goosander. Long-tailed Ducks have wintered in small numbers (1–6) in several years. There are also frequent records of Slavonian, Red-necked and Black-necked Grebes, Red-throated, Black-throated and Great Northern Divers and, following gales, small flocks of Shags. Some of these individuals may stay for lengthy periods but an unfortunately high percentage of the divers seem to show some signs of oil contamination.

There is a large gull roost on the reservoir, mostly Common and Black-headed Gulls with a few Herring and Great Black backed Gulls. In addition to this there is a constant stream of mostly Common Gulls, which feed during the day inland on the Wolds and fly to roost on the coast, pausing to bathe on the reservoir from mid afternoon until after dark in the autumn and winter months. These gulls usually collect on adjacent fields to preen, before flying off to the coast, where they can be scanned for vagrant Mediterranean, Glaucous and Iceland Gulls. The mass of constantly changing birds, however, makes finding rarer species difficult, and once found, they are easily lost. The surrounding fields have flocks of Lapwing and Golden Plover in midwinter and often large flocks of Fieldfares, while the rough grass on the dyke banks attracts hunting Short-eared and Barn Owls. The latter species is still particularly common in the surrounding area and birds can be seen drifting over their hunting territories throughout the year. A good sized flock of Yellowhammers and Chaffinches with odd Brambling and a few Tree Sparrows is attracted to the farmyard and field in the southeast corner near the hide. Sparrowhawks are now a daily sight and wintering Merlins can usually be located on the surrounding fields with perseverance.

The reservoir walls and banks are exceptionally good for migrant Yellow and White Wagtails in spring due to the abundance of insects. Peak April counts of Yellow Wagtails may exceed 100 birds, and individuals of various other races, Blue-headed, Grey-headed and Ashy-headed, have been identified, with at least two yellow-headed birds, possibly of the eastern race *lutea*, having been photographed. A few migrant Northern Wheatears occur on the banks and odd Black Redstarts appear, often around the pumping station in the northeast corner. Adult Mediterranean Gulls in full breeding plumage are fairly regular in late March, which is also a good time for Iceland and Glaucous Gulls dropping in, often during the day rather than at roost time. Migrating flocks of Arctic, Common and Black Terns and Little Gulls pass through from mid April but seldom linger for long in the spring.

The concrete banks offer little wader habitat but Common Sandpipers are frequent and the site seems to have something of an attraction for the odd Temminck's Stint while small flocks of breeding-plumaged Sanderling and Turnstone also appear in May. On the south side of the reservoir a small plantation of ash has a thriving rookery, which can be viewed at eye level from the reservoir wall, and a few pairs of Tree Sparrow. The grassy banks often attract feeding flocks of Fieldfare, Redwing and Blackbird with a few migrant Ring Ouzels. The path around the top of the bank has a good growth of weeds, which brings feeding Linnets, Goldfinches, Greenfinches and Yellowhammers. Meadow Pipits breed in areas of rougher grasses, with attendant Cuckoos always present, but in general the range of breeding species is a limited one. Large flocks of Swifts feed over the reservoir all summer, with good numbers of House Martins, in particular, Swallows and Sand Martins during April–May and August–September.

Autumn migration brings with it a wider range of passage waders, and with birds lingering for longer periods, species such as Black Terns are more easily found. Common Sandpipers are the most regular wader but may well be outnumbered by influxes of other species like Ruff, Little Stint and Curlew Sandpiper in bumper years for these arctic breeders. A wide variety of species from Turnstone to such unlikely species as Grey Plover, Spotted Redshank, Wood Sandpiper and Black and Bar-tailed Godwit have been recorded feeding on the inpenetrable concrete banks. Regular vagrants include Red-necked and Grey Phalaropes in addition to which Black-winged Stilt, Pectoral Sandpiper, Lesser Yellowlegs and Wilson's Phalarope have all occurred. Slavonian and Black-necked Grebes may make lengthy stays during the autumn as do the vagrant sea-ducks, Velvet Scoter, Long-tailed Duck and Scaup, which appear from October onwards. Gales on the coast may bring a few seabirds onto the reservoir, there being records of Manx Shearwater, Leach's Petrel, Shags, Arctic, Pomarine and Great Skuas, and in the late autumn even Little Auks may put in a brief appearance. Being within easy sight of the coast, however, few of these birds stay long unless exhausted. Parties of Common and Black Terns and Little

Gulls vary in numbers as individuals come and go, with most Black Terns and Little Gulls following easterly winds in August.

Raptors seem to be attracted by large bodies of water, although the immediate habitat would seem to offer little in the way of suitable feeding for most species. Migrant Marsh Harriers and Ospreys are regular in spring and autumn, the winter months may produce a few Hen Harrier records and vagrants such as Red Kite and Honey Buzzard have been recorded.

Obviously a well watched large reservoir within easy flying distance of the east coast has turned up a good crop of rare birds over the years. In addition to the waders mentioned earlier, the grassy banks have played host to no fewer than three spring Ortolan Buntings, Lapland and Snow Buntings and even odd Shorelarks. Red-breasted Goose, American Wigeon and Ring-necked Duck head the list of rare wildfowl and rare terns have included Gull-billed, Whiskered and four White-winged Blacks.

Timing

Although some birds will be present at any time of year, the best periods are winter, November to March, and the spring and autumn migra-

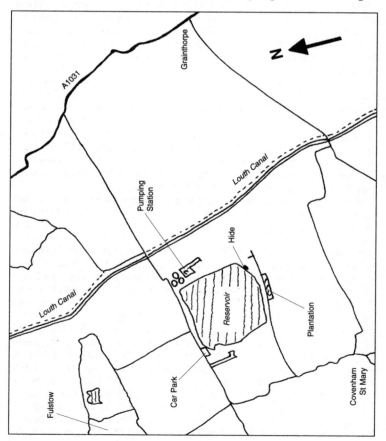

tion periods, April, May and August to October. As there is open access to all the banks of the reservoir, it is possible to compensate for the position of the sun at any time of day and the hide is well situated for scanning most of the reservoir, except in the late evenings when the sun will be shining across the water surface. With increasing use of the reservoir for a variety of water sports, early morning visits are recommended as the birds will be more settled. Late afternoon and evening are the time to view the gull roost, the exact position of which will vary with the prevailing wind direction, but the west and south banks are usually best.

Access

Covenham Reservoir is situated 5 miles (8 km) north of Louth and is equidistant between the main A16 Louth to Grimsby road and the A1031 Mablethorpe to Cleethorpes coast road. From the A16, 0.6 mile (1 km) south of Ludborough, take the minor road signposted to Covenham and Grainthorpe, 2 miles (3.2 km) farther on go straight over a crossroads and the reservoir is visible on the right. A car park is located at the first, northeastern, corner (TF 342 963). A series of steps leads up to the top of the bank, from where it is possible to walk all the way around the reservoir. From the A1031 turn west into Firebeacon Lane, signposted to Ludborough, 1 mile (1.6 km) north of Grainthorpe village. It is then 2.5 miles (4 km) to the car park as above. A hide, useful in windy and cold weather, overlooks the protected area in the southeast corner of the reservoir. The door is left unlocked but please be sure to fasten it securely on leaving as this is a very windy location and wind damage is frequent.

Calendar

Resident: Barn Owl, Meadow Pipit, Yellowhammer.

October–March: Little Grebe, Great Crested Grebe, Red-necked Grebe, Slavonian Grebe, Cormorant, Wigeon, Gadwall, Teal, Pintail, Pochard, Tufted Duck, Scaup, Long-tailed Duck, Velvet Scoter, Goldeneye, Goosander, Sparrowhawk, Merlin, Golden Plover, Lapwing, Green Sandpiper, Mediterranean Gull (rare), Iceland Gull (rare), Glaucous Gull (rare), Woodpigeon (large flocks), Short-eared Owl, Rock Pipit (scarce), Grey Wagtail (scarce), Stonechat (scarce), Fieldfare, Redwing, Brambling, Reed Bunting, Corn Bunting.

April–September: Black-necked Grebe, Marsh Harrier (passage), Sanderling, Common Sandpiper, Turnstone, Little Gull, Common Tern, Arctic Tern, Black Tern, Cuckoo, Swift, Yellow Wagtail, White Wagtail, Black Redstart, Stonechat, Northern Wheatear, Ring Ouzel, Rookery, Tree Sparrow.

OS Map 112

Habitat

Where the north–south oriented limestone ridge reaches its northern limits in the vicinity of Scunthorpe there are a few remnants of the once vast heathlands which developed on the blown sands left over from the last glacial periods. There are also large blocks of woodland with old deciduous plantations interspersed with younger conifers, some of which are already being clear-felled and replanted. Extraction of sand and gravel in the area around Messingham has created a number of recently abandoned workings, some of which have been purchased by the Lincolnshire Trust (LTNC) as a reserve. Further to the east lies the open expanse of the Ancholme Valley, offering a differing range of habitats adjacent to the woodlands, the interface between woodland and valley often being attractive to raptors.

RISBY WARREN

Habitat

The largest single remaining remnant of the old heathlands is found on Risby Warren, where heather and bracken flourish on the sandy soils, still dominating the open areas between the shelter-belts of pines. Large areas are heavily grazed by rabbits, while around the edges subsidence from past mining operations has led to some extensive tracts being fenced, to prohibit access, allowing them to revert to rough grassland. A true eyesore is the NP power lines, which stretch the length of the warren, but they do provide an unusual nesting site for a colony of Rooks.

Species

Winter interest on the warren is created by the possibility of large raptors. Common Buzzards are fairly regular, if elusive, feasting on the abundant population of rabbits, while Hen Harriers put in regular appearances. The huge winter Woodpigeon roost no doubt accounts for the visits by Peregrines, and Sparrowhawks are quite common. There is also a large roost of corvids, with a significant total of Jackdaws (up to 1,000), and Stock Doves often total 2–300 birds. Curlew are normally present along with Green Woodpeckers and the odd Short-eared Owl. A small pond near the farm on the southeastern edge of the warren sometimes has wintering Green Sandpiper and Grey Wagtail, and a Woodlark spent some days on a sandy track there one January. Spring migration brings variable numbers of Northern Wheatears, the odd Ring Ouzel and occasional sightings of Hobby. A few pairs of Curlew breed as do Green Woodpecker, Mistle Thrush and Sparrowhawk, and there is an interesting Rookery on the electricty pylons which cross the warren.

Timing

The site is used mainly as a Pheasant shoot and is usually shot on Saturdays from 1 September to 1 February, so it is best to avoid

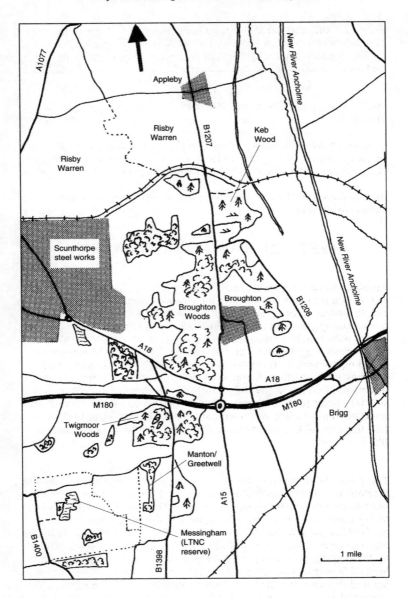

Saturdays during this period. Late afternoon is often the best time to catch up with raptors, but a sunny day with light to moderate winds will often tempt birds aloft.

Access

The Warren is all private and is managed as Pheasant shoot but there is one public footpath which crosses the whole area and allows the best sites to be studied. From the B1207 Broughton to Winterton road, turn left in Appleby village onto a minor road signed to Scunthorpe. After 1.5

miles (2.4 km) another minor road is signposted to Roxby to the right. Turn left here onto a track, marked as a dead end, and park somewhere on the roadside. The public footpath continues to the end of this track and then is well signed across the warren.

Calendar

Resident: Sparrowhawk, Kestrel, Stock Dove, Green Woodpecker, Mistle Thrush.

October–March: Hen Harrier, Common Buzzard, Rough-legged Buzzard (scarce), Merlin, Peregrine, Curlew, Green Sandpiper, Woodpigeon (large roost), Short-eared Owl, Grey Wagtail (scarce).

April–September: Hobby (scarce), Curlew, Northern Wheatear, Ring Ouzel (April, May).

GREETWELL, MANTON AND TWIGMOOR

Habitat

Another important grazed sandy heath occurs at Greetwell, here most of the area is private but some can be viewed from the roadside and a public footpath. These natural heathlands have a combination of open grazed sandy grassland with longer heather patches and stands of birch scrub, with bracken being more dominant in the summer. The old, rather acidic, 'gull ponds' at Twigmoor no longer hold the teeming breeding colonies of Black-headed Gulls which gave them their name but they form an interesting part of the old woodland complex which was planted on the sandy ridges and valleys. Many of the old trees are standard Scots pines but there are also beech and sweet chestnut and areas of younger birch scrub with alders around the edges of the lakes and the inevitable plantations of Corsican and Scots pine and a few blocks of larch.

Species

The sandy fields around the edge of Twigmoor Woods and Manton Warren are fairly unproductive agricultural areas and have recently been turned over to free-range pig rearing. This has attracted large wintering flocks of finches, mainly Chaffinch and Brambling with lesser totals of Greenfinch, Goldfinch and Linnet. Sparrowhawks are always in attendance and the recent glut of rabbits on the open warrens has led to the regular apearance of Common Buzzards. Green and Great Spotted Woodpeckers are present all year, with rare reports of Lesser Spotted Woodpecker, which are no doubt more common but are easily missed in large areas of suitable habitat. The extensive rhododendrons at Twigmoor act as a winter roost site for large numbers of finches which flock in from the surrounding fields in the late winter afternoons. Alders around the lakes host feeding flocks of Siskin and Redpoll.

The song of the Mistle Thrush is evident everywhere in the early spring, with birds particularly numerous on the heathlands where, with luck, a singing Woodlark may also be heard. A few pair of Curlew still breed and summer visitors include Tree Pipit on the heaths joining the plentiful Yellowhammers. There remains a small relict population of

Redstart in Twigmoor Woods. A few pairs of Lapwing breed on rough ground by Greetwell crossroads where feeding Turtle Doves are regular. Twigmoor Woods have a good breeding population of Jay, Treecreeper, Great Spotted and Green Woodpecker and Garden Warblers and summer sightings of the elusive Hawfinch suggest they may breed somewhere locally. A vantage point overlooking the woodlands may produce sightings of Hobby or even a rarity such as Honey Buzzard, although Common Buzzard and Osprey are better bets.

Timing
Early mornings are the best time for singing birds in spring and summer and avoid some of the dog walkers at Twigmoor. Mosquitoes can be a real problem at Twigmoor in the evenings in summer.

Access
Footpaths around the gull ponds and some of the best areas of woodland, mostly designed to show off the huge areas of flowering rhododendron in the brief summer flowering period, have recently been opened to the public in what is essentially a private woodland. Access is via two tracks, obvious to the west of the B1398, 1 mile (1.6 km) south of where it leaves the A18 (SE 943 058). Well worn tracks lead around the gull ponds in a circular route. Manton and Greetwell Warren can be overlooked from a lay-by on the side of the B1398, 800 yds/m south of Greetwell crossroads, adjacent to Aldham Plantation. Alternatively a public footpath runs north–south across the western edge of the best areas of Warren from Greetwell Hall farm to Manton village. From the B1398 turn west at Greetwell crossroads (SE 943 049) onto a minor road signposted to Messingham. The road descends a small hill amongst woodland and then turns right as it comes out into the open. Park on the left at the bottom of the hill (SE 934 046) and the public footpath heads off south across the warren, rising over a small ridge after about 800 yds/m, which offers good views over the valley to the west towards Messingham Sand Quarries reserve and over the heath/warren to the east. This footpath comes to Manor Farm after 1.25 miles (2 km) from where another path goes off right, down into the valley, and eventually joins up with the minor road (SE 923 043) on which you parked, providing a circular route back to the car park area.

Calendar
Resident: Sparrowhawk, Kestrel, Woodcock, Stock Dove, Tawny Owl, Long-eared Owl, Green Woodpecker, Great Spotted Woodpecker, Lesser Spotted Woodpecker, Meadow Pipit, Mistle Thrush, Willow Tit, Coal Tit, Treecreeper, Jay, Redpoll, Hawfinch, Yellowhammer.

October–March: Common Buzzard, Brambling, Siskin, Common Crossbill.

April–September: Osprey (annual, April, May), Hobby, Turtle Dove, Cuckoo, Nightjar, Tree Pipit, Redstart, Ring Ouzel (April, May), Garden Warbler, Wood Warbler (scarce), Spotted Flycatcher, Siskin, Common Crossbill (irregular).

MESSINGHAM SAND QUARRIES

Habitat

Extraction of sand and gravel at Messingham has led to the creation of an interesting series of pits, which are now in the later stages of succession, with reed fringes, willow and sallows clumps and birch scrub on the surrounding sandy spits and ridges. The area is now a reserve of the Lincolnshire Trust (LTNC) and management work has created some open areas amongst the invading wetland scrub and in the conifer plantation which backs the reserve, while three hides have been erected overlooking the largest shallow open water areas and one deeper water pit.

Species

This excellent reserve holds a good range of species throughout the year, being of most interest from spring through to autumn, and as well as for birds is a very important site for dragonflies.

Wintering wildfowl include good totals of Wigeon, Gadwall, Teal sometimes Shoveler, Pochard and Tufted Duck, with smaller numbers of Goldeneye and fairly regular appearances by odd Goosander and Scaup. The semi-resident flock of Canada and Greylag Geese sometimes attract other oddities, Barnacle and Pink-footed Geese occurring in most winters. Small parties of Bewick's and Whooper Swans are infrequent visitors. A few winters have brought Bittern but they are usually very difficult to catch up with even in such a resticted area of reedbeds.

The plantations and birch woodland have the usual feeding tit flocks, and there have been several wintering records of Chiffchaffs, with one of the race *tristis*. Flocks of Redpoll and Siskin feed in the alders and birch and the marshy areas have a few Snipe and odd Jack Snipe, which again are very elusive. The site is a good one for watching for raptors, seen over the heaths and woods away to the west or over the fields around the reserve. Winter sightings usually include a few Peregrine records, with odd Common Buzzard, Hen Harrier and Merlin, while spring and summer bring passage Marsh Harrier, Osprey and fairly regular sightings of Hobby.

Migrant waders in spring and autumn are attracted to the muddy areas around the pits and also to flooded areas on the grass field, the site of an old rubbish tip, to the west of the reserve proper. Ringed and Little Ringed Plovers breed, and there is often a notable gathering of young Little Ringed Plovers from nearby breeding sites, in the late summer. A few pairs of Lapwing, Snipe and Redshank nest on the fields with odd pairs of Oystercatcher. The most frequent passage waders are Green and Common Sandpiper and Greenshank, but Wood Sandpiper are annual and a wide range of species has appeared including both Bartailed and Black-tailed Godwits, Avocet, Sanderling, Turnstone, Little and Temminck's Stint, Curlew and Pectoral Sandpipers and Red-necked Phalarope.

The flooded pits have a thriving breeding colony of Black-headed Gulls, and in recent years a single male Mediterranean Gull has paired with a Black-headed Gull, rearing several hybrid young which now also appear in the colony having reached adulthood. Large numbers of Lesser Black-backed Gulls visit the pits in midsummer and bring with them the odd Yellow-legged Gull. Other breeding birds include Great Crested and Little Grebe, Shelduck, Shoveler, Tufted Duck, Pochard, Ruddy Duck and probably Gadwall.

Sand Martins

The pits are particularly rich in insect life, which proves a magnet for feeding flocks of Swallows, House Martins, Swifts and Sand Martins, the latter nesting in nearby operational sand quarries. Migrating parties of Common, Arctic and Black Terns make brief visits in the spring and autumn and a few Little Gulls are recorded most years (April–May). The combination of a wide range of habitats and an area of open water in an isolated location have brought a wide variety of rarities to the site in recent years in addition to the waders mentioned previously. Rare herons, Little, Cattle and Great White Egret and Purple Heron have all put in an appearance, American Wigeon, Green-winged Teal, Ring-necked Duck, White-tailed Eagle, Spotted Crake and Common Crane, no fewer than three Caspian Terns, a White-winged Black Tern, Red-rumped Swallow, two singing Marsh Warblers and Red-backed Shrike are all on the Messingham list. Even a pelagic species, Leach's Petrel, has occurred once following westerly gales.

Timing
The only problem at this locality is the local farmer who insists on shooting wildfowl on land adjacent to the reserve during the winter months (September to January). This usually takes place on a Saturday, when the wildfowl become well dispersed, so this day is best avoided. Spring offers the greatest variety of species and the best chance of a scarce migrant.

Access
Access is limited to permit holders only, this being a reserve of the Lincolnshire Trust. The entrance to the reserve car park (SE 908 032) is off the B1400, 800 yds/m south of the T junction from the B1400 at Messingham, signposted to Kirton Lindsey, and is approached down a rough track on the left. Some of the pits and surrounding fields can be overlooked from the minor road which runs from the B1400 at Messingham village to Scawby and also from the B1400 adjacent to Mells Farm.

Calendar
Resident: Sparrowhawk, Woodcock, Long-eared Owl, Meadow Pipit, Green Woodpecker, Jay, Yellowhammer.

October–March: Greylag Goose, Wigeon, Gadwall, Teal, Shoveler, Pochard, Goldeneye, Peregrine, Lapwing, Jack Snipe, Snipe, Brambling, Siskin.

April–September: Osprey (annual, April, May), Hobby, Oystercatcher, Little Ringed Plover, Ringed Plover, Lapwing, Dunlin, Ruff, Wood Sandpiper, Green Sandpiper, Mediterranean Gull (and hybrids), Little Gull, Black-headed Gull (colony), Common Tern, Arctic Tern, Black Tern, Turtle Dove, Cuckoo, Swift, Yellow Wagtail, Sedge Warbler, Reed Warbler, Garden Warbler.

13 CROWLE WASTE OS Sheet 112

Habitat

Crowle Waste or Moor, which lies in the far northwest corner of Lincolnshire, is the eastern extension of the far more extensive area of Thorne Moors. The whole area is an exceptionally important natural history site, being a remnant lowland raised peat bog, the largest remnant of such a site in the UK, and is designated as a SSSI. Three hundred acres (121 ha) of the section at Crowle is owned and managed by the Lincolnshire Trust, the remainder being owned by local small scale peat extraction concerns, which continue to remove the peat for sale for horticultural use.

All of the area has been affected by the activities of man over the last 400 years, with peat cutting being the most significant operation. The majority of the sections owned by the Trust have previously been subjected to peat extraction and then left to revert to semi-natural status. The result is a rich mixture of shallow acid pools, which in the northern section run in long strips or ribbons, as they are known locally, forming quite extensive areas of open water bordered by mire vegetation and separated by higher peat banks dominated by typical plants of dry acid heath such as two species of heather and bracken. Some of the deeper pools on the northern section have small reedbeds and areas of sallow scrub. The northern waymarked route around the reserve follows some of the original raised banks used as tramways during peat extraction when small trains and trucks were used to move the peat. Drier parts of the Waste are dominated by bracken and birch scrub but there is also a variety of other trees present from rowan to elder and ash, all of which are restricted in occurrence. The area as a whole is an exceptionally important one for its variety of flora, including such acid-loving species as cotton grass, hare's-tail cotton grass, purple moor-grass, two species of heather and rarities like round-leaved sundew, bog rosemary and cranberry. A total of over 3,000 species of insects has been recorded from the Thorne complex as a whole and there are large populations of typical acid heath dragonflies, such as black darter and four-spotted chaser, with a local population of the large heath butterfly.

Recent management work has centred upon clearing the invasive birch scrub from the southern part of the Trust reserve to create more open areas typical of the original peat bog, with shallow pools also having been dug to enhance the value of the site. Unfortunately, a series of dry years and deep drainage by peat extraction concerns have damaged the site over the years and the low water table has resulted in habitat degradation. The surrounding farmland is flat and was formed by warping silt onto the original rich peat, which has now turned it into productive arable land with deep open drainage ditches but no hedgerows and precious few old willows standing sentinel. Deep ploughing still brings fossilised bog trees to the surface and these can be seen piled around the field edges in some areas.

Species

Winter is a relatively quiet time on the Waste. Wildfowl include a few Teal but the pools are too acid to attract many duck. The birch scrub holds flocks of Redpolls, which vary in size with the fruiting birch crop and any autumn arrival from the continent, and roving flocks of tits, with Long-tailed Tits often being quite numerous and Willow Tits a sure bet.

The main interest is formed by the wintering raptors, which are best seen as they gather to roost. Most of the birds roost on the Thorne side of the county boundary but several arrive, from hunting over the Isle of Axholme, and gather before roosting over the Crowle side. Sparrowhawks have become rather common in recent years and there are usually Kestrels over the nearby fields. The communal roost of Hen Harriers and Merlins at Thorne may produce up to five or more of each species passing through Crowle in the late afternoon, with birds often stopping off to hunt the nearby fields before heading for the roost site. In good winters for the species there have also been regular sightings of Short-eared Owl and Rough-legged Buzzard and, of late, even wintering Marsh Harriers have appeared. Carrion Crows have communal roosts on the moors and up to 50 birds may be seen gathering in nearby fields before flying into their roosts on late winter evenings. Raucous Jays are also regular and a feature of the early spring.

Spring and summer bring a wealth of birdsong with high densities of breeding Willow Warbler, Whitethroat, Wren, Chaffinch and Yellowhammer. A few singing Nightingales, at their most northerly regular location in Britain, can be heard from the southern section of the reserve, although most seem to be on the Yorkshire side of the border. Typical heathland species include Woodcock, Tree Pipit and Nightjar, the latter typically totalling about four to six churring males, while Long-eared Owls also breed as do Green and Great Spotted Woodpeckers, Grasshopper Warbler and small numbers of Teal. A few pairs of Water Rail are present, with their squealing calls making them obvious in the early spring, while drumming Snipe and roding Woodcock are also features of late evenings and early mornings.

The abundant insect population attracts feeding flocks of Swifts and hirundines, and the emergent four-spotted chaser dragonflies are a favourite quarry of the Hobbies, which have become a regular summer feature of the area as have Marsh Harriers, which have increased on passage in spring. Whinchats bred in the past and odd pairs may still do so as birds are often seen on passage around the edges of the reserve. Adders and grass snakes are quite common from March onwards and it has to be said that this is one of the worst (or best) places for mosquitoes on warm summer nights and also for biting midges and horseflies in summer when the bracken often grows well above head height.

Timing

To see winter raptors a visit from mid afternoon is recommended, although there will be chances of seeing odd birds throughout the day. During the spring and summer anytime is suitable but early morning produces the best birdsong and evening the chance of Woodcock and Nightjar.

Access

Entrance to the Lincolnshire Trust Reserve is now generally unrestricted but visitors are requested to adhere to the restrictions which apply to other Trust reserves, to keep to waymarked routes and take special care with regard to the very high fire risk in the area. Raptors can also be seen from the unclassified roads which approach the area from Crowle town.

Heading north from the A161 in Crowle town turn left onto a minor road at the northern edge of the town, just before a sharp right-hand bend, which runs for 1 mile (1.6 km) northwest to the edge of Crowle Waste. The Lincolnshire Trust Reserve is split into two main sections: the northern section has limited parking (at SE 759 145) and a waymarked route of 6 km, while there is a larger car park for the southern

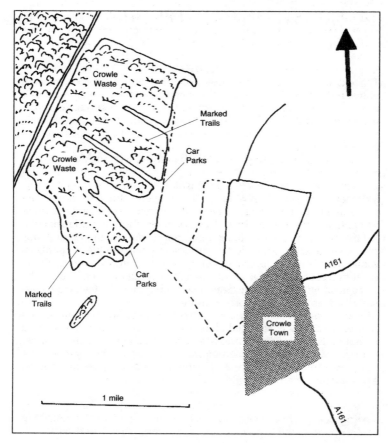

section (at SE 756 137) where a 1.25-mile (2 km) route takes in the most interesting areas of the reserve.

To see raptors in winter it is best to stay on the edge of the woodland to give a wide view over the surrounding fields, or watch from the north-western corner of the northern walking route, or watch from farther back up the approach road to gain views over the heath and fields,

Calendar

October–March: Hen Harrier, Sparrowhawk, Merlin, Rough-legged Buzzard (rare), Short-eared Owl, Willow Tit, Jay, Carrion Crow (roost), Redpoll, finch flocks, Yellowhammer.

April–September: Teal, Water Rail, Marsh Harrier (scarce), Hobby, Snipe, Woodcock, Long-eared Owl, Green and Great Spotted Woodpeckers, Nightjar, Swift, Nightingale, Whinchat, Tree Pipit, Grasshopper Warbler, Reed Warbler, Willow Tit, Redpoll, Reed Bunting, Yellowhammer.

14 KIRKBY-ON-BAIN DISTRICT OS Map 122

Habitat

This extensive district is composed of a number of relict and working gravel pits in the valley of the River Bain, along with some impressive areas of heathland and woodland on the sand and gravel deposits to the west of the river.

KIRKBY MOOR AND MOOR FARM

Habitat

The heathlands at Kirkby Moor and nearby Moor Farm are both Lincolnshire Trust (LTNC) reserves and together have an extensive area of open sandy warren, which was typical of much of the Lincolnshire heathlands up to the late 1950s when the demise of the rabbit popula-tion led to their being overrun with longer, coarser grasses and more robust vegetation. A large percentage of the heath is made up of very short rabbit-grazed turf and bare sand around the warrens, with patch-es of heather and bracken around the periphery. Shelter-belts of pine, some old standard Scots pines, and birch scrub make up most of the rest of the reserves but Moor Farm has a good acidic bog, and a pond at Kirkby Moor is surrounded by older conifers and some old oaks. The adjacent Forestry Commission-owned Ostler's plantation is mostly conifers, with a lot of Scots pine, but recent clear-felling and subse-quent replanting has opened up some of the area adjacent to Kirkby Moor itself.

Species

Roving flocks of finches and tits, Goldcrests and odd woodpeckers make up the staple winter species mix on these heathland sites, which are at their best when the fruiting of the birch and pine trees coincides with a winter influx of northern finches. Large flocks of Redpolls and Siskin will then predominate in most winters but Common Crossbills may also be in evidence especially at Moor Farm and Ostler's plantation. The old Scots pines by the roadside were popular with a wintering flock of Common and Parrot Crossbills in the 1990–91 winter when up to 40 of the rarer Parrot Crossbills were in the area. In the same winter a flock of up to 200 Redpolls at Kirkby Moor contained several Mealy Redpolls and up to four Arctic Redpolls. Woodcock feed on the wet woodland floor but are seldom seen unless flushed accidentally. Sparrowhawks are quite common and there have been past records of Common and Rough-legged Buzzards and Goshawk. Kirkby Moor was formerly quite a regular spot for a wintering Great Grey Shrike but this species' recent decline has reduced the chances of locating one of these birds, although the habitat remains excellent for the species.

Woodlark

All three species of woodpecker breed in the area, and Green Woodpeckers are particularly in evidence at Moor Farm where they feed on the open sandy warren along with exceptional numbers of Mistle Thrushes. Jays are also very common at both sites and can be seen in good numbers in March, especially, when a singing Woodlark may well be present. A few pairs of Tree Pipit breed and in most summers there are a few Common Crossbills in the vicinity, which may themselves nest in some springs. The copse and block of woodland by the pond at Kirkby Moor are a local stronghold for Nightingales with up to six males present most years. They seem to be rather easy to observe at this locality in contrast to most other sites. The same could not be said of the male Golden Oriole which sang in the copse one June day, but the other recent star attraction, a female Red-footed Falcon in May 1994, was very cooperative and often sat in small elders on the heath with one of the local Cuckoos, both birds dropping down to feed on worms and caterpillars.

Timing

The most productive time of year is spring/summer when most birds are in song and the heathland flora at its best. On warm spring days there is a reasonable chance of seeing a grass snake or the locally common

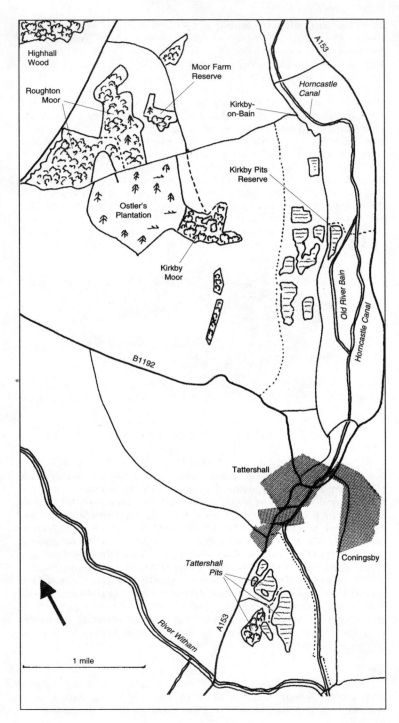

adder on the heaths. Wintering finch flocks are present from November through to February and arrivals of Common Crossbills often take place in June.

Access

Kirkby Moor and Moor Farm, both Lincolnshire Trust reserves (access by permit only), lie either side of a minor road which leaves the B1191, Woodall Spa to Horncastle road, on the eastern side of Woodall Spa and is signed to Kirkby-on-Bain. Leaving Woodall there is a public car park (TF 215 630) for the Forestry Commission Ostler's plantation walks, after 0.8 miles (1.3 km) on the right of the road. After a further 0.6 miles (1 km) another minor road runs off to the left just before a large house on the left with a stand of mature Scots pines on the roadside. Turn left here, down the side of a tree nursery, and the entrance to Moor Farm is on the left after 500 yds/m. Entrance is by permit only. Kirkby Moor reserve entrance is opposite the left turn (at TF 225 629) down a track leading across the open heath to the marked trails around the pools and woodland.

Calendar

Resident: Sparrowhawk, Kestrel, Woodcock, Stock Dove, Tawny Owl, Green, Great Spotted and Lesser Spotted Woodpeckers, Mistle Thrush, Goldcrest, Long-tailed Tit, Willow Tit, Coal Tit, Treecreeper, Jay, Redpoll, Bullfinch, Yellowhammer.

October–March: Common Buzzard, Rough-legged Buzzard (rare), Fieldfare, Redwing, Brambling, Siskin, Common Crossbill.

April–September: Turtle Dove, Cuckoo, Tree Pipit, Nightingale, Garden Warbler, Chiffchaff, Spotted Flycatcher, Common Crossbill (irregular).

KIRKBY-ON-BAIN PITS

Habitat

The sand and gravel pits at Kirkby-on-Bain are expanding in area all the time with continued extraction for the gravel workings there. The more recent pits are not visible from the roads but the older workings are now a reserve of the Lincolnshire Trust (LTNC). Here one large pit is maintained as a shallow water habitat, with gravel and sand islands and spits appearing when the water level is lowered. There is little encroaching vegetation to date but the other older pits to the west of the road now support a dense cover of willows, sallows and birch scrub on the surrounding sand spits and banks. The steep-sided banks mean that there is very little reed growth. The most recently worked-out pits to the south of the works are still in a largely just abandoned condition, with little successional vegetation, but some tree planting has taken place around the edges. Two of the pits at the northern end of the workings are presently in use as a landfill site rubbish tip, with their attendant supply of food for scavenging gulls and corvids.

Species

A number of species of wildfowl are present throughout the year, with highest totals in the winter months. There is a lot of interchange between this locality and Tattershall Pits so if a good bird is not at one site it is well worth checking the other. Key species of wildfowl are Gadwall, Shoveler, Pochard, Tufted Duck and Ruddy Duck, all of which also breed in most years or at least are present through the summer. There are occasional records of Smew, and gulls, which feed on the landfill site, mainly Black-headed and Herring, sometimes attracting the odd Glaucous or Iceland Gull in the late winter (February–March). A few Green Sandpipers winter around the pits.

Spring brings early records of Sand Martin, and there are thriving breeding colonies of this species around the pits, which no doubt accounts for the regular visitations by Hobbies during the summer months. The gravel working and the reserve pit hold good numbers of breeding Little Ringed and Ringed Plovers, a few Lapwing and Redshank and a few pairs of Common Terns. There are two thriving colonies of Black-headed Gulls, one on the Lincolnshire Trust reserve, which have drawn in the odd Mediterranean Gull during the summer months. The presence of the tip close to the colony no doubt also led to the first county breeding by a pair of Lesser Black-backed Gulls, in 1993, in amongst the Black-headed Gulls. With large numbers of non-breeding Lesser Black-backed Gulls present in the summer there are also regular appearances by Yellow-legged Gulls in July and August. Spring migration often brings a few Little Gulls and Black Terns, and odd first-summer Little Gulls may stay for long periods.

When the water levels are lowered in spring and autumn the site attracts a good variety of migrant waders, which may include such unexpected species as Knot, Bar-tailed Godwit, Turnstone and Sanderling. More regular species are Greenshank, Spotted Redshank, Green, Wood and Common Sandpipers, Ruff, Little Stint and Curlew Sandpiper. Curlew tend to feed in the grass fields to the west of the pits and are occasionally joined by a few Whimbrel in April and May. Rarities have included Temminck's Stint, Red-necked Phalarope and an exquisite adult Sociable Plover, which consorted with Lapwing on adjacent sandy fields in spring 1993. Apart from Hobbies, there are regular records of passage Marsh Harrier, and Common Buzzards can sometimes be seen over Tumby Woods to the east, where both Red and Black Kites were also reported in 1993. Grey Wagtails have bred nearby in recent years and odd pairs of Nightingale summer in the dense willow clumps around the older workings.

Timing
The best times to visit are from mid March through to September for the migrant and breeding birds, winter being less productive as a rule.

Access
Most of these pits are visible from the minor road which runs north–south from Kirkby-on-Bain to Coningsby. The first pits, with the landfill site to the right, are obvious 1 mile (1.6 km) south of Kirby-on-Bain. It is possible to park opposite the entrance to the landfill site (TF 238 613) and view the reserve pit on the left and the mature workings on the right. A public footpath leads off to the left, crossing the old River Bain and the Horncastle canal and ending at the A153 Horncastle to Coningsby road. Another mile (1.6 km) along the minor road are further pits on the right of the road, which can be seen from the roadside (TF 232 603). There is also a public footpath, which runs along the west-

ern side of all the pits from Kirkby-on-Bain to Tattershall Thorpe, a distance of 2.5 miles (4 km).

Calendar

Resident: Little Grebe, Great Crested Grebe, Greylag Goose, Gadwall, Shoveler, Pochard, Tufted Duck, Sparrowhawk, Kestrel, Stock Dove, Kingfisher, Bullfinch, Yellowhammer.

October–March: Cormorant, Wigeon, Goldeneye, Green Sandpiper, Iceland and Glaucous Gulls (both rare).

April–September. Garganey (scarce), Ruddy Duck, Hobby, Oystercatcher, Little Ringed Plover, Ringed Plover, Lapwing, Dunlin, Ruff, Wood Sandpiper, Green Sandpiper, Common Sandpiper, Mediterranean Gull (rare), Little Gull, Black-headed Gull (colony), Lesser Black-backed Gull, Yellow-legged Gull, Common Tern, Black Tern, Turtle Dove, Cuckoo, Sand Martin (colony), Tree Pipit, Grey Wagtail, Yellow Wagtail, Nightingale, Sedge Warbler, Reed Warbler, Garden Warbler, Chiffchaff, Spotted Flycatcher.

TATTERSHALL PITS/RIVER WITHAM

Habitat

South of Tattershall village a further expanse of disused gravel pits has been turned into a leisure complex, with water sports and fishing dominating the activities. The habitat is much the same as that at Kirkby, with large expanses of open deep water surrounded by tracts of birch woodland and mown grassland.

From where the River Bain joins the River Witham at Chapel Hill a minor road runs alongside the Witham back up to Woodall. This section is usually ice-free, even in hard weather, and thus provides an easily accessible and well used refuge for wildfowl forced off the pits during severe freeze ups.

Species

Winter wildfowl are the key interest at this locality. There is a large semi-resident flock of feral Greylag Geese, with substantial numbers of Canadas also present, and these inevitably attract other oddments, but the Egyptian Goose appears to be a local release. Bean and White-fronted Geese and Whooper and Bewick's Swans have been recorded in hard weather, however, and any large gathering of wildfowl is liable to bring in other species. This is one of the centres of the increasing Lincolnshire Gadwall population, with up to 160 birds already recorded in November and December from peaks of only 30–40 in the early 1980s. Other peak winter counts include 3–400 Wigeon, 6–700 Pochard, 2–300 Tufted Duck and a significant gathering of Coot, which exceed 700 in all months and may reach the 1,000 mark in some years. A few Goosander make regular visits, and in good Smew years there will be a few birds on the pits. Increasingly regular records of Red-crested Pochards may well be accounted for by the presence of a wildfowl collection on the nearby River Witham. Variable numbers of Great Crested Grebe winter and there are odd records of the rarer grebes. The nearby stretch of the River Witham often holds a few Goosander and has played host to Black-throated Diver, Slavonian Grebe, Smew and the recent unfortunate White-billed Diver.

Timberland Delph is a good winter site for Short-eared Owl, with up to 7–8 birds noted in some years over the banks and adjacent fenland fields.

Timing

Winter visits are the most profitable as in the summer large numbers of visitors and a high degree of water sports and other activities cause excessive disturbance.

Access

The entrance to the leisure park at Tattershall is off the A153, 1 mile (1.6 km) south of Tattershall village (TF 204 571). Ask permission before driving into the park, there is usually no objection to birdwatchers, especially in the winter months when the pits are at their most interesting.

Continue south on the A153 another mile (1.6 km) to Tattershall Bridge and take a sharp right turn immediately over the bridge itself onto a minor road, which then runs along the bank of the Witham as far as Martin Dales on the B1191, where a right turn leads back into Woodall Spa. Timberland Delph, a large drainage canal, runs away to the left, 3 miles (4.8 km) after leaving Tattershall Bridge.

Calendar

Resident: Little Grebe, Great Crested Grebe, Greylag Goose, Gadwall, Shoveler, Pochard, Tufted Duck, Sparrowhawk, Kestrel,

October–March: Cormorant, Gadwall, Wigeon, Goldeneye, Smew, Goosander, Coot.

ADDITIONAL SITES

Name	Marston Sewage Farm.
Grid Reference	SK 906 427
Habitat	Old style sewage farm with wader scrape.
Species	Winter and passage waders, wagtails, pipits.
Timing	All.
Access	Owned by Anglian Water: public hide overlooks scrape.

Name	Bradley Woods.
Grid Reference	TA 245 058
Habitat	Old deciduous woodland.
Species	Woodland species includes Nuthatch and Lesser Spotted Woodpecker.
Timing	All.
Access	Public access dawn to dusk.

Name   Snipe Dales.
Grid Reference TF 330 685
Habitat   Rough grass and plantations in steep-sided valley with spring line and small streams, in the Wolds.
Species   Barn Owl, Short-eared Owl, Snipe, Green Woodpecker, Meadow Pipit, Grasshopper Warbler, Yellowhammer.
Timing   All.
Access   Nature Reserve, footpath from Winceby village.

Name   Bourne Woods.
Grid Reference TF 080 205
Habitat   Mixed old and young deciduous and conifer woodland.
Species   Woodland species include Nuthatch, Marsh Tit, Common Crossbill (fairly regular).
Timing   All.
Access   Footpaths from picnic site (TF 076 201).

Name   Normanby Park.
Grid Reference SE 887 168
Habitat   Old parkland with mature deciduous trees, some conifers.
Species   Good variety of woodland birds, includes Great and Lesser Spotted Woodpecker, Treecreeper, Little Owl, Brambling.
Timing   All.
Access   Open to the public, car parking fee; from B1430 Scunthorpe to Burton-upon-Stather road.

Name   Oxcombe/Farforth/Scamblesby Valleys.
Grid Reference TF 29–31/76–78
Habitat   Set-aside rough grassland on steep Wolds valleys with plantations.
Species   Hen Harrier, Rough-legged Buzzard (rare), Common Buzzard, Merlin, Peregrine, Barn Owl winter.
Timing   Winter.
Access   Views over valleys from Bluestone Heath road.

Name   Cleethorpes Country Park.
Grid Reference TA 305 070
Habitat   Artificial lake set amongst rough grassland with newly planted copses.
Species   Great Crested and Little Grebe, rarer grebes fairly regular, Meadow Pipit, Sedge Warbler, Whitethroat, passage migrants.
Timing   All.
Access   Two entrance points at TA 312 171 off Chelmsford Avenue (Cleethorpes), and in Humberston at TA 309 061.

Name   Belton Park.
Grid Reference SK 9338
Habitat   Old deer park with open grazed grassland and ancient trees, many oaks, small ornamental lakes.

Species   Woodland species including Nuthatch, Marsh Tit, Treecreeper, all three woodpeckers.
Timing   All.
Access   National Trust property open to public during restricted hours, with daily charge.

Name   Wilsford/Rauceby Warren/Ancaster Valley.
Grid Reference TF 034 439 and SK 9842
Habitat   Shallow gravel pits with willow and hawthorn scrub, sandy heathland; agricultural valley with copses.
Species   Hobby, Common Buzzard, Green Woodpecker, Marsh Tit, Nuthatch, tits and finches, formerly Great Grey Shrike.
Timing   All.
Access   Rauceby Warren is a Lincolnshire Trust reserve, access off A153 Sleaford to Grantham road; Ancaster Valley from A153 in Ancaster, public footpath runs south.

Name   Bardney Forest.
Grid Reference TF 1473
Habitat   Coniferous woodland with some deciduous plantings and some meadows.
Species   Woodland species, Sparrowhawk, Nightingale, Coal Tit, Treecreeper, Blackcap, Garden Warbler, Grasshopper Warbler, Tree Pipit, Common Crossbill (irregular), Siskin, Redpoll.
Timing   Spring and summer.
Access   Off B1202 Bardney to Wragby road onto minor road, signed to Chambers Plantation, where park car (at TF 149 739).

NORTHAMPTONSHIRE

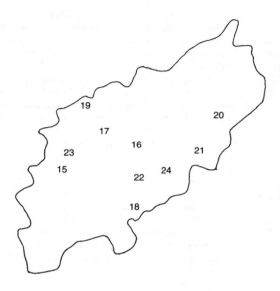

15 BADBY WOOD AND FAWSLEY PARK

Habitat

Badby Wood is one of the very few natural looking woodlands to be found in Northamptonshire, comprising largely mature deciduous trees. The wood grows on a sandy soil, and in May the woodland floor is carpeted with bluebells. There are many footpaths criss-crossing the wood, allowing extensive exploration, and an obvious high point, called Hazeley Knob, which seems to attract woodland species more usually associated with the western side of Britain. Large oak, ash, sweet chestnut, sycamore and cherry trees are scattered throughout the wood, in addition to which one or two clearings and a plantation of conifers at the southeast end of the wood add to the variety of habitats and increase the variety of bird species attracted to the woodland.

Adjoining the wood is Fawsley Park, an ancient parkland encircling the church. There are a large number of mature standard oaks spread across the open grassland of the park which is grazed by sheep and horses. This is a specialised habitat, almost unique within the county in as much as the whole area is open to the public. Within the park are three small lakes, two of which have *Phragmites* reedbeds and are surrounded by alders and other species typical of this type of habitat. Coarse fishing is allowed on two of the lakes from mid June to mid March, with trout fishing on the third, although none of the lakes is heavily fished.

Species

The woodland is alive with birdsong in spring, and this is the best site to see Redstart and Wood Warbler in Northamptonshire at this time of year, although neither is guaranteed. Redstarts prefer the older trees, especially the oaks, where they habitually nest in holes in the trees. The males advertise their territories with their distinctive song, given from a perch, often, however, situated high in the canopy, making the location of even such brightly coloured birds as the summer-plumaged males quite difficult. Spotted Flycatchers are quite common in the woodland and parkland, and its cousin, the Pied Flycatcher, a county rarity, occurs every couple of years or so in either area. Great Spotted Woodpeckers are common and there are still one or two Lesser Spotted Woodpeckers to be found but, as everywhere, this sparrow-sized woodpecker can be very difficult to spot in the tops of the old trees where they prefer to feed. Green Woodpeckers prefer the more open parkland, also a good spot to listen for the loud ringing call of the Nuthatch, which can be found in either habitat though favouring the older trees with dead branches and holes for nesting.

The common warblers such as Willow Warbler, Chiffchaff, Blackcap and Garden Warbler are widespread, with Chiffchaff particularly attracted to the rhododendrons. Tawny Owls frequently call at dusk but the wood is too high and the lack of a developed scrub layer also makes it unsuitable for Nightingales. The parkland is also home to breeding Jackdaws, the small cackling corvid, which reaches good numbers amongst the old oaks as they offer good nesting sites in the larger old holes also favoured by Tawny Owls.

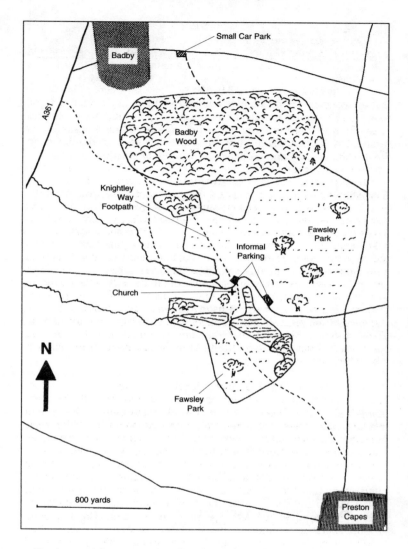

The largest lake next to the church has a reedbed which attracts Reed
Warbler during the summer, and Water Rail has bred. The Great Crested
Grebes, Mute Swans and Ruddy Ducks are, however, more easily seen.
The alders sometimes hold feeding flocks of Siskins and Redpolls in the
winter but these birds are easily overlooked as they feed quietly in the
upper branches only becoming obvious when they explode out in a calling frenzy at the approach of a predator such as a resident Sparrowhawk.
During the winter months Grey Wagtails are often found, preferring the
fast-flowing overflows of the lakes. In the spring and summer they are
replaced by graceful brightly coloured Yellow Wagtails which like the
damper areas of grassland. The summer abundance of insects draws in
feeding flocks of hirundines and Swifts, which can be seen swooping
over the woodland canopy as well as around the parkland.

Timing

Early morning in early to mid May is the best time to visit the woodland as all the summer visitors will have arrived, and with the territorial males in full song, establishing their breeding territories, they will be much easier to locate in the oaks which are still relatively open at this time. As the canopy closes and birdsong diminishes later in the breeding season there is still plenty of activity but the birds are harder to pinpoint. In the winter months fine sunny days with little wind offer the best chances of bumping into the mixed-feeding flocks of tits, Goldcrests, Nuthatches and Treecreepers which characterise the woodland. The parkland and lakes can be interesting at any season.

Access

Travelling south from Daventry on the A361 turn left after 2 miles (3.2 km) into Badby village, and pass through on the Everdon road. After 200 yds/m there is a very small car parking area on the right surrounded by horse chestnut trees. Walk up the dirt track to the wood, which is 200 yds/m from the road. A mass of footpaths enables ample exploration of the wood. To reach Fawsley Park continue along the road and turn right again to enter the parkland. The road passes close to all three lakes and there are plenty of places to pull in and footpaths to follow.

Calendar

Resident: Great Crested Grebe, Mute Swan, Tufted Duck, Ruddy Duck , Coot, Moorhen, Kestrel, Water Rail, Tawny Owl, Green, Great Spotted and Lesser Spotted Woodpeckers, Goldcrest, Treecreeper, Nuthatch, Marsh Tit, Willow Tit, Jackdaw.

October–March: Pochard, Grey Wagtail, Siskin, Redpoll.

April–September: Sand and House Martin, Swallow, Swift, Yellow Wagtail, Redstart (scarce), Reed Warbler, Blackcap, Garden Warbler, Willow Warbler, Chiffchaff, Pied Flycatcher and Wood Warbler (rare), Spotted Flycatcher, Reed Bunting.

16 PITSFORD RESERVOIR   OS Maps 141/152

Habitat

Constructed in 1955, this 800-acre (324 ha) reservoir, owned by Anglian Water, is subjected to intensive recreational use for sailing, trout fishing and walking. Apart from the dam, the entire reservoir has natural clay banks, which in turn have a number of mixed woodland plantations of varying ages.

The larger south side of the reservoir is all open to the public, apart from the sailing club grounds, but the area north of the causeway, on the road between Holcot and Brixworth, is an SSSI and a reserve of the Northamptonshire Wildlife Trust, with access limited to permit holders only. The fishing lodge is also in this section and is situated adjacent to the causeway. Most of the mature plantations, including a mature copse of oak, are found on the reserve itself. The grassy banks are often grazed by sheep, particularly south of the causeway and on the reserve side where there are many willows and hawthorns between the water's edge and the plantations. The surrounding fields, a mixture of arable and pasture together with a network of hedgerows which can be seen from within the reserve perimeter, often attract migrants, particularly passerines. A footpath around the perimeter fence is a full 13 miles (21 km) long.

Species

This site has attracted more than 220 different species in its 40-year history, and is the premier site for birding in Northamptonshire. During the winter months large numbers of wildfowl are attracted to the ample feeding opportunities provided by the reservoir and its environs, with average totals of over 3,500 birds, and a peak of 6,200 birds in December 1993. It is for this reason that the site was designated an SSSI. Wigeon are the most numerous of the dabbling ducks, with regularly over 1,000 birds present, but there are also up to 800 Mallard and 750 Teal. Of the diving ducks, Tufted Ducks have recently peaked at more than 1,200, particularly in the early part of the winter, and the site is of national importance for this species and also Goosander, which average 59 individuals. Fewer Pochard are now present than in the past, with 250 the usual peak, and over 100 Goldeneye are recorded in the coldest months. Ruddy Duck numbers build up throughout the winter and some may remain throughout the year.

Of the scarcer species, Pintail and Shoveler are present throughout the autumn, with a few of the latter remaining to breed along with Gadwall, which usually successfully rear a few broods. Scaup, Common Scoter, Red-breasted Merganser and Smew are annual and Red-crested Pochard can turn up at any time. The much rarer American Wigeon and Ring-necked Duck have both occurred once, and Eider, Velvet Scoter and Long-tailed Duck visit every two or three winters. Bewick's Swans usually pass through in November *en route* to Slimbridge, and large flocks of Canada Geese, which can be found grazing on the open fields adjacent to the southeast bank, often attract scarcer species such as Brent, White-fronted and Pink-footed Geese.

Great Crested Grebes average nearly 200 birds, and this site is ranked the eleventh most important in Britain for the species. When sailing commences on a Sunday morning, the birds in the deeper water areas

Wigeon

near the dam and the sailing club tend to move towards the causeway, which offers excellent views over a large part of the water area. All three of the scarcer species of grebe, Slavonian, Black-necked and Red-necked, are annual visitors and at least one diver species is attracted each year, most often Great Northern. A small band of enthusiasts watch the assembling hordes of gulls coming in from all directions, to roost near the dam, nightly from August to March, with numbers varying depending on wind direction and temperature. The roost is composed mainly of Black-headed and Common Gulls with fewer Herring, Lesser Black-backed and Great Black-backed Gulls. The total is regularly around 20,000 birds and a few Mediterranean, Glaucous and Iceland Gulls are picked out annually, the former right through the autumn and winter and the latter two species from Christmas onwards.

Corn Buntings and Yellowhammers can usually be found in the fields adjacent to the dam, often attracted to the sheep-feeding troughs for an easy meal. Small flocks of Linnets, Goldfinches and Meadow Pipits roam around the banks and attract the attention of the resident Sparrowhawks and occasional Merlin, while Tree Sparrows are thinly distributed. October is the best time to find Rock Pipits feeding on the dam or causeway and single Snow Buntings also occur most often at this time.

Springtime brings White and Yellow Wagtails to the causeway along with a few Northern Wheatears. The first parties of Sand Martins hawk insects over the water and singing warblers appear in the plantations and thickets, with eight species staying to breed, mostly on the reserve side of the reservoir. On cool or overcast days in May, hundreds or even thousands of hirundines and Swifts may be hunting for insects low over the water surface, producing a spectacular sight. A few Common Terns are present throughout the summer, although none breeds yet, while the numbers of visiting Arctic and Black Terns vary enormously from year to year, with counts into three figures in some springs, but much rarer are Sandwich and Little Terns, one or two individuals of each being annual. Several species of waterbird breed and broods of Little and Great Crested Grebes, Mute Swans and Tufted Duck are often conspicuous during the summer months.

During late summer and early autumn, when water levels can fall dramatically, acres of mud are exposed on the shallower reserve side of the reservoir, to the obvious delight of many wader species. Six hides can afford close views of some of the 25 species of wader which are regular, along with the occasional vagrant. Lapwing, Golden Plover, Ringed Plover, Dunlin, Ruff and Greenshank are the most numerous waders, with a scattering of Little Stint, Spotted Redshank, Knot, Black and Bar-tailed Godwits, Turnstone, Common, Green, Wood and Curlew Sandpipers. In all, 39 species of wader have been recorded at the site, including the following rarities: Sociable Plover, Black-winged Pratincole, Wilson's Phalarope, American Golden Plover, Long-billed Dowitcher, Lesser Yellowlegs and Buff-breasted Sandpiper.

The completion of the new pumping-in facilities means that the likelihood of drawing down the water level is now in the hands of Anglian Water, which may mean that the regular autumn draw-off of water may not occur with such regularity, which will have a detrimental effect on the summer/early autumn water levels in the future.

Black-necked Grebes often arrive in August, along with wandering Marsh Harriers, and it is the best time to catch sight of an Osprey flying

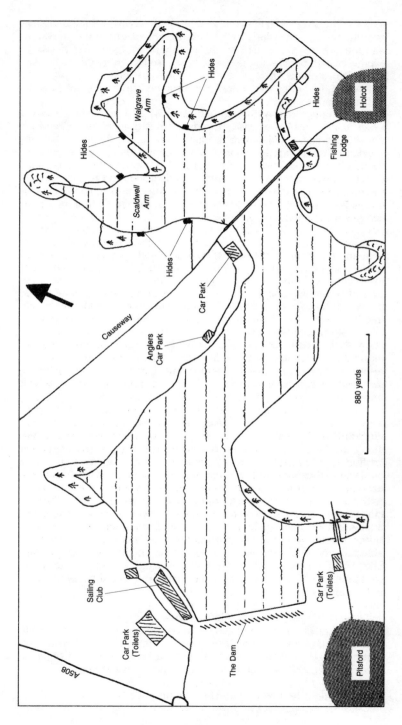

over the causeway with a fish, while Hobbies regularly hunt dragonflies over the water, particularly in the evenings. A walk from the causeway into the Scaldwell arm can produce migrant warblers, Whinchats or even Redstart on the hedges which are visible from the perimeter fences. Cormorants, now present throughout the year, roost on the tall Willows in the Waldgrave arm of the reservoir and may number up to 60 birds.

A search through any autumn parties of Black Terns and Little Gulls, which usually arrive on easterly winds at this time of year, could be rewarded with a White-winged Black Tern, a southeastern vagrant species which has appeared on no fewer than eight occasions. By contrast, gale force westerly winds in September and October have produced regular sightings of seabirds, including the most regular species such as Shag, Leach's Petrel, Manx Shearwater and Arctic Skuas, with occasional Gannet, Fulmar, Great and Pomarine Skuas, although some years pass with no records at all.

Timing

Something of interest can usually be found at any time of year, but the spring and autumn passage periods are the most rewarding, particularly the latter, right through the winter when there are always large numbers of waterfowl. Some areas remain free of ice even in the deepest freezes and hundreds of birds can then be concentrated into small ice-free holes, affording exceptional viewing. Which bank to choose for a walk from the causeway to the dam depends on the time of day, to enjoy the best light conditions, particularly if the sun is out. Gull watchers tend to assemble near the sailing club at the southwest corner of the reservoir an hour or more before dusk but have to wait until the windsurfers and yachtsmen have finished at weekends, before the gulls will settle.

Access

Pitsford Reservoir (Water) is 6 miles (9.6 km) north of Northampton along the A508 Northampton to Market Harborough road, between Pitsford and Brixworth villages. This road provides access to the dam end, where there are car parks and toilets at either end of the dam, and also an information centre at the Brixworth end. Alternatively from the A43 Northampton to Kettering road, turn left after Moulton, through Holcot village to the causeway half a mile (0.8 km) beyond, which gives access to the reserve side to the north and open access to the south side. A permit is required for the reserve (no dogs allowed), and is available daily or annually from the fishing lodge by the causeway or from The Wildlife Trust for Northamptonshire, Lings House, Billing Lings, Northampton, NN3 8BR. Six hides are always open on the reserve north of the causeway.

Calendar

Resident: Little and Great Crested Grebes, Cormorant, Grey Heron, Mute Swan, Canada Goose, Ruddy Duck, Gadwall, Tufted Duck, Sparrowhawk, Tawny Owl, Great Spotted Woodpecker, all five tit species, Goldcrest, Tree Sparrow, Yellowhammer, Reed Bunting, Corn Bunting.

October–March: Red-necked and Slavonian Grebe (both scarce), Black-necked Grebe, Bewick's Swan (passage), Brent Goose (scarce),

Wigeon, Teal, Pintail, Shoveler, Pochard, Goldeneye, Smew, Goosander, Merlin (rare), Golden Plover, Lapwing, gulls; Mediterranean, Iceland, Glaucous Gulls (all rare), Meadow Pipit, Grey Wagtail, Stonechat, Fieldfare, Redwing.

April–September: Black-necked Grebe (Scarce), Garganey, Marsh Harrier (passage), Osprey (passage), Hobby, Ringed Plover, Dunlin, Ruff, Greenshank, Green Sandpiper, Common Sandpiper, other waders depending on water levels, Little Gull, Common, Arctic and Black Terns, Cuckoo, Swift, Sand Martin, Yellow and White Wagtails, Whinchat, Northern Wheatear, warblers, Rookery.

17 HOLLOWELL RESERVOIR   OS Sheet 141

Habitat

Hollowell is a relatively old reservoir (opened in 1938), used for domestic water storage and owned by Anglian Water. The reservoir nestles in a narrow sheltered valley, with the banks being surrounded by grazed grassland. Recreational usage includes sailing, with a sailing club being based at the west end of the dam, and yachts being very much in evidence on Sunday afternoons. There is also coarse fishing, with an open season from mid June to mid March, the reservoir being renowned for its large pike. Most anglers prefer to fish from the dam. Along the west bank there is a margin of sedge and reed, and within the perimeter of the reservoir grounds there are several mature plantations, some of pine and some mixed, which together make this an attractive place for birds and birdwatchers alike.

If the water level falls in late summer, the Guilsborough bay, on the western bank, provides a good band of mud, attractive to waders and wildfowl. The agricultural landscape forming the reservoir's immediate environs is one of wheat fields and sheep-grazed pasture.

Species

The reservoir and its immediate environs offer a good mix of wetland and woodland birds, with species more associated with hedgerows and scrubland also being present nearby. The late autumn wildfowl counts have topped 2,700 birds, which makes this the fourth most important site in Northamptonshire for this group of species. Most of the ducks start to arrive in the late autumn and build up to winter peaks before they start to depart again, often as early as February if the weather remains mild. Resident Greylag and Canada Geese, Great Crested Grebes and Mute Swans are joined by a good variety of dabbling and diving duck, which also regularly attract a few rarer species. Wigeon are the most numerous dabbling duck, with up to 650 birds being present, followed by Teal (400), Gadwall (250) and Shoveler (140). Highest totals of diving duck are for Tufted Duck, with up to 200 birds, and then Pochard (50), while the recent colonist, the Ruddy Duck, has numbered over 100 individuals on occasions. The deeper water adjacent to the dam has also attracted regular Scaup and Common Scoter but also

Long-tailed Duck, Eider, Velvet Scoter and Ring-necked Duck as well as both Red-throated and Great Northern Divers and Red-necked, Slavonian and Black-necked Grebes. The shallower water at the northern end of the reservoir is more attractive to the dabbling ducks, and amongst the other species mentioned above, there have been records of American Wigeon and Green-winged Teal, both vagrants from North America, as well as fairly regular Red-crested Pochards.

There is a winter gull roost, with the main species being Black-headed and Common Gulls but, inevitably, Mediterranean Gulls have occurred in recent years, although they remain rare. The area has resident Kestrels and Sparrowhawks, often seen hunting during the short winter days. In the woodlands, flocks of tits and finches may include a few Common Crossbills in good years for this species, while the hedgerows and grass fields hold flocks of wintering Redwing and Fieldfare. The wealth of winter wildfowl and small passerines also brings in hunting Merlin and Peregrine on occasions during the winter months.

Garganey

The transition period from late winter to early spring sees an increase in the numbers of Goosander and Goldeneye, which peak at this time prior to their departure to their breeding grounds. Goldeneyes, the males stunning white with bottle-green heads, can often be seen in their exaggerated head-throwing displays, accompanied by their distinctive calling, as they attempt to impress accompanying females on warm sunny days from early March onwards.

The first warm days of the spring, from early March, will often reveal Sand Martins hawking emergent insects over the water, the odd immaculate male Northern Wheatear on short-grazed pastures, Chiffchaffs singing their own name from the trees around the water and Yellow Wagtails hunting insects by the water's edge or following livestock in nearby fields. Little Ringed Plovers are often early arrivals too, with birds attracted to even small areas of exposed mud where they can be very difficult to spot. However, their distinctive butterfly-like display flight and their obvious calls draw attention to any birds which remain for any length of time. All of these species are frequently present before the end of March but most of the other summer residents arrive from mid April onwards.

As well as a good variety of summer migrants such as warblers, hirundines and Swifts there is often a good passage of the three commoner inland tern species, with good totals of Common, Arctic and Black being recorded in suitable weather conditions. Sandwich Tern has also occurred, and that most delightful little duck, the Garganey, is a scarce visitor at this season. Passage raptors include almost annual visits from Ospreys and increasingly regular Marsh Harriers. The commoner waders pass through in small numbers, with Common Sandpiper and Greenshank the most frequent, but anything is possible and both Avocet and Collared Pratincole have paid visits, while other rarities have included species as diverse as Spoonbill, Little Bittern and Hoopoe.

Breeding waterbirds are relatively few in variety, with Moorhen, Coot, Great Crested Grebe and Canada Goose the principal species. The plantations hold a good variety of breeding woodland birds such as tits, Treecreeper, Chaffinch, Great Spotted and Green Woodpeckers, the latter advertising their presence with their characteristic yaffling calls. Sparrowhawks and Kestrels also nest, and the hedgerows and areas of scrub hold Whitethroat, Lesser Whitethroat, Blackcap, Garden Warbler and Yellowhammer.

A fall in the level of the water during the early autumn, from late August onwards, will reveal areas of mud which may attract a few passage waders. The most frequent visitors are species such as Ruff, Dunlin, Green, Wood and Common Sandpipers, Ringed Plover, Redshank and Greenshank but a few scarcer species occur in most years, with species such as Black-tailed Godwit, Whimbrel and Spotted Redshank being the most frequent, while Pectoral Sandpiper has occurred on several occasions and Temminck's Stint and Grey Phalarope have also appeared. Wagtails and Meadow Pipit congregate on the short-cropped turf and there is the usual late autumnal build-up of hirundines feasting on the insect bonanza before their flights to winter quarters.

Timing

Autumn is probably the best time of year for a visit, when wildfowl are continually arriving for the winter and, depending on the water level, there is a good chance of a few waders. These will be most likely at the northern feeder stream end or in Guilsborough bay on the west bank. Wildfowl are present all winter but numbers begin to fall by late February. There is also a small gull roost during the winter months. The light conditions mean that the reservoir is best viewed from the east bank in the morning and the west bank in the afternoon. On Sunday afternoons most of the wildfowl will be concentrated at the northern end of the reservoir due to the activities of the sailing club.

Access

It is necessary to obtain a birdwatching permit, available from: The Fishing Lodge at Pitsford Reservoir, Brixworth Road, Holcot, Northants. The permit allows you to walk right around the reservoir, which will take about 1–2 hours. Hollowell lies 10 miles (16 km) north of Northampton. From the M1 motorway, junction 18, at Crick, follow the A428 southeast to West Haddon, then left onto the B4036 towards Cold Ashby. Turn right here towards Guilsborough and through to Hollowell village. There are car parks at the northern end between Guilsborough and the A50 by the feeder stream and at the southern end by the access

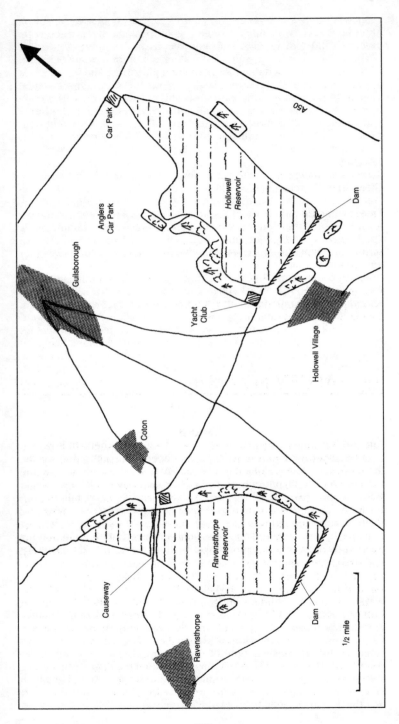

road to the sailing club. Alternatively, heading north from Northampton on the A50, after 10 miles (16 km), turn left along a minor road to Guilsborough, and the feeder stream car park is on the left after 500 yds/m. There are no hides.

On Sundays, when the wildfowl are disturbed by sailing, many move to nearby Ravensthorpe Reservoir, just 1 mile (1.6 km) to the southwest. This latter reservoir can be viewed from the causeway at its northern end, to the north of which is a small reserve with no access. The southern section is heavily fished for trout.

Calendar

Resident: Great Crested Grebe, Greylag Goose, Canada Goose, Mute Swan, Sparrowhawk, Kestrel, Moorhen, Coot, Tawny Owl, Green and Great Spotted Woodpeckers.

October–March: Little Grebe, Wigeon, Teal, Gadwall, Pintail (scarce), Shoveler, Red-crested Pochard (scarce), Pochard, Tufted Duck, Goldeneye, Goosander (scarce), Ruddy Duck, Black-headed and Common Gull roost, Fieldfare, Redwing, Common Crossbill (scarce).

April–September: Garganey (scarce), Little Ringed Plover, Ringed Plover, Dunlin, Ruff, Snipe, Redshank, Greenshank, Common Sandpiper, Green Sandpiper, Black-tailed Godwit, Common Tern, Arctic Tern, Black Tern, Yellow Wagtail, woodland species.

18 SALCEY FOREST   OS Sheet 152

Habitat

Salcey is an ancient royal hunting forest of 1250 acres (500 ha), owned and managed by the Forestry Commission, and situated alongside the M1 motorway. It is rectangular in shape, with a private farmed area in the centre called Salcey Lawn, once used to provide hay and pasture for deer, the quarry of the royal hunt. The forest was and still is famous for its ancient oaks, which now remain in much reduced numbers as the active forestry industry has felled the old trees and replanted mainly with the more economic fast-growing softwoods. With an increasing awareness of the conservation importance of the woodland, however, some oaks have again been planted in recent years. There are still some fine stands of mature oaks, covering 250 acres (100 ha), some of which, planted in 1847, are part of a 34-acre (13.5 ha) reserve, shared by the Northamptonshire Wildlife Trust and neighbouring BBONT, which is part of a 382-acre (153 ha) designated SSSI. Other trees in the reserve are mainly native ash and field maple with introduced sycamores, sweet chestnut and turkey oaks, while willows and sallows grow mainly along the ride edges. Some of the largest standard oaks are to be found dotted around the farmed area and along the edge of the forest.

The forest stands on heavy boulder-clay soils, and the paths which have not been reinforced with stone chippings can become very muddy during wet weather and in the winter months.

Once a mecca for entomologists, large areas of the forest were at one time sprayed with the chemical 2.4.5-T, which had a dramatic effect on these insect populations, but thankfully some rare species still exist today. There are several small ponds used by birds throughout the day for drinking and bathing. Of the large network of rides some are wide and grassy and managed to provide a diverse ground flora, and some are narrow and overhung by shrubs and trees. There are three well marked trails of different lengths leading through the different areas of the forest and its habitats.

Species

Fifty-two species breed in the forest, including all three species of woodpecker, which can at times be strikingly obvious and, at others, difficult to locate. During the winter, when the broadleaf trees are bare, and in the early spring, when the male Great and Lesser Spotted Woodpeckers are drumming, are the best times to connect with these two species. Green Woodpeckers are more often heard than seen, giving away their presence with their loud, laughing yaffle calls. They do, however, spend long periods on the ground foraging for ants and other invertebrates and may well be first seen as they are flushed from one of the grassy rides, flying up into the nearest large tree before returning to feed when the disturbance has passed.

During the winter months resident tits, of all five common species, will join together with Goldcrests, Treecreepers and the odd Nuthatch to form large foraging flocks moving through the woods searching for food. Listen for the chorus of noisy contact calls, especially from the Long-tailed Tits, and watch for the birds moving through the upper branches of the oaks; the Nuthatches and Treecreepers preferring the trunks and older, often dead branches on the oaks. By spring, the flocks disperse but territorial males can be located by song and calls, with the Treecreepers and Nuthatches being very vocal from late March.

The early spring is also the best time to see raucous Jays, which frequent the forest, as they are often at their most visible at this time. Tawny Owls are widespread and broadcast their presence at dusk, while Long-eared Owl, which has bred, is much rarer. The calls and song of the adult birds is quiet compared to the far-carrying calls of the Tawny Owl, but the squeaky calls of the fledged young are more obvious in the late spring.

In spring and summer the site is well known for the Nightingales, which prefer the coppiced areas and plantations with a shrub layer. To listen to the beautiful song of the male Nightingale in all its glory a visit in the early morning or late evening from late April to early June should pay dividends. Although some birds will sing throughout the day in the early part of their stay, there is nothing quite like listening to the full-blown song on a calm, warm spring evening to the background of an attendant chorus of newly arrived summer migrants and resident woodland birds. Grasshopper Warblers are fairly common in the younger plantations shortly after replanting, and their high-pitched trilling song is at its strongest during the night. While listening to the calls of the Tawny Owls and the reeling of the Grasshopper Warblers the grunts and squeaks of roding Woodcock may be obvious as dusk approaches, although this species has declined somewhat of late. The newly cleared areas of the forest, especially those where odd trees and snags have been left standing, are attractive to Tree Pipits which use the isolated trees as perches

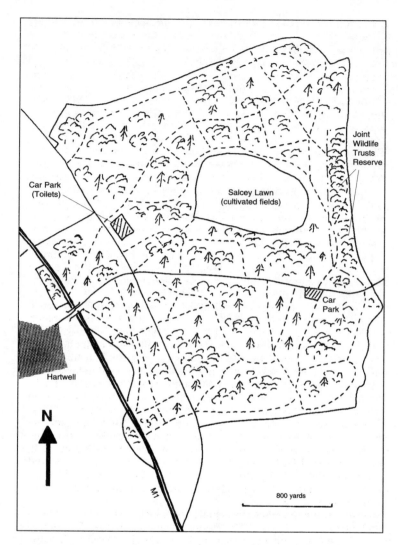

Car Park
(Toilets)

Joint
Wildlife
Trusts
Reserve

Salcey Lawn
(cultivated fields)

Car
Park

Hartwell

N

M1

800 yards

from which to launch their characteristic parachuting song flights.

Wood Warblers and Redstarts are both unusual visitors to the older woodland areas, with the former species usually announcing its arrival with its clear descendent shivering song performed from the bright green newly opened leaf canopy. The dawn chorus includes the far-carrying song of the Mistle Thrush, or stormcock, mixed in with the songs of all the usual summer migrants typical of broadleaved woodland, and good numbers of Blackcap, Garden Warbler, Chiffchaff and abundant Willow Warblers. Whitethroat and Lesser Whitethroat prefer the more scrubby areas around the clear-fells and the woodland rides where Cuckoos also repeat their name in song. These woodland edges are also good spots to hear the quiet piping of the Bullfinch and to look for this delightfully smart finch in the spring when they often feed on the buds of blackthorn and sallows. Kestrels and Sparrowhawks both breed and there has recently been an increase in sightings of Common Buzzards, which may well breed in the forest in the future if the population continues to expand in the East Midlands.

Timing

Spring is the best time to visit, and the dawn chorus is particularly impressive, especially when the Nightingales are in full song from late April. Song diminishes throughout the summer and the increasingly dense foliage makes it harder to actually see the birds, although early autumn is often the best time to see families of Spotted Flycatchers darting out from the bare branches catching insects. To see roding Woodcock a visit near dusk between February and June will pay dividends. The site is very popular with dog walkers, families and walkers, and Sunday afternoon is the peak period of human activity and hence the worst time to look for birds. Having said this, there are plenty of footpaths off the marked trails which can still be of interest even at the busiest of times.

Access

Leaving Northampton southwards on the A508, take a minor road left to Wootton and continue through the village to Quinton on the Hanslope road. Two miles (3.2 km) beyond Quinton is a large car park on the left just within the forest (at SP 795 516). There are information boards, picnic tables and toilets and two of the trails start from here. The Lesser Spotted Woodpecker trail takes about an hour and the longer Great Spotted Woodpecker trail about two hours at a leisurely pace. Leaving the main car park and turning left and then left again at the crossroads along the minor road towards Horton and Stoke Goldington there is another car park on the right after 1 mile (1.6 km) (at SP 811 508) where the longer Green Woodpecker trail starts; this trail takes 2.5 hours, with wellington boots being needed. This same car park gives access to the reserve section of the forest on the northern side of the road. A main track passes down the western edge of the reserve but access is restricted to Trust members to prevent trampling of the rare plants growing here.

Calendar

Resident: Sparrowhawk, Kestrel, Red-legged Partridge, Woodcock, Little Owl, Tawny Owl, Long-eared Owl, Stock Dove, Green, Great Spotted and Lesser Spotted Woodpeckers, Mistle Thrush, Nuthatch, Treecreeper, Goldcrest, Redpoll (scarce), Blue, Great, Long-tailed, Marsh and Willow Tits, Jay, Tree Sparrow, Greenfinch, Goldfinch, Linnet, Bullfinch, Reed Bunting, Yellowhammer.

October–March: Fieldfare, Redwing, Siskin.

April–September: Turtle Dove, Cuckoo, Tree Pipit, Nightingale, Redstart (rare), Grasshopper Warbler, Whitethroat, Lesser Whitethroat, Blackcap, Garden Warbler, Wood Warbler (scarce), Willow Warbler, Chiffchaff, Spotted Flycatcher.

19 STANFORD RESERVOIR

Habitat

The Leicester and Northamptonshire county boundary bisects this 180-acre (72 ha) drinking water reservoir owned by Severn Trent Water Authority. However, because of the large bay on the southeast bank of the reservoir, most of the water is in Northamptonshire. This bay, called Blower's Lodge Bay, and the surrounding bank, extending to the disused railway line, has been a 13.6-acre (6 ha) reserve of the Northamptonshire Wildlife Trust since 1968. There are two hides on either side of the mouth of the bay.

The northwest Leicestershire bank is flanked by a narrow belt of trees, which grow close to the water's edge, while the southern section is more open, with adjoining arable fields, but there is plenty of hawthorn scrub in the reserve with fast-growing willows being found at intervals around the water's edge. There are also a few small patches of reeds in places around the perimeter. Coarse fishing is allowed between mid June and mid March but not on the reserve. There are two deciduous woods to the north and south of the reservoir and a footpath encircles the whole site.

Species

Stanford Reservoir varies between the third and eighth most important site for wildfowl in Northamptonshire, with more than 3,200 birds present in January 1992. Recent totals have included 1,850 Wigeon, 320 Teal, up to 90 Gadwall, 300+ Shoveler, 240 Pochard and 420 Tufted Duck. Large numbers of Coot often find this site to their liking and peak counts have included an exceptional 2,115 in October 1989. Consequently, this locality is currently ranked the ninth most important wintering site for this species in Britain, with an average winter population of over 1,557 in the last five winters; it is also the eighth most important locality for Ruddy Duck, with an average of 118 birds present. Wild geese are sometimes encountered, usually in flight, and have included White-fronts, Pink-feet and Brent. All three species of swan, Mute, Bewick's and Whooper, have been recorded in some winters.

There is a large winter gull roost, with the number of Lesser Black-backed Gulls often totalling over 2,000 birds. Among the numerous Black-headed and Common Gulls the much rarer Mediterranean, Glaucous and Ring-billed Gulls have all occurred. Long-eared Owls have occasionally been seen roosting in the scrub on the reserve section. These birds are always difficult to observe when settled into their winter roost sites, which are often in dense hawthorns. On sunny mornings, after a frosty night, however, they may occasionally be seen warming themselves in the sun on the outside of bushes; close views will reveal their glaring brilliant orange eyes and raised ear tufts, always a sign of anxiety.

All three of the scarcer grebes, Red-necked, Black-necked and Slavonian, have appeared more than once as have Red-throated and Great Northern Divers, particularly at the dam end where the deeper water is found.

A ringing group, active since 1974, has trapped more than 70 different species, including spring records of such rarities as Marsh Warbler, Hoopoe and Red-backed Shrike, with Golden Oriole, Great Reed

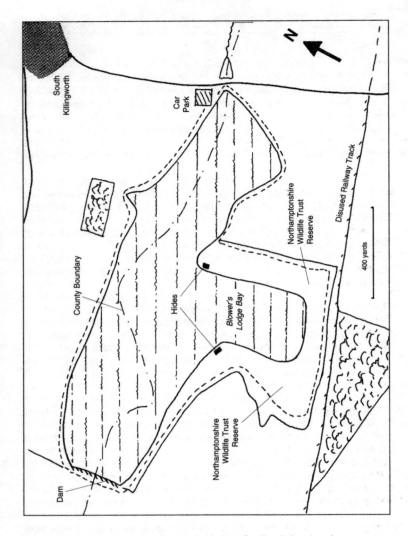

Warbler, Lesser Grey Shrike and Alpine Swift all having been seen, demonstrating the ability of lost migrants to find suitable areas of habitat around inland reservoirs. The *Phragmites* reed patches attract breeding Reed Warblers, which are present from May through to August. About 30 different species breed on the reserve, including Common Terns, which have adapted to nesting on specially constructed rafts.

Rare passage waders have included all three phalaropes, Red-necked, Grey and Wilson's, Lesser Yellowlegs (twice), Purple Sandpiper, Temminck's Stint and Avocets, but on the majority of visits the more usually encountered species are likely to be Ringed Plover, Dunlin, Ruff and Greenshank, with a few Green and Common Sandpiper and Little Stint, Turnstone, Curlew Sandpiper, Spotted Redshank, Wood Sandpiper and both godwits occurring more frequently when the water level falls after a hot summer. Peregrines seem to occur here more often than at any other local site and Merlins and Hen Harriers have also been seen.

Tern passage can be interesting, with one or two of the more unusual species, for example Little and Sandwich or even the much rarer Caspian, Whiskered and White-winged Black Terns, which have all appeared, turning up among the usual Common, Arctic and Black Terns. Strong winds and heavy showers in the autumn have produced a good number of gale-blown seabirds including Leach's Petrel, Gannet, Shag, Arctic and Great Skuas and Little Auk, an impressive list for a reservoir which lies about as far from any coast as anywhere in Britain.

Timing

This site is worth visiting at any time of year with usually something of interest to be seen, although the winter and passage periods are the best times. If approaching from the feeder stream end the best viewing conditions will be had in the morning, and if watching the gull roost, the hide nearer the dam may be better in the late afternoon.

Access

A minor road from the A50 at Welford towards Kilworth goes along the northern edge of the reservoir where there is a car park at the feeder stream end at (SP 612 812). On approaching from the B5414 South Kilworth to Stanford on Avon road, the entrance to the dam is on the left after 1 mile (1.6 km). Access is restricted to permit holders only, permits obtainable from Severn Trent Water Authority, Avon House, Demountford Way, Cannon Park, Coventry, CV4 7EJ, or from the Northamptonshire Wildlife Trust, Lings House, Billing Lings, Northampton, NN3 4BE.

Calendar

Resident: Great Crested and Little Grebes, Mute Swan, Canada Goose, Coot, Moorhen, Reed Bunting, Yellowhammer.

October–March: Black-necked Grebe (scarce), Wigeon, Teal, Gadwall, Shoveler, Pintail, Pochard, Tufted Duck, Goldeneye, Goosander (scarce), Ruddy Duck, Peregrine (rare), Snipe, Black-headed Gull, Common Gull, Mediterranean Gull (rare), Lesser Black-backed Gull, Long-eared Owl (rare), Grey Wagtail, Brambling (scarce).

April–September: Hobby, passage waders depending on water levels, Little Ringed and Ringed Plover, Dunlin, Ruff, Redshank, Spotted Redshank, Greenshank, Common, Green and Wood Sandpiper, Common Tern, passage Arctic, Black Terns, Little and Sandwich Terns (scarce), Grasshopper, Sedge and Reed Warblers.

20 THRAPSTON GRAVEL PITS AND TICHMARSH RESERVE

Habitat

This locality consists of a chain of former gravel pits, stretching a distance of nearly 3.5 miles (5.6 km) along the River Nene northeastwards from Thrapston, with the most recently excavated pits situated at either end. Part of the complex is the 180 acre (110 ha) Tichmarsh Reserve, managed by the Northamptonshire Wildlife Trust. This reserve includes a former duck decoy, now nearly clogged with vegetation, and surrounded by willows, alders, silver birch and Scots pine, which were planted by Lord Lilford in 1885. This decoy has been the site of an important heronry for many years. Adjacent to the heronry at the west end is a small lake, partly surrounded by willows and overlooked by a hide. The largest reserve lake, flooded in 1986, has several islands which are managed to keep the vegetation in check in order to enable Common Terns, ducks and waders to breed.

There are five hides, including two which give good views of this and adjacent pits and two which overlook purpose built scrapes. This lake is surrounded by rough grassland grazed by many wildfowl, and there is a *Phragmites* reedbed at the western end where one of the hides is situated. There are young deciduous plantations at intervals around the reserve, with one alongside the heronry into which it is hoped that the herons will eventually spread when the trees reach maturity. The lake at the northeast end of the complex has recently become a carp fishery, with a resultant increase in disturbance.

The large lake nearest Thrapston village is the deepest and the home of an active sailing club but at the eastern end of the pit are several narrow islands covered in mature trees and offering a safe haven for nesting waterbirds. Coarse fishing is allowed on this lake from mid June to mid March. The track of the former railway line running northeast out of Thrapston is a popular footpath, affording good views of this lake but not Tichmarsh Reserve, although access can be gained to the reserve from it. The mature trees and associated scrub which have grown up along this track attract an interesting range of woodland bird species. To the east and north of Harper's Brook are three smaller lakes, one of which is a private trout lake with few surrounding trees, the others being encircled by a variety of trees, predominantly willows.

Species

This site has consistently been the second most important site in Northamptonshire for wildfowl, hosting over 3,600 individuals in December 1991. Wigeon are the most numerous, with sometimes over 1,000 birds present, but there are also over 800 Coot and 100 each of Gadwall, Teal and Shoveler, over 300 Pochard, and 250 Tufted Duck. Up to 75 Goldeneye occur and over 100 Goosander are regular in February, making this site currently the eighth most important in Britain for the latter species. Rarities have included American Wigeon and Blue-winged Teal. Greylag and Canada Geese are both prolific breeders and both regularly number over 300 birds including young at the end of the breeding season. Up to 90 Great Crested Grebes are present annually in the autumn months, with up to 50 throughout the year. The Grey Heron colony fluctuates in number, falling after hard winters, but over 40 nests have been regular in the 1990s. Four species of rare herons, Purple Heron, Night Heron, Great White Egret and Little Egret have all been attracted to neighbouring lakes.

Tichmarsh Reserve holds the highest number of breeding species, at least 34, including such significant inland breeding species as Oystercatcher, Ringed and Little Ringed Plovers and Common Tern. Reed, Sedge and Grasshopper Warblers, Garden Warbler, Blackcap and two or three species of woodpecker also nest, along with Treecreeper and the declining Tree Sparrow, which prefer to nest in the mature alder trees. Parties of Yellow, Pied and White Wagtails like to feed on emergent insects along the water's edge during their spring migration in April and May.

Greenshank

In both spring and autumn, migrating waders such as Dunlin, Ruff, Grey Plover, Greenshank and Common Sandpiper, Turnstone and Bar-tailed and Black-tailed Godwits find plenty of feeding opportunities along with Redshank, Snipe and Curlew, all of which breed nearby. Pectoral Sandpiper and Grey Phalarope are the rarest waders to have appeared.

The footpath leading from Thrapston is called 'Town Walk' and passes through some excellent mature trees, shrubs and scrub, which proves attractive to many passage migrants including seven or eight species of warbler and sometimes Nightingale. This is often the best place to seek out the first arriving migrants in spring. The mature trees also occasionally produce records of Hawfinches during the winter months.

Hobbies can be seen hawking insects over the reserve during the summer, and Ospreys and Marsh Harriers seem to turn up about every two to three years, while a splendid Red-footed Falcon found the environs of one of the smaller lakes to its liking during one hot spring spell, as it stayed for a week. In winter Hen Harrier has also occurred.

The lake nearest Thrapston has a habit of attracting terns and Little Gulls after easterly winds, with sometimes large numbers of both Arctic and Black Terns appearing. Occasionally Little and Sandwich also arrive as well as the widespread Common Tern. Both White-winged Black and Whiskered Terns have also been recorded here.

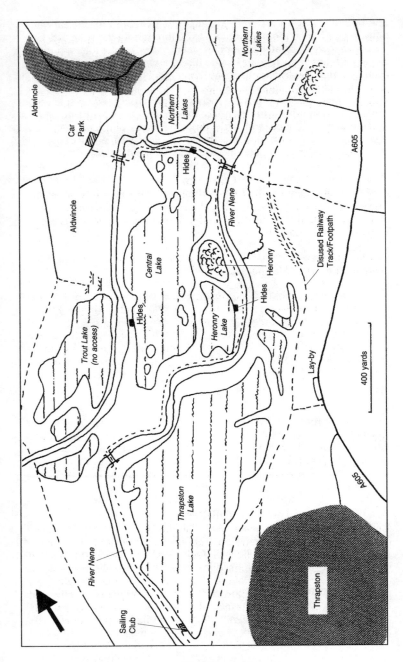

Timing

The site is worthy of a visit at any time of day and any time of year in any season as there is always something of interest, and yet the site is remarkably underwatched.

Access

From Thrapston take the A605 for 2 miles (3.2 km) northeastwards and turn left into Thorpe Waterville village, follow the road past the pit to Aldwincle and then first left into Lowick Lane. The entrance to the reserve is after 300 yds/m (at TL 007 815) where there is a small car park and information boards. The Nene Way long-distance footpath also runs alongside the reserve. Alternatively, park in the lay-by off the A605, 500 yds/m northeast out of Thrapston and take the footpath down the side of the field to the old disused railway line which gives views of the main lake adjacent to Thrapston. This path is called Town Walk and leads back into Thrapston but is popular with dog walkers.

Calendar

Resident: Little Grebe, Great Crested Grebe, Grey Heron, Cormorant, Greylag and Canada Geese, Gadwall, Tufted Duck, Kingfisher, Green and Great Spotted Woodpecker, Lesser Spotted Woodpecker (scarce), Tree Sparrow, Reed Bunting.

October–March: Wigeon, Teal, Shoveler, Goldeneye, Water Rail, Fieldfare, Redwing, Hawfinch (scarce).

April–September: Shelduck, Garganey (scarce), Osprey and Marsh Harrier (rare passage), Hobby, Ringed Plover, Little Ringed Plover, Redshank, Curlew (scarce), Dunlin, Ruff, Bar-tailed and Black-tailed Godwit, Little Gull, Common Tern, Arctic Tern, Little and Sandwich Tern (both scarce), Yellow Wagtail, Nightingale (scarce), Northern Wheatear, Reed Warbler, Sedge Warbler and Grasshopper Warbler, Blackcap, Garden Warbler.

21 DITCHFORD GRAVEL PITS

OS Sheets 152/153

Habitat

This single site has added more species to the county bird list and more British rarities have occurred here than at any other site in the county and probably in the entire Midlands region. Its secret lies in the fact that it occupies a riverside location on an east–west flyway, is visible for miles to migrating birds, and offers a huge variety of habitats suitable for both feeding and breeding purposes. The large network of new and worked-out gravel pits exhibits the full range of successional vegetation, from open bare sand and gravel with shallow floodwater pools and a minimum of vegetation to areas of mature willow carr.

The largest pit, immediately to the west of Higham Ferrers, was designated as an SSSI on account of its important selection of breeding bird species and the number of passage waders using the locality as a regular stop-over. This status, however, still did not stop a new road being built across one side of the pit in 1985 and its subsequent upgrading to dual carriageway ten years later. The associated diversion of the river along a new course seemed to affect the water levels in the pit, which no longer rose and fell as quickly, an important factor in maintaining muddy edges and feeding areas for waders. Since that time the banks have become increasingly vegetated with willows and patches of reedmace, and some of the narrow islands left after mineral extraction have also become covered in willows. In some respects the pit does not seem, from a human viewpoint, to look as good as it was, but nevertheless it is obviously still just as attractive to birds, and rarities continue to put in an appearance.

More pits have since been excavated, and the newest stretch to the west of Ditchford Lane (joining the A45 just west of Rushden to the B571 Wellingborough to Irthlingborough road), extends almost to the eastern outskirts of Wellingborough. A hide on the riverbank overlooking the main pit was soon destroyed by vandals but two new ones on an area leased by the Northamptonshire Wildlife Trust may fare better.

Species
Sooty Tern, Bee-eater, Penduline Tit, Red-rumped Swallow, Alpine Swift, Broad-billed Sandpiper, Night Heron, Green-winged Teal, American Wigeon, Ring-necked Duck, Sabine's and Ring-billed Gulls are just a few of the exciting species to have visited this site over the years. The current list of species recorded stands at 225, even more than recorded at Pitsford Reservoir.

Ditchford varies between the fifth and eighth best county wildfowl site, with the January 1992 count of 1,350 birds being the highest total in recent years. Wigeon predominate, with up to 350 birds, followed by Tufted Duck (285), Teal (185), Pochard (175), Gadwall (145) and Shoveler (80), as well as Mallard and a few Goldeneye. Something rarer often appears during the course of a year, for example Scaup, Common Scoter or Red-crested Pochard, but even extreme rarities such as Ferruginous Duck, Eider, Long-tailed Duck and Velvet Scoter have appeared over the years. Ducks tend to move around the complex of pits, with their movements dependent upon local environmental conditions such as wind strength and direction and the amount of disturbance, but in general, the largest lake immediately west of Higham Ferrers holds the best variety and totals. Pochard, Shoveler, Shelduck, Gadwall and Tufted Ducks have all recently bred, with Wigeon, Garganey and Teal summering.

This is also the best site in the county for Water Pipit, with up to three birds wintering annually. The birds tend to favour the area alongside the river but, as is often the case with this flighty species, they can be difficult to observe well as they often fly long distances once flushed and are not quick to return to favoured locations. Stonechat also like this area in the winter and a pair have even stayed to breed nearby on one occasion. Water Rails too can usually be found around any of the older more vegetated pits, being most easily observed during spells of hard weather when their favoured feeding areas in the shallower water around the reed and sedge fringes may be iced over and the birds forced out to feed in the more open ice-free areas where they may become more visible. Bearded Tits have found the mass of waterside vegetation to their liking but are not annual in occurrence. They are often first located due to their habit of giving their obvious pinging call notes as they feed in amongst the reedbeds or even in patches of dead willow herb and nettles, which can also provide seeds for their winter diet. When not calling, they can be very inconspicuous, feeding quietly in the vegetation.

Gulls often gather in the late afternoon but their choice of pit seems to vary. Large numbers of Lesser and Great Black-backed Gulls are sometimes present and these have been accompanied by Iceland and Glaucous Gulls on several occasions, with Mediterranean Gull also having occurred amongst the commoner Black-headed and Common Gulls. Most birds fly off just before dusk to roost elsewhere, probably at Grafham Water across the county boundary in Cambridgeshire.

Water Pipit

In spring the bushes are alive with Sedge and Willow Warblers, and Reed Warblers too are not uncommon. Cetti's Warblers took up residence at Ditchford for several years, with most of the county records coming from this site, and a rare singing Savi's Warbler also spent some time here one spring. There is a small heronry, with up to ten pairs of Grey Heron nesting annually. Several Purple Herons have been recorded on neighbouring pits, in addition to Spoonbill, Little Egret and several Bitterns over the years, the latter mainly occurring during the winter months. Waders are now mostly found at the western end of the complex, with 34 species having been recorded from the locality including all the commoner species as well as several Temminck's Stints, two Kentish Plovers, Marsh Sandpiper, Lesser Yellowlegs, Pectoral and Purple Sandpipers, Avocet and Grey Phalarope. The pits also have a good range of breeding waders, with Redshank, Lapwing, Ringed and Little Ringed Plovers all nesting annually, and hopefully Oystercatcher will soon follow suit as birds are occurring with more frequency in the spring and summer months.

Common Terns no longer breed but are ever present during the summer and when inland movements of flocks of migrating terns are taking place. At such times, Arctic and Black Terns also arrive with regularity, and the much scarcer Little and Sandwich Terns are also possible, while there is additionally one record of a vagrant White-winged Black Tern.

Waders are more numerous in autumn, with the usual passage of small flocks of Dunlin, Ringed and Little Ringed Plovers, Ruff, Greenshank and Common and Green Sandpipers plus the usual scarcer species such as both godwits, Little Stint, Curlew and Wood Sandpipers. Even some seabirds have been attracted, following displacements from either the east or west coasts, with Shag, Fulmar, Leach's Petrel and three species of skuas, Pomarine, Arctic and Long-tailed, all having been recorded. Diligent searching of the site during the autumn has

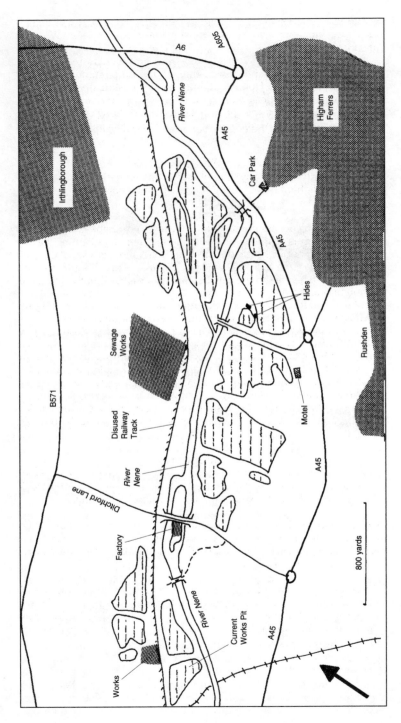

even led to the discovery of vagrants normally associated wth coastal localities, including two Yellow-browed Warblers, Firecrest, Wryneck and Hoopoe.

As would be expected with so many birds and such a variety of habitats many raptors have been encountered, from the ubiquitous Kestrel and Sparrowhawks to Hobby, all three species nesting nearby. Osprey, Marsh Harrier and Merlin are seen every two years or so and even Goshawk and Hen Harrier have been recorded. Long-eared Owls are sometimes seen in the winter and through into spring and may breed in the area as they can be very elusive when nesting.

Timing

A visit is worthwhile at any time of day or any time of year. There is so much good habitat here to explore and anything can turn up.

Access

There are many access points but the easiest to describe is from the A6 in Higham Ferrers. Approaching from the south on the A6 turn left at the Queen's Head public house down Wharf Road, there is a small car park at the bottom of the hill (at SP 953 687). Walk over the footbridge over the dual carriageway to the pits beyond. Access is virtually unlimited, although one private lake is fenced off, but a new hide even overlooks this lake. Another hide overlooks the small lake adjacent to the dual carriageway and a scrape has recently been constructed here.

To view the newer pits take Ditchford Lane just west of Rushden, travelling north for two-thirds of a mile (1000 m) and crossing the river bridge with the traffic lights; just beyond on the left is a gravel track (at SP 930 684), which can be walked down or is driveable (after the gravel lorries have stopped running in the evenings or at weekends). A pit on the left is heavily fished but beyond this is a pit used as a dump for the gravel residues from the washing process at the works, which makes areas attractive to waders. The newer pits are further along the track on the left.

Calendar

Resident: Little Grebe, Great Crested Grebe, Grey Heron, Mute Swan, Greylag Goose, Canada Goose, Gadwall, Tufted Duck, Ruddy Duck, Sparrowhawk, Kestrel, Kingfisher, Willow Tit, Reed Bunting.

October–March: Cormorant, Wigeon, Teal, Shoveler, Pochard, Red-crested Pochard (scarce), Scaup and Common Scoter (scarce), Water Rail, Long-eared Owl (rare), Water Pipit, Snipe, Green Sandpiper, Grey Wagtail, Stonechat, Redpoll.

April–September: Shelduck, Garganey (scarce), Osprey and Marsh Harrier (scarce), Hobby, Oystercatcher, Redshank, Little Ringed Plover, Ringed Plover, Common Sandpiper, (other passage waders), Common, Tern, Arctic Tern, Black Tern, Sandwich and Little Terns (rare passage), Cuckoo, Sedge Warbler, Reed Warbler, Whitethroat.

Habitat

This extensive area comprises one large and five small, flooded, worked-out gravel pits alongside the southern bank of the River Nene at the southeast edge of Northampton. The largest lake, which has been enclosed by a giant clay and earth bank, is designed as a flood catchment area to receive floodwater when the River Nene is swollen after periods of heavy rainfall. Automatic sluices allow the level of the basin 'Washlands' to fill up and hence lower the level of the river, thereby protecting areas downstream from the threat of flooding. Originally it was thought that the basin would only fill about once every seven years but flooding is at present, at least, an annual event, which can occur at any time of year following a period of extended heavy rainfall.

When not covered in floodwater the area is grazed by sheep and geese. A large spit of land and a narrower point extend into the lake, and waders, gulls and terns often find these spots to their liking. There is also a small gravel island at the southwest corner of the basin with, at present, a few small willows growing on it. This has consistently been the best of the lakes, but in late 1995 the owner granted access to coarse fishermen, which could have a dramatic effect on the birdlife at this site. The small lakes to the east are not open to the public. The deepest of these lakes is a trout fishery which can, however, be easily scanned from the rim of the largest lake, while another can be viewed from a public footpath which runs along the southern edge. This footpath is the track of a former railway line, still used for access purposes by gravel lorries. The latter lake is surrounded by willows, many of which overhang the water, and there is a small *Phragmites* reedbed in the southeast corner.

Species

The locality is the eighth most important wintering site in Britain for Golden Plover, with large numbers, up to 5,000 birds, being present from October through to April, unless there is a major freeze-up, when they depart to the west, returning with the thaw. Several thousand Lapwing are also usually present along with up to 100 Dunlin and a Green Sandpiper or two. Clifford Hill averages the third best site in the county for wildfowl, with up to 2,900 individuals present in December 1993, comprising over 1,500 Mallard, up to 600 Wigeon, 130 Pochard, and 160 Tufted Duck, with smaller numbers of Gadwall, Teal, Shoveler and Goldeneye and, especially after Christmas, up to 50 Goosander. Of the rarer ducks, Scaup, Smew and Common Scoter are almost annual. Wigeon find the short grassy banks around the main lake to their liking and are often accompanied by large numbers of Greylag and Canada Geese, up to 350 and 450 respectively in late 1995. These feral flocks often attract wandering wild geese, and White-fronted, Pink-footed and Brent Geese, usually singles, have occurred regularly, with also the odd Barnacle and Egyptian Goose of unknown origin. Mute Swan numbers often total 50–100, even during the summer months, and Bewick's Swans sometimes pay a visit in November.

The point area acts as a gathering site for Cormorants and gulls in the late afternoon prior to going to roost. The gulls consist mainly of Black-

Northern Wheatear

headed, with smaller numbers of Common Gulls, Lesser Black-backs and Herring Gulls. As with most well watched gull haunts, there have been occasional records of the more regular scarce species, with Yellow-legged, Glaucous, Iceland and Mediterranean Gulls all having occurred once or twice.

The adjacent trout lake is very deep, and consequently, even during the most prolonged frosts, there is always an ice-free hole acting as a magnet for the remaining wildfowl, which has also attracted Red-necked Grebe during such conditions.

In March, Northern Wheatears and Sand Martins sometimes make their first county appearance at this site, and the former can on good days reach double figures. White and Yellow Wagtails like the grassy edges and Ring Ouzels have been recorded a couple of times. Of the passage waders, Redshank, Ringed and Little Ringed Plovers are certain and a good selection of other passage waders move through but seldom stay for more than a day or so. Of the rarer spring migrants, Sanderling, Whimbrel and Bar-tailed Godwit are often the most reliable. Common Terns are present throughout the summer as they breed farther down the valley, coming to the pits to fish and bringing their fledged young later in the summer. Little and Sandwich Terns are almost annual on passage, with Black Terns and Little Gulls being more reliable given a hint of east or southeast in the winds during May and July–September. Great Crested Grebes, Mute Swans, Greylag and Canada Geese, Coots, Moorhens and Tufted Duck breed on adjacent pits, and Shelduck are often seen in summer. Reed and Sedge Warblers also frequent the reedbeds and sedges around these pits where they both breed. Birds of the more open grassland habitats include breeding Meadow Pipit and Skylark, while that darting blue-backed fisherman, the Kingfisher, Little Owl and Reed Bunting are all breeding birds.

Such a well watched site with a good range of habitats is sure to produce a number of rare birds amongst its wealth of commoner species. Hoopoe, Red Kite, Osprey and Marsh Harrier have all been attracted in spring, Spoonbills have occurred twice and Little Egret has appeared in late summer. Following periods of gale force westerly winds during the autumn, even a Leach's Petrel has put in an appearance, proving that just about anything can turn up at well watched inland sites. Vagrant passerines more usually associated with the coastal salt-marshes also

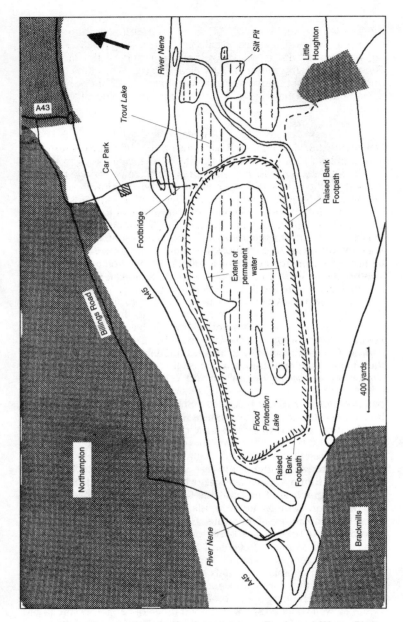

appear from time to time in the late autumn. Rock and Water Pipits, Shorelark, Snow Bunting and Twite have all been recorded at this locality, a very good range of coastal species for a site in central England.

Timing

The best times to visit on a dry day are either early morning or just before dusk, as the main lake area is popular with joggers and particularly dog walkers, who seldom keep to the footpaths and let their dogs run free. On wet and windy days there is less disturbance, and any time of day can be good. It is easy to gain the best viewing position by walking around the rim to view any particular part of the large lake. Tuesday, during the winter months, is perhaps the worst time to visit as there is often shooting over the adjacent private lakes and the wildfowl in particular will have been disturbed, and the Golden Plovers also move off.

Access

Leaving central Northampton eastwards on the Billings road turn right after 2 miles (3.2 km) down Weston Mill Lane, signposted to Weston Favell Mill. After 300 yds/m over the dual carriageway bridge there is a car park on the right. (NB leave nothing of value on show in your car as break-ins are frequent.) Walk south down the lane towards the boat club, cross, first, the lock gate then the footbridge across the river, and the main lake is immediately in front of you. The footpath encircles the Washlands flood storage reservoir. Alternatively, at the A45 (Nene Valley Way)/A43 (Lumbertubs Way) interchange, go north on the A43 for just 200 yds/m before turning left along Bewick Road then left down Weston Mill Lane after half a mile (800 m), then as above. Access can also be gained from the A428 Bedford road which passes the southern edge of the main lake.

Calendar

Resident: Little Grebe, Great Crested Grebe, Cormorant, Mute Swan, Greylag Goose, Canada Goose, Gadwall, Tufted Duck, Grey Partridge, Red-legged Partridge, Lapwing, Little Owl, Kingfisher, Meadow Pipit, Skylark, Reed Bunting.

October–March: Wigeon, Goldeneye, Smew (scarce), Goosander (from December), Golden Plover, Dunlin, Snipe, Green Sandpiper, Black-headed, Common, Lesser Black-backed Gulls, Rock Pipit, Grey Wagtail, Linnet.

April–September: Shelduck, passage waders, Little Stint, Sanderling, Dunlin, Ruff, Bar-tailed Godwit, Greenshank, Wood Sandpiper, Common Sandpiper, Turnstone, Redshank, Little Gull, Yellow-legged Gull, Common Tern, Arctic Tern, Black Tern, Northern Wheatear and Whinchat (passage), Reed Warbler, Sedge Warbler.

23 DAVENTRY RESERVOIR COUNTRY PARK AND BOROUGH HILL

Habitat

Constructed in the nineteenth century, the 130-acre (52 ha) Daventry Reservoir is owned by the British Waterways Board and is used to supply water to the canal feeder system. In the early 1980s it was designated as a country park, administered by Daventry District Council, which leases the area and also owns the land immediately to the west of the reservoir. Apart from the dam situated at the northern end of the reservoir, it is completely surrounded by a narrow belt of mature deciduous woodland with some willows, which grow right down to the water's edge. The immediate surroundings also encompass small areas of short-mown grassland and areas of rough grassland with bushes. The banks shelve gently down to the water's edge. Coarse fishing is permitted between mid June and mid March, with the dam being the most popular site with anglers. There is also an adventure playground for children alongside the car park and an information centre, toilets (including facilities for the disabled), and a cafe along the path to the dam. The land to the north and east of the dam is arable farmland. A footpath of 2 miles (3.2 km) in length encircles the reservoir and provides an attractive walk.

Only 1 mile (1.6 km) to the southeast of Daventry Reservoir is Borough Hill, the highest point in the area, rising to a height of 650 feet (200 m). Until recently this was the site of the BBC World Service Radio Station, but now all but one of the 14 masts have been removed and the area opened up to the public, with a circular walk of 2 miles (3.2 km) around the 140-acre (56 ha) summit, offering spectacular views over the surrounding countryside.

An ancient hill fort occupied the site long before the presence of the BBC! The area is grazed by sheep, with some rather unkempt hedgerows attractive to migrants.

Species

Nearly 190 species of bird have been attracted to this relatively small area. The reservoir has resident Great Crested Grebes and Canada Geese, while Shoveler have bred. Winter wildfowl numbers reach about 400, with Pochard, Tufted Duck and Wigeon being the most obvious species, along with Mallard, but most of the regular sea-duck species have occurred, including Scaup, Long-tailed Duck, Eider, Common and Velvet Scoter, the latter having now become almost annual. Surface-feeding ducks are often accompanied at the water's edge by flocks of Lapwing, Golden Plover and Common Snipe, particularly on the south and west banks. Winter has also produced records of both Great Northern and Black-throated Divers and Slavonian Grebe. Shags, which are of course very scarce inland, especially in Northamptonshire, have visited this site on several occasions in recent years. There is a small gull roost, usually holding a few hundred birds, mostly Black-headed Gulls, easily scrutinised from the Carvell hide. Close scrutiny of the roosting birds has enabled observers to locate both Yellow-legged and

Mediterranean Gulls on an annual basis, while Ring-billed and Sabine's Gulls have also recently visited the site.

Spring brings a profusion of insects and hence an abundance of food for passage migrant passerines, with a variety of species of warbler being numerous and odd Redstart and Ring Ouzel also being noted. The scrub and rough grassland areas have Whitethroat and Lesser Whitethroat, Blackcap and occasional Grasshopper Warbler. Most of the terns to be seen are Common Terns, which have taken to breeding on the purpose built rafts installed on the reservoir. During easterly winds, however, small parties of Black Terns and Little Gulls often make an appearance, and even White-winged Black Tern has recently been added to the area's list of species. Arctic Terns are annual in occurrence, sometimes reaching double figure counts, and both Little and Sandwich Terns occur every two to three years, although their visits may well be rather brief! Ospreys also pass through with increasing regularity and other odd birds at this time have included a fine summer-plumaged Red-necked Grebe, which stayed for more than two months recently.

Wryneck

With the continual loss of water from the canal system, through losses at the locks, which is at a peak in summer months as the canals are at their busiest, there is the necessity to draw water from the reservoir to top up the system. This almost inevitably results in a drop in the water level of the reservoir during the late summer and early autumn, coinciding nicely with the start of the autumn wader migration. The exposed mud then attracts small numbers of a good variety of passage waders, with Ruff, Greenshank, Dunlin, Common and Green Sandpipers being the most numerous. There is always a good chance of something scarcer at this time, Little Stint, Curlew Sandpiper and Spotted Redshank being the next most reliable species, but even rarer birds like Pectoral Sandpipers have stopped off several times; Temminck's Stint, Kentish Plover and both Purple Sandpiper and Red-necked Phalarope have all been recorded, the latter two feeding, on and just off, the stony dam respectively.

Other oddities have included Little Egret and Spoonbill, with Wryneck and Black Redstart having been attracted to the dam area. This is also the best time of year to look out for Black-necked Grebes,

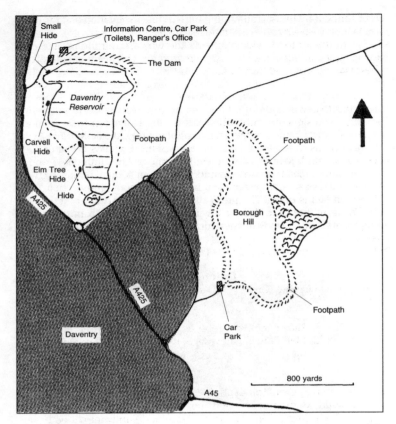

which may be rather inconspicuous, needing serious scanning to pick them out. Rock Pipits are also a scarce late autumn visitor to the stony dam area, while passage flocks of Meadow Pipits are to be found in the grass areas.

Borough Hill has only just been opened up to the public and thus its full potential has yet to be realised. In its first autumn it has, however, attracted a trickle of interesting migrants such as several Redstarts, Pied Flycatchers, a Richard's Pipit and also Merlin, Peregrine, Marsh Harrier and Common Buzzard. Its elevation above the surrounding countryside should make it an obvious place for attracting soaring raptors and pulling in passage migrants. Green Woodpeckers are resident on the hill and, although it has yet to be explored in spring, the likelihood of passage Ring Ouzels occurring seems high.

Timing

The area will repay a visit at any time of year but the autumn period, with the chance of passage waders and Black-necked Grebe, and the winter, with the highest totals of wildfowl and the chance of scarce species, are the best two times. Migrants may be numerous in spring and there are a few interesting breeding species. All three hides are situated on the west bank of the reservoir and thus the light is at its best from these hides in the afternoon. As the hides are shielded from the direct sunlight by the surrounding belt of trees, however, the sun is not directly in the observer's eyes in the mornings. As the reservoir is accessible from the footpath which goes all the way around the perimeter, varying light conditions can be compensated for. The evening gull roost is best viewed from the Carvell hide.

Access

Daventry Reservoir Country Park is on the northeastern edge of Daventry, well signed from the B4036 Daventry to Welton road, with a car park situated in the northwestern part of the reserve (at SP 577 642). A footpath runs right round the reservoir, two hides always being open, access to the middle hide, Elm Tree hide, being by key, obtainable from the Ranger's Office at the western end of the dam. A small hide near the office overlooks a feeding station situated in the woodland.

Borough Hill is only 0.75 miles (1 km) to the southeast of the reservoir. The single mast will act as a guide. Leave the A45 northwards along the A425 for 500 yds/m then turn right again after 300 yds/m at the base of the hill. A small car park is provided at the top. A footpath of 2 miles (3.2 km) encircles the top of the hill.

Calendar

Resident: Great Crested Grebe, Canada Goose, Green and Great Spotted Woodpecker.

October–March: Black-necked Grebe (rare), Shoveler, Teal, Pochard, Tufted Duck, Golden Plover, Lapwing, Snipe, gulls, Rock Pipit (scarce), Fieldfare, Redwing.

April–September: Common Scoter (scarce), Dunlin, Ruff, Greenshank, Green Sandpiper, Common Sandpiper, other waders, depending upon extent of mud, Mediterranean Gull (rare), Yellow-legged Gull (scarce), Common Tern, Arctic Tern (passage), Little and Sandwich Terns (rare on passage), Black Tern (passage), hirundines, Redstart, Ring Ouzel (scarce passage), warblers.

24 SUMMERLEYS NATURE RESERVE AT EARLS BARTON GRAVEL PITS

OS Sheet 152

Habitat

Following cessation of mineral extraction in 1989, this large gravel pit was purposefully and thoughtfully landscaped and developed into what has quickly become an excellent reserve. It forms part of a chain of both restored and still active gravel pits, in the Wollaston–Earls Barton section of the River Nene Valley, which extend for 3.5 miles (5.6 km). Officially opened in 1994, Summerleys Reserve has already attracted a large number of bird species in its own right and has become very popular with local birdwatchers. It is bounded by gently sloping banks which shelve down into the open water, there is also a series of gravel-topped islands to attract breeding terns, waders and wildfowl and a purpose built scrape on which the water level is controlled to produce optimum conditions for attracting migrant and breeding waders. Additionally, a small stream runs into and out of the lake.

Two well placed hides overlook the best part of the reserve, including the scrape. Thousands of mixed deciduous trees have been planted on the reserve and there are hawthorn hedgerows and standard ash trees around the perimeter. The reserve is managed by Northamptonshire County Council. A former railway line which runs along the northern edge of the pits complex, is now used as an access track by gravel lorries servicing the ongoing aggregate extraction industry. Beyond this, grazed meadows lead down to the River Nene, while to the east and west lie older gravel workings and to the south beyond the road is mixed arable farmland.

Species

Winter is an interesting time at the pits with good totals of wildfowl and a good variety of species. Up to six Smew have now become annual including a couple of spectacular 'white nuns', Goldeneye peak at 40, Wigeon 450, Pochard 180, and Tufted Ducks 470. One or two Red-crested Pochard appear in autumn, with Common Scoter and Black-necked Grebe being almost annual as are Brent and White-fronted Geese, which are attracted by the large number of Greylag and Canada Geese breeding here. Eider, Long-tailed Duck and Ferruginous Duck have all occurred as well as the three rarer grebes, Red-necked, Slavonian and Black-necked, and also Great Northern Diver. Even a vagrant Little Auk put in an exhausted appearance during a recent early November movement on the east coast.

Gulls tend to accumulate on one of the islands on an adjoining pit, with numbers rarely more than 200 birds, but even so, the occasional Mediterranean Gull and Kittiwake have accompanied what are mainly Black-headed with a few Common and Lesser Black-backed Gulls. Water Rails occur but are easier to hear than see, their eerie calls being a feature of cold still winter evenings. The hawthorn hedgerows support feeding flocks of winter thrushes, Blackbirds, Fieldfare and Redwing and flocks of Meadow Pipits winter, frequenting short-grass areas around the newer workings. Snipe find the shallow water areas with sedges and wet grassland to their liking, and odd Green Sandpipers occur throughout the winter months, often feeding on the newly worked pits.

On a spring day the reserve is alive with birds, Black-headed Gulls and Common Terns along with Redshank, Lapwings and Little Ringed and Ringed Plovers all calling, displaying and competing for space. Singing Sedge and Reed Warblers vie for territories and mates amongst the reedbeds and rough scrub areas around the pit, with attendant Cuckoos watching for likely nests in which to lay their eggs. The ever present Cormorants are often to be observed resting on the gravel islands with outstretched wings.

As the water level in the scrape is allowed to fall to create muddy edges there will probably be a selection of waders in a mixture of winter, summer and transitional plumages. There may be Dunlin, Ruff, Turnstone, Sanderling, Grey Plover, Bar-tailed Godwits, Whimbrel and

Greenshank, all annual in spring, and even Little Stint and Curlew Sandpiper on occasions. Passage waders in spring are usually short-stayers, however, as the urge to press on to their breeding grounds drives them northwards. Rarer waders have included near annual Temminck's Stint as well as Buff-breasted and Marsh Sandpipers, Red-necked Phalarope and Kentish Plover, the latter two species having appeared on two occasions.

Smew

This is one of the best sites in the county to chance upon a Sandwich Tern, now just about annual in occurrence, or a Little Tern which are nearly so. Arctic Terns often pass through in parties in April, Black Terns and Little Gulls often arriving together, with May being the best month for these two species. The combination of a period of east or southeast winds and rain is a sure bet to produce these delightful spring transients. Hobbies are seen almost daily throughout the summer, often hawking for insects, especially dragonflies, over the pools. The two open country chats, Northern Wheatear and Whinchat, are regular passage migrants during the spring, occurring mainly in April and early to mid May.

When conditions are overcast there can be literally hundreds of Swifts swooping low over the water along with the breeding Sand Martins, and also House Martins and Swallows, all taking advantage of the emergent insect populations. Yellow Wagtails like the edges of the lakes where they gather to feed, and migrant White Wagtails are regular spring visitors. One or two Wigeon stay throughout the summer and Teal linger late into May. Garganey do not breed but odd birds appear throughout the spring and summer. Shoveler sometimes breed and Gadwall usually do so. Tree Sparrows nest on the reserve, and both Grey Herons and Oystercatchers on neighbouring pits, which have also played host to three rarities, two Red-footed Falcons and a truly exceptional inland bird, a Bridled Tern, all in spring.

Little Egrets have arrived in August several times recently, in line with the species recent increase in numbers in southern Britain, with most individuals preferring to feed on the scrape. In the autumn the myriad teasels attract delightful charms of Goldfinches. On the scrape the waders seen in spring can again be seen in autumn, with the addition of Black-tailed Godwit, while Little Stint and Curlew Sandpiper are more

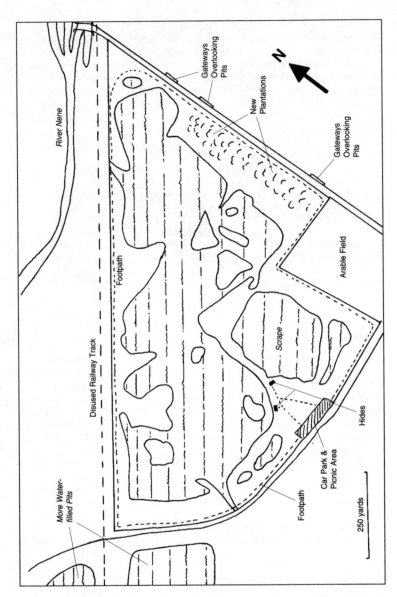

likely and Sanderling less likely than in spring. Golden Plover numbers often build up to around the 1,000 mark as they feed in nearby fields and come into the reserve to bathe and roost.

Timing

This site can be rewarding at any time of the day or year but early morning during the migration seasons is probably the most exciting time to visit as there is always the prospect of something new having arrived overnight, especially after heavy rain.

Access

The reserve is easily reached from the A45 dual carriageway between Northampton to the west (5 miles (8 km)) and Wellingborough to the east (2.5 miles (4 km)), by leaving at the Great Doddington turn-off, then turning left and first right and past the mill at the bottom of the hill. After a further 500 yds/m the car park and reserve is clearly signposted on the left (at SP 885 633). Two hides, both with access for wheelchairs, the left-hand one being purpose built for disabled people, are both within 50 yds/m of the car park. A well marked footpath surrounds the reserve and affords views of all parts of the reserve. There are guided walks at intervals throughout the year.

The two water-filled pits to the east are always worthy of a look and can be viewed from the gateways along the single-track road, which is first left after turning left into the car park. The pit further to the west and the newer ones to the east can also be explored.

Calendar

Resident: Great Crested Grebe, Little Grebe, Cormorant, Grey Heron, Mute Swan, Greylag Goose, Canada Goose, Gadwall, Tufted Duck, Kestrel, Sparrowhawk, Grey Partridge, Red-legged Partridge, Coot, Moorhen, Lapwing, Black-headed Gull, Green Woodpecker, Tree Sparrow.

October–March: Bewick's Swan (scarce), White-fronted and Brent Goose (both rare), Wigeon, Teal, Pintail, Shoveler, Pochard, Goldeneye, Smew, Water Rail, Golden Plover, Snipe, Green Sandpiper, Common and Lesser Black-backed Gulls, Meadow Pipit, Fieldfare, Redwing.

April–September: Garganey (scarce), Hobby, Oystercatcher, Little Ringed and Ringed Plovers, Redshank, passage waders, Grey Plover, Sanderling, Knot, Little Stint, Temminck's Stint (rare), Curlew Sandpiper, Dunlin, Ruff, Black and Bar-tailed Godwits, Curlew, Whimbrel, Spotted Redshank, Greenshank, Common, Green and Wood Sandpipers and Turnstone. Common Tern, Little and Sandwich Terns (scarce), Black Tern, Little Gull, Cuckoo, Yellow and White Wagtails, Reed and Sedge Warbler.

ADDITIONAL SITES

Name	Harrington disused airfield.
Grid Reference	SP 771 769
Habitat	Rough grassland with old wartime buildings and set-aside fields surrounded by wheat fields, all over 500 feet.
Species	Resident Corn Bunting, Green Woodpecker. Short-eared Owl, Merlin and Tree Sparrow in autumn/winter; Golden Plovers, finch and bunting flocks in Winter; Quail in May/June.
Timing	All.
Access	Four miles (6.4 km) southwest of Rothwell off the B576 turn right towards Draughton and airfield is on the right. A minor road and bridleway cross the area.

Name   Stanwick Gravel Pits.
Grid Reference SP 973 717
Habitat   Shallow, water-filled gravel workings in the Nene Valley between Higham Ferrers and Raunds. Some landscaped islands and a marshy area.
Species   Wildfowl and Water Rail winter, Common Tern and some common waders breed; passage waders and terns in spring and autumn; Hobby and Marsh Harrier in spring/summer. Attractive to rare migrants, recently including Little Egrets, Spotted Crake, Ferruginous Duck, Stone Curlew, Temminck's Stint, Baird's Sandpiper, Kentish Plover and Savi's Warbler.
Timing   All.
Access   One and a half miles (2.4 km) northeast of Higham Ferrers on the A605 to Stanwick roundabout where there are lay-bys on either side of road after 300 yds. Follow marked footpaths around area.

Name   Wakerley Great Wood and Fineshade Wood.
Grid Reference SP 963 987 and SP 978 983
Habitat   Forest Enterprise woodlands of 600 (243 ha) and 900 acres (364 ha) respectively, part of the once vast Rockingham Forest royal hunting area. Mixed woodlands with large old larch trees by the main car park at Wakerley.
Species   Best county site for Common Crossbills, often in larch tree by Wakerley car park; also recorded, Parrot and Two-barred Crossbill in 1990–91; Hawfinch, Lesser Spotted Woodpecker and Long-eared Owl all scarce residents; Tree Pipits breed; Hen Harriers have roosted in winter.
Timing   All.
Access   The woods straddle the A43, 10 miles (16 km) north of Corby. The car park at Wakerley, with marked trails, picnic area and toilets (at SP 963 987), the car park at Fineshade (at SP 978 983).

Name   Kinewell Lake, Ringstead Gravel Pits.
Grid Reference SP 978 752
Habitat   Disused gravel workings and pits with islands.
Species   Winter wildfowl and passage terns.
Timing   All.
Access   Public footpath surrounds the lake, with car park (at SP 982 751).

Name   Sywell Reservoir Country Park.
Grid Reference SP 832 655
Habitat   Natural banked reservoir with deciduous and mixed woodlands.
Species   Winter wildfowl; passage terns and breeding Common Terns. Green and Great Spotted Woodpeckers. Passage migrants attracted to dam area, e.g. Yellow Wagtail.
Timing   All.
Access   Public access dawn to dusk; a footpath runs around the reservoir and a hide available, key from ranger. Toilets, information, picnic areas. Car park (at SP 834 652).

Name	Boddington Reservoir.
Grid Reference	SP 498 534
Habitat	Natural banked reservoir. pool and small reedbed with scrub and mature woodland.
Species	Winter wildfowl, passage waders and terns and typical woodland birds.
Timing	All.
Access	Owned by British Waterways Board, with a small reserve called Byfield Pool on the western edge, leased by Northamptonshire Wildlife Trust. Footpath all around area.

DERBYSHIRE

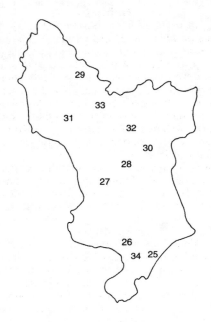

25 Staunton Harold Reservoir
26 Willington Gravel Pits
27 Carsington Water
28 Cromford Canal and Shiningcliff
    Wood
29 The Upper Derwent Valley

30 Ogston Reservoir
31 The Derbyshire Dales
32 The East Moors
33 Padley Gorge SSSI, Longsham
    Estate Country Park
34 Foremark Reservoir

25 STAUNTON HAROLD RESERVOIR

Habitat

This is an attractive reservoir lying in a natural valley surrounded by mainly deciduous woodland and open farmland. A comparatively new reservoir (216 acres (87 ha)), only completed in 1964, it is owned and managed by the Severn Trent Water Authority and is used for sailing and coarse fishing. Disturbance is therefore quite extensive and only the southern third of the reservoir remains for the most part free from this problem. The southeastern corner of the reservoir borders the county of Leicestershire and lies adjacent to the mixed woodland of Spring Wood, a Derbyshire Wildlife Trust reserve. To the southwest is Calke Park, an area of mature oaks set amongst open grass parkland, owned by the National Trust.

The geography of the reservoir means that the water is fairly shallow throughout, and it has gently sloping sandy banks, attractive to wading birds and wildfowl. The water surface is dotted with buoys, used for sailing, which in turn form perches for a variety of birds.

Species

During the winter period the reservoir is locally important for the concentrations of Great Crested Grebes, which in some winters may exceed 100 birds. Visitations by rarer species include Red-throated, Black-throated and Great Northern Divers and Red-necked and Slavonian Grebes, all of which are rare but have proved to be not too infrequent during recent winters. A resident flock of Canada Geese sometimes attracts individuals or small parties of Greylag, Pink-footed and Barnacle Geese, and there have been typically brief visits from some largish flocks of Bewick's Swans and even the normally strictly coastal Brent Geese over the years. The buoys scattered over the water surface provide useful drying-out perches for Cormorants, and after periods of gales on the coast there have been odd occurrences of a few Shags.

The winter wildfowl scene is headed by Wigeon, Teal, Pochard, Goldeneye and Goosander with regular appearances from the scarcer species, Pintail, Shoveler and Ruddy Duck, whilst there have been single records of Red-crested Pochard, Eider and Long-tailed Duck. The dabbling ducks tend to concentrate at the far end of the southern arm, where there are a number of grass fields used for grazing by the flocks of Wigeon, and shallows attractive to feeding Teal, which may reach three-figure counts. A relatively small and underwatched gull roost, of 1–3,000 birds is present during the early winter but it is probable that most of these birds leave close to dark and fly to the nearby Foremark Reservoir to roost. Even so there have been sightings of Glaucous and Iceland Gulls at the reservoir but occurrences are rare.

The surrounding arable fields are also of interest, with flocks of Lapwing, coveys of Grey Partridge and flocks of finches. The latter consist mainly of the declining Linnet and may also hold parties of Twite, a notable inland occurrence. Little Owls can be heard calling towards dusk and the area has also played host to a wintering Great Grey Shrike in the past. The trees at the southern end of the reservoir hold parties of tits and Goldcrests and on rare occasions have held Firecrest, while the alders as usual attract flocks of Siskin and Redpoll. The road bridge at this southern end is a good place to watch for Water Rails, which occur infrequently in cold weather. Of the raptors, Sparrowhawks are fairly common, there are sporadic visits from Common Buzzards and Peregrine has also been seen on a number of occasions.

Spring is one of the best times to visit the reservoir as it proves attractive to both migrant land and waterbirds and offers the potential for locating scarce passage migrants. It is certainly the best time to look for the exquisite summer-plumaged Black-necked Grebes, which along with small flocks of Common Scoters, may appear *en route* to their breeding areas farther north. Sightings of passage raptors are often a case of pot luck but Ospreys are not infrequent and probably under recorded, while that dashing little falcon, the Hobby, is best looked for in the evenings when they arrive to hunt the flocks of House and Sand Martins, Swallows and Swifts which feed over the reservoir.

The shallow sandy banks make attractive feeding areas for a number of waders, if the water levels are not too high. These include the regular Ringed and Little Ringed Plovers, Dunlin, Ruff and Greenshank, with good numbers of Common Sandpiper. In addition to which there is always the chance of a Grey Plover, Spotted Redshank, Black-tailed Godwit or Whimbrel, or even something rarer. The movement of flocks of terns, Common, Arctic and Black, with occasional Little Gulls, takes place during April and May in the right weather conditions. The birds build up in numbers during the day but almost invariably seem to depart just prior to dusk. Little and Sandwich Terns have also rarely been reported, and there is one record of a party of four Roseate Terns having been seen.

The banks and the dam wall are attractive to large numbers of insects, and make good feeding areas for Yellow and White Wagtails and Northern Wheatears. Singing Sedge Warblers and Whitethroats appear along the western banks of the reservoir and Grasshopper Warblers are not too infrequent, while Cuckoos are always present, but Turtle Doves seem to be in decline.

During high summer the amount of disturbance reaches a peak and the birdlife interest is in consequence much reduced, but the surrounding fields may hold a calling Quail.

Autumn migration sees the return wader passage under way, with larger numbers than in spring, and species such as Dunlin, Ringed Plover, Ruff, Green and Common Sandpipers often staying for longer periods and sometimes being joined by a few Curlew Sandpiper and Little Stint. Tern passage is mainly of Common and Black Terns, with the latter peaking at some 220 birds during good periods. Little Gulls also appear and gales on the coast may bring in the odd Arctic and Great Skua. Black-necked Grebes are again possible at this season but records usually involve the less spectacular but dainty juvenile birds. Passerine migrants to be found around the hedgerows along the footpaths, as well as the usual warblers, often include small numbers of Redstarts and Whinchats.

A number of rare birds have been recorded over the reservoir's 30-year history, including Little Egret and two White-winged Black Terns in autumn, in addition to which good inland county birds have included Purple Sandpiper, Razorbill, Little Auk and a Pomarine Skua which lingered for four days.

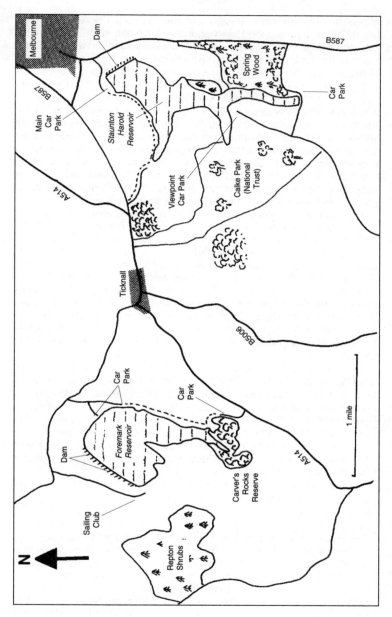

Timing
The best times of year for a visit are during the winter period, November–March, and during the spring and autumn migration, April–May and August–October. As access to the main body of water, at the dam end of the reservoir, is only permitted along the western side, the early morning sun can create a problem and thus afternoon and early evening visits are best on sunny days. Unfortunately this is

countered by the greater degree of disturbance from water sports during the afternoon and evening periods so birds are most settled in the early mornings. The gull roost is best viewed from the west bank just south of the sailing club, where the birds can sometimes be reasonably close.

Access

Staunton Harold Reservoir is situated 5 miles (8 km) south of Derby, just to the south of Melbourne and to the east of Foremark Reservoir. The dam car park is reached from the B587, 800 yds/m south of Melbourne, and is well signposted. This is a pay and display car park and the entrance gates are locked at dusk. The south arm can be reached by taking the B587 south of Melbourne for 2 miles (3.2 km) then taking a right turn and following this minor road for a further 1 mile (1.6 km) to a road bridge which overlooks the water area. A further 800 yds/m along this road a right turn leads to a watchpoint and large car park which overlooks the central part of the reservoir.

Calendar

Resident: Great Crested Grebe, Little Grebe, Canada Goose, Sparrowhawk, Grey Partridge, Little Owl, Kingfisher, Willow Tit, Linnet.

October–March: Divers (all three species rare), Red-necked Grebe (rare), Cormorant, Grey Heron, Bewick's Swan (scarce), Wigeon, Teal, Shoveler, Pintail (scarce), Pochard, Goldeneye, Goosander, Ruddy Duck (scarce), Lapwing, Snipe, Common Gull, Grey Wagtail, Stonechat (scarce), Fieldfare, Redwing, Goldfinch, Linnet, Reed Bunting.

April–September: Black-necked Grebe (rare), Common Scoter (scarce), Osprey (rare), Hobby, Quail (scarce), Little Ringed and Ringed Plover, Grey Plover, Little Stint, Curlew Sandpiper (all scarce), Dunlin, Ruff, Greenshank, Green Sandpiper, Common Sandpiper (all passage), Little Gull (scarce), Common Tern, Arctic Tern, Black Tern, Little Tern (rare), Turtle Dove, Cuckoo, Swift, Yellow Wagtail, White Wagtail, Northern Wheatear, Redstart, Whinchat (all passage), Grasshopper Warbler (scarce), Sedge Warbler, Whitethroat, Chiffchaff.

26 WILLINGTON GRAVEL PITS OS Sheet 128

Habitat

Excavated in the late 1970s, Willington Gravel Pits form part of an extensive chain of workings extending along the Trent valley floodplain. The area covers approximately 183 acres and contains a variety of wetland habitats, ranging from large stretches of open water, some with islets, to small shallow secluded pools, fringed with *Phragmites* and willow scrub. In addition there is a small area of water meadow in the extreme southwestern corner of the site and an area of gravel flats and sand mounds in the northwest corner. Several of the pits have very shallow margins, created by partial infilling with pulverised flyash from the local power stations, and these prove attractive to passage waders, gulls, terns and wildfowl. Although there is no woodland on the site, the hedgerows along the approach lane contain oak, ash and sycamore along with thickets of blackthorn and gorse, and many 'woodland' birds can be found here.

Species

As with most other water bodies in the Trent valley, wildfowl are the main attraction during the winter months. Although numbers are smaller than on some of the neighbouring reservoirs, there is usually a wide range of species to be seen. Shelduck, Wigeon, Teal, Mallard, Shoveler, Pochard, Tufted Duck and Goldeneye are everyday birds, and these are sometimes joined by Gadwall and, more rarely, Pintail, Scaup and Smew. The flock of Cormorants peaks during the period, with numbers often in excess of 70 individuals, while the group of wintering Goosanders has reached over 100 in recent times. There are good numbers of Canada Geese and the flock often harbours a few Pink-footed, White-fronted and Greylag Geese, though most of these are probably of feral origin. Brent Geese have been recorded as have Bewick's Swans but both are unusual.

Waders are a little thin on the ground but Jack Snipe are quite often found amongst the larger numbers of Common Snipe which frequent, in particular, the water meadow area. A few Redshank and Ringed Plovers can be found, along with the odd Green Sandpiper among the larger groups of Lapwing and Golden Plovers which like to loaf on the flyash areas. Although there is no gull roost at the site, all the common winter species are usually present and Glaucous and Mediterranean Gulls have both been found. Kestrel and Sparrowhawk are the most likely raptors to be encountered at this season but both Peregrine and Merlin have been noted and Long-eared Owls have roosted in hawthorn thickets along the lane on at least one occasion.

Spring is probably the best time to visit this site as it acts as a magnet for migrants moving along the Trent valley. The early part of the period often produces Kittiwakes and, more rarely, Garganey, but it is not until late April or early May that the first migrating flocks of Common, Arctic and Black Terns appear, bringing with them a few Little Gulls, some in full summer plumage. Both Sandwich and Little Tern have been noted in recent years, including a group of four of the latter, but they seldom linger. Waders are always in evidence and no fewer than 29 species have been recorded, of which over half are regular visitors. A typical May should produce records of Oystercatcher, Little Ringed and Ringed Plovers, Grey Plover, Lapwing, Sanderling, Dunlin, Ruff, Black and Bar-tailed Godwits, Whimbrel, Curlew, Redshank, Greenshank and Common Sandpiper, with Knot, Spotted Redshank, Wood Sandpiper and Turnstone all possible additions.

Raptors, either resident or passage birds, are often noted during the spring period: Marsh Harriers have been attracted to the small reedbed and occasionally stay to roost, Ospreys put in regular appearances as they commute between the Trent valley and nearby Foremark Reservoir, sometimes using the electricity pylons as perches, and Common Buzzards have drifted over the area on rare visits from their woodland haunts a little farther to the south. Kestrels and Sparrowhawks are everyday sights and Peregrines have been seen causing havoc among the waders on hunting forays from their cooling tower eyrie at the power station. Hobby numbers have increased dramatically over the last few years and they are now an almost expected sight as they hawk insects and occasionally display over the pits before moving on to their breeding sites.

Searching the flocks of Pied and Yellow Wagtails, which forage in the more stony areas of the overgrown flyash beds, will produce a few White Wagtails in April. Northern Wheatears may appear anywhere but they do tend to favour the gravel flats at the northwestern end of the site. The approach lane is also not without interest as all three woodpeckers have been encountered, although Green is by far the most likely to be seen, or rather heard, on a casual walk. Whitethroat, Lesser Whitethroat, Blackcaps and Garden Warblers can all be heard singing amongst the more numerous Willow Warblers, Wrens, Robins, Blue, Great and Long-tailed Tits.

By the time Reed Warblers set up their territories in the reedbed they share with Sedge Warblers, summer is not far off. Several pairs of Reed Warbler breed here in what is a rare habitat in county terms. Other breeding birds are much more easily seen, the most obvious being the large numbers of Black-headed Gulls which nest on the islets. Around 150 pairs bred in 1995, making this the second largest colony in the county. A pair of adult Mediterranean Gulls visited the colony in 1992 and the possibility of their breeding in the future should not be dismissed. Sharing the islets with the gulls are up to eight pairs of Common Tern, and in recent years a single pair of Oystercatcher have take advantage of the aggressive nest defence of the gulls to allow them to rear young without interference from predators. Now a scarce breeding bird in the county, up to eight pairs of Redshank share the overgrown flyash pits with Lapwings, Ringed Plovers and, occasionally, Little Ringed Plovers, though the latter prefer the gravel flats. Breeding wildfowl include Mallard, Tufted Duck, and more rarely, Pochard. Shelduck have appeared with young and Garganey have summered at least once. Several pairs of Great Crested Grebes nest and a pair of Red-breasted Mergansers have been noted with young. Mute Swans nest annually and a small colony of Sand Martins exists in the sand mounds nearby. In addition, Meadow Pipits, Pied Wagtails and Kingfishers all breed around the pits, while the hedgerows along the lane harbour several species of warbler, finches and tits.

Many birds are still feeding young when the first returning migrants arrive. As in the spring waders are much in evidence, with Greenshank, Green Sandpiper, Ruff and both godwits often on view, while this is also the best time to catch up with Little Stint and Curlew Sandpiper. Common and Arctic Terns, many in juvenile plumage, pass through on their return migration and, as in the spring, are occasionally joined by small numbers of Black Terns and Little Gulls.

In view of its position on a major flyway it is no surprise that the area has turned up a number of both national and local rarities, which have included Black-throated Diver, Fulmar, Little Egret, Green-winged Teal, Blue-winged Teal, Ring-necked Duck, Avocet, Kentish Plover, Temminck's Stint, Caspian Tern, Shorelark, Water Pipit and Firecrest.

Timing

The best times to visit Willington are during the spring and autumn migration, April and May and August to October, although the remainder of the year is seldom without interest. As the main wader haunts are

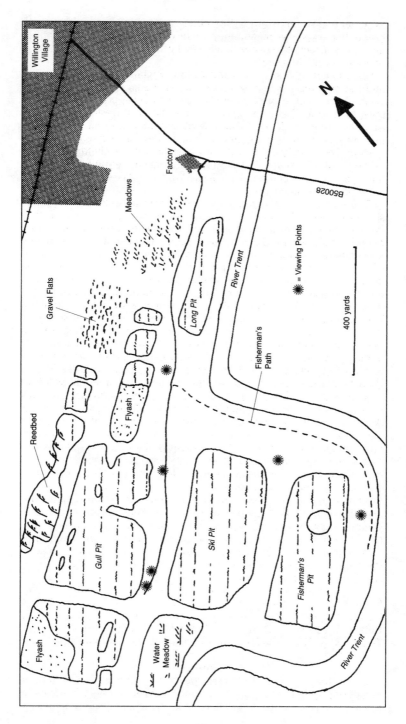

to the west of the approach lane, and viewed from it, the morning is the best time to watch on sunny days.

Access

Willington Gravel Pits are situated 6 miles (10 km) southwest of Derby and just to the southwest of Willington. From the A38 take the A5132 eastbound towards Willington. Once in the village take the B5008 towards Repton. The approach lane is found on the south side of the road, 100 yds/m beyond the village church and 100 yds/m before the river bridge (SK 295 280). The lane runs southwest for three-quarters of a mile (1.25 km) and provides ample parking. At present this is the only public access but even so most of the pits and the main flyash area can be viewed from somewhere along its length. A fisherman's path runs south along the River Trent bank via a stile, 700 yds/m along the lane, and this gives good views over both the fisherman's (pylon on island) and skiing pits.

At the time of writing (1995) there are plans to turn the northwest side of the lane into a local nature reserve and this could affect future access arrangements.

Calendar

Resident: Great Crested Grebe, Cormorant, Canada Goose, Grey Heron, Redshank, Black-headed Gull, Kingfisher, Green Woodpecker, Yellowhammer.

October–March: Bewick's Swan and Brent Goose (both rare), Wigeon, Gadwall (scarce), Teal, Mallard, Pintail (scarce), Shoveler, Pochard, Tufted Duck, Scaup (rare), Goldeneye, Smew (rare), Goosander, Ruddy Duck, Sparrowhawk, Golden Plover, Lapwing, Jack Snipe (scarce), Common Snipe, Green Sandpiper, Mediterranean and Glaucous Gulls (both rare), Kittiwake, Long-eared Owl (rare), Meadow Pipit, Fieldfare, Redwing, Tree Sparrow, Linnet, Reed Bunting.

April–September: Red-breasted Merganser (scarce), Marsh Harrier Osprey, Hobby, Peregrine, Oystercatcher, Ringed and Little Ringed Plovers, Grey Plover (scarce), Knot (rare), Sanderling, Little Stint, Curlew Sandpiper, Dunlin, Ruff, Black and Bar-tailed Godwits, Whimbrel, Curlew, Spotted Redshank (scarce), Greenshank, Wood Sandpiper (scarce), Common Sandpiper, Turnstone, Little Gull, Sandwich Tern (rare), Common, Arctic and Black Terns, Little Tern (rare), Cuckoo, Lesser Spotted Woodpecker (rare), Sand Martin, Yellow Wagtail, Northern Wheatear, Reed Warbler, Lesser Whitethroat, Whitethroat, Bullfinch.

27 CARSINGTON WATER   OS Sheet 119

Habitat

Carsington Water, the most recently constructed large reservoir in Britain, is set in beautiful countryside on the southeastern edge of the

Peak District National Park. Construction of this Severn Trent reservoir began in 1981 and was finally completed in 1991, being officially opened in 1992. It has a maximum water surface area of 300 hectares. Water is pumped into the reservoir via a 6.5-mile (10.5 km) aqueduct from the River Derwent at Ambergate (see Cromford Canal), during high levels of water flow, to act as a storage facility used in regulating the flow of the River Derwent. At times of low water flow in the river, water is returned from the reservoir to maintain water supplies to abstraction points near Derby. The reservoir is thus still in its infancy and is still being developed by Severn Trent as a show case which is expected to attract an estimated 300,000 visitors a year.

A large visitor centre on the west bank of the reservoir forms the focus of recreational facilities and provides exhibitions, shops, toilet and refreshment facilities. There are facilities for the disabled with access to all the hides and the visitor centre. A specific Wildlife Centre, situated in a fully centrally-heated double-glazed hide, is located to the north-east of the main visitor centre. This wildlife centre is used for educational purposes and has display boards and other facilities. Views from the windows reveal nests of Lapwing and Little Ringed Plovers. The two other hides, Lane End hide and Sheepwash hide, are also situated on the west bank of the reservoir which is more gently sloping than the east bank, with the shallower water areas being attractive to a wider range of species.

The retaining dam, which forms the southwestern side of the reservoir, rises to a height of 128 feet (38.5 m) at its highest point but the banks are gently sloping and grassed. The grass here is kept short and proves attractive to small passerines. The remainder of the reservoir's surroundings are mainly cattle- and sheep-grazed fields, with dividing hawthorn hedgerows, along with some mature woodland and several younger plantations. The principal areas of mature woodland are found in Hall and Middle Woods, both on the eastern side of the reservoir. Hall Wood has extensive areas of coniferous trees, with pine and larch, but the mixed central section contains old oaks, beeches and ash trees, with a woodland carpet of bluebells, wood anemones and wood sorrel being particularly attractive in the spring. The younger recently planted areas, which are found all around the site, consist mainly of a mixture of willow, alder, ash, guelder rose, rowan and hawthorn. Over half a million trees and shrubs have been planted in these new woodland areas since the construction of the reservoir to establish attractive wildlife habitats. At the southeastern end of the reservoir rough grassland with patches of gorse dominate the hillside.

There are several small islands dotted around the reservoir, most of which are covered in rough grassland. Active management in 1994, however, created a shingle spit on Horseshoe Island, which immediately attracted breeding Little Ringed Plovers in 1995. Additionally a number of scrapes have been dug in front of the Sheepwash hide during October 1995, which it is hoped will attract migrant waders as the water level falls in coming years. There are also tern rafts situated in Sheepwash and Shiningford Creeks which it is hoped will eventually attract breeding Common Terns. The northern part of the reservoir has been set aside as a wildlife study zone with limited public access at present. The southern part is used for a variety of other recreational pursuits including fishing and sailing and is thus more disturbed.

An active Bird Club established in 1992 collects records from the reservoir and produces an annual report, which also details annual developments at the reservoir. Visitors are invited to record details of their sightings in a log book kept in the Sheepwash hide.

Species

Carsington Water is still very much a reservoir in its infancy and hence the list of bird species recorded continues to grow annually as more birds and more birdwatchers are attracted to this developing site. Opened as recently as 1992, the reservoir already has a list of 178 species recorded to date, with up to ten species being added per annum. With further management and developments aimed at attracting specific species to breed and feed at the reservoir, there are exciting prospects for the coming years at this splendid reservoir.

Winter wildfowl totals may peak at over 1,000 birds, with the main species being Wigeon (300), Mallard (3–400) and Teal (160) while Tufted Duck (up to 350) and Pochard (350) peak later in the winter in February/March. Small numbers of Goosander and Goldeneye are also regular and a variety of other scarcer species, from Pintail, Shoveler, Scaup, Smew, Red-breasted Merganser to Eider and Long-tailed Duck, have also all been recorded to date. Coot numbers peak at over 100 and a local flock of Canada Geese may number 180 birds. In addition to these species, flocks of Pink-footed Geese are seen flying over on passage during October to March, and small parties of Whooper and Bewick's Swans have been seen in November/December. Already Cormorants have adopted the reservoir on a regular basis and up to 70 birds roost in Hall Wood during the winter months. The best area for dabbling ducks and waders is the northeastern section between Shiningford Creek and Big Island where the shallowest water occurs. Diving duck and Cormorants favour the western, deeper side of the reservoir. There are already records of Red-throated and three of Black-throated Diver, and Red-necked Grebe has occurred in winter amongst the resident Great Crested and Little Grebes.

There is a small gull roost with up to 600 Black-headed Gulls and smaller numbers of Common and the larger gulls during the winter, which is best watched from Lane End hide. Peak numbers of roosting gulls are found, however, in November/December when up to 4,000 Lesser Black-backed Gulls occur. Mediterranean, Glaucous and Iceland and Yellow-legged Gulls have all been found amongst the roosting birds. Lane End hide, which is situated southwest of Sheepwash car park, is the best spot from which to watch the roost and may also offer good views of large flocks of Lapwing and Golden Plover, which gather in front of the hide in winter during times of low water levels.

Feeding stations at the Wildlife Centre and in Sheepwash car park attract parties of tits, Greenfinch, Goldfinch, Tree Sparrows, and small numbers of Yellowhammer and Reed Bunting with odd Great Spotted Woodpeckers. The rough grass on the islands sometimes draws in a hunting Short-eared Owl, while raptors include Sparrowhawk, Kestrel, fairly regular Common Buzzard and occasional Merlin and Peregrine. Stonechats sometimes winter in the areas of rough grass and gorse around the reservoir edges but their numbers vary from year to year.

Spring sees Canada Geese, Tufted Duck and Mallard breeding on the islands, which may also hold odd pairs of Redshank. As there is little shelter on the open water, nests of Little and Great Crested Grebes and Coot are often subject to losses in strong winds. Similarly Coot,

Moorhen and Ruddy Duck are more successful on the adjacent Hopton and Green Ponds. Up to six broods of Tufted Duck have been noted and Pochard have also bred. A few pairs of Lapwing nest, and a specially created shingle spit quickly attracted a pair of Little Ringed Plovers in 1995, which reared two broods, immediately in front of the Wildlife Centre hide. A pair of Common Sandpipers bred in 1992.

The woodland residents such as Tawny Owl, Green and Great Spotted Woodpeckers, tits and Treecreepers are joined by a good selection of warblers, with Chiffchaff, Willow Warbler, Blackcap and Garden Warbler in good numbers. The more scrubby areas and adjacent hedgerows play host to Whitethroats and Lesser Whitethroats, while the rough grass areas and new plantations echo to the songs of both Meadow and Tree Pipits. Skylarks breed and a few pairs of Whinchat also nest, especially in the rougher areas around Sheepwash Creek. Grasshopper Warbler also favour this type of habitat but are not recorded breeding every year, although reeling birds are a feature of spring periods. Another attractive summer visitor, which usually breeds is the Redstart. A few pairs have even been attracted to nest in specially placed nesting boxes around the reservoir. There is a small Rookery in Hopton Wood with up to 27 nests of late. Little Owls are resident and can be seen from the path encircling the reservoir, while the odd Long-eared Owl may also be present throughout the year.

Little Ringed Plover

Spring migration can be an exciting time as it offers the chance to find scarce migrants. The short-grazed grass on the dam wall is particularly attractive to insect-eating passerines, wagtails and pipits in particular. Northern Wheatears, Yellow and White Wagtails occur during April and early May, while resident Pied Wagtails are always present but usually reach a peak of up to 100 birds in September. Grey Wagtails also appear at this season but may also be seen in winter and during the autumn when they are most numerous. Flocks of hirundines and Swifts feed over the water and easterly winds may drift in parties of Common, Arctic and Black Terns during April and May, while Little and Sandwich Terns have also been encountered. Flocks of Kittiwakes seem prone to arriving early, mainly in March. Common Scoters on the other hand are most regular in April and May and to a lesser extent in July and August. Spring has also so far proved to be the best season for seeing delightful summer-plumaged Black-necked Grebes, which have occasionally stayed for several days, and also for the odd Garganey. Osprey and Marsh Harrier are the two most regular of the spring vagrant raptors, neither, however, staying for long.

Although waders of a few species occur throughout the year it is during the autumn, from July onwards, that the best variety of species is to be found as the water level falls and exposes muddy margins along the shallower eastern banks. The best areas are Shiningford Creek, Flat Island, the Spit and tower bank. Dunlin, Redshank, Common Sandpiper and Little Ringed Plovers are regular but a good variety of waders occurs every year including such regulars as Greenshank, Ruff, Black-tailed Godwit and Green Sandpiper. Whimbrel are, however, most regular in spring, often as fly-overs.

Seeded grasses and weeds hold a good sized flock of Linnets and other finches, the former often peaking at over 300 birds during September. Also at this time a pre-roost gathering of Jackdaws at the northern end of the reservoir has held up to 3,000 birds. Incoming Redwing and Fieldfare feast on the hawthorn berries and passage flocks of Meadow Pipits congregate around the dam.

Although no national rarities have yet been recorded at Carsington it has hosted several local rarities including Black-throated Diver, Manx Shearwater, Leach's Petrel, Eider, Avocet and Pomarine, Arctic and Great Skuas, and its potential is surely as yet largely untapped.

Access

Carsington Water is situated in southern Derbyshire about 12 miles (19.2 km) northwest of Derby and 4 miles (6.4 km) northeast of Ashbourne. Access to the visitor centre and Sheepwash car parks is off the B5035 Ashbourne to Wirksworth road. The visitor centre, which also incorporates an exhibition, shops, restaurant, refreshments, toilets and first aid as well as a children's play area, is open all year except Christmas day from 10 am. The reservoir site, however, is open every day of the year from 7 am until sunset. The Millfields car park is approached via a minor road which runs along the dam wall southeast from the visitor centre. Car parks at Millfields and Sheepwash are free but that at the main Visitor Centre is a pay and display. The car parks at Sheepwash and Millfields are locked at night, just after dark; a notice board in the car park states the time the gates are locked. The pay and display car park at the Visitor Centre is open at all times. Coach parties are welcome but are asked to give prior notice if at all possible.

There is a circular walk which runs right around the reservoir, a distance of 7–8 miles (12–13 km), which for 2 miles (3.2 km) follows minor public roads and is shared with a horse riding and cycling route.

Timing

As the reservoir is very popular and used for a wide range of water-based recreational pursuits, a visit in the early morning or evening sees the least disturbance. Weekends and bank holidays are obviously the busiest times for visitors. The northern section of the water is, however, a wildlife study zone and is thus not disturbed, so visits at any time will still be productive. Owing to the location of the sun, evening visits offer

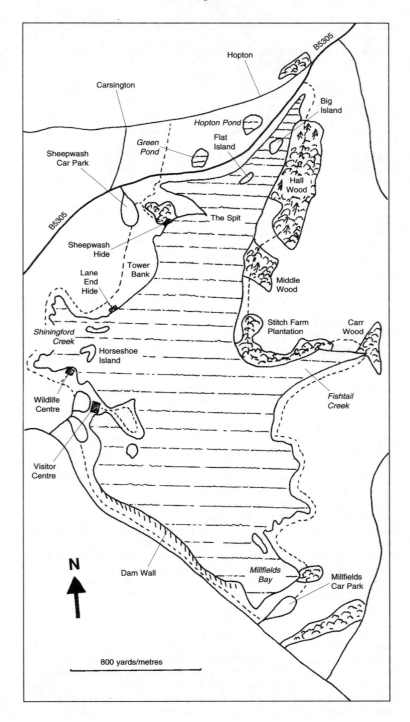

Hopton

B5305

Carsington

Big
Island

Hopton Pond

Flat
Island

Green
Pond

Sheepwash
Car Park

Hall
Wood

B5305

The Spit

Sheepwash
Hide

Tower
Bank

Lane
End
Hide

Middle
Wood

Stitch Farm
Plantation

Carr
Wood

Shiningford
Creek

Horseshoe
Island

Fishtail
Creek

Wildlife
Centre

Visitor
Centre

N

Dam Wall

Millfields
Bay

Millfields
Car Park

800 yards/metres

the best light conditions for watching from the west bank, which is generally the best area for wildfowl and waders and also for viewing the gull roost. Any time of year will prove productive.

Calendar

Resident: Great Crested and Little Grebes, Mute Swan, Canada Goose, Pochard, Tufted Duck, Ruddy Duck, Lapwing, Little Owl, Tawny Owl, Green Woodpecker, Great Spotted Woodpecker, Pied Wagtail, Treecreeper, Tree Sparrow, Yellowhammer, Reed Bunting.

October–March: Vagrant diver or grebe, Cormorant, Wigeon, Teal, Pochard, Tufted Duck, Goosander, Goldeneye, Coot, Golden Plover, gull roost, Lesser Black-backed Gulls, Short-eared Owl, Stonechat.

April–September: Little Ringed Plover, Dunlin, Curlew, Whimbrel, Redshank, Greenshank, Green Sandpiper, Common Sandpiper, Common, Arctic and Black Terns passage, Swift, hirundines, White and Yellow Wagtails, Redstart, Whinchat, Northern Wheatear, Garden warbler, Lesser Whitethroat, Whitethroat, Spotted Flycatcher, Jackdaw.

28 CROMFORD CANAL AND SHININGCLIFF WOOD OS Sheet 119

Habitat

All of this area lies to the southwest of Matlock, and in combination the two sites form an interesting birdwatching area with a good mix of typical woodland species, along with some local specialities, and species associated with streams and meadows. Cromford Canal, which runs from Cromford Wharf to Whatstandwell, lies adjacent to the River Derwent, and like Shiningcliff Wood is an English Nature SSSI. The latter site is owned by the National Trust. There are 4 miles (6.4 km) of disused canal, some of which is being reclaimed, with a border of surrounding deciduous woodland and riverside meadows. The area of interest extends southwards to Ambergate, with the stretch from Whatstandwell to Ambergate being a nature reserve managed by the Derbyshire Wildlife Trust. Shiningcliff Wood rises from the River Derwent up the western bank, from just south of Whatstandwell, and stretches south nearly to Ambergate. It is a mixed deciduous and coniferous woodland.

Species

The site is at its best during the spring and summer months but there are special birds to be found in the winter, while species such as Grey Wagtail, Little Grebe, Sparrowhawk and the woodpeckers are resident. Large roving flocks of tits, Treecreepers and a variety of other woodland birds are a major feature of the winter months in Shiningcliff Wood, with smaller numbers present along the canal. Chaffinches and variable numbers of Brambling are also in evidence and there may well be a sizeable roost of a variety of finches in Shiningcliff Wood. Riverside alder trees produce suitable food for wintering flocks of Siskin and Redpoll and the winter thrushes, Fieldfare and Redwing, may appear in good numbers, often feeding in the riverside meadows and roosting in the woodlands, where large numbers of Blackbirds and other thrushes may join them.

One special and seldom seen species which attracts birdwatchers to Cromford is the impressive Hawfinch. Small numbers are regularly observed during the winter near Cromford Wharf in particular. These large, heavy-billed finches always create a lasting impression, when seen well they are one of our most beautiful passerines and yet their appearances are so often fleeting, offering little time for prolonged study. The best way to locate the feeding birds is to learn to recognise their hard 'tic' call notes, somewhat reminiscent of a Robin. Once the call is heard, search the tree-tops carefully, looking for large 'lumps' stuck onto the upper branches. Above all else be as quiet and unobtrusive as possible as Hawfinches are very wary birds indeed.

Hawfinch

By early spring all three woodpeckers are proclaiming their territories, with the two spotted species drumming on favoured dead branches, while the loud and distinctive yaffle of the Green Woodpecker gives away its presence.

Dippers may be found along the canal, particularly in the region of the aqueduct, and Grey Wagtails join them on the river and canal. Kingfishers are also regular, often giving away their presence with their high-pitched distinctive calls as they flash across the water. They are particularly noisy and obvious in April, when displaying, as they often indulge in rapid chases over their chosen stretch of river or canal.

The woodlands come to life with the arrival of the first singing Chiffchaffs in late March, followed from mid April by singing Willow Warblers and then a progressive arrival of Blackcap, Garden Warbler, Whitethroat and Lesser Whitethroat. Spotted Flycatchers have a very unobtrusive song and yet they make themselves very obvious with their flycatching sorties, often performed from branches which hang low

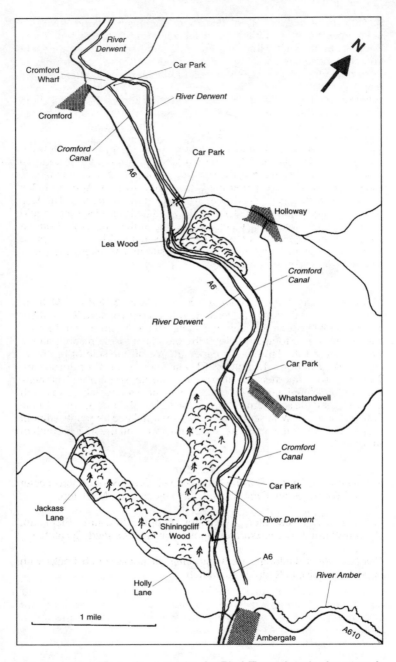

over the water. Their close cousin, the Pied Flycatcher, is also spreading into the area and the delightful shivering song of the Wood Warbler can be heard from suitable spots in the woodlands. Redstarts breed in the more open woodland edges, which are a favoured feeding area of

Green Woodpeckers. Lesser Spotted Woodpeckers are more often encountered in old timber with dead upper branches, often in association with the acrobatic Nuthatch, which is best located by its distinctive piping call notes. Shiningcliff Wood also has roding Woodcock during the spring and summer months in the early mornings and late evenings. Of late, the Cromford Canal has also played host to breeding Goosanders, a rather special breeding species this far south in the country.

Timing

The best chance of locating Hawfinches is offered by an early morning visit between October and March on a bright day with little wind, optimum conditions for hearing the birds call. For the summer visitors it is usually best to visit soon after the birds have arrived in April and May when they are singing and displaying and are most obvious. The resident woodpeckers and Kingfishers, Grey Wagtails and Dippers should be displaying in March and a fine sunny day at this time would offer a good opportunity for searching for these species. This is a popular tourist and walking area and thus sunny summer weekends are best avoided unless you start very early.

Access

All the car parks in the area are accessed off the A6 Derby to Matlock road which runs through the Derwent Valley. For Cromford Wharf there is a car park opposite the church just east of the A6 from Cromford village. From here a footpath follows the old canal towpath south all the way to Ambergate. Further car parks are just off the side of the A6 at Highpeak junction, 1.2 miles (2 km) south of Cromford, and Whatstandwell, another 1.25 miles (2 km) further south from Highpeak junction. For Shiningcliff Wood there is a car park, which serves both the wood and the southern section of the canal, at Ranch Corner, 1 mile (1.6 km) south of Whatstandwell, and additional access points without proper car parks off Holly Lane, which runs west off the A6 just south of Ambergate.

Calendar

Resident: Little Grebe, Sparrowhawk, Green, Great Spotted and Lesser Spotted Woodpecker, Grey Wagtail, tits, Treecreeper, Nuthatch.

April–August: Goosander, Kingfisher, Dipper, Redstart, Blackcap, Garden Warbler, Wood Warbler, Spotted Flycatcher, Pied Flycatcher.

October–March: Fieldfare, Redwing, large tit flocks, finch flocks with large roosts, Siskin, Redpoll, Hawfinch.

Habitat

This very impressive area, located in the High Peak region of the Peak District, is one of great scenic attraction, and being within easy reach of several large centres of population, notably Sheffield, Chesterfield and even Manchester, it is very popular with large numbers of visitors from hill walkers to cyclists and general sightseers. The major feature of the valley is the three reservoirs, Howden, Derwent and Ladybower, which were formed when the valley was flooded at the turn of the century, to provide water for the urban areas nearby. The reservoirs are deep with steep sides and lack any extensive areas of emergent vegetation around their edges. In times of drought or very dry summers, as in 1976, when the water level falls considerably in Ladybower Reservoir, the remnants of the flooded village of Derwent may be visible. In several places the surrounding woodlands run right down to the water's edge. The water in the reservoirs is relatively acid, as most of the water drains off the surrounding acidic peat moorlands, and thus they provide relatively little of interest in the way of birds, in direct contrast to the surrounding forests and moorland.

The valley sides have been extensively planted with coniferous woodlands, mainly larch and pine but with some spruce and areas of deciduous trees, there also being some remnants of old oak woodlands on some of the hillsides. Above the plantations the valley slopes are covered with large expanses of rough sheep-grazed grassland and mixed heather and grass moorland, dominating the tops of the surrounding hills, which rise to over 1700 feet (520 m). The gritstone moorland in this region is widely known as the Dark Peak, in contrast to the more verdant areas of the lower or White Peak.

Species

Winter birding is highly dependent upon the weather, as, with all upland areas, where rain, wind and low cloud/fog and mist will ruin any chance of seeing the speciality species of the area. Although the reservoirs may have the odd Goosander and occasionally a few Tufted Duck and Pochard, there is usually little to see on the open water, but it is always worth a scan as all three species of diver, Bewick's and Whooper Swan, Long-tailed Duck and Grey Phalarope have all been recorded over the last ten-year period. Watch out for the resident Grey Wagtails around the water's edge and near the dams and inlet streams, where Dippers can also occasionally be found.

A walk through the lower woodlands will reveal the typical flocks of tits and small passerines, dominated by Coal Tits, with a few Treecreepers and Goldcrests in variable numbers. Flocks of Siskins adorn the larches and areas of alders but are easily passed as they feed quietly and often only announce their presence on being flushed, when their high-pitched calls make them so obvious. The flocks may be accompanied by Redpolls and Goldfinches.

Flocks of Redwing and Fieldfare are often seen throughout the winter in the dale in addition to which good numbers pass through on migration. One of the key species of the area is the Common Crossbill

Red Grouse

and this bird is best looked for in the plantations of larch, where their regular chipping calls are the best way of locating feeding flocks in the high tree-tops. Numbers of this species vary as everywhere, but in good winters there may be over 200 birds in the valley, and in the winter of 1982–83, large flocks of Common Crossbills were accompanied by flocks of Parrot Crossbills and a male Two-barred Crossbill.

Resident raptors such as Sparrowhawk are to be seen hunting the woodlands, and on fine sunny days from the turn of the year they will be indulging in display flights over the plantations and the lower moorland. This is one of the best areas in the country to observe the other very special resident accipiter, the Goshawk, as the birds can be seen from the public roads and footpaths without causing disturbance. At any time from January to April local pairs may be seen displaying over the plantations around the valley, with one of the best spots being the the larch plantation north of windy corner, to the west of Howden Reservoir. As with all raptors, patience, perseverance and luck are the key elements to succesful sightings, but given a fine day with some blue sky and light to moderate winds then a watch of an hour or two should produce one or more sightings of these magnificent raptors over the plantations and the intervening ridges. They may well be in the air with Sparrowhawks, allowing the obvious differences in size and proportions to be compared. As they are resident, the Goshawks can be seen in midwinter, when they also hunt over the adjacent moorland, but when not in display a larger degree of luck is required to locate them.

As well as the two accipiters the moorland has an enviable reputation for producing other raptors during the winter months, with regular appearances by Peregrines, which are also resident, Hen Harriers, up to 11 individuals having been seen in the local roost, Merlin and occasional Common and Rough-legged Buzzards.

The resident Red Grouse will also be present on the heather tops and in midwinter it is worth keeping an eye out for mountain hares in their winter dress. A pair of Stonechat sometimes winter up the valley beyond Howden Reservoir. A visit in mid to late March may also produce sightings of displaying Peregrines and even a pair of Ravens, which have returned to the area in recent years. These impressive croaking corvids always adding extra spice to a good list of raptors.

The path which leads up onto the moorland, following the River Derwent valley from Slippery Stones to the north of Howden Reservoir, offers good views over the surrounding crags for raptors. On clear winter days with blue skies, skeins of Pink-footed Geese may often be seen high over the moorland on one of their complicated midwinter migrations between feeding sites in the northwest, Scotland and East Anglia. Dippers can be found on the Derwent downstream of the Ladybower dam. Any Common Crossbills which are nesting will have young by March and April, when roving family parties may be obvious in the plantations. The area has produced several records of wintering Great Grey Shrikes in the past and there is always the possibility of one of these fine northern winter visitors being located around the plantations and clear-fells.

During April and May, Red-breasted Mergansers and Common Sandpipers return to breed around the reservoirs, and the piping display song of the fluttering sandpipers is a sure sign of summer. The resident woodland bird population is swelled by the arrival of Chiffchaffs and Willow Warblers, with Tree Pipits on the woodland slopes and a few pairs of Redstart and Wood Warbler in the older deciduous blocks. On the moors the Red Grouse become more visible as the cocks display and their 'go-back go-back' calls echo around the tops. Raptors are less obvious when nesting but the hunting male Sparrowawks are a regular sight around the plantations, preying on the newly fledged small passerines; Goshawks are also seen and the distinctive silhouette of a Peregrine may be see drifting over distant ridges and moorland. Odd pairs of Merlin breed on the moors but they are seldom seen during the summer months.

On the moorland tops breeding Curlew and Golden Plovers, and in some years the occasional pair of Dunlin, take up summer territories. Take care not to disturb breeding birds which alarm call as you pass. That most attractive of our thrushes, the Ring Ouzel, also breeds on the valley slopes, and the song of the male can often be heard from late March or early April but the birds can be particularly elusive when nesting and are best seen early in the season.

Timing

This is a very popular tourist site and attracts very large numbers of people at all times of year, even in midwinter and in bad weather, and this has to be borne in mind when planning a visit. The worst times are midsummer and on bank holidays and weekends when congestion, due to the high number of cars, can be a real problem for access to the best areas. The area as a whole, however, is extensive, and the numbers of people in any one site, away from obvious attractions like the dams and car parks, are not usually a problem, especially as regards raptor watching.

The most important factor to bear in mind here is the weather. This is an upland region and as such the weather can turn suddenly from glorious sunshine to torrential rain with strong winds, and the temperature can change dramatically. The chances of bad weather are obviously worse in the winter but the main point to bear in mind is to be prepared for the worst and never set off up onto the moorland, in particular, without due preparation and sufficient warm and waterproof clothing. The upland areas are also prone to low cloud and mist, which ruins any attempt to watch raptors and thus it is important to get a good weather forecast before contemplating a visit for these birds. In general, winter is good for raptors but the best time to see Goshawks is from February to early April, they are least obvious in summer and early autumn. Good

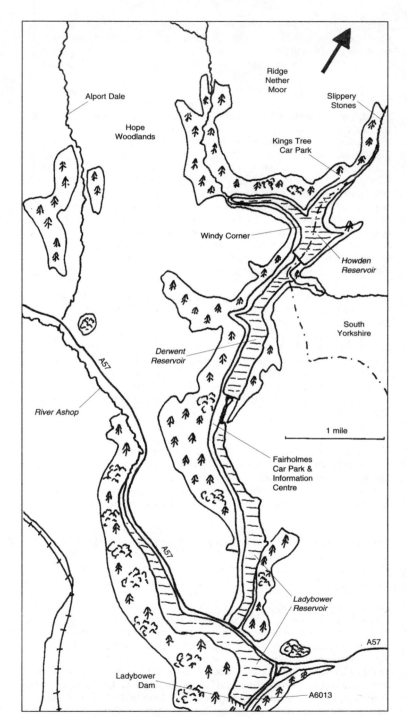

Alport Dale

Hope
Woodlands

Ridge
Nether
Moor

Slippery
Stones

Kings Tree
Car Park

Windy Corner

Howden
Reservoir

South
Yorkshire

A57

*Derwent
Reservoir*

River Ashop

1 mile

A57

Fairholmes
Car Park &
Information
Centre

*Ladybower
Reservoir*

A57

Ladybower
Dam

A6013

raptor weather does not necessarily mean sunshine but high cloud and some blue sky with light or moderate winds is often best, although at peak display periods the birds will be aloft at some time during the day in all but the worst weather. Sunny days bring the largest numbers of tourists.

Access

The upper Derwent valley lies about 10 miles (16 km) west of Sheffield and 16 miles (25 km) northwest of Chesterfield. The main A57 Sheffield to Glossop, trans-Pennine road (Snake Pass), passes the bottom end of Ladybower Reservoir. A road runs north along the western edge of the three reservoirs, signposted to Derwentdale, to the head of the valley at Kings Tree, at the northern end of Howden Reservoir where there is a small car park. There are a few other car parks along the road where it is possible to park and there are a number of public footpaths leading up onto the moorland. On Sundays throughout the year, during the summer, from April to the end of October, at weekends and on bank holidays, the road is closed at the southern end of Derwent Reservoir, at Fairholmes, where there is a car park and information centre. This car park soon becomes congested and an early arrival is an advantage at weekends. Cycles can be hired and there is a shuttle service on a minibus around the northern end of the two northernmost reservoirs, which saves a walk of 2.5 miles (4 km) to Windy Corner, along the road, the best spot for Goshawks.

One of the best sites for looking for wintering raptors is located by following the path which leads up onto the open moorland from the head of the valley, at the northern end of Howden Reservoir, at Kings Tree. Easier access to the higher areas of open moorland is gained by driving west along the A57 to the summit of Snake Pass where the Pennine Way crosses the road. The moorland has open access but is very popular with hill walkers.

Calendar

Resident: Sparrowhawk, Goshawk, Peregrine, Red Grouse, Dipper, Grey Wagtail, Coal Tit, Raven (2–3), Siskin (small numbers only in summer), Common Crossbill (some years).

September–March: Hen Harrier, Common Buzzard (rare), Rough-legged Buzzard (rare), Merlin.

April–August: Red-breasted Merganser, Merlin, Golden Plover, Curlew, Common Sandpiper, Tree Pipit, Ring Ouzel, Redstart, Wood Warbler.

30 OGSTON RESERVOIR   OS Sheet 119

Habitat

This reservoir was created in 1958 when the River Amber was dammed near Ogston Hall, flooding a total of 206 acres (83 ha). The reservoir banks are all natural, those on the northern and western sides shelving

gently, while those on the east are much steeper. The water level usually falls in the summer and autumn periods exposing muddy margins.
A few small woodlands lie close to the water's edge, including the
Derbyshire Wildlife Trust's reserve, for which an entry permit is
required. Otherwise the surrounding land is farmland, largely pastoral
and fairly typical of the region. Recreational sailing, which was introduced soon after the reservoir was flooded, takes place over much of
the existing water area. This, however, causes much less disturbance to
the wildlife than the trout fishing, which takes place during the period
April to October.

Species

The main interests for birdwatchers at Ogston are the gull roost, the wintering wildfowl populations and, especially when water levels are low
and muddy margins revealed, migrant waders.

The most numerous wildfowl in winter are Mallard, Teal and Wigeon,
all of which are usually present in three-figure flocks. Diving ducks by
contrast occur in generally small numbers, though Tufted Duck have
reached over 100 birds and Pochard nearly 400. Goldeneye have been
rather erratic in their appearance of late but Goosanders are increasing,
with small numbers often present. Also showing signs of a rapid recent
increase are Cormorants, which arrive in small flocks in the early morning from their roost site at Attenborough Gravel Pits, 19 miles (30.4 km)
away in Nottinghamshire. A flock of Canada Geese is usually present,
with their numbers peaking during the autumn when over 300 have
been counted. Small numbers of both Little and Great Crested Grebes
overwinter, the latter often increasing considerably when severe weather freezes small surrounding waters. Grey Herons are present in all but
the most severe weather.

More occasional visitors amongst the wildfowl include Shoveler,
Pintail, Gadwall, Red-breasted Merganser, Smew and Velvet Scoter
(both very rare), Long-tailed Duck and Scaup, a flock of 17 of which has
overwintered on one occasion. Bewick's and Whooper Swans occasionally call in on migration but rarely stay for long. Bitterns have been
seen on a very few occasions, usually in the willows at the northwest
and southwest ends of the reservoir.

All of the three 'common' diver species and the three rarer grebes
have been recorded, with Great Northern and Black-throated Divers
having on occasions stayed for long periods, while the less regular Red-
throated Diver tends to be more transitory. One of the Great Northern
Divers was a summer-plumaged bird on the unusual date of 30 June.
The rarer grebes, Red-necked, Slavonian and Black-necked, are all very
infrequent visitors, with the latter most often seen in spring, although
the highest count of four birds of this species occurred in December.

The winter gull roost is of considerable interest to birdwatchers as it
tends to attract some of the rarer species and is easily viewed from the
roads and car parks. Typically, the roost forms in late October reaching
its largest numbers in the new year and is abandoned in late March or
early April. In recent years the largest counts of the regular species have
been: Black-headed Gull (8,300), Common Gull (70), Lesser Black-
backed Gull (1,100), Herring Gull (1,400) and Great Black-backed Gull
(620). Yellow-legged Gull is being recognised more frequently in small
numbers. However, it is for the fairly regular presence of Iceland,
Glaucous and Mediterranean Gulls that many birdwatchers visit Ogston.

In recent years Iceland Gull has taken over from Glaucous Gull as the most reliable of the three species, with up to a dozen or so different individuals identified in some winters. Mediterranean Gulls have become much more frequent winter visitors and a few have been seen as migrants at other times of year. Gales in winter, and sometimes at other times of year, may bring in small numbers of Kittiwakes. Intense scrutiny of the gull roost has also resulted in sightings of Ring-billed Gull (three), Bonaparte's Gull, Laughing Gull and birds showing characteristics of Kumlien's- and Thayer's-type Iceland Gulls.

In some winters small flocks of Brambling feed on the reservoir banks and roost at night in rhododendron cover in Carr Wood. The latter also often holds large numbers of roosting corvids, Woodpigeons and Stock Doves. Woodcocks lie up here in bracken cover during the day and can often be seen at deep dusk as they fly out to feed in fields and boggy spots beyond the reservoir.

Spring is usually rather a quiet time at Ogston as trout fishing commences and the banks are lined with fishermen, in addition to which the water levels are usually high. Migrant waders seen at this time are often, by consequence, fly-over records. Easterly winds (as in autumn) may produce such scarce migrants as Common Scoter, Little Gull and Black Tern, while Arctic Terns are regular and have occasionally peaked at over 100 birds. Ospreys have been seen on occasions, usually fleetingly, but one bird stayed the whole summer. Several pairs of Mallard and Coot and smaller numbers of Little and Great Crested Grebes, Tufted Duck and Canada Geese all breed. If the water levels are suitable, Little Ringed Plover and Lapwing may nest. The installation in 1990 of two rafts for Common Terns had immediate effect with both being used successfully. There is a well established heronry with 15–20 pairs of Grey Heron breeding in the larch trees in adjacent Carr Wood, which can be viewed from the road. Kingfishers and Grey Wagtails breed on some of the surrounding streams, Little Owls on the farmland and Sparrowhawks and probably all three woodpeckers in nearby woodlands. The scrubbier parts of the reservoir margins and adjacent hedgerows support Sedge and Grasshopper Warblers, Whitethroats and Lesser Whitethroats.

In a reasonably dry summer the water levels will begin to fall by the early autumn, producing areas of exposed mud and shallow water attractive to waders. Regular species include Common Sandpiper, Greenshank, Ringed and Little Ringed Plovers and Dunlin. Less frequent are Ruff, Oystercatcher, Knot, Sanderling, Whimbrel, Wood Sandpiper and Spotted Redshank. Rarer still there are records of Kentish Plover, Purple Sandpiper, Temminck's Stint and Grey and Wilson's Phalaropes. As well as waders the shallow water margins attract surface-feeding ducks, with a few Shoveler, Pintail and Garganey being seen most autumns. Ospreys are occasional at this time when they are more likely to stay for a few days. Later in the autumn, usually in October, the presence of one or two Rock, and more rarely Water Pipits is betrayed by their sibilant calls.

Ogston Reservoir is undoubtedly the most regularly watched site in Derbyshire, which has resulted in the longest bird list of any place in the county. Unusual species, in addition to those mentioned above, include: Fulmar, Gannet, Storm and Leach's Petrels, Shag, Little Egret, Bean and Brent Geese, Green-winged Teal, Red-crested Pochard, Ferruginous Duck, Eider, Honey Buzzard, Marsh and Hen Harriers, Goshawk, Rough-legged Buzzard, Common Crane, Corncrake, all four skuas, Caspian, Roseate and White-winged Black Terns, Red-rumped Swallow, Woodlark, Black Redstart, Firecrest, Great Grey Shrike and Snow Bunting.

Timing

The best time of year to visit is from October to March when disturbance is lightest and waterbird numbers are at their highest. In spring and early summer there may be relatively few birds present. The gull roost is generally best viewed from the road and car park at the western side of the reservoir.

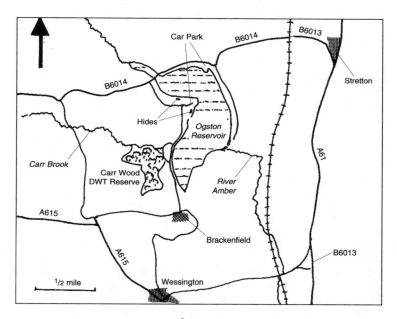

Access

Ogston Reservoir lies 1.5 miles (2.4 km) southwest of Clay Cross and immediately north of the village of Brackenfield. It is most easily reached from the B6014 Stretton to Matlock road, which runs along the northern edge of the reservoir, cutting off a small water area known as Milltown Inlet. Immediately west of the latter a minor road runs south to Woolley and Brackenfield and gives good views of the southern two-thirds of the reservoir, though periodically these are restricted by a dense growth of scrub. There are public car parks at the northeastern end of the reservoir and on the central west bank at Woolley. There is no access to the water's edge. Ogston Bird Club owns three hides on the west and northwest banks, for which a key is provided on joining the club; the club also publishes an annual report. Details are obtainable from Alan Bennet, 64 High Street, Stonebroom, Derbyshire, DE5 6JY.

Calendar

Resident: Little Grebe, Great Crested Grebe, Cormorant, Grey Heron, Canada Goose, Mallard, Tufted Duck, Sparrowhawk, Coot, woodpeckers, Little Owl, Kingfisher, Grey Wagtail.

October–March: Wigeon, Teal, Pochard, Goosander, Snipe, Woodcock, Glaucous, Iceland and Mediterranean Gulls, Brambling.

April–September: Little Ringed Plover (scarce), Common Tern, hirundines, Swift, Sedge and Grasshopper Warbler, Lesser Whitethroat.

31 THE DERBYSHIRE DALES   OS Sheet 119

Habitat

The Peak District is typified by two distinctly different regions, in the north and northwest the Dark Peak, typified by gritstone moors such as those found in the Upper Derwent region, and to the south and south-west, the White Peak, where the underlying carboniferous limestone forms a gentle landscape of rolling hills with occasional deep valleys. The carboniferous limestone extrudes in places along the sides of some of the valleys, forming imposing crags typical of the more spectacular of the dales.

The area to the east of Buxton, within the White Peak, is one of beautiful wooded limestone valleys, with craggy gorges and more open meadows in the lower reaches of the valleys where the streams meander down to join the River Derwent. The valley sides in the upper reaches climb steeply to the higher regions of lush pasture with their drystone walls and isolated farms. These higher pastures have few trees but small copses often exist around farms and odd wind-battered trees stand sentinel, forming perching posts for some of the upland birds. The valleys are typified by fast-flowing clear trout streams bubbling over stretches of rapids, which alternate with quieter sections, often where the flow of the rivers has been dammed by old mills such as that at Cressbrook. Here, wider stretches of water offer a differing habitat suitable to species like Little Grebe. The woodlands are mainly of ash, with some alders evident in the lower river sections, but as you climb up from the valley floor the trees thin and are replaced with more scattered trees and patches of hawthorn scrub, gorse and broom.

Species

The resident species of the dales are relatively few and the winter months usually have little to offer apart from the typical birds of the streams and some woodland species. Grey Wagtails are always present on the fast-running streams and can be seen feeding around the water's edge or from exposed rocks in midstream. They frequently give away their presence with their typical 'ptinck' flight calls. The other special bird of the rapids is the inimitable Dipper, with its comic bobbing action. Sitting on exposed rocks amongst the rapids or on the bank sides flashing its white bib and brown and black belly, the Dipper is a wonderful sight. Dippers quite often nest under bridges, which are a good place to stand when looking for them. Watch for the flash of black and white and listen for their distinctive call above the noise of the stream as they fly low to the water's surface, often passing straight under bridges, or scan the exposed boulders in the stream bed for perched birds bobbing up and down.

The slower stretches of river also have Kingfishers, Little Grebes and Tufted Duck as breeding birds. The woodlands have a typical collection of tits and finches, with Marsh Tit being of interest, and the larger woods hold odd pairs of Nuthatch and Great and Lesser Spotted Woodpeckers. Green Woodpeckers are more likely to be encountered in the grassland areas where the trees thin out above the valley floor. Flocks of Woodpigeons, Stock Doves and corvids roam the upland pastures and roost in the valley woodlands, while wintering Fieldfares and Redwings join the resident thrushes in feasting on the winter berry crop, later feeding out on the pastures in mild weather. Jackdaws are prominent among the corvid flocks and by March they gather around their breeding sites on the limestone crags where they wheel around noisily, laying claim to suitable breeding holes.

Dipper

Spring and summer bring a wealth of special migrants to the area, adding their songs to the local chorus. Willow Warblers, Chiffchaffs and both Blackcap and Garden Warbler frequent the woodlands, along with a few pairs of Wood Warbler. Spotted Flycatchers are late arrivals, often being found along the stream sides, making feeding sorties from favoured overhanging branches out over the water to catch their favoured insect prey. Of late, a few Pied Flycatchers have also spread into the area but with the trees in full leaf they can be very elusive.

Higher up the valley sides Redstarts are a regular sight often perching on the low stone walls, while Tree Pipits occupy the interface between wood and pasture, with their close cousin, the Meadow Pipit, taking over on the higher pastures and rough grassland where the song of the Skylark is always obvious. Other summer visitors to the higher pastures are Northern Wheatears, which arrive from mid March, and a few pairs of Whinchat. Breeding Lapwings and Curlew arrive from February and indulge in their spectacular display flights before settling to breed on the upland fields. Areas of scrub often harbour Whitethroats and Yellowhammers.

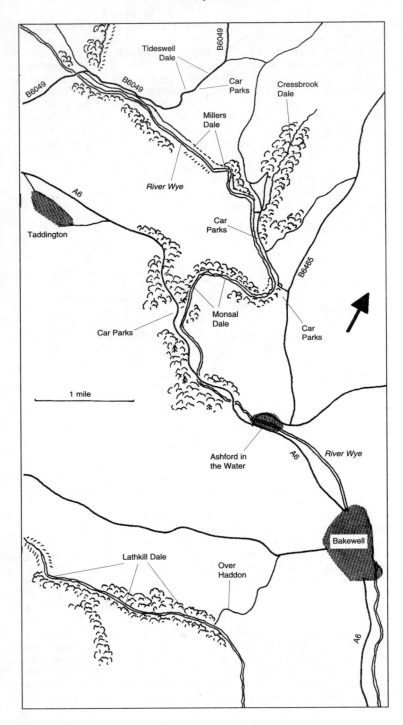

Timing

This area is extremely popular with tourists, rock climbers, hikers and fishermen and therefore disturbance along the main footpaths is a real problem. On sunny summer days or weekends and bank holidays the area becomes rapidly overcrowded and the chances of seeing even resident birds decrease. It is therefore best to visit in midweek and also early in the morning before the crowds build up. The winter period is usually rather quiet and the best period is undoubtedly from March through to June or even July when the summer migrants are in residence.

Access

Millers Dale, Monsal Dale, Cressbrook Dale and Chee Dale are all just north of the A6 Buxton to Bakewell trunk road. For Millers Dale the B6049 leaves the A6 3 miles (4.8 km) east of Buxton and crosses the River Wye, continuing to Tideswell Dale where there is a car park and toilets.

For Monsal Dale and Cressbrook Dale and Cressbrook Mill the B6465 runs northwest from the A6 out of Ashford in the Water, 1.5 miles (2.4 km) west of Bakewell. There is a car park at Monsal Head, where an unclassified road follows the river to Cressbrook, with a car park 800 yds/m farther along this minor road at Upperdale. Lathkill Dale is 2 miles (3.2 km) south of Bakewell and approached on the B5055 and then unclassified roads from Bakewell to Over Haddon, or the B5056 then unclassified roads from the A6, 2 miles (3.2 km) west of Bakewell to Youlgreave. Footpaths and rights of way are well signed, but all the fields are private and those without public rights of way should not be walked.

Calendar

Resident: Sparrowhawk, Kestrel, Kingfisher, Stock Dove, Jackdaw, Dipper, Grey Wagtail, Green and Great Spotted Woodpecker, Marsh Tit, Nuthatch, Jackdaw, Rook, Yellowhammer.

March–August: Curlew, Lapwing, Northern Wheatear, Whinchat, Redstart, Tree Pipit, Willow Warbler, Chiffchaff, Blackcap, Garden Warbler, Whitethroat, Wood Warbler, Spotted Flycatcher, Pied Flycatcher (scarce).

32 THE EAST MOORS   OS Sheet 119

Habitat

This is the most southeasterly block of moorland in the Pennines and comprises East Moor, Bramton East Moor, Gibbet Moor, Harewood Moor and Beeley Moor. For simplification, most birdwatchers refer to the area north of Harland Edge as 'East Moor' and the section to the south as Beeley Moor. The moors lie at around 1000 feet (300 m) above sea level, reaching a maximum of 1203 feet (360 m) at the eastern end of Harland Edge.

Most of the land is gently undulating and is dominated by heather, which is burned on a rotational basis for grouse management purposes. There are also extensive grassy stretches, mainly of purple moorgrass, and some small boggy areas where plants such as round-leaved sundew can be found. There are very few trees, just a few scattered small birches and hawthorns. On the fringes of the area tracts of bilberry support small colonies of the localised green hairstreak butterfly. The rocky 'edges', which are such a feature of the Peak District landscape, are represented here by the south-facing Harland Edge and the smaller west-facing Fallinge Edge.

Species

Only a few species are regularly present during the winter months and it is possible to spend some time here and see little more than Carrion Crows and Red Grouse. The latter have declined here in recent years to the extent that organised shoots are nowadays very infrequent.

Most birdwatchers visit the moor to look for raptors, Hen Harriers and Merlins in particular. Hen Harriers are usually present from September or October to April. Up to five birds have been seen and in some years there has been a small communal roost on East Moor, though in other years birds have been seen in late autumn but have not stayed through the winter. Recording of the colours of efficacious wingtags has revealed that at least some of these birds had been reared in northern Scotland. Hen Harriers are most often seen by scanning the horizons as the birds quarter low over the heather in search of small birds and rodents. Sometimes Merlins can be seen flying very close to them and it may seem that the smaller bird is mobbing the harrier but it is more likely that the Merlin is waiting to attack any small birds put to flight by the hunting harrier. Another good way to find Merlins here is to scan large boulders out on the moor, where they spend a lot of time sitting and preening.

Common Buzzard, Peregrine and Raven are three species currently increasing in the Peak District, and may also be seen feeding on or around the moors, especially in winter, but sometimes at other times of year. Common Buzzards are invariably seen singly but Ravens seem to remain paired for much of the year and are often seen in twos. Peregrines can sometimes be seen sitting on the same rocks used by the Merlins. Goshawk sightings are not rare, despite an unacceptably high nest failure rate at the hands of egg collectors and falconers. Other raptors recorded here include Marsh Harrier, which has been seen on several occasions, mainly in spring, Montagu's Harrier, Red Kite, Osprey and Red-footed Falcon. Short-eared Owls have nested but are usually encountered as migrants.

Small birds in the winter period are usually few and far between but up to seven Stonechats have overwintered, perhaps attracted by some of the heather-eating moth caterpillars to be found at this season; a pleasant surprise occurred in 1995 when a pair stayed to breed. Great Grey Shrikes and Snow Buntings have wintered in the past but have both become considerable rarities of late.

At any time between October and March transient skeins of Pink-footed Geese may be seen flying over, invariably heading either ESE or WNW as they commute on an unerringly direct route between their feeding areas in southwest Lancashire and the southern Wash. Mid to late morning is usually the best time of day to connect with these flocks

Hen Harrier

but occasionally they occur at other times of day and, on rare occasions, have rested and fed on the moor and adjacent fields.

The early spring sees the return of Curlews and Skylarks to the moors, followed in March and April by Meadow Pipits, which may occur in large flocks, Northern Wheatears and Ring Ouzels, though the latter are now very scarce here, with maybe one or two pairs in some years and none at all in others. A few pairs of Whinchat breed, mainly in the large bracken beds along the rocky edges. Twite formerly bred, but numbers in the eastern Peak District have plummeted and the few birds seen now are thought to be migrants. Curlew numbers seem prone to quite wide annual variations but these waders are very obvious in spring as they perform their rising and falling aerial display flight and in midsummer flocks of 30 or so birds can be seen in the newly mown hayfields adjacent to the moors. A few pairs of Snipe frequent the boggy stretches, and Golden Plovers breed in some years, usually in newly burnt heather. A pair of Redshank bred once on Beeley Moor, and Dunlin have been seen here in midsummer, though whether they breed or not is uncertain. Migrant Dotterel, in trips of up to six birds, have been seen on several occasions, mainly in late April and May, frequenting the bare areas created by recent heather burning.

Another attraction of the moors is the regular presence in mid to late summer of Hobbies, especially around Beeley Moor, where up to four birds have been seen together. Though seen annually, these falcons are most obvious in odd-numbered years, which is when northern eggar moths fly in large numbers. In the even-numbered years, Cuckoos, sometimes in small groups, can be seen devouring the larvae of the same moth.

Timing

A visit at any time of year can be rewarding but the winter months are generally the most productive time for seeking raptors. Bright and reasonably calm late autumn and winter days are best for seeing Pink-footed Geese movements. Breeding waders are most conspicuous here during their spring display period while late April and May offer the best chance of finding Dotterel. Hobbies might be seen during any of the summer months but July seems to be the most likely month.

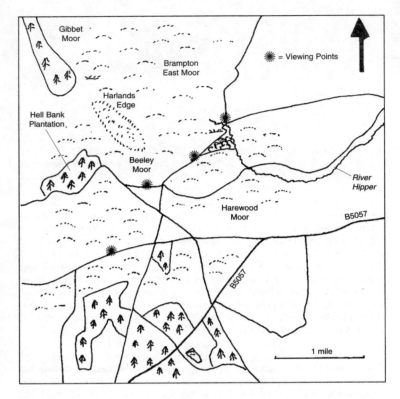

Access

The East Moors lie a few miles southwest of Chesterfield and south of the A619 Chesterfield to Baslow road. Very few footpaths cross the moors, which are all private, and almost all local birdwatchers view from the minor roads which cross the area and offer good vantage points. Particularly good spots are west and north of Slagmill Plantation, the north side of Beeley Triangle and between the small gas plant and Wragg's Quarry on Beeley Moor.

Calendar

Resident: Red Grouse, Goshawk, Sparrowhawk, Common Buzzard, Kestrel, Peregrine, Raven.

October–March: Pink-footed Goose, Hen Harrier, Merlin, Short-eared Owl, Stonechat.

April–August: Hobby, Golden Plover, Snipe, Curlew, Cuckoo, Skylark, Meadow Pipit, Whinchat, Northern Wheatear, Ring Ouzel.

33 PADLEY GORGE SSSI, LONGSHAW ESTATE COUNTRY PARK

Habitat

Padley Gorge, a notified SSSI, lies more or less centrally within the National Trust's Longshaw estate, on the Derbyshire side of the county boundary with South Yorkshire and to the west of the major urban area of Sheffield. The main part of the gorge itself lies between Lawrence Field, an open gritstone moor to the north, and the Sheffield plantation, an open coniferous woodland to the east.

The gorge itself consists of a very steep-sided valley, with Burbage Brook running through the valley bottom, on a general northeast to southwest orientation, to join the River Derwent just to the north of Grindleford. Although the area has been well known to naturalists as Padley Gorge since the 1950s, most maps refer to the site as Yarncliff Woods. Trees are mainly sessile oak, with some sycamores in the lower reaches and silver birch becoming dominant at higher elevations. Areas of moorland which have been fenced against sheep have areas of heather and bilberry. The higher areas of moorland rise to around 1000 feet (300 metres) above sea level, falling to around 500 feet (150 m) in the lower reaches of Burbage Brook.

Species

There are very few birds to be found on the Longshaw estate during the winter months except for corvids, Carrion Crows and Jackdaws on the open areas, with odd Red Grouse on the moorlands. Odd tit flocks occur in the valley woodlands in the gorge, and the local Dippers are resident on the brook. In some years Common Crossbills occur in the Sheffield plantation.

Birdlife begins to come into its own in March when the early returning waders, Lapwing and Curlew, arrive back from their wintering areas to display over their chosen breeding territories. The first of the true summer visitors, Northern Wheatears and Ring Ouzels, follow shortly afterwards in early April and are a sure sign that spring is really on the way. As more summer visitors appear in the woodlands in the valley, and the lengthening days even make evening visits possible, the area becomes most attractive to birdwatchers from late April into May.

A good walk commences from the bottom of the valley, from Grindleford railway station, and then follows the brook upstream. By the top of the railway tunnel the trees usually harbour singing Wood Warblers, and the fast-flowing brook should produce sightings of both Dipper and Grey Wagtail.

Typical, but often elusive birds of the sessile oak woods, which occur in good numbers and should be encountered during a typical day's visit, include Green and Great Spotted Woodpeckers, Treecreeper and Nuthatch. Scattered through the trees on the steep banks of the brook are a large number of nest boxes, many made of steel, to protect the nesting Pied Flycatchers from the ravages of Great Spotted Woodpeckers and even egg collectors. About 15 pairs of this super black-and-white flycatcher usually nest in the purpose-built boxes along with small numbers of Redstart and much larger numbers of Blue and Great Tits. Being at a relatively high altitude, however, the tits do not compete with the much rarer Pied Flycatchers for the nest boxes.

Raptors in the area, which may be seen overhead include Kestrel and Sparrowhawk and the occasional Goshawk, if you are very lucky, while Tawny Owls nest in the woodlands but as everywhere are most easily located at dusk when calling or feeding young. Although usually present, those two special woodland bird species, Lesser Spotted Woodpecker and Hawfinch, present a much harder target for the prospective visitor and a large slice of luck is often needed to bump into them. At the head of the gorge, as the woodlands thin to open moorland, Tree Pipits and Redpolls occur amongst the birch trees and Whinchats occur on the more open moorland. At higher elevations the breeding Northern Wheatears are fairly common but the local population of Ring Ouzels has declined considerably and pairs are now rather thin on the ground. The breeding populations of Meadow Pipit no doubt account for the high concentrations of Cuckoos, which are more common here than in lowland Derbyshire.

A bonus bird on the moorland would be a Merlin and a late evening walk should also turn up a few roding Woodcock.

Pied Flycatcher

Timing

April and May are without doubt the best months to visit for a range of woodland and open moorland species combined with the special birds of the brook. Longshaw is a country park, right on the edge of Sheffield, however, and thus attracts large numbers of visitors so it is best to avoid Sundays as the whole area is popular with ramblers. Early morning visits are the best, allowing most of the singing birds to be located before the disturbance and excess noise of picnickers and day trippers causes the birds to become less audible and visible. Visitor pressure can be bad on hot sunny days when children playing in the stream will also reduce the chance of Dipper and Grey Wagtail!

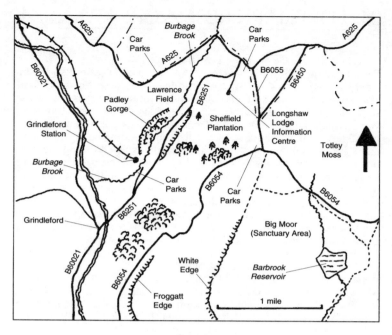

Access

There are four main car parks at the following locations:

1. Lawrence Field by the north side of the A625, Sheffield to Hathersage road, 1.5 miles (2.4 km) west of Hathersage village (SK 252 801).
2. Grindleford Railway Station, just off the north side of the B6521 at Nether Padley, 1 mile (1.6 km) northeast of Grindleford village (SK 251 789).
3. Near the junction of the B6055 with the A625, at the Fox House Inn (SK 267 802).
4. Near the junction of the B6055 with the B6054 (SK 269 789).

The whole of the area has open public access at all times.

Calendar

Resident: Sparrowhawk, Red Grouse, Tawny Owl, Green Woodpecker, Great Spotted Woodpecker, Dipper, Coal Tit, Nuthatch, Treecreeper.

April–May: Curlew, Tree Pipit, Grey Wagtail, Redstart, Whinchat, Northern Wheatear, Ring Ouzel, Wood Warbler, Pied Flycatcher, Redpoll.

Habitat

Completed in 1977, this 230-acre (93 ha) reservoir is owned and managed by the Severn Trent Water Authority and is used for sailing and trout fishing, with the far end of the south arm, which forms part of the Carver's Rocks Nature Reserve, being free from disturbance. The reservoir is situated to the east of the Trent Valley floodplain, at an altitude of 365 feet (110 m) above sea level. The surrounding banks are sandy and steeply sloping, with shallow banks only exposed during dry periods when the water levels are low. The dam, which is covered with rock, has an attractive steep grassy bank. The surrounding land is mainly hilly farmland but a large mature coniferous plantation, Repton Shrubs, lies to the southwest of the reservoir.

Carver's Rocks Nature Reserve, owned and managed by the Derbyshire Wildlife Trust, is a mainly deciduous woodland with some bracken areas, and is situated to the south of the reservoir.

Species

Winter is the best time to visit this site, especially in severe cold spells when the reservoir becomes an important site for diving duck and roosting gulls. Being situated high up in the Trent Valley, the reservoir acts as a beacon to overflying migrants, in particular wildfowl, for whom it is an obvious place to rest and feed. Winter species include Great Crested Grebe, Cormorants, Tufted Duck, Pochard, Goldeneye and Goosander, with Ruddy Ducks occurring occasionally. Large numbers of some species may be recorded, with up to 180 Great Crested Grebes and 80 Cormorants having been counted. The reservoir, however, is best known for its wintering flock of Goosander, which have peaked at some 200 birds in severe cold weather. Dabbling ducks are infrequent, but Wigeon, Teal and Shoveler occur, with records of Pintail and Gadwall not being too uncommon.

Red-throated, Black-throated and Great Northern Divers have all occurred, with some individuals lingering for lengthy periods. Of the rarer grebes there have been a number of records of Red-necked and one of Slavonian. Sea-duck, always rare at inland localities, have included Long-tailed Duck, Eider, Velvet Scoter and Scaup, while on rare occasions flocks of Brent Geese and Bewick's Swans have been seen, usually, however, only lingering for a few hours. Skeins of Pink-footed Geese pass through the area, usually high overhead, and there is one winter record of a Bittern frequenting the south arm of the Carver's Rocks Nature Reserve section.

One of the main attractions of the site is the large gull roost which usually peaks at 10–15,000 birds, mostly Black-headed Gulls but with good numbers of Common, Herring, Lesser and Great Black-backed Gulls. The roost usually pulls in the odd Glaucous and Iceland Gull at some time in most winters and sightings of Mediterranean Gulls are increasing and odd Kittiwakes sometimes occur in the late winter period. The farmland to the east of the reservoir usually holds flocks of Lapwing, with occasional Golden Plover, while coveys of Grey Partridge can still be found and flocks of finches and Tree Sparrows frequent the areas around the farm buildings. Barn Owls are attracted to the areas to the northwest and south where they can be seen quartering the rough grassland. Tawny and Little Owls are both fairly common but not so visible. Of the other two owls, Short-eared Owls were once regular winter visitors but have become scarce of late, while there are a few records of Long-eared Owls from the area to the north of the dam.

Birch and alder trees in Carver's Rocks Nature Reserve attract flocks of Siskins and Redpolls and most of the common woodland birds including the elusive Lesser Spotted Woodpecker.

Spring migration brings Northern Wheatears and Yellow Wagtails to the concrete walls and grassy banks of the dam. Swallows, Sand Martins, House Martins and Swifts can reach good numbers, with up to 1,000 of the latter species, taking advantage of the profusion of flying insects. The small plantations along the banks echo to the sound of singing Willow Warblers, with 20–30 males present, and smaller numbers of Whitethroat and Lesser Whitethroat. The rough grass areas, near the entrance to Carver's Rocks Reserve, hold a few pairs of Grasshopper Warbler, and the same areas are good for Woodcock, which can be seen roding over the area on late spring evenings. The nature reserve

Mediterranean and Black-headed Gulls

itself has Blackcaps and Garden Warblers and there is always the chance of a Wood Warbler or Redstart, both species probably being underrecorded in this little watched area. The first regional Cuckoo of the spring is recorded with frequency on the reserve, while the open bracken areas to the west have a few breeding pairs of Tree Pipit and Yellowhammer. Corn Buntings were formerly a common sight singing in the fields along the bridle path which runs from the nature reserve to the dam end of the reservoir, but records have declined seriously and sightings are now scarce.

The reservoir attracts early migrant Common and Arctic Terns, the latter species sometimes occurring in good sized flocks, which, however, seldom linger for long before pressing on north to their far northern breeding grounds. A good passage of terns may also produce records of Black and Sandwich Terns but the Blacks seem to favour the nearby Staunton Harold Reservoir, which has a near local monopoly on this species. Small parties of Common Scoter pause briefly on their cross-country migrations in spring when they are well worth checking for the rarer Velvet Scoter, four of which turned up with Common Scoters in 1992. The steep sandy banks are not attractive to feeding waders and thus most of the wader records are of birds announcing their presence as they fly over calling. The exception is the dam wall which does attract Common Sandpipers and the occasional Greenshank.

Foremark is well known for its records of Ospreys and is the most favoured haunt of this species in the south of the county during the spring and late summer. The individuals which occur are usually immatures and may linger for long periods, taking advantage of the ready supply of tasty trout. Also seen on passage are odd Marsh Harriers, while sightings of both Hobby and Common Buzzard are increasing, with the latter being seen at all seasons.

Summer tends to be a very quiet time, with a high level of disturbance from water sports, and the only birds of note tend to be the breeding species, which include good numbers of Turtle Dove. The set-aside fields to the north and south of the reservoir have, however, accounted for a few records of that elusive summer visitor, the Quail.

Autumn migration brings movements of Common Terns with occasional Black and Arctic Terns, while Little Gulls are not uncommon. Fly-over waders, such as Whimbrel and Grey Plover, announce their flying visit with calls. In hot dry summers low water levels may expose some sandy and muddy shorelines, which will sometimes tempt down small passing flocks of Dunlin and Ringed Plover, with occasional Little Stint and Curlew Sandpiper in good years for these species. Great Crested Grebe numbers begin to build towards their winter peak and there is always a chance of a Red-throated Diver, Black-necked Grebe or Common Scoter, all of which have been recorded during this period. Late autumn brings returning Goldeneye and Goosander and the odd flock of Wigeon.

The reservoir is, generally speaking, underwatched and, as yet, no major rarities have been located, but a number of good county birds have occurred, which include two records of Fulmar, Long-tailed Duck, Velvet Scoters, Eiders, Great Skua and Hen Harrier, the latter a good bird for the south of Derbyshire.

Timing

The best periods to visit the site are during the winter, November–March, and in the spring, April–May. As the reservoir is very deep the water seldom freezes and thus it is well worth paying a visit during spells of extreme hard weather as birds from the surrounding frozen areas will concentrate at the reservoir. Mornings are the best time as access is only allowed on the eastern side of the reservoir and the sun becomes a problem during the afternoon and evenings. Late evenings in the winter are best for viewing the gull roost, which is best watched from the side of the toilet block, in the main dam car park, as it offers some shelter from the elements.

Access

Foremark Reservoir is 5 miles (8 km) south of Derby and lies to the west of the A514 Ticknall to Hartshorne road. From the A514 at the west end of Ticknall, take the minor road west towards Milton. One mile (1.6 km) farther along this road take a left turn at the entrance gates, which leads to the dam end of the reservoir, the two public car parks and toilet blocks. Public access is only allowed on this side of the reservoir, where walking south will lead to Carver's Rocks Nature Reserve. The reserve can also be reached from the entrance gates which lie on the A514,

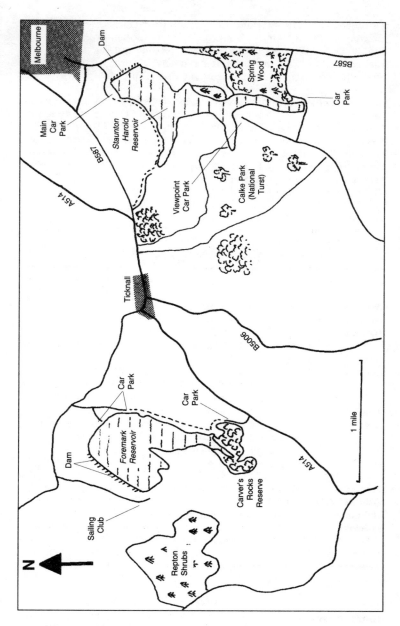

equidistant between Ticknall and Hartshorne. Please note that all entrance gates are locked at around dusk.

Calendar

Resident: Great Crested Grebe, Little Grebe, Sparrowhawk, Common Buzzard (scarce), Tawny Owl, Barn Owl, Grey Partridge, Lesser Spotted Woodpecker, Marsh Tit, Yellowhammer.

October–March: Divers (rare), Cormorant, Grey Heron, Bewick's Swan (scarce), Wigeon, Pintail (scarce), Pochard, Goldeneye, Goosander, Ruddy Duck, Lapwing, Golden Plover, Mediterranean, Iceland and Glaucous Gulls (all rare), Short-eared Owl (scarce), Grey Wagtail, Stonechat (scarce), Fieldfare, Redwing, Brambling.

April–September: Common Scoter (scarce), Osprey (rare but regular), Hobby, Quail (scarce), Ringed Plover (passage), Common Sandpiper, Greenshank (passage), Little Gull (scarce), Common Tern, Arctic Tern (passage), Sandwich Tern (rare), Black Tern (scarce), Turtle Dove, Cuckoo, Tree Pipit, Yellow Wagtail, Northern Wheatear (passage), Grasshopper Warbler, Lesser Whitethroat, Garden Warbler, Willow Warbler, Corn Bunting (scarce).

ADDITIONAL SITES

Name	Shipley Country Park.
Grid Reference	SK 4344
Habitat	Open grassland with two lakes, and two ponds, mixed deciduous and conifer woodland and gardens; hide on Mapperley Reservoir.
Species	Little and Great Crested Grebes, Little and Tawny Owl, Reed Warbler, thrushes, tit flocks, finches, Common Sandpiper, common passage waders, Short-eared Owl (autumn).
Timing	All.
Access	Off A608 at Heanor through industrial estate to a car park and visitor centre or via car park at Mapperley Reservoir off minor road north of Mapperley village.

Name	Erewash Valley/Brinsley Flash.
Grid Reference	SK 4449
Habitat	Shallow water flashes created by mining subsidence.
Species	Ruddy Duck, passage waders, occasional rarities such as Spoonbill, Red-footed Falcon.
Timing	All.
Access	Lane from Brinsley village.

Name	Willamthorpe.
Grid Reference	SK 4366
Habitat	Small reserve with extensive reedbed.
Species	Great Crested Grebe, Water Rail, Jack Snipe, Little Ringed Plover, Reed and Sedge Warbler, Bearded Tit (occasional), Swallow, Pied Wagtail and Corn Bunting roosts.
Timing	Winter and spring/autumn.
Access	Just north of Holmewood; from A6175 onto Park Road; car park and hide near sewage farm.

Name   Cresswell Craggs.
Grid Reference SK 5374
Habitat   Wooded magnesian limestone gorge with a small lake; important archaeological site.
Species   Spotted Flycatcher, warblers, three woodpeckers, winter tit and finch flocks.
Timing   Busy site and early mornings preferable.
Access   From A616 at Cresswell or onto B6042 from A60 north of Welbeck Abbey.

Name   Elvaston Castle Country Park.
Grid Reference SK 405 330
Habitat   Deciduous woodland in old parkland with a lake.
Species   Nuthatch, all three woodpeckers, Hobby, Sparrowhawk, Siskin and Redpoll winter, Canada Geese, tits and finches, Collared Dove roost.
Timing   All.
Access   From A6 Derby–Leicester road onto B5010, park entrance is 1 mile (1.6 km) north, large car park with visitor centre.

Name   Drakelow Wildfowl Reserve.
Grid Reference SK 2220
Habitat   Disused gravel working with open water, reedbeds, scrub and gravel islands; a National Power reserve.
Species   Cormorant, Canada Geese, wildfowl, Gadwall, Teal, Goldeneye; Peregrine, Water Rail, Jack Snipe, Oystercatcher, Ringed and Little Ringed Plovers, Reed and Sedge Warbler, Common Tern.
Timing   All.
Access   By permit only from National Power at Drakelow Power Station. From A38 take minor road to Walton-on-Trent, entrance is 1 mile (1.6 km) north of village.

Name   Church Wilne Reservoir.
Grid Reference SK 460 325
Habitat   Deep, steep-banked reservoir with grassed banks and scrub; disused gravel pit used for water-skiing adjacent to reservoir.
Species   Cormorant, wildfowl include Goldeneye, Gadwall (50+), Wigeon (1,000), Pochard, winter gull roost largest in county, passage Common, Arctic, Black Terns, Little Gull, Yellow and Pied Wagtails, hirundines, Swifts, rarities.
Timing   All.
Access   By permit only from Severn Trent Water Authority; entrance to reservoir is off minor road between Sawley and Breaston.

Name   Chatsworth Park.
Grid Reference SK 260 700.
Habitat   Old parkland with open grazed grassland, deciduous woodland, scattered ancient deciduous trees, fast-flowing stream.

Species	Three species of woodpecker, Nuthatch, Hawfinch, Dipper and Grey Wagtail, Kingfisher, Little Grebe, Common Sandpiper, Yellow Wagtail, Goosander.
Timing	All but weekends and summer are very busy.
Access	From A6 Matlock to Bakewell road at Rowsley onto A623 Baslow road. Park private property but southwestern section usually open to the public.

Name	Wyver Lane
Grid Reference	SK 354 486
Habitat	Water Meadows alongside River Derwent.
Species	Teal, Wigeon, Shoveler, Ruddy Duck, Tufted Duck, Hobby, Common Sandpiper, Water Rail, Jack Snipe, Green Woodpecker, warblers.
Timing	All.
Access	From the A6 at north end of Belper onto Wyver Lane; view from the lane over water meadows to left; park near hide.

Name	Goyt Valley and Axe Edge.
Grid Reference	SK 015 758 to 020 700
Habitat	Gritstone valley with large reservoirs, plantations and open moorland.
Species	Red Grouse, Golden Plover, Curlew, Whinchat, Ring Ouzel, Twite, Northern Wheatear on moors; Common Sandpiper, Grey Wagtail and Dipper on river; Redstart, Wood Warbler, Pied Flycatcher woodlands; Red-breasted Merganser in spring.
Timing	Best in spring and summer; popular tourist area.
Access	From old A6 Buxton to Manchester road, now A5002, or from A537 Buxton to Macclesfield road near Cat and Fiddle inn. Several car parks in valley.

LEICESTERSHIRE

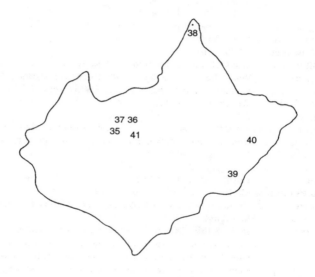

35 Bradgate Park and Cropston
    Reservoir
36 Swithland Wood
37 Swithland Reservoir

38 Belvoir Area
39 Eyebrook Reservoir
40 Rutland Water
41 Soar Valley Gravel Pits

35 BRADGATE PARK AND CROPSTON RESERVOIR

Habitat

Bradgate Park lies at the southeastern edge of Charnwood Forest, and is the county's largest remaining area of semi-natural moorland, covering some 850 acres (374 ha). It was established as a deer park in the thirteenth century (herds of fallow and red deer still roam in a semi-wild state), and was given to the people of Leicestershire by Charles Bennion in 1928. Today it is managed, along with nearby Swithland Wood, by the Bradgate Park trustees on behalf of Leicestershire County Council.

The park vegetation is dominated by bracken, with a few small patches of wet heath and drier grassy areas. These consist mainly of purple moor-grass, and contain several locally rare plants including cross-leaved heath, lesser skullcap and lemon-scented fern. There are many scattered oaks, some very old, and several newer plantations of mixed deciduous and coniferous trees. These are surrounded by drystone walls, creating undisturbed oases where many birds nest. The northern end of the park rises to around 600 feet (200 m) and has many rocky outcrops, one of which is the well known local landmark of Old John Tower. Several small ponds provide excellent habitat for dragonflies, amphibians and water plants.

A fast-flowing stream, fringed with alders, runs along the southern edge of the park, past the ruins of Bradgate House, and eventually into Cropston Reservoir. This drinking water reservoir forms the eastern edge of Bradgate Park and is separated from it by a drystone wall. Public access is not allowed to the reservoir margins. The shallow southern end, which is easily watched from the park, usually has muddy areas in autumn, which attract waders. The deeper water at the dam is favoured by diving ducks and grebes.

Species

BRADGATE PARK

The vast areas of bracken can often appear relatively birdless even in summer, Yellowhammers and Meadow Pipits being the commonest breeding species, with a few Reed Buntings and Yellow Wagtails in the wetter areas. In spring and summer Tree Pipits perform their parachute song flights from the oaks and the edges of the plantations. Whinchats, until a few years ago a breeding species, appear to have gone, but odd birds may still arrive on passage. Redstarts have also declined dramatically but still hang on in small numbers, with a handful of pairs breeding in the old oaks each year. The quiet scratchy song of the males can often be heard near the Newton Lindford entrance but the singing birds are difficult to locate in the crowns of the large spreading oaks.

The plantations hold good numbers of the commoner breeding warblers, plus the occasional Wood Warbler. Hallgates Spinney and Dale Spinney have recently been the favoured sites for this species. Grasshopper Warblers sometimes hold territory in the park, the scrubby area between Hallgates and the inflow of the reservoir is probably the best place to look and listen for this often elusive species. All three species of woodpecker occur in the oaks and plantations, although Lesser Spotted is rarely seen. Green Woodpeckers can often be found feeding on the ant hills around the ruins. Nuthatches also like the old oaks, with their abundance of suitable nesting holes.

The introduced Little Owl is another characteristic bird of the park, with several pairs breeding in most years. The enclosed area behind the ruins is one of the more reliable places to see them, although they are well camouflaged when sitting motionless against the trunk of an oak. Several pairs of Tawny Owls also breed and Woodcocks probably do so. Woodcocks can be seen roding over the plantations at dawn and dusk in spring and summer, and are occasionally flushed from the wetter areas in the winter. Sparrowhawks may be seen hunting over the park at anytime of the year, and one or two pairs breed in the plantations. Very occasionally a Common Buzzard or Merlin may appear.

Grey Wagtails and Kingfishers can often be seen along the stream, and both have bred in the past. Little Grebes nest in the broader stretches created by the weirs, and also on the pond in the ruins enclosure. Northern Wheatears and Ring Ouzels sometimes appear on passage, the former may be seen almost anywhere in the park, but the latter favour the rockier terrain similar to their upland breeding habitat.

The park is quiet in winter but is the most reliable site in the county for Stonechat, with up to four birds being present in most years from November through to March. The birds frequent the dead bracken and drystone walls, particularly around the ruins and the reservoir inflow. Flocks of Siskin and Redpolls may be found feeding in the streamside alders.

Rarer visitors to the park in recent years have included Short-eared Owl, Hen Harrier, Honey Buzzard, Great Grey Shrike and both Richard's and Tawny Pipits.

CROPSTON RESERVOIR

The reservoir is usually at its best in the autumn, when falling water levels can expose a large expanse of mud at the inflow end. This regularly attracts waders, of which the most numerous are Ringed and Little Ringed Plovers, Dunlin, Greenshank, Redshank, Ruff, Common and

Ring Ouzel

Green Sandpipers and Snipe. Many other species have, however, been recorded including Wood Sandpiper, Knot, Sanderling, Little Stint, Black and Bar-tailed Godwits, Whimbrel, Spotted Redshank and Turnstone. Quite large numbers of moulting duck are also usually present in late summer and may include one or two Garganey. Terns are regular on autumn passage and occasional Little Gulls may drop in. Hobbies may be seen hunting over the reservoir and the park, particularly in late summer, when family parties may be in evidence.

In winter the reservoir holds reasonable numbers of most of the common ducks: Wigeon, Mallard, Teal and small numbers of Gadwall and Shoveler feed at the inflow end and around the edges, whilst Pochard, Tufted Duck, Goldeneye and Ruddy Ducks favour the deeper water off the dam. Up to 40 Great Crested Grebes and a few Little Grebes winter, and Cormorants may also be present. The only waders apart from the ubiquitous Lapwings are up to 50 or so Snipe and the occasional Green Sandpiper and Jack Snipe.

A gull roost sometimes forms on the reservoir, but more usually the site acts as a pre-roost assembly for the large gathering on nearby Swithland Reservoir. Recent unusual winter visitors have included Black-throated Diver, Slavonian and Red-necked Grebes, Scaup, Common Scoter, Red-breasted Merganser, Mediterranean Gull and Kittiwake.

The water level is often high in spring and the reservoir is therefore relatively quiet. Small numbers of duck breed including occasional Gadwall and Ruddy Duck; Little Ringed Plover and a few pairs of Lapwing may also do so if the water level drops sufficiently. In the right weather conditions, easterly winds being best, terns including a large proportion of Arctics, and Little Gulls may visit briefly.

Timing

Bradgate Park is by far the most popular recreational area in Leicestershire, and is often very crowded, particularly on fine days in both summer and winter. Fortunately the birds using the reservoir do not seem to be unduly disturbed by the hordes of people, but bear in mind that parking may be difficult or impossible at weekends and on bank holidays.

Autumn is generally the best season for the reservoir, as the water level usually drops from July onwards, attracting waders. As with nearby Swithland Reservoir, the winter duck population can fluctuate markedly from day to day.

Time of day seems to be unimportant as regards migrant waders, and there is often evidence of continuing passage throughout the day, with a different mix of species present in the morning to the evening. Obviously to avoid the crowds in the park, early morning is best, although the inflow of the reservoir may be difficult to watch on bright days, and is better in the afternoon.

Access

The park is open throughout the year and is served by three major car parks, at Newton Linford (SK 523 097), Hunt's Hill (SK 523 117) and Hallgates (SK 542 114). Park at any of these and explore the many pathways on foot. Hallgates is nearest to Cropston Reservoir; follow the road through the park to view the inflow, which is the best area for waders. The reservoir can also be watched from the dam; park in the lay-by on the B5330 (at SK 551 111).

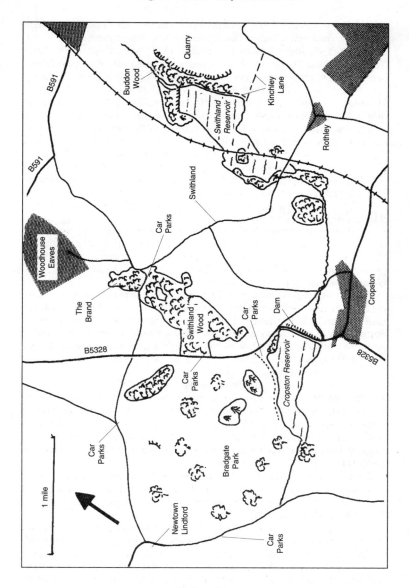

Calendar

Resident: Little Grebe, Great Crested Grebe, Mallard, Tufted Duck, Ruddy Duck, Sparrowhawk, Little Owl, Tawny Owl, Kingfisher, Green, Great Spotted and Lesser Spotted Woodpeckers, Grey Wagtail, Meadow Pipit, Nuthatch, Treecreeper, Reed Bunting.

November–March: Wigeon, Teal, Gadwall, Shoveler, Pochard, Goldeneye, Jack Snipe, Snipe, Green Sandpiper, Stonechat, Fieldfare, Redwing, Siskin, Redpoll.

April–June: Garganey (scarce), Hobby, Little Ringed Plover, Common Sandpiper, Little Gull (scarce), Common Tern, Arctic Tern, Black Tern, Tree Pipit, Yellow Wagtail, Redstart, Whinchat (now scarce), Northern Wheatear, Ring Ouzel (rare), Grasshopper Warbler, Wood Warbler (occasional).

July–October: Garganey, Hobby, Little Ringed Plover, Ringed Plover, Dunlin, Ruff, Redshank, Greenshank, Green Sandpiper, Wood Sandpiper (scarce), Common Sandpiper, Little Gull, terns, Yellow Wagtail, Whinchat, Northern Wheatear.

36 SWITHLAND WOOD   OS Sheet 129

Habitat
Together with the adjacent private woodland, known as The Brand, Swithland Wood forms the largest remaining area of the original Charnwood oak woodland covering some 180 acres (72 ha) in total. Pedunculate and sessile oak predominate with stands of birch, small-leaved lime and alder, the latter particularly along the stream at the southern end of the wood. The shrub layer is mainly hazel with some holly but this has been much reduced by the effects of many visitors and their attendant dogs straying from the main pathways.

The woodland is very rich in wildlife, with over 250 plant species and 200 species of butterflies and moths having been recorded. A small herb-rich meadow at the northern end of the wood adds to the variety of habitats in the area and in spring it is carpeted with common spotted orchids and also holds the locally rare adder's tongue fern. Also within the wood are two very deep, water-filled slate quarries, which provide a habitat for Mallard, Tufted Duck and Little Grebe and once hosted one of the county's most bizarre records, a Puffin!

Species
All three species of woodpecker are resident, and Swithland Wood is one of the best places in the county to see the secretive Lesser Spotted. Several pairs breed and the birds are most easily located in spring by listening for their distinctive 'pee pee pee' calls. Nuthatch and Treecreeper are also easily seen and it is possible to compare identification of both Marsh and Willow Tits, the latter usually being found in the damper areas of the wood. A visit at dawn or dusk in spring is required to see Woodcocks roding, with one of the best places being the large spoil heap next to the southernmost quarry. From this vantage point the birds can be easily seen as they pass over the tree-tops, giving their distinctive grunts and squeaks, at eye level.

Grey Wagtails sometimes breed in the steep-sided slate quarries and Little Grebe and Mallard have also done so in the past. Predators are represented by Sparrowhawks and Tawny Owls. The latter species may sometimes be found roosting during the day in the favoured large holly trees at the southern end of the wood.

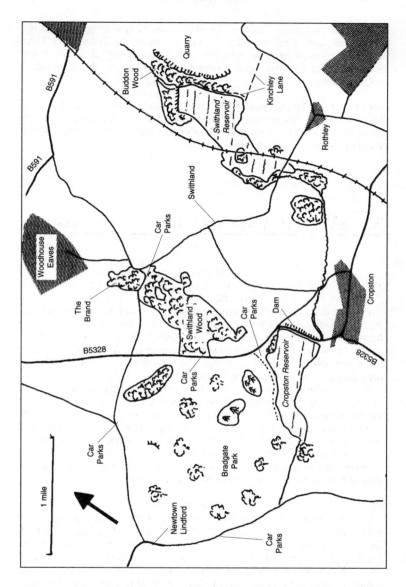

In spring the wood holds a good selection of summering warblers including Blackcap, Garden and Willow Warblers and Chiffchaff. In addition this is the most reliable site in the county for Wood Warbler, with up to two or three males usually singing each spring, but whether they still nest is open to question. The numbers of this species have certainly declined in recent years probably because of the destruction of much of the shrub layer. Although Wood Warblers may sing from anywhere in the wood, the most regular sites are at the northern end near the Brand car park and in the fenced-off section at the eastern edge of the wood.

Spotted Flycatchers occur in reasonable numbers and there are a few spring records of Pied Flycatchers, which could conceivably breed in the future as they have been seen inspecting nesting holes on more than one occasion. One former breeding species which may hold on in small numbers is the Hawfinch, which although reported less than annually, usually from The Brand, may still breed in that wood, which is private and therefore rather less disturbed.

The wood is relatively quiet in the winter but tits and woodpeckers are perhaps easier to see at this time of year, and Redpolls and Siskins, the latter sometimes in good numbers, frequent the alders along the stream.

Timing

Most of the warblers are present and singing by early May but Wood Warblers may not arrive until mid May in some years and have usually stopped singing by the first week of June. Early morning is definitely the best time of day in spring, as birds sing almost continuously for the first two hours after dawn but tend to be much less vocal later in the day. Woodcocks can be seen roding at dawn and dusk. In winter the time of day is less critical as the birds are active all day in their never-ending search for food.

Access

There are car parks at the northern and southern end of the wood (at SK 537 130 and SK 537 117), the latter about half a mile (0.8 km) west of Bradgate Park Hallgates car park off the B5330. Keep to the main foot-paths as erosion and trampling of the undergrowth are a serious prob-lem in the wood. The paths can be very muddy even in summer, and wellingtons are recommended.

Calendar

Resident: Sparrowhawk, Woodcock, Tawny Owl, Green, Great and Lesser Spotted Woodpeckers, Grey Wagtail, Marsh Tit, Willow Tit, Nuthatch, Treecreeper, Jay, Hawfinch (rare, possibly extinct).

Summer: Garden Warbler, Blackcap, Wood Warbler, Chiffchaff, Willow Warbler, Spotted Flycatcher, Pied Flycatcher (rare passage visitor).

Winter: Siskin, Redpoll.

37 SWITHLAND RESERVOIR   OS Sheet 129

Habitat

Swithland Reservoir is approximately 1 mile (1.6 km) long by half a mile (0.8 km) wide, and lies at the eastern edge of Charnwood Forest. It is bisected by the Great Central Railway, and the northern and south-ern sections are both easily watched from public roads. At the southern (inflow) end a shallow lagoon has formed, cut off from the rest of the reservoir by the road bridge; it is surrounded by reed-swamp and willow carr. The northeast shore was formerly bounded by Buddon Wood, but this has now been sadly reduced to a narrow strip by the ever expanding Mountsorrel granite quarry. This wood, originally oak, is now mainly composed of birch. There is, however, another small area of oak woodland on Brazil Island, connected to the banks by the railway viaduct, but this along with the rest of the reservoir grounds is private.

There are several marshy areas around the reservoir, with stands of bulrush and reed canary-grass. These, along with willows and alders, provide a habitat for Reed Warblers, Reed Buntings and occasional Water Rails. The fields and hedges along Kinchley Lane (see Access) are worth a look, particularly in autumn and winter, as is the railway embankment at Rabbit's Bridge (SK 554 144).

Swithland is now mainly used to top up nearby Cropston Reservoir, from where drinking water is taken; consequently the water level fluctuates considerably, although the shoreline is largely stony and thus disappointing for waders. The reservoir is relatively undisturbed, water sports have fortunately been resisted, and only a small amount of coarse fishing takes place. During the winter months shooting in the reservoir grounds and surrounding fields can temporarily affect the number of wildfowl, which may then disperse to Cropston Reservoir or the Soar Valley gravel pits.

Species

One of the main attractions at this site is the gull roost. In winter up to 15,000 gulls have been counted, although numbers, particularly of large gulls, have declined somewhat with the recent closure of the nearby Mountsorrel tip. The roost can sometimes be difficult to watch as the best viewpoint, halfway along Kinchley Lane, faces directly into the setting sun. Overcast evenings are therefore better.

Since the mid 1980s a small group of enthusiasts, with permits to enter the reservoir grounds, have watched the roost every winter. Mediterranean Gulls have proved to be regular visitors, with up to three birds at a time being recorded, and their occurrence is almost guaranteed from November to March, although patience, good light and a good telescope are required to pick them out! Glaucous Gulls were virtually annual until the closure of the tip, and several Iceland Gulls have been recorded. The real prizes, however, have been the first and second county Ring-billed Gulls, in 1988 and 1989 respectively. The roost is also worth watching in late summer and autumn, this being the peak time for Yellow-legged Gulls. Swithland provided the first county record in 1987, since when they have become regular and expected visitors, with up to eight individuals present at a time. One or two occasionally winter, although great care is needed with identification after December.

The reservoir has a good winter population of wildfowl: Wigeon, Gadwall, Teal, Shoveler, Tufted Duck, Pochard and Goldeneye are all regular, with occasional Pintail and Goosander. Swithland is one of the main Leicestershire wintering sites for Ruddy Duck, with over 250 birds recorded on recent counts. Smew are infrequent visitors as are seaducks: Common and Velvet Scoters, Scaup, Long-tailed Duck, Eider and Red-breasted Merganser all having been noted. In hard weather any of the the three rarer grebes may join the Great Crested and Little Grebes, Red-necked Grebe being the most likely. All three divers have occurred with Red-throated being the most frequent. A recent addition to the winter scene has been a roost of Cormorants, with up to 50 birds gathering on the tern rafts in the late afternoon before flying to roost in the trees on the south side of the reservoir. It seems likely that this species may well start to breed at this locality in the near future.

The water level is generally high in the winter and so waders are scarce, Green Sandpiper being the only regular species. One or two Water Rails may be found in the marshy areas at the inflow and along Kinchley Lane. Buddon Wood and the trees around the dam area hold woodpeckers, including Lesser Spotted, Marsh and Willow Tits, Siskin, Redpoll and Brambling, the latter being most frequent on passage in late March and April. Sparrowhawks are frequently seen and Mountsorrel quarry is the most regular wintering site for Peregrine in the county, with up to three birds having been noted together at times. Grey Wagtails are usually about the dam and Kingfishers may be seen anywhere around the reservoir but especially at the inflow lagoon and behind the dam.

Easterly winds in spring often bring a passage of Arctic and Black Terns, occasionally in good numbers, while two to three pairs of Common Terns nest on the special rafts. Little Gulls are sometimes associated with movements of terns, and Kittiwakes may also appear in March or April, especially after gales. Wader passage is slight and dependent upon the water levels, but Common Sandpipers, Little Ringed Plovers and occasionally odd birds of other species turn up on the sloping stonework of the dam.

Breeding ducks include Mallard, Tufted Duck and Ruddy Duck. Pochard, Gadwall and Shoveler have also bred and Garganey is a scarce passage migrant. Large gatherings of Swifts and hirundines may attract the attentions of hunting Hobbies. Rarer raptors have appeared on passage including Osprey and Buzzard. Several pairs of Reed Warbler breed around the reservoir, along with Reed Buntings and the occasional pair of Sedge Warbler. Wood Warblers sometimes sing for a day or two on spring passage, in Buddon Wood, but quickly move on.

Midsummer is often quiet. Post-breeding flocks of Lapwing start to appear as early as June, and there is a regular flock of moulting diving ducks. Pochard and Tufted Duck predominate in the flock, which may number 300 birds, but there have also been past records of odd Goldeneye. Black-necked Grebes are almost annual in late July and August and may stay for a week or more. Passage waders are less numerous than at Cropston Reservoir but most of the regular species have been recorded. Ringed and Little Ringed Plovers, Common Sandpiper, Greenshank and Dunlin are the most frequent. The return passage of terns is not usually as large as in spring but small flocks of Black Terns may occur in the right weather conditions from July to October. Records of Arctic Terns are rare in autumn and usually involve juveniles. Migrant passerines can turn up in any area of cover around the reservoir and all areas of bushes and trees should be searched for warblers, chats and other species.

Swithland is a well watched locality and has amassed a good list of rare birds over the years, with the most recent being Leach's Petrel, Bittern, Spoonbill, Ferruginous Duck, Killdeer, Red-necked and Grey Phalaropes, Great and Arctic Skuas, White-winged Black Tern, Firecrest, Great Grey Shrike and Common Crossbill.

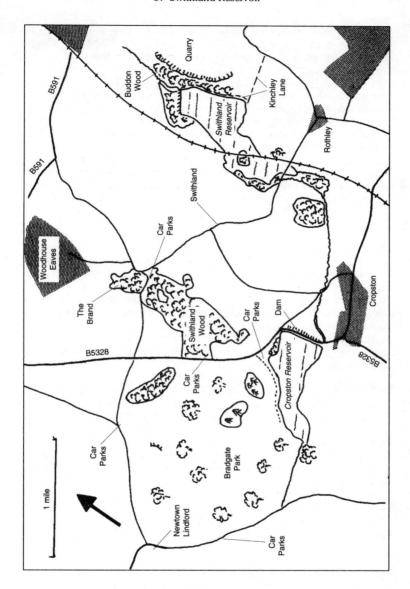

Timing

Winter is the best time to see large numbers of birds, although spring and autumn probably offer better chances of finding something unusual. In winter the gull roost assembles an hour or two before dusk, but as mentioned previously, be sure to pick an overcast afternoon for best viewing conditions. On really cold days, if the reservoir is frozen over, the gulls may be present all day.

Time of day for migrants is not too important, although early morning is usually best. Shooting occasionally takes place in the grounds during the winter months, causing temporary disturbance to ducks, which move to nearby Cropston Reservoir. The gull roost may also be disrupted and on some evenings may also shift to Cropston. The shoots are mostly on Saturday mornings but times are irregular throughout.

Access

The south side of the reservoir can be watched from the minor road between Swithland and Rothley. Park on the bridge (at SK 563 133). To reach the north side follow this road for half a mile (0.8 km) and turn left onto Kinchley Lane, which skirts the eastern shore and dam of the reservoir. Drive and park carefully as the lane is winding and narrow, and is frequented by numbers of dog walkers and horse riders. On no account enter any of the reservoir grounds, Buddon Wood or the railway line as all are private. A small number of local birders have permits to enter the grounds, however, so do not automatically assume that anyone in the grounds is trespassing.

Calendar

Resident: Little Grebe, Great Crested Grebe, Cormorant (more in winter), Pochard, Tufted Duck, Ruddy Duck, Sparrowhawk, Kingfisher, Lesser Spotted Woodpecker, Grey Wagtail, Marsh Tit, Willow Tit.

November–March: Divers (rare), Red-necked Grebe (scarce), Wigeon, Gadwall, Pintail (scarce), Teal, Shoveler, Goldeneye, sea-duck (rare), Smew (rare), Goosander (scarce), Peregrine, Water Rail, Green Sandpiper, Mediterranean Gull, Yellow-legged Gull, Iceland Gull (rare), Glaucous Gull (scarce), Kittiwake (after gales), Fieldfare, Redwing, Siskin, Redpoll, Brambling.

April–June: Garganey (rare), Osprey (rare), Hobby, Little Ringed Plover, Common Sandpiper, Little Gull, Common, Arctic and Black Terns, Yellow Wagtail, Reed Warbler, Wood Warbler (scarce).

July–October: Black-necked Grebe (scarce), Garganey (scarce), Gadwall, Hobby, Little Ringed Plover, Ringed Plover, Dunlin, Greenshank, Green Sandpiper, Common Sandpiper, Little Gull, Yellow-legged Gull, Black Tern.

38 BELVOIR AREA OS Sheets 129 and 130

Habitat

The Belvoir area, which lies to the north of Melton Mowbray and to the southwest of Grantham, is mostly within Leicestershire but lies on the boundaries with Nottinghamshire to the northwest and Lincolnshire to the northeast. The region is dominated by the Belvoir ridge, which rises to a height of 500 feet (150 m), with Belvoir Castle, at its eastern end, forming a well known landmark. Along the ridge from Belvoir west to Stathern are extensive stands of mature mixed deciduous woodland with smaller areas of conifers. Barkestone, Plungar and Stathern Woods, which are all part of one large block, are all accessible on their southern edge via the Jubilee Way footpath.

To the east and south lie areas of private parkland, which include two small lakes and Knipton Reservoir (also private), but which can be viewed at its western end from the minor road between Knipton and Branston. To the north runs the disused Grantham Canal, with adjacent areas of rich arable farmland and grazed grassland. Additionally there are some lengths of old dismantled railway track, overgrown with scrub, mainly hawthorn but with some birch and a mix of other self-sown species, as well as bramble and rough grass. Much of the Vale of Belvoir, north of the canal, runs into Nottinghamshire.

Species

Winter birdwatching in the Belvoir area concentrates on woodland birds and raptors but there are a few Goosanders on the lakes and the reservoir, where they join the resident Great Crested Grebes and Tufted Ducks.

Raptor watching is at its best in winter, especially late winter, when the resident birds are starting to display. The wooded ridge offers raptors a suitable source of uplift which they need when soaring, whilst the open but varied countryside offers good hunting grounds. The area holds several pairs of the increasingly common Sparrowhawk with the ubiquitous Kestrel, and also two to three pairs of Common Buzzards. The latter species do seem, at last, to be spreading back into the East Midlands counties as a breeding bird, with increasing sightings of birds during the summer months and also widespread wintering individuals being encountered.

The best way of locating raptors in winter is to locate a good vantage point and watch for birds soaring over the ridge or hunting over the open fields and, in particular, any areas of rough grassland, set-aside or pasture fields. Watching for sudden panic amongst feeding flocks of passerines, Woodpigeon, Lapwing and corvids will often reveal a hunting raptor in their midst. Of the rarer species, the dashing Merlin and the Peregrine are the most common during the winter. Merlins spend a lot of time sitting around on fields, old straw bales or fenceposts, watching

Common Buzzard

for their favoured prey of small birds, so scanning such perches may produce extended views of the birds.

Many observers were attracted to the area during the 1994–95 winter when, following a national influx, a Rough-legged Buzzard took up residence in the area from October 1994, staying the whole winter in the area north of Branston. That ghostly evening hunter, the Barn Owl, may be encountered hunting along the minor road south of Barkestone-le-Vale.

The open arable fields hold coveys of Red-legged Partridge, with some Chukars and hybrids, which are easily found, whilst the Grey Partridges are typically more elusive.

The woodlands have a typical mix of flocks of tits, including Marsh Tit, Goldcrests, Treecreepers and Nuthatch. Marsh Tits and Nuthatch are quite common here and are fairly easy to find. All three species of woodpecker are resident, though, as everywhere, Lesser Spotted is the most difficult to locate. Large flocks of Chaffinches frequent suitable fields, and in some years are joined by a few Brambling.

In the early spring, before the trees are in full leaf, some of the nests of the 25–30 pairs of Grey Heron, which nest on the Belvoir Estate, can be seen in the woodland by looking west from the minor road north of Harston. Woodcock may be seen roding over Stathern Wood in the early morning and late evenings.

From May onwards Hobbies return to the area and undoubtedly breed in the vicinity. As the habitat here is mainly one of parkland and open country, however, with few water bodies to attract hunting birds, seeing them is often a matter of pot luck. Hunting adults, which are feeding young in the summer, are, however, attracted to House Martin colonies in the villages and also to places where Swifts and hirundines feed over the woodlands on the ridge. These are also suitable spots to look for displaying birds in May. Probably the best chance of seeing the birds though is from late August when the young are on the wing and making their first hunting flights. In summer, Quail are regular in the south-facing barley and wheat fields north of Branston village.

Along the canal banks Yellow Wagtails are attracted to the wetland habitat, which also plays host to all three of the traditional 'wetland' warblers, Grasshopper, Sedge and Reed. Grasshopper Warblers, with their trilling buzz of a song, often sing throughout the night in late April and early May as they establish territories in areas of rough grassland, often with clumps of brambles, willow herb or low scrub. Reed Warblers are found most frequently in the reedbeds, which are to be found where the minor road crosses the canal north of Stathern. The disused railway line presents a wide ribbon of what soon becomes secondary woodland with tall scrub soon encroaching over the old track bed. This can be an important habitat in agricultural landscapes and here provides breeding sites for Turtle Doves and a good variety of warblers including Blackcap, Garden Warbler, Willow Warbler, Whitethroat and Lesser Whitethroat. The declining Corn Bunting has been heard in song north of Branston village and should be looked for elsewhere as this is still a relatively good area for the species.

Autumn is the least promising time to visit the area. A few Green Sandpipers visit Knipton Reservoir and there may be diurnal movements of Lapwings, Skylarks and thrushes but otherwise little may be seen apart from the common resident birds.

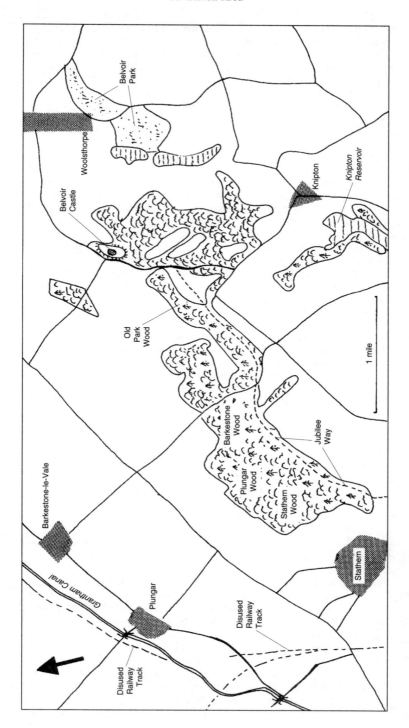

Timing

Interesting species may be seen throughout the year but the winter and midsummer periods are likely to be the most productive. Fine weather offers the best prospects for finding a good range of species within the area.

Access

From the A607 Grantham to Belvoir road take minor roads northbound, signposted to Belvoir, Knipton and Branston. The estate is owned by the Duke of Rutland and much of the rest of the area is private. Visitors should keep to public roads and footpaths.

Good vantage points for watching raptors are found (at SK 818 300) to the southeast of Knipton Reservoir, half a mile (0.8 km) north of Harston village (at SK 836 325) on the minor road to Woolsthorpe, and 1 mile (1.6 km) southwest of Barkestone-le-Vale, on a minor road which gives views over Barkestone and Plungar Woods and the valley to the northwest (at SK 792 333). Woodland birds may be seen along the Jubilee Way, which passes along the southern edge of a large block of woodland just east of Stathern village. At Stathern bridge on the Grantham Canal (SK 756 324) there are reedbeds which hold breeding Reed Warblers. The canal footpath is open to the public all year round. Many of the roads in the area have verges wide enough to park a car on: visitors should use discretion and show respect for other road users.

Calendar

Resident: Great Crested Grebe, Tufted Duck, Sparrowhawk, Kestrel, Common Buzzard, Red-legged and Grey Partridge, Barn Owl, Green, Great and Lesser Spotted Woodpeckers, Nuthatch, Marsh Tit, Chaffinch.

October–March: Goosander, Merlin, Peregrine (both scarce), Brambling.

April–September: Woodcock, Quail, Hobby, Turtle Dove, Yellow Wagtail, Grasshopper Warbler, Reed and Sedge Warbler, Blackcap, Garden Warbler, Lesser Whitethroat, Whitethroat, Corn Bunting.

39 EYEBROOK RESERVOIR   OS Sheet 141

Recently somewhat overshadowed by its larger neighbour, Rutland Water, Eyebrook has a long record as an excellent inland locality for birdwatching and has attracted an impressive range of species over its 50-year history. It remains one of the most important localities in the county of Leicestershire.

Habitat

Completed in 1940, this 400-acre (160 ha) reservoir is owned by Corby Steel and Tube works. It is used for trout fishing in season, but is otherwise little disturbed. The reservoir occupies a sheltered position in a valley and has natural, gently shelving banks with a grassy fringe. The northern end is marshy, with vegetation including water mint, silver weed and amphibious bistort, whilst the eastern shore has a coniferous plantation of pine, larch and spruce. Below the dam there is an avenue of European hardwoods and there are several small stands of willows around the reservoir, for example on the island. The surrounding land is mainly arable with hawthorn hedgerows and odd scattered older trees.

Species

In winter the main attractions are the large numbers of wildfowl and the roosting gulls. Wildfowl include small numbers of Bewick's Swans, 100+ feral Greylag Geese, which are sometimes joined by stray wild geese (especially White-fronted), nearly 1,000 Wigeon, small numbers of Pintail and regular Smew and Goosander. Over 100 Ruddy Ducks are sometimes present. Waders congregate to roost on the exposed mud at the northern end of the reservoir and include up to 2,000 Golden Plover, 1,000 Lapwing and 150 Dunlin.

The gull roost may be observed from anywhere along the western shore road, depending on conditions; the principal species being Black-headed, Common, Herring and Great Black-backed Gulls. In recent years Mediterranean Gulls have become regular in small numbers, especially in the late autumn and early spring but with a few birds throughout the winter. Iceland and Glaucous Gulls are much rarer, though records of the former are currently increasing.

Flocks of Fieldfares strip the berries from the hawthorns along the southwestern shore, whilst stubble fields around the reservoir attract small numbers of Tree Sparrows, finches and Yellowhammers. Over 1,000 Woodpigeons gather to roost in the plantation.

Black-necked Grebes sometimes arrive on passage from late March onwards. Garganey are regular and Common Scoters occasional at this season. Ospreys have become annual visitors and the northern end of the reservoir is a good place to watch hunting Hobbies from May onwards. Spring waders include Little Ringed and Ringed Plovers, Redshank and Common Sandpiper with occasional visits by other species depending on conditions. Little Gulls, Kittiwakes, Common, Arctic and Black Terns are all regular, the last two sometimes in impressive numbers, but fluctucating from year to year. Over 50 Yellow

Bewick's Swans

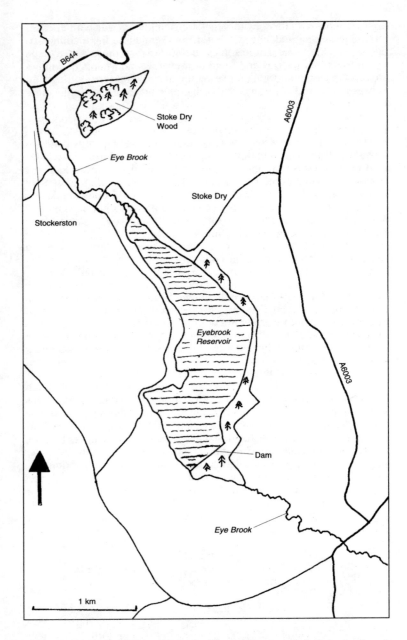

Wagtails and a few White Wagtails are usually present in late April and give good close views around the reservoir margins. A few Whinchat and Northern Wheatears usually pass through, whilst the hedgerows support a good population of Whitethroats. Breeding birds include Great Crested Grebe, Shelduck (occasional), Gadwall and Tufted Duck. A few Ruddy Duck normally summer.

Sparrowhawks breed in nearby woods and may be seen hunting around the reservoir. Little Owls sometimes hunt at dusk from telegraph poles along the road towards Stockerston. Tree Sparrows can be seen in the trees near the inflow at the northern end and the plantation has Goldcrest, Spotted Flycatcher, Willow Tit and Treecreeper.

Autumn passage brings probably the greatest variety of birds to the reservoir. In addition to those species which occur in spring the following are all regular; Red-crested Pochard, Little Stint, Curlew Sandpiper, Ruff, Black-tailed Godwit, Spotted Redshank, Greenshank, Wood Sandpiper and Yellow-legged Gull (late summer onwards). Siskins often arrive in the plantation from September. The number of waders obviously varies according to the success of their respective breeding seasons and the amount of exposed muddy margins, and it would not be normal to see all these species on a single visit. Surprises are always possible, however, and over the years these have included Night and Squacco Herons, Little Egret (4), American Wigeon (3), Ring-necked Duck (2), Ferruginous Duck (1), White-headed Duck (1), Black-winged Pratincole, Killdeer, Baird's Sandpiper (2), Caspian Tern (3), White-winged Black Tern (4) and Citrine Wagtail.

Timing
Interesting birdwatching can be enjoyed here throughout the year. Wildfowl numbers are at their highest from November to March, whilst migrants are more numerous from April to early June and August to October. For viewing the western shore the light is best during the afternoons, and during inclement conditions most of the reservoir can be seen from a car.

Access
The reservoir is situated to the west of the A6003, Oakham to Corby road, 2 miles (3.2 km) south of Uppingham. Leave Uppingham south on the A6003, turn right at the crossroads after 1.5 miles (2.4 km). Follow the minor road down through Stoke Dry to the reservoir. The minor road then runs north and bends left around the northern inlet end of the reservoir to a T junction where a left turn leads down the western side of the water to the dam at its southern end. There is room to park cars (at SP 853 965, SP 844 968 and SP 850 955).

Access to the plantation and the hide on the island is only granted to members of the LROS, but most birds on the reservoir can be seen from the road.

Calendar
Resident: Great Crested Grebe, Tufted Duck, Ruddy Duck, Sparrowhawk, Little Owl, Tree Sparrow, Willow Tit, Yellowhammer.

April–October: Black-necked Grebe (scarce), Gadwall, Garganey, Red-crested Pochard, Common Scoter, Osprey, Hobby, Little Ringed Plover, Ringed Plover, Dunlin, Little Stint, Curlew Sandpiper, Ruff, Black-tailed Godwit, Spotted Redshank, Greenshank, Wood Sandpiper, Green Sandpiper, Common Sandpiper, Little Gull, Mediterranean Gull, Yellow-legged Gull, Kittiwake, Common Tern, Arctic Tern, Black Tern, Yellow Wagtail, White Wagtail, Spotted Flycatcher.

November–March: Bewick's Swan, Greylag Goose, Wigeon, Pintail, Smew, Goosander, Ruddy Duck, Golden Plover, Lapwing, Dunlin, Mediterranean Gull, Iceland Gull, Glaucous Gull, (both scarce), Fieldfare.

40 RUTLAND WATER   OS Sheet 141

Habitat

Constructed as recently as 1975, Rutland Water is the largest man-made reservoir in Britain, with 3100 acres (1250 ha) of open water. It is under the ownership of Anglian Water Services, with an impressive one-third of the shoreline, at the western end of the reservoir (a 350-acre (130 ha) area), having been set aside as a nature reserve, which is managed by the Leicestershire and Rutland Trust for Nature Conservation (LRTNC). The reservoir is extensively used for other recreational pursuits, such as cycling, fishing and sailing, but the reserve end is relatively undisturbed. The reservoir has very quickly become established as an exceptional place for attracting birds, in particular, wildfowl. An idea of its importance can be gained from the fact that it regularly holds over 10,000 birds during the winter months, which has contributed to its designation as an SSSI, SPA and Ramsar Site.

The reservoir was formed by the construction of a dam at the eastern end and subsequent flooding of two shallow valleys of formerly agricultural land. The surrounding area is thus one of gentle shelving natural banks given over to mainly arable farmland away from the immediate vicinity of the reservoir.

The reserve consists of a range of habitats including three shallow lagoons, with purpose built islands and rafts to attract breeding terns, reedbeds, ancient meadows, hedgerows and small areas of scrub. Continuing planting of trees around the reserve, mainly willow, ash and alder, will lead to more extensive woodland cover in time and, presently, there are mature deciduous woodlands around Lax Hill and Gibbet Gorse.

Away from the reserve area there are plantations of young conifers and hardwoods at the base of the Hambleton peninsula and mature deciduous woodland at Hambleton, Armley and Barnsdale Woods. The dam itself provides a vantage point for looking over the eastern end of the reservoir and also provides a large area of stonework and open grassland as additional habitats.

Species

During the winter months the sheer numbers of wildfowl and gulls make this area outstanding and certainly the single most important inland site in the region. In addition to the totals of wildfowl and roosting gulls there are some waders and usually large wintering flocks of finches around the reservoir edges.

The area has a reputation for attracting vagrant divers of all three species, with Great Northern being almost regular and Black-throated increasingly more common in recent winters. Wintering Great Crested

Grebes reach 400–800, with over 1,000 recorded on occasions, and both Red-necked and Slavonian Grebes are regular visitors. The recent increase in numbers of inland Cormorants often sees an impressive 500+ birds around the reservoir, with large numbers drying their wings on perches around the reserve lagoons. A few Bewick's Swans are sometimes present and the resident flock of feral Greylag and Snow Geese may be joined by stray Pink-footed and White-fronted Geese. The principal species of duck by weight of numbers are: Wigeon (3,500), Mallard and Tufted Duck (1,000 each), Gadwall (1,000, early winter), Shoveler and Pochard (500), Ruddy Duck (400) and Goldeneye (300). The above are of course general numbers which are exceeded at certain times and in some winters when larger arrivals of certain species may be evident. Additionally a wide range of other duck occur, with up to 50 Goosander the most common, but regular records of Smew and small numbers of such marine species as Long-tailed Duck, Common Scoter, Scaup and Red-breasted Merganser.

Most species are outnumbered by the impressive total of up to 3,500 Coot. Water Rails winter around the lagoons and are often heard calling, with the patient observer sometimes being treated to good views from the hides. Raptor interest includes the resident Sparrowhawks and Kestrels, with regular if brief visits from the spectacular Peregrine, turning some good days into exceptional ones. Wintering waders are principally those of inland grasslands with flocks of Golden Plover and Lapwing but in addition a significant flock of Ruff are usually present, a few Dunlin and odd Green Sandpiper winter. Snipe are to be seen around the lagoons, but although present in small numbers, Jack Snipe rarely offer views, being secreted in the short vegetation around the water's edge.

With such a large body of water the roosting flocks of gulls can be dispersed over a wide area but are best watched from Gadwall or Goldeneye hides on Egleton reserve. The roost contains mainly small gulls, Black-headed and Common but also numbers of Herring Gull and up to 400 Great Black-backed Gulls. The rarer species are indeed rare, with few records of Glaucous or Iceland Gulls, whilst Mediterranean Gulls, which are most regular in the late autumn and early spring, are becoming more regular in midwinter. Owing to the huge size of the reserve, few observers watch the gull roost at Rutland on a regular basis and no doubt more scarce species would be recorded given better and more comprehensive observer coverage.

Although both Long-eared and Short-eared Owls occur, their numbers have apparently declined in recent years. Old hedges of hawthorn around the reserve may harbour flocks of Fieldfare and Redwing until their berry crop is exhausted, and Tree Sparrows can be seen at close quarters coming to the feeders in front of the Birdwatching Centre. Alder plantations behind lagoons II and III and along the Lyndon Reserve usually hold feeding flocks of both Siskin and Redpoll, and Barnsdale Avenue is a good place to look for Brambling.

The first Sand Martins and Chiffchaffs pass through during mid March but spring migration is at a peak from mid April onwards, with all the regular summer visitors such as Willow Warblers and Blackcaps arriving to breed. Black-necked Grebes in their full breeding finery are regular in small numbers, mainly favouring lagoon III or the North Arm, while that exquisite little duck, the Garganey, is also a regular visitor to the lagoons. With a wealth of potential food available it is perhaps not

Osprey

surprising that passage Ospreys have become a regular sight, with some individuals staying off passage for a few days when they may adopt a favoured old tree for feeding, sometimes offering prolonged views.

Hobbies have undergone something of an increase in the North Midlands in recent years and they can be watched hunting over the reserve from May onwards, usually feeding on emergent insects, but later in the summer chasing the flocks of hirundines and Swifts; up to 4,000 of the latter may be present at the western end of the reservoir in May.

The shallow lagoons provide good feeding habitat for migrant waders and, in addition to the regular inland species such as Little Ringed and Ringed Plovers, Redshank, Greenshank and Common Sandpiper, there are regular visits from normally more coastal species such as Black-tailed Godwit, Oystercatcher, Grey Plover, Whimbrel and Turnstone. A small population of 20–25 (maximum 50) pairs of Common Terns have been attracted to nest on specially constructed rafts on the reserve, while early May also sees a regular passage of other species, in variable numbers, mainly Arctic and Black Terns, given the right weather conditions, but also Little Gulls and Kittiwakes, the former often associated with the Black Tern movements.

Sedge and Reed Warblers nest in the reedbeds and rough vegetation around the reserve, the latter often attracting the attentions of the local Cuckoos which parasitise them regularly at this site. Other breeding warblers include Grasshopper and Garden Warbler and Lesser Whitethroat. The numbers of breeding Nightingales seems to be in decline but their far-carrying song can still be heard from Barnsdale and in Hambleton Wood. Northern Wheatears may frequent open grassy areas, for example at the dam, during the spring passage periods and occasional Redstarts also pass through the reserve area.

The reserve attracts a good variety of breeding species, of which the most interesting include Great Crested Grebe, 15–20 pairs of Cormorant, Egyptian Goose, Shelduck, Gadwall and Ruddy Duck. In common with some other sites in the region, odd Goldeneye have summered in recent years. Little Ringed Plovers breed in most years and a single pair of Oystercatcher are almost annual in their breeding attempts. As mentioned, up to 50 pairs of Common Tern can be seen (nesting on the tern rafts in the lagoons) from the hides. The plantation of ash trees behind the Birdwatching Centre has a series of nest boxes which support a thriving colony of Tree Sparrows, and amongst the other summer visitors, Turtle Doves can be heard purring from the old hedgrows around the meadows.

Autumn passage starts in mid July with waders and continues in earnest through to November when wintering thrush flocks will often be arriving. Black-necked Grebes are again regular and there are normally up to ten Garganey around the lagoons during the early autumn period. Peak numbers of some wildfowl species also occur at this time when there have been counts of, for example, 1,800 Gadwall, 700 Shoveler and 2,000 Tufted Duck. Red-crested Pochards are regular in small numbers, although as everywhere their origins are open to question.

As well as the hunting Hobbies raptor interest may again include Osprey and the occasional passage Common Buzzard and Marsh Harrier. Open muddy areas around the edges of the reservoir, especially the lagoons, Manton Bay and the North Arm, attract increasing numbers of waders, with the same species present as in the spring but also an increasing variety, often with records of Knot, Little Stint, Curlew Sandpiper (sometimes in small flocks in good years), Spotted Redshank and Wood Sandpiper. Easterly winds on the coast will bring in flocks of Black Terns, which may peak in excess of 100 individuals, and small parties of Little Gulls and Kittiwakes. Similar conditions in the late autumn, from late September onwards, also regularly produce a few records of Rock Pipits which favour the stony areas such as those at the dam.

Rutland Water's inland location, away from any major river system, makes the occurrence of rarities infrequent and unpredictable in spite of its large size. Some outstanding birds have been found over the years since its construction, however, and there is always the chance of locating a rarity amongst the wealth of commoner birds. Rarities have included Night Heron, Cattle Egret, Little Egret (4), Great White Egret (2), Ring-necked Duck, Lesser Scaup, Red-footed Falcon, Collared Pratincole, White-rumped and Pectoral Sandpipers, Ring-billed Gull, Caspian, Bridled and White-winged Black Terns, Alpine Swift, Red-throated Pipit, Cetti's and Savi's Warblers.

Timing

First-class birdwatching may be enjoyed here at any time of year. The sheer size of the reserve easily fills a full day's birdwatching. It is best to visit the eastern areas of the reservoir in the early morning before they are disturbed and while the light is good. For viewing the reserve the light is best in the afternoons and is behind the observer for viewing the gull roost from the hides. Visitors to the Egleton Reserve should walk to the Goldeneye hide arm in the mornings, with the sun behind the viewing positions, and then watch from Lagoons II and III in the afternoon to again take advantage of the best light conditions.

Access

Rutland Water lies one mile (1.6 km) southeast of Oakham and is easily reached from the A1 via the A606 west of Stamford, and from the A47 along the A6003 north of Uppingham. The Anglian Water Birdwatching Centre and Egleton Reserve are reached by turning off the A6003, 1 mile (1.6 km) south of Oakham towards Egleton and following the signposted road to the Centre (at SK 878 073). Staff at the Centre are very help-

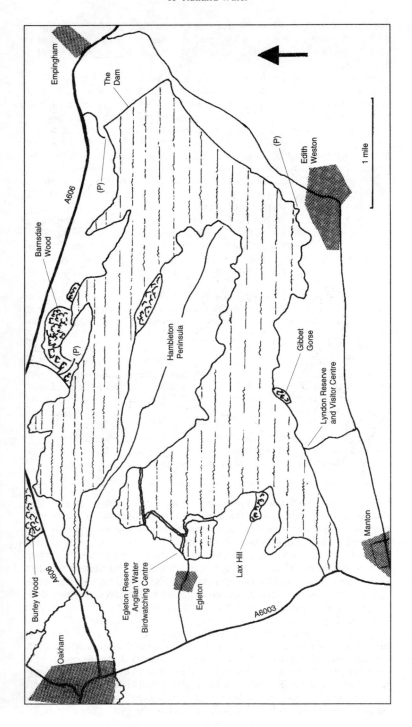

Empingham

The Dam

(P)

(P)

Edith Weston

1 mile

A606

Barnsdale Wood

(P)

Hambleton Peninsula

Gibbet Gorse

Lyndon Reserve and Visitor Centre

Burley Wood

A606

Egleton Reserve Anglian Water Birdwatching Centre

Egleton

Lax Hill

Manton

A6003

Oakham

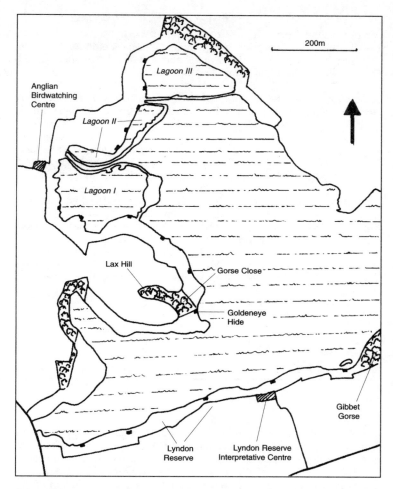

ful and have up-to-date information about birds on the reserve. The reserve is open between 9 am and 5 pm from April to October, and between 9 am and 4 pm during the remainder of the year. A permit is required and is available from the Centre.

The Lyndon Centre is reached by turning east off the A6003, 2.5 miles (4 km) south of Oakham through Manton village and then taking the signposted minor road to the Centre (at SK 893 056). Lyndon Reserve is open from 10 am to 4 pm at weekends and on Tuesdays, Wednesdays, Thursdays and Fridays from May to October. A permit is required and is available from the Centre upon arrival. The cycle track east of the centre gives good, elevated views over the South Arm. To view the dam and adjacent areas of open water, which is good for grebes and diving duck during the winter, park in the signposted car park at the northern end of the reservoir. The North Arm is best viewed from the end of the minor road (at SK 888 086) or from the car park (at SK 895 080). It is worth scanning for raptors over Burley Wood to the north but access is restricted to members of the Rutland Natural History Society.

Calendar

Resident: Little Grebe, Great Crested Grebe, Cormorant, Grey Heron, Greylag Goose, Snow Goose, Egyptian Goose, Shelduck, Gadwall, Shoveler, Tufted Duck, Ruddy Duck, Sparrowhawk, Great Spotted and Green Woodpeckers, Nuthatch, Tree Sparrow.

November–March: Red-throated Diver, Black-throated Diver and Great Northern Diver (all scarce), Red-necked Grebe, Slavonian Grebe, Bewick's Swan (scarce), Wigeon, Pintail, Pochard, Scaup (scarce), Red-crested Pochard (scarce), Long-tailed Duck (rare), Goldeneye, Smew, Goosander, Peregrine, Water Rail, Golden Plover, Dunlin, Ruff, Jack Snipe, Green Sandpiper, gull roost, Short-eared Owl and Long-eared Owl (both scarce in recent years), Fieldfare, Redwing, Redpoll, Siskin.

April–October: Black-necked Grebe, Garganey, Hobby, Little Ringed Plover, Ringed Plover, Little Stint, Curlew Sandpiper, Dunlin, Black-tailed Godwit, Redshank, Spotted Redshank, Greenshank, Wood Sandpiper, Common Sandpiper, Little Gull, Common Tern, Arctic Tern, Black Tern, Turtle Dove, Cuckoo, Rock Pipit (scarce autumn), Yellow Wagtail, Nightingale, Northern Wheatear, Grasshopper, Reed and Sedge Warblers, Garden Warbler, Lesser Whitethroat, Spotted Flycatcher.

41 SOAR VALLEY
GRAVEL PITS
OS Sheets 129 and 140

Habitat

The River Soar flows roughly south to north through Leicestershire, and in places the meandering river has been straightened and canalised. Since the 1950s sand and gravel have been extracted from the Soar Valley, for a distance of about 3 miles (4.8 km) north of Leicester, leaving a chain of flooded disused gravel workings from Cossington in the north, to Watermead, which lies just inside the city boundary, to the south. Although many of these pits are now used for leisure activities, in particular water sports, and others have been filled in, there are still relatively undisturbed areas to be found which provide suitable habitats for many species of birds.

The stretch from Wanlip south to Watermead is now a country park, controlled by Leicestershire County Council. There are car parks, footpaths and even two hides situated at Birstall. All this has, however, been something of a mixed blessing for wildlife, for although the habitats are now protected, and to some extent managed, the benefits have been countered by a large increase in disturbance from the growing numbers of visitors attracted to the site.

The principal habitats in this section include the River Soar itself and its banks, along with various flooded pits, some with islands, grazing fields, reedbeds, scrub, hedgerows and trees. The whole area is subject to winter flooding, which can greatly increase the areas of standing water.

Species

In spite of the large number of human visitors the pits support some interesting breeding species, including a few pairs of Grey Heron at Wanlip. Several pairs of Common Terns have been attracted to breed on islands at Cossington and Watermead and also on special tern rafts at the latter locality. Breeding waders are typical of grassland and gravel pit sites, with Lapwing, Little Ringed Plover and Redshank, the latter species having declined seriously in recent times, however, a feature of many inland and coastal localities.

Passerine breeders include Yellow Wagtails, in the meadows and on grassy islands, with that typical songster of wet scrub edges, the Sedge Warbler, being common along the riverbanks. A few pairs of Grasshopper Warbler also breed, but Reed Warblers are virtually restricted as breeding birds to the reedbed at Wanlip, although birds may be heard singing from the newly planted stands of reed at Watermead. The trees and scrub around Wanlip also harbour the declining Turtle Dove, but here the purring song is more often heard than the birds are seen.

A recent success story for local habitat management and conservation in action is found at Wanlip, where an artificial Sand Martin bank has been constructed, and is now occupied by the breeding martins. Kingfishers may be seen flashing along the river and canal at any time of year and they probably breed somewhere in the area.

Spring passage may enhance the numbers of terns present, with parties of Arctic and Black Terns joining the breeding Commons during spells of east to southeasterly winds in late April and May. Flocks of hirundines feeding over the water may attract the unwelcome attentions of a hunting Hobby, and that master fisherman, the Osprey, is sometimes encountered on passage by a few lucky observers. The Soar Valley seems to have a particular attraction for migrant passerines, possibly enhanced by its north–south orientation. In April and May the grassy areas may hold large flocks of Yellow Wagtails, with a few White Wagtails, the odd Whinchat and Northern Wheatear. Any of the scrub areas are worth a look for warblers such as Willow Warbler, Whitethroat, Lesser Whitethroat and Blackcap, and even Redstarts have been located within the city boundary.

Waders are scarce in spring but the autumn passage brings the odd Greenshank, Dunlin, Ruff or Common Sandpiper in addition to the breeding species, but most of these birds move on quickly, as a rule, probably due to the high level of disturbance.

Wildfowl numbers reach a peak in winter when the pits are often at their most productive with lower levels of disturbance being an obvious factor. The large feral flocks of Canada and Greylag Geese are sometimes joined by parties of wild geese, and Bewick's and Whooper Swans will sometimes join the herds of Mute Swans feeding out on the flooded fields. Principal duck species are Mallard, Wigeon, Teal, Gadwall, Shoveler, Tufted Duck and Pochard, with a few Goldeneye and Goosander also being regular, the latter usually at Birstall or Watermead. The Birstall section is the best locality for finding Water Rail, a few of which regularly winter and may sometimes be located in front of the hides. Wintering waders include Green Sandpiper and both Snipe and Jack Snipe, the latter as usual being difficult to see, but they can occasionally be flushed from the 'floodplain' between Birstall and Watermead.

This area also occasionally holds Short-eared Owls, as does the private area immediately north of Wanlip. Long-eared Owls occur in some winters but they are irregular, although when present they have been seen roosting in the hawthorn and willow scrub at Birstall. There may be a small gull roost at Watermead or Wanlip, where odd Mediterranean Gulls have been noted, but more usually the gulls gather here in a pre-roost assembly before flying off to roost at Swithland Reservoir.

Timing

The Country Park is rarely as full of people as Bradgate Park can be, but sailing, fishing and windsurfing cause more direct disturbance which affects the numbers of birds present. An early start to a visit is therefore recommended between April and October. Timing is less crucial in the winter but bear in mind that many of the footpaths may be impassable when the area floods after heavy rain.

Access

The gravel pit complex can roughly be divided into four sections from north to south: Cossington, Wanlip, Birstall and Watermead. Cossington is the least disturbed section as it is farthest from the main car parks and parts of the area are private. The northernmost pit can be viewed from the lay-by on the B5328 between Rothley and Cossington (at SK 601 130). From here a public footpath leads past two pits to the canal towpath and south to Wanlip Gravel Pits. The area between Cossington and Wanlip is now mostly private.

Access to the Wanlip section is off the B673 between Wanlip and Syston. Approaching from Wanlip the car park is on the right at (SK 606 108). This is the start of the Country Park, and well marked footpaths cover the whole area. There are four large pits, most of which are used for sailing and windsurfing, but a small, shallow pit just to the west of the car park, has a reedbed and extensive willow scrub and is well worth a look. From here it is possible to walk south to the Birstall section or alternatively park in the car park at the end of Meadow Lane in Birstall (SK 603 095). This area is designated as a nature reserve and has two hides, but these are usually only open at weekends. Most of the pits are well vegetated with reed and bulrush and the surrounding areas are thick with willow and hawthorn scrub.

The final section at Watermead is best reached on foot along the canal towpath from Birstall. This leads past a large overgrown field, once a gravel pit, but now filled and left as a floodplain. Watermead has two large pits, one of which is used for windsurfing but terns and waders still breed on the island in the pit. The other pit adjacent to the busy ring road, and actually within the city boundary, is a nature reserve and has two small hides. The fields on the opposite side of the river are often flooded in the winter and are worth scanning for wildfowl.

Calendar

Resident: Great Crested Grebe, Little Grebe, Grey Heron, Tufted Duck, Sparrowhawk, Kingfisher, Tree Sparrow.

November–March: Cormorant, Wigeon, Gadwall, Teal, Shoveler, Pochard, Goldeneye, Goosander, Ruddy Duck, Peregrine (rare), Water

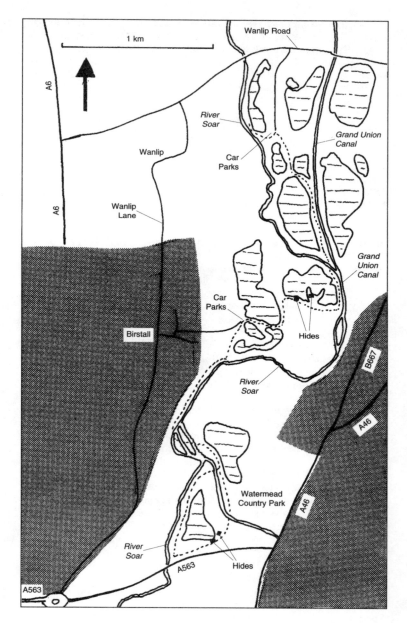

Rail, Snipe, Jack Snipe, Green Sandpiper, Long-eared and Short-eared Owl (both scarce).

April–June: Garganey (scarce), Osprey (rare), Hobby, Little Ringed Plover, Ringed Plover, Redshank, Common Sandpiper, Common Tern, Arctic Tern, Black Tern, Turtle Dove, Yellow Wagtail, White Wagtail, Grasshopper, Reed and Sedge Warblers, Northern Wheatear, Whinchat.

July–October: Garganey (scarce), Hobby, Little Ringed Plover, Ringed Plover, Dunlin, Ruff, Redshank, Greenshank, Common Sandpiper, Green Sandpiper, Common, Arctic and Black Terns, Yellow Wagtail, Whinchat.

ADDITIONAL SITES

Name	Launde.
Grid Reference	OS sheet 141, SK 79/04
Habitat	Open parkland with scattered oaks; medieval fishponds, deciduous woodland along the upper reaches of the River Chater.
Species	Sparrowhawk, Kingfisher, all three woodpeckers, 2–3 pairs of Redstart, six species of warbler, Nuthatch.
Access	Roads and public footpaths provide adaquate access. Please respect the privacy of the Abbey. Kingfishers (at SK 798 047). Lesser Spotted Woodpeckers and Redstarts in oaks near Abbey (SK 796 044) and along valley towards Sanvey Castle.

Name	Exton Park.
Grid Reference	OS Sheet 130, SK 91–2/11, SK 95/12
Habitat	Private park; mature deciduous woodland (mainly ash, beech and oak), small lakes, arable fields, some recent conifer plantations.
Species	Fort Henry lakes (SK 950 120) have breeding Great Crested Grebe, Tufted and Ruddy Duck. Tunneley Wood (SK 932 123), Woodcock, all three woodpeckers, Tree Pipit, Grasshopper Warbler. In winter small numbers of Hawfinch occasional around hornbeams in the northwest corner of the wood.
Timing	Spring and winter.
Access	No vehicular access but pedestrian access is allowed along certain roads and footpaths. A 2-mile (3.2 km) walk along the road northeast of Exton village leads past Tunneley Wood and Fort Henry Lakes.

Name	Welland Valley (Caldecott–Barrowden).
Grid Reference	OS Sheet 141, SK 87–93/94–99
Habitat	Flat river valley with grazing meadows, hawthorn hedgerows and scrub along dismantled railway.
Species	Mandarin used to breed at Barrowden. Turtle Doves and Lesser Whitethroat along the railway in summer. Barn Owl and Short-eared Owl sometimes in winter, (especially at SP 883 953). Kingfishers, a few pairs of Corn Bunting around Seaton.
Timing	Summer and winter.
Access	By road along the B672 east of Caldecott from where there are several roads and footpaths south to the river.

Name   Thornton Reservoir.
Grid Reference SK 474 075
Habitat   Open water reservoir.
Species   Wildfowl, grebes, terns (spring–autumn), small gull roost.
Timing   Peak numbers in winter.
Access   South of Markfield.

Name   Beacon Hill.
Grid Reference SK 51/14
Habitat   Heath, scrub and woodland.
Species   Woodpeckers, Tree Pipit, Wood Warbler, Nuthatch, Brambling, Siskin.
Timing   All year.
Access   Situated near Woodhouse Eaves.

Name   Outwoods.
Grid Reference SK 51/17
Habitat   Mixed woodland.
Species   Woodpeckers, Wood Warbler.
Timing   Spring/summer.
Access   Southwest of Loughborough.

Name   Ulverscroft.
Grid Reference SK 48–49/11
Habitat   Heath, scrub, woodland.
Species   Tree Pipit, Redstart, Pied Flycatcher (occasional).
Timing   Spring/summer.
Access   North of Markfield; a LRTNC reserve.

Name   Aylestone Meadows.
Grid Reference SK 575 018
Habitat   River and flood meadows.
Species   Kingfisher, Reed and Sedge Warbler, Ring Ouzel (occasional on passage).
Timing   All year.
Access   Southwest of Leicester City Centre.

NOTTINGHAMSHIRE

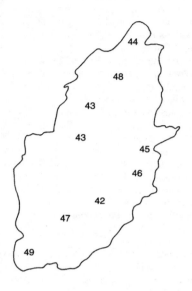

42 Hoveringham Gravel Pits
43 Sherwood Forest District
44 The Idle Valley
45 Girton and Besthorpe
46 South Muskham Pits

47 Colwick/Netherfield/Holme
    Pierrepont
48 Lound
49 Attenborough Nature
    Reserve/Attenborough and
    Long Eaton New Workings

Habitat

Much of the land between Hoveringham and Bleasby, to the northeast, has had extensive gravel and sand extraction by Tarmac Roadstone for many years, and there are currently plans for further expansion of the workings. Many of the pits created by these extractions have proved to be of ornithological interest over the years, but in contrast to many other such complexes, many have now been filled and returned to agricultural use. However, a small number remain, which, because of their size and location, are considered to make Hoveringham one of the premier birdwatching sites in Nottinhgamshire. The Trent Valley is a major overland migration route for birds and the lakes at Hoveringham are often a magnet for such migratory species.

The largest pit in the complex, recently enlarged and reflooded, is used by Nottinghamshire County Sailing Club for sailing and windsurfing during the months of March to December. There is a very small lake to the west of the main lake, used as a training lake by the sailing club, and another slightly larger lake to the northeast of the main lake, which is undisturbed by water sports. These lakes are bordered on one side by the River Trent and on the other two sides by farmland with, on the west side, a meadow which has SSSI status.

The main lake itself has rather steeply sloping, grassed sides but the other lakes are surrounded with more mature vegetation and have some shallow edges. The river has many bushes along its bank nearest the lake, and on the other side there is a steep wooded escarpment.

There are, in addition, several other lakes or pits in the area, but only one is accessible to the public. This pit which lies to the north of Hoveringham village, directly alongside Thurgaton railay station, is currently drained for further extraction. This pit or lake has the railway running alongside but is otherwise surrounded by farmland and has a small mixed deciduous wood next to it.

Species

The winter months bring wildfowl and gulls to the complex and a variety of species to the surrounding farmland and small woodlands. Typical wintering species include Great Crested and Little Grebes, Cormorant, Mute Swan, Mallard, Tufted Duck, Wigeon, Teal and Gadwall, with Goldeneye and Pochard also regular. Frequent records of rarer species such as Pintail, Goosander and Shoveler are logged, and occasionally odd Scaup or Smew may be found. There have also been records of the rarer grebes and divers in recent years and as the main lake is now much larger in area there is an increasing chance of the occurrence of these species in the future.

There has been a gull roost on the main lake in past years, with the principal species being Black-headed, and lesser numbers of Common Gulls with a few of the larger species. There have been occasional records of Mediterranean, Iceland and Glaucous Gulls so the roost is always worth close scrutiny during the winter months.

The surrounding fields often have flocks of Lapwings and Golden Plover during the winter, and flocks of Redwing and Fieldfare may often be encountered in the early winter period. Wild geese and swans often pass through but seldom linger in the area. Small passerines are represented by such species as Linnet, Reed Bunting, Yellowhammer, Long-tailed Tit and Meadow Pipit, all of which are common, whilst Rock Pipits are occasional and one or two Stonechats and Grey Wagtails usually winter around the main lake. Green and Great Spotted Woodpeckers are often heard and seen in the areas of woodland and raptor sightings include regular Sparrowhawks, with occasional Merlin and Peregrine hunting the surrounding fields.

The first summer migrants, Sand Martin, Chiffchaff and a few Northern Wheatears, arrive during late March when local breeding birds such as Shelduck, Redshank and Oystercatcher first appear on the surrounding fields. The banks of the lakes and the River Trent unfortunately offer little suitable wader habitat so only small numbers of Common and Green Sandpipers are regular in spring, with occasional visits from Greenshank, Sanderling and Turnstone. The drained pit adjacent ot the railway line offers better wader habitat, especially for Ringed and Little Ringed Plovers and passage Dunlin. Common Terns also breed in this pit and flight to feed over the river and the main lake, which also attracts passage parties of Arctic and Black Terns in suitable weather conditions.

The main sailing lake also attracts feeding flocks of Swifts, Swallows, Sand and House Martins during the spring and summer when insects are emerging and on the wing, and summer migrants such as Willow Warbler, Whitethroat, Sedge Warbler and Yellow Wagtail all join resident Meadow Pipits and Reed Buntings in breeding on areas around the main lake. The small woodland across the River Trent has breeding Tawny Owl and most of the common woodland species, and in addition has a small heronry. That dashing falcon, the Hobby, is also an occasional visitor during the late spring and summer months.

The autumn return migration period often brings in good numbers of Black Terns, which can be seen hawking insects over the main lake, joined by the occasional Arctic Tern and Little Gull. The more regular waders such as Common and Green Sandpipers are sometimes joined by rarer species including Little Stint, Ruff, Grey Plover, Wood Sandpiper, Bar and Black-tailed Godwits and the occasional Curlew Sandpiper. Passage Whinchat are regular, often perching on tall weedy stems and small bushes, and Garganey are also most regular at this season, although in their more sombre eclipse plumage they are less easy to identify.

Over the years, with its strategic location on the Trent Valley route, the site has produced a creditable list of scarce and rare birds for an inland county, from the three rarer grebes, Black and Red-necked and Slavonian, to Black-throated and Great Northern Divers, and to lost seabirds such as Fulmar and Leach's Petrel. Wader highlights range from Temminck's Stint and Red-necked Phalarope from the east, to Buff-breasted Sandpiper from the nearctic, with more expected finds including Osprey and Bittern; the best of the passage passerines being Black Redstart, Water Pipit and Snow Bunting. Ring-billed Gull is the most recent rarity to have occurred with nearby Bleasby Pits holding the first Redhead for the Western Palearctic in March 1996.

Timing

Hoveringham pits have something of interest to birdwatchers at all times of year and because they are large stretches of water on a migra-

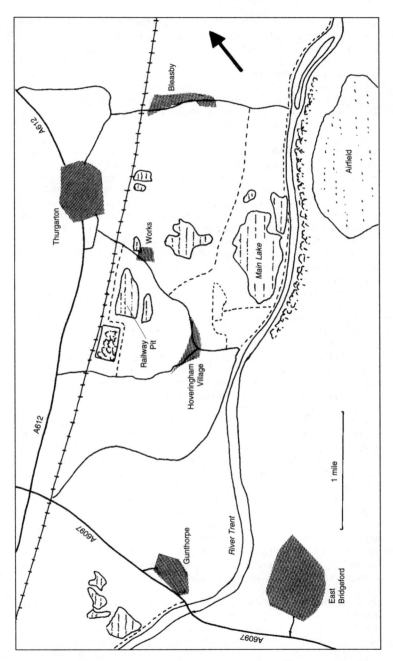

tion route, unusual birds can drop in at any time. However, the best periods are probably November to March when there is little disturbance from water sports on the sailing lake, and during the spring and autumn migration periods. Late afternoon and evening during the winter months is the time to watch the gull roost but at other times of year early morning visits are best, before disturbance from sailing begins.

Access

Hoveringham village is situated 2 miles (3.2 km) east of Lowdham, which is about 6 miles (9.6 km) northeast of Nottingham. It is also 2 miles (3.2 km) south of Thurgaton, which is about 11 miles (17.6 km) from Newark-on-Trent. If travelling from Nottingham, pass through Lowdham on the A612 and after 1 mile (1.6 km) turn right onto a minor road singposted to Hoveringham. In the village turn right at the T junction near the church, continue to a sharp right-hand bend in the road, and a few hundred yds/m further on, park in the large car park on the left (SK 702 462).

If travelling from Newark or Southwell, go through Thurgaton and immediately after the village take a left turn onto a minor road and cross the railway crossing. After 1 mile (1.6 km) the road passes through Hoveringham village; continue on this road to the sharp right-hand bend and park in the car park on the left (see above). Walk back along the road to the bend and go through the gate onto the public footpath along the River Trent, with the river to the right. Continue along the footpath through the SSSI meadow for a few hundred yds/m then through another gate, and the main sailing lake is on the left (SK 712 472). The best views of the lake are obtained a little farther on, when the riverbank path is closer to the lake. There is also another smaller lake at the far end of the sailing lake. It is not possible to walk all the way around the lake since much of the land is private.

To reach the railway pit (SK 697 481), park near the railway crossing and take the public footpath to the southwest, adjacent to the railway line. Please note that parking is severely limited and that visitors to this working site should stay strictly to the footpaths.

Calendar

Resident: Little Grebe, Great Crested Grebe, Grey Heron, Mute Swan, Lapwing, Grey Partridge, Red-legged Partridge, Sparrowhawk, Little Owl, Tawny Owl, Kingfisher, Green Woodpecker, Great Spotted Woodpecker, Skylark, Meadow Pipit, Long-tailed Tit, Linnet, Yellowhammer, Reed Bunting.

October–March: Wigeon, Teal, Gadwall, Shoveler, Pochard, Tufted Duck, Goldeneye, Goosander, Golden Plover, Snipe, Green Sandpiper, gulls, Grey Wagtail, Stonechat, Fieldfare , Redwing, Goldfinch, Redpoll, Bullfinch; in addition scarce but regular visitors to look out for include: Pintail, Common Scoter, Smew, Red-breasted Merganser, Merlin, Peregrine, Jack Snipe, Rock Pipit, Brambling, Siskin, Twite.

April–September: Shelduck, Garganey, Oystercatcher, Little Ringed Plover, Ringed Plover, Sanderling, Little Stint, Dunlin, Ruff, Whimbrel, Curlew, Redshank, Greenshank, Common Sandpiper, Turnstone, Common Tern, Black Tern, Turtle Dove, Cuckoo, Swift, Sand Martin, Swallow, House Martin, Yellow Wagtail, White Wagtail, Whinchat, Northern Wheatear, warblers. Scarce visitors may include Hobby, Curlew Sandpiper, godwits, Wood Sandpiper, Little Gull, Kittiwake, Sandwich Tern, Little Tern and Grasshopper Warbler.

43 SHERWOOD FOREST DISTRICT

Habitat

The area of central Nottinghamshire, between Nottingham and Worksop, long associated with the myths and legends of Robin Hood and the Sheriff of Nottingham, has changed a great deal since the time when the Royal Forest of Sherwood stretched in an unbroken belt of ancient woodland for 20 miles (32 km) north and south and 8 miles (12.8 km) east to west. The area of ancient forest has been reduced to small fragments, but successive generations of landed gentry have created estates with areas of parkland, ornamental lakes and younger woodlands which have all added to the diversity of the landscape, still such an exceptional area for birdwatching. The present landscape is a wonderfully varied mix of old deciduous woodland, parkland, lakes, heathlands, shelter-belts and younger coniferous plantations interspersed with arable farmland.

For convenience therefore this section deals with a number of different birdwatching sites, all of which lie within the Sherwood Forest district, including the following three major sites: Sherwood Pines Forest Park (Clipstone Forest), Sherwood Country Park and Budby South Forest (the Birklands) and finally Thoresby, and Welbeck estates and Clumber Park (the Dukeries). Some of the estates and woodlands are well known due to their special attractions in the form of scarce breeding and wintering birds, and the area as a whole is a very popular tourist attraction.

Of the remnants of the ancient forest, characterised by its stunted, gnarled old oaks, one of the best known is Sherwood Country Park, sometimes referred to as the Birklands, a tract of woodland which holds the famous Major Oak. This woodland is managed by Nottinghamshire County Council and has been designated an SSSI due to the wealth of wildlife associated with the old oak woodland, and in particular, the large variety of insects attracted to the oaks. Many of the other woodlands in the region are managed by Forest Enterprise (Sherwood and Lincolnshire Forest District), and recent management within many of these forests has seen a marked shift to more wildlife-orientated developments, increasing their value to birds and birdwatchers alike.

The Sherwood Pines Forest Park (Clipstone Forest), the largest area of forest open to the public in the East Midlands, acts as the flagship for the Nottinghamshire Forest Enterprise. The main habitats in the Forest Park are coniferous woodland, which is at varying ages and states of harvesting and replanting, and areas of open sandy heathland. Wide open rides and tracks dissect the woodland blocks, and three trails of 1 mile (1.6 km), 2.5 miles (4 km) and 6 miles (9.6 km) are colour-signed, leading through the variety of habitats. The forest conservation plan has been designed to benefit the wildlife of the site. Here, sandy heathland found in the forest is being maintained for its wildlife, in particular Nightjars, Woodlark, Tree Pipit and other heathland birds, and the coniferous woodland is also being managed in an attempt to increase its potential value to wildlife.

There are other Forest Enterprise woodlands open to the public in the nearby area including Thieves and Harlow Woods, Blidworth Wood and Haywoods Oaks, the latter named after the collection of ancient oaks which have now been made more visible by conifer harvesting. Details of the facilities available at all of these woodlands can be found on a well produced Forest Enterprise brochure, available from the Forest Enterprise Edwinstowe Office, and entitled *Forest Walks in Sherwood*.

Of the old estates in the region, the best known are Clumber Park, Thoresby Park and Welbeck, all of which are known together as the Dukeries, the latter two being large private estates, some of which can, however, be adequately viewed from public roads. The 3800 acres (1530 ha) of Clumber Park are owned and managed by the National Trust. The park boasts the longest continuous avenue of lime trees anywhere in Europe amongst its wealth of woodlands, which includes large blocks of old oak, sweet chestnut, horse chestnut and beech, interspersed mainly along the park boundaries with younger plantations of conifers. There are also splendid ornamental trees and an understorey of rhododendron around the chapel area, where a block of yews is of importance to the Hawfinch population. Farmland and some open heathland make up most of the rest of the area, with a series of large man-made lakes set in the valley of the River Poulter, which runs through the centre of the park. The wide roadside verges are mainly short grass which spread into a mixed cover of longer rough grasses, bracken and birch scrub around the heathland clearings.

Thoresby Park is mainly private land with restricted access, and viewing is from a minor road which passes the northern side of the park. The Welbeck estate, presently owned by the Bentinck's, an offshoot of the Duke of Portland's estate, has much the same mix of woodland and farmland, with again an impressive series of ornamental lakes, some of which can be overlooked from the minor road which runs from Carburton to Cuckney.

Species

The coniferous woodlands, especially Sherwood Pines Forest Park (Clipstone Forest), hold a typical cross-section of associated species, with good numbers of Goldcrest, Coal Tit, Treecreeper, Great Spotted and Green Woodpecker. As with all coniferous woodlands, however, winter can seem a very bleak time for birds as the communal feeding flocks of small passerines rove over large areas of woodland, being absent from extensive blocks for long periods when such spots can seem totally birdless. Depending on the fruiting of the birch trees and the pines there will be variable sized flocks of of Redpolls and Siskins, with a few of both species staying into late spring and breeding occasionally. Common Crossbills also occur annually but again their numbers vary with the size of the irruptions from their strongholds in Scandinavia and northern Siberia. The first signs of irruptions occur in June when the first birds arrive, often with the peak in July. The number of birds staying to winter will then depend upon the local pine and larch cone crops.

The area of heathland to the north at Budby is good for all three of the above species and in many years played host to wintering Great Grey Shrikes, although none has been seen for the last few winters, but of course where the habitat is suitable there is always the chance of others appearing in future winters.

In the spring the heathlands at Sherwood Pines (Clipstone),

Sherwood Country Park (the Birklands), Budby and Clumber come to life with an abundance of insects. The songs of Willow Warblers and Chiffchaffs are added to the local chorus, and on the heaths Whitethroats and Yellowhammers are numerous. By mid April the heathlands resound to the delightful sound of that free-fall parachutist, the Tree Pipit. These birds are present through to mid August when they again depart for winter quarters in Africa. Redstarts breed in many areas, and a small population of Whinchats until recently were regular breeders at Sherwood Pines. Of late, however, no birds have bred for a few years, a decline which may be in line with other east coast counties where the species no longer breeds.

As evening draws in during June to August, young owls may be heard calling from the edges of the plantations of conifers; Tawny Owls always seem to be most common but a few pairs of Long-eared Owls are present and the squeaky-gate call of the young is a characteristic heathland sound on long warm evenings as are the grunts and squeaks of roding Woodcock which traverse the evening skyline. The other heathland specialist, the Nightjar, also breeds in good numbers in the forest and on the heaths. Appropriate habitat management should hopefully ensure the continued presence of this very special bird within the Sherwood Pines (Clipstone) Forest where they inhabit the clear-fells as well as on the natural heathland sites. Full census work in the Sherwood District as a whole in recent years has shown a peak population of up to 70 churring males, although totals in 1994 and 1995 have been lower.

The areas of mainly old deciduous woodland found in the Dukeries and Sherwood Country Park (the Birklands) support a rich variety of woodland birds, which occur in high numbers. During the winter months, Clumber Park is a particularly good locality, with feeding flocks usually apparent in the woodland blocks around the main car park area, the chapel and the oak woodland near the main road. As the birds are regularly fed by visitors, they can become very tame and give superb views at very close quarters. Species such as Nuthatch, Great Spotted Woodpecker, Marsh Tits and to a lesser degree Willow Tits and even the normally timid Jay will come down to take food from right next to people and make the use of binoculars almost redundant. Blue, Great and Long-tailed Tits also frequent the oaks, along with Treecreeper and Goldcrests. Large flocks of Chaffinches, up to 400 birds occur, and, depending on the size of the previous autumn's arrival from the continent, there will be variable numbers of Brambling in the finch flocks.

One of the major attractions of the site in winter, however, is the gathering of Hawfinches in the trees behind the chapel, where yews and a well watched hornbeam provide food for these specialised heavy-billed finches. They are best seen in the early mornings, before disturbance from the large numbers of tourists can soon force the birds to quieter areas. The birds' presence is often given away by their distinctive 'tic' call notes, as they are far from obvious even when perched in the tops of the leafless trees. Another scarce wintering species, the Firecrest, has also occurred in a few winters in the rhododendron scrub around this particular spot and they are worth looking and listening for on any visit.

The lakes have the inevitable large flock of Canada Geese and good numbers of Gadwall, some of which breed. A wide variety of wildfowl occur, however, from the ubiquitous Mallard to flocks of Pochard (up to 230 birds), Wigeon, Teal, Tufted Duck and a local population of

Ruddy Duck, which have on occasions numbered in excess of 80 birds, although about 40 are more often seen, while even odd Goldeneye are regular, and locally high concentrations of Moorhens may reach 150 birds. The lake edges and the flooded fields near the ford even attract a few passage waders when the levels are suitable, with Green and Common Sandpiper the most frequent.

In the late winter/early spring (February–April) on warm mornings the local Lesser Spotted Woodpeckers become much easier to locate as they indulge in their spring drumming and territorial displays in the older trees, where they are usually to be found right up in the tops. Clumber Park and Sherwood Country Park are the best locality for this species. The woodland bird population is swelled with summering Willow Warbler, Chiffchaff, Blackcap, Garden Warbler, Spotted Flycatchers and, occasionally, the odd Wood Warbler may take up a territory in suitable habitat.

Honey Buzzard

Welbeck is best known for one species, the Honey Buzzard, for this was one of the first well known breeding sites of this species in the British Isles, where the birds could be watched from a public road without disturbance. Honey Buzzards have been present in summer here for over 30 years, and have bred in some years. They generally arrive in late May and are present through to late August but often become more difficult to see later in the year. They are best seen from the minor road which runs along the southern edge of the estate (see Access), as they soar and display over the woodlands to the north. It should be noted that the birds, although sometimes showing well, can be very difficult to see as they spend a great deal of time just sitting around in trees watching for wasps and bees passing to their nests, which hold the larvae favoured by feeding Honey Buzzards. On some days the birds are not seen at all or just for a few minutes. Warm sunny days with scattered broken cloud and a light to moderate wind during the early part of their stay are often the best as this is when they will be most active and can sometimes be seen in their wing-clapping display flight.

Honey Buzzards are not the only large raptors in the area, however, as an increasing number of Common Buzzards now nest in the same locality and, as they spend much more time on the wing, they are therefore more likely to be seen than the Honey Buzzards, so caution is needed with identification.

Another spring/summer attraction here is the large heronry, with numerous Grey Heron nests visible, in Cat Hills plantation just across the Carburton Forge lake from the roadside car parking area. Large noisy flocks of Jackdaws also breed in the woodlands hereabouts and their sudden cackling eruptions may give away the impending appearance of a raptor. Also on the lake are a good population of Gadwall, with a few Ruddy Ducks. Ospreys are frequent visitors in spring and may stay in the area for days or even weeks, making regular fishing sorties to the lakes, while Marsh Harriers seem annual on passage in recent years. Midsummer watches will often produce sightings of Hobby, while Sparrowhawks and Kestrels are abundant, giving a possible day list of seven species of raptor. Goshawk and Peregrine are also annual, while Merlin is seen in most winters, with the occasional Hen Harrier, and there is one record of Red Kite.

Hawfinches breed in the vicinity but the best way of locating them is to listen for their distinctive 'tic' calls as they fly over the tree-tops. Nuthatch, Marsh Tit and all three species of woodpecker also breed locally.

Rarities in the Dukeries over the years have included Ring-necked Duck, Parrot Crossbills and, in the autumn of 1994, three Red-rumped Swallows which frequented the area around the Carburton entrance to Clumber Park.

Timing

Woodland birds will be present throughout the year but best views are obtained during winter when the birds are being fed. Lesser Spotted Woodpeckers are best looked for in March/April. Large post-breeding mixed flocks of passerines are present in July/August. The Honey Buzzards arrive in late May and are best seen in June and early July but may show through to late August. Common Buzzards are resident but Ospreys and Hobbies most likely from May to July. Best days for raptors vary but a long vigil may well be necessary so an early start is recommended on a day with broken cumulus cloud, sunshine and moderate winds.

Access

Clumber is 4.5 miles (7.2 km) southeast of Worksop and 6.5 miles (10.4 km) southwest of Retford. Access is from the A1/A57/A614 roundabout. Follow the A614 for half a mile (0.8 km) and turn right into the park through a stone archway. The drive runs between the avenue of limes for 4 miles (6.4 km) to two stone pillars at Carburton. There are numerous parking places off the side of this main road but for the chapel and the main car park and lake take a left turn after 2 miles (3.2 km) to the car park. An access fee of £2.50 is charged for cars and motorcycles which actually park off the road, for non National Trust members, pedestrians are free. The park is open all year. There are toilets, a cafe and bicycle hire facilities at the main car park.

For Welbeck turn right off the B6034 Worksop to Budby road at a crossroads 3 miles (4.8 km) southeast of Worksop, or from Clumber continue on the road which runs through the middle of the park and straight over the crossroads at Carburton. Carburton Lake appears on the right and 1.5 miles (2.4 km) along this road there is a right-hand bend, followed by a left, and an obvious parking area on the right of the road, with Carburton Forge Lake off to the right and in front. Park here

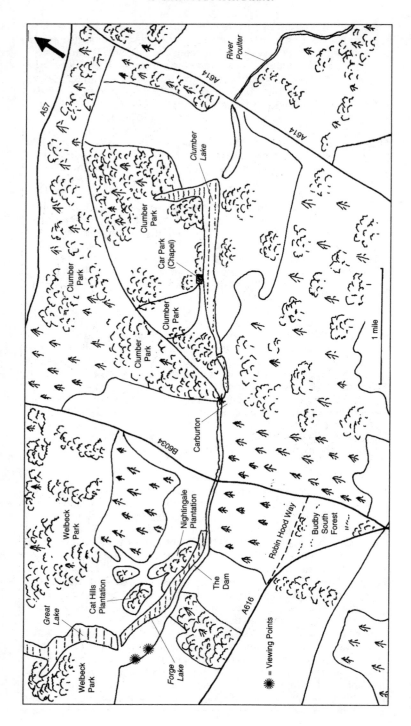

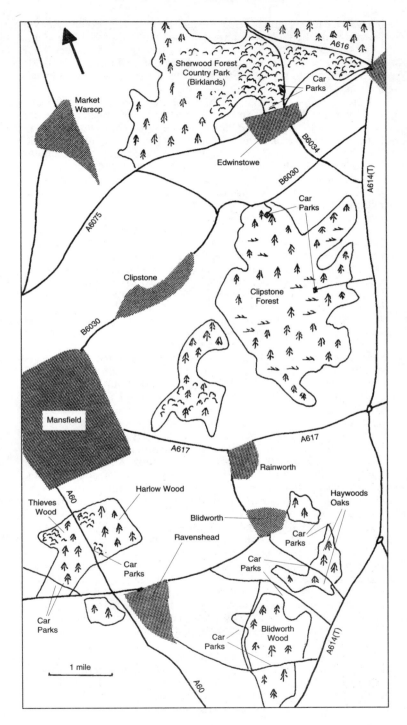

and watch over the woods across the lake for raptors, or continue along the road to the Bentinck monument on the right (with limited parking), or another 200 yds/m along the road to where a tree trunk has been layed on the north side of the road, and watch from there over the fields and woodlands to the north. Do not enter the fields or private woodlands here.

Sherwood Pines Forest Park (Clipstone Forest) lies 13 miles (20.8 km) north of Nottingham and 3 miles (4.8 km) east of Mansfield. There are two car parks, the major one with visitor centre, catering and toilet facilities and a childrens play area, is reached by leaving the A614(T), 1 mile (1.6 km) south of New Ollerton, turning right onto the B6030 for 2 miles (3.2 km) then left into the signed park where there is a charge of £1 per vehicle. There is also a car park at Deerdale, accessed by turning right (west) off the A614(T), 3.5 miles (5.6 km) south of North Ollerton. Three trails lead from the main car park and visitor centre, with the shorter 1-mile (1.6 km) walk being surfaced for pushchairs and wheelchairs.

For Sherwood Country Park, Birklands, take the A6075 Mansfield to Ollerton road, turn left (north) onto the B6034 at Edwinstowe and drive for half a mile (0.8 km) then turn left to the visitor centre where there are toilet facilities and a wayfaring course. A car park fee of £1 is charged.

Budby South Forest (known locally as Budby Common) is not signposted but lies to the west of the A616 in a triangle formed by the A616, the B6034 and the Robin Hood Way footpath. From the A616 at Budby, travelling north, turn right onto the B6034 and the main area of heath is on the left after half a mile (0.8 km). This is a military training area and visitors must keep to designated footpaths.

Blidworth Wood has three car parks, all accessed from minor roads off the A614(T) northwest of Calverton. Travelling south on the A614, 7 miles (11.2 km) south of New Ollerton is a roundabout. From here successive minor roads lead off to the right (west) to car parks for Blidworth and Haywoods Oaks. From the roundabout, another 1 mile (1.6 km) south, turn right onto a minor road and then 0.8 miles (1.2 km) further on are two car parks for Haywoods Oaks. Back at the A614, a further half a mile (0.8 km) south, another right turn leads after 1 mile (1.6 km) to a car park for Blidworth Wood on the left. Another half a mile (0.8 km) south off the A614, a right turn leads to the second car park after a further half a mile (0.8 km). Continue along this minor road for another half a mile (0.8 km) and turn right again for half a mile (0.8 km) to the third car Park for Blidworth Wood.

Thieves and Harlow Woods lie just south of Mansfield, either side of the A60. For Harlow Wood, park either in the small car park at the Portland Training College on the east side of the A60, 1.5 miles (2.4 km) south of Mansfield or alternatively park at Thieves Wood and walk through to access Harlow Wood on foot. The Friar Tuck trail leads through the woodland. There are two car parks serving Thieves Wood. Turn right southbound from the A60 onto the B6020 for half a mile (0.8 km) then right again onto the B6139, with two car parks on the right and left. Two waymarked trails lead through this popular recreational area.

Calendar

Resident: Grey Heron, Gadwall, Ruddy Duck, Common Buzzard, Sparrowhawk, Stock Dove, Green Woodpecker, Great Spotted Woodpecker, Lesser Spotted Woodpecker, Marsh Tit, Willow Tit, Nuthatch, Treecreeper, Jay, Jackdaw, Hawfinch.

October–March: Merlin (scarce), Firecrest (scarce), Siskin, Redpoll, Common Crossbill (occasional), Hawfinch.

April–September. Honey Buzzard, Common Buzzard, Osprey, Hobby, Woodcock, Nightjar, Tree Pipit, Redstart, Wood Warbler (occasional), Common Crossbill (has bred), Pied Flycatcher (rare).

44 THE IDLE VALLEY   OS Sheets 111 and 112

Habitat

In the far north of Nottinghamshire the River Idle forms the county boundary with the western extremities of Lincolnshire in the Isle of Axholme. The carrlands either side of the river, once regularly flooded and with extensive marshes, have all long since been drained and brought under arable cultivation but odd fields, especially at Idle Stop, do still flood in most winters. The main crops on this rich, black peaty soil are cereals, sugar beet and peas. Drainage has left the area crossed with wide straight dykes, which are a source of permanent water and, in the case of the wider ones, may hold small reedbeds. Hedgerows and trees are a rare sight but there are some rough areas around field edges which can prove attractive to feeding finches and buntings. Recent set-aside policy has also created more attractive winter feeding in some areas as fields are left after harvest for the ensuing winter.

An old turbary at Langholme, in the Isle of Axholme, a reserve of the Lincolnshire Trust, a small conifer plantation near Carr Farm, and the old bombing range at Misson stand as isolated pockets of mainly birch woodland in the wide open landscape. Another fairly extensive area of scrub is located just west of Idle Stop bridge.

Species

In spite of the apparently overall barren appearance of the landscape, winter can bring large numbers of passerines, with flocks of Skylarks, Linnets and Yellowhammers, flocks of up to 500 birds of each species have been noted, occasional Twite and exceptional flocks of the declining Corn Bunting, with peak counts of up to 500 birds, and up to 60 Tree Sparrows. The wide open fields also hold large flocks of Lapwing and Golden Plover, Rooks (up to 7,000) and Jackdaws, 1,000 of both species flight into Lincolnshire to roost. Both Woodpigeon and Stock Doves can be in impressive numbers, up to 3,000 and 110, respectively.

Winter thrushes arrive from October, with large flocks of Redwing, Blackbird and Fieldfare passing through during the late autumn and good numbers often still present through to February or March. This avian fodder attracts the attention of Merlin and Hen Harrier in most winters. The resident Barn Owls and the occasional Short-eared Owl drift over the rough dyke banks in their hunt for voles and other small rodents, and in addition Long-eared Owls and Hooded Crows were once both regular winter visitors.

One of the main attractions of the area in the winter, however, is the wintering flock of wild swans. Bewick's and Whoopers usually arrive from late October and often stay until early March. Totals vary from year to year, but up to 60 Bewick's and 35 Whoopers have been noted in some recent years. These birds do move about considerably during the course of the winter with favoured feeding areas changing as fields are ploughed and crops grow, in addition to which this flock of birds is thought to also visit Lound Pits to the south on occasions. Flooded fields along the river, in particular those at Idle Stop, have in recent winters attracted good numbers of wintering Gadwall, Wigeon, Shoveler, Teal and Shelduck.

Winter vagrants have included Red Kite and Red-necked Grebe. By early spring wet marshy areas attract feeding Snipe, up to 60 birds being recorded in good years in March, and flooded fields may hold small flocks of Curlew and Redshank.

During April, flocks of northern Golden Plovers often pass through the area, staying off to feed for a few days, while newly arrived Yellow Wagtails proclaim their territories over the growing crops. Passage migrants such as Northern Wheatears and Whinchats, which have bred in the area in the past, are seen in small numbers, often on the young pea fields, which also act as something of a magnet for the regular trips of Dotterel occurring from the last week of April. These birds are probably annual in occurrence but in some years trips may stay for extended periods when numbers build and fall as further birds arrive and depart. One of our most attractive waders, Dotterel, are always much appreciated by birders.

In good years for the species, up to 12 Quail have been heard calling from the fields during the late spring or summer. At Idle Stop Bridge a series of small ponds with small areas of reedbeds hold breeding Sedge, Reed and Grasshopper Warblers, with Lesser Whitethroat, Whitethroat and Turtle Dove in the scrub, while Water Rails, which occur on passage, may also breed. A vagrant Golden Oriole was found at Idle Stop in spring 1994.

Raptors are represented by Kestrel and Sparrowhawks but there are passage records of Marsh Harrier and Osprey and even occasional Montagu's Harrier.

Dotterel

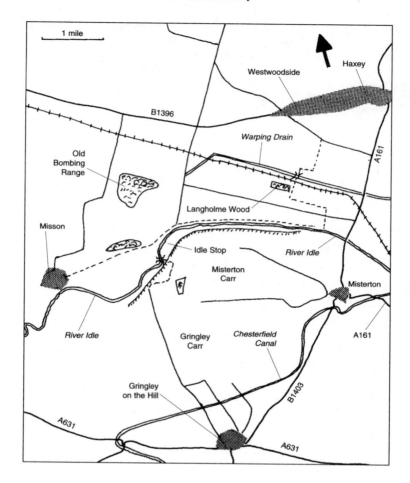

The dykes and drainage channels are important areas for dragonflies and damselflies during the summer and these, along with the large flocks of Swifts and hirundines which feed over the summer cereal fields, prove attractive to Hobbies, which are regular in the area from May to early September and may well breed.

Autumn sees the start of the build-up of flocks of feeding finches and the return of the first Golden Plovers, which over the years have brought with them odd Dotterel and even American Golden Plover.

Timing
Winter is probably the best time to see large numbers of birds and for the wild swans. Dotterel arrive anywhere from mid April onwards but are most frequently seen on the carrlands during early May.

Access
The whole area between Misterton, Gringley on the Hill and Misson can only be watched from the series of minor unclassified roads which dissect the carrlands, and a public footpath which runs along part of the

length of the northern bank of the River Idle. Many of these unclassified roads are open to the public at the discretion of the local farmers, and any local signs should be obeyed.

Two minor roads run west from Misterton village off the B1403 into Misterton Carrs. Another minor road runs northwest from Gringley on the Hill, off the A631, into Gringley Carrs and to Idle Stop, which is accessed via an unclassified road which turns right off the minor road after 3 miles (4.8 km), then left to a bridge over the River Idle. The northern side of the valley can be viewed from a minor road running west from the A161, Beckingham to Epworth road, 1.6 miles (2.6 km) north of Misterton village. A further 2.8 miles (4.5 km) along this minor road a T junction leads north and south, the latter route leading down to the Idle bank where a public footpath leads off both east and west. The westward route leads via Idle Stop to an area of scrub which has in the past held Long-eared Owls.

Calendar

October–March: Bewick's and Whooper Swan, Hen Harrier, Merlin, Golden Plover, Lapwing, Snipe, Barn Owl, Short-eared Owl (scarce), Long-eared Owl (occasional), Stock Dove, Woodpigeon (large flocks), Fieldfare, Redwing, Blackbird, Rook, Jackdaw, Tree Sparrow, Linnet, Twite (rare), Yellowhammer, Corn Bunting.

April–September: Marsh Harrier (scarce), Hobby (scarce), Quail (scarce), Golden Plover, Dotterel (scarce April–May), Turtle Dove, Yellow Wagtail, Whinchat, Northern Wheatear (both passage), Sedge, Reed and Grasshopper Warblers.

45   GIRTON AND BESTHORPE   OS Sheet 121

Habitat

Sand and gravel extraction in the vicinity of the villages of Girton and Besthorpe, to the north of Newark, has created a series of pits, several of which are now disused and flooded, with areas of scrub having grown up around their periphery. The pits and associated gravel workings all lie within the broad valley floodplain of the River Trent. The surrounding area is composed of old grazing marshes to the south of Girton and Besthorpe pits and to the west across the River Trent, with some remnants of the old mature hawthorn hegderows which were used to divide up the grazing pastures.

In very wet winters, the River Trent may occasionally flood some of these fields, making them particularly attractive to wildfowl. Other land has been turned over to arable farming and some of the larger lagoons at Besthorpe were used as settlement lagoons for flyash, which was pumped there from power stations further along the Trent Valley. The two sites have been brought to life in words and drawings in *Shorelines: Birds at the Water's Edge*, a collection of paintings and drawings by local artist, Michael Warren, published in 1984 and now out of print.

The pits all lie to the east of the River Trent, which at this point is a relatively wide and open river with high grass banks grazed in places by cattle and sheep but with longer rough grass dominating in other stretches.

The largest of the pits at Girton is used for water sports, with a sailing club in existence, while the smaller pits have an extensive growth of sallow and willow scrub around their edges, with some small areas of *Phragmites* also present. Further south at Girton, The Fleet, a small stream, widens into a broad shallow sheet of water, backed by old gnarled willows, it has sedges round the edges and often muddy margins, which can prove attractive to waders and wagtails.

A small marshy area at Besthorpe opposite the settling lagoons, the first of which is now filled and totally dry, is particularly attractive, with shallow water areas interspersed with clumps of sedge, reed and some willow and sallow scrub. The water levels here vary greatly, however, as the extraction company pump in water at certain times. The area is now managed jointly by Redland Aggregates and the Nottinghamshire Wildlife Trust. Again large old hawthorn hedges flank some of the area.

Species

The area is of interest throughout the year but is best known for the high numbers of wintering wildfowl which make the site of particular importance within the county of Nottinghamshire. During the winter months, however, there is considerable movement of birds between different sites in the Trent Valley in response to disturbance, feeding conditions and weather. During severe freezing weather, when areas of open water may be ice-bound, the birds will move to the open water of the Trent to feed. Of most local interest is the flock of wintering Goosanders, which favour the pits at Girton and have peaked at 90 in some years. Other diving duck are also present in good numbers, with Tufted Duck and Pochard, up to 56 Goldeneye and fairly regular Smew, while Scaup, Long-tailed Duck and Red-crested Pochard are all occasional visitors. A large flock of Wigeon move between the pits and feeding areas on grazing meadows, especially when the fields are flooded, and small numbers of Gadwall also winter. A large flock of Canada Geese may reach 500 birds in midwinter, and Greylag Geese are also on the increase with odd pairs breeding at Besthorpe. Flocks of Pink-footed Geese more often than not just overfly the area but small numbers sometimes linger for a few days on the wetter arable fields. Similarly Bewick's Swans are mainly a late autumn passage species, but when the grazing meadows are flooded a flock may spend days or even weeks in the area. Teal favour the marshy areas at Besthorpe, where their population has peaked at 400 birds in February. Other vagrant waterfowl have included Common Scoter, Mandarin and Bean and Brent Geese.

As with most inland wetland sites, the number of Cormorants using the sites has increased dramatically of late, from peaks of about 45 in the early 1990s to 120 in recent winters. Shelducks are often present in small numbers, and rarer species have included wintering Slavonian Grebe and visits from Red-throated and Great Northern Divers, Red-necked Grebe and Bittern. The muddy edges and sedge beds of The Fleet and the marsh at Besthorpe prove attractive to Snipe, which have reached totals of 80 or so birds at peak passage periods, and in winter they usually hold one or more Jack Snipe but, as everywhere, a considerable amount of good fortune is needed to bump into one of these superbly camouflaged waders.

Short-eared Owl

There is a gull roost at Girton comprising mainly small gulls, Black-headed and Common, but with some Great Black-backed, and it has in the past produced records of Glaucous and Mediterranean Gull. The surrounding fields attract large flocks of Lapwing (up to 800, January), and Golden Plover, usually only 200 to 300. Small numbers of Ruff are fairly regular and a few Dunlin are often to be found at Besthorpe when the area is not frozen over. Flocks of finches, Chaffinch, Brambling, Greenfinch, Goldfinch and Redpoll feed on the rough ground around the pits, where seeding weeds provide a winter bounty, while the fields and hedgerows hold Yellowhammers and the hedges act as a roost for a few Reed and Corn Buntings. Merlins and Hen Harriers are seen on occasions and odd Short-eared Owls may pass through or even stay to winter in good years. Sparrowhawks and Kestrels are a common sight.

March brings the change from winter to spring and breeding Ringed Plovers are often already be back on territory. March is the best month to find a Rock Pipit, a decidedly rare species at inland locations. Spring brings a good variety of passage migrants and breeding birds. The latter include such interesting inland species as a few pairs of Shelduck, 2–3 pairs of Redshank, odd pairs of Lapwing and the usual Ringed and Little Ringed Plovers. Good numbers of Great Crested and Little Grebes breed at Girton, and Kingfishers are seen frequently.

May is the best month for bumping into breeding-plumaged Black-necked Grebes, which have occurred in some years. Warblers include Willow, Sedge and odd Grasshopper, with Whitethroat and Lesser Whitethroat, and the reedmace beds at Besthorpe also played host to the first Savi's Warbler for the county, in May 1990. Wagtails may be rather common on passage, and Yellow Wagtails turned in a record 81 on 14 May 1990. Some of these birds stay to nest along with Reed Buntings and Yellowhammers and a few pairs of Turtle Dove. Small numbers of Northern Wheatear appear in spring and odd Ring Ouzels have been found. Large numbers of hirundines and Swifts may be found feeding over the water areas in cold weather and it is inclement weather which brings in the highest numbers of passage terns in the spring. Common, Arctic and Black Terns all pass through in most years, with the last days of April and the first week of May being the most productive periods, while Sandwich Tern has also occurred.

The variety and number of migrant waders, in both spring and autumn, is highly dependent upon the availability of suitable muddy habitat, and while species such as Green and Common Sandpipers can be relied upon, the appearance of rarer species is rather more unpredictable. Ruff, however, are fairly regular at Besthorpe as are Greenshank and Dunlin, which may total 20 birds at their peak. Oystercatcher have also become more regular, especially in spring, when up to seven birds have been present. Much rarer species such as Whimbrel, Black and Bar-tailed Godwit, Little and Temminck's Stint and Curlew Sandpiper, Spotted Redshank, Sanderling and Wood Sandpiper are often annual. Green Sandpipers may be in double figures and Golden Plover numbers build up to 2–300 on adjacent fields.

The autumn also sees local Turtle Doves congregating before their departure to the south, with small flocks coming to drink and bath at the pits, and Shoveler peak at Besthorpe, reaching 40 or so birds in August/September, sometimes with the odd Garganey also being present. Later in the autumn, flocks of Stock Doves may exceed 100 birds, and passage Skylarks and Meadow Pipits have totalled 250 and 100 per day respectively in October. Westward moving flocks of Redwing and Fieldfare stop off to feed on the hawthorn berry crop, sometimes staying for several weeks in productive autumns.

Situated in the Trent Valley on a major flyway this site receives its fair share of vagrants, which have ranged from storm-driven Leach's Petrels, Gannet, Arctic and Great Skuas to Little Egret, Avocet, American Golden Plover, Buff-breasted Sandpiper and a well watched Great Snipe, found in nettle beds along the Trent bank.

Timing

The site is a good place to visit at any time but is at its most productive in midwinter and during both passage periods. At weekends, early morning visits are best at Girton, where sailing may well disturb the waterfowl later in the day.

Access

The area is situated 5 miles (8 km) north of Newark, off the A1133 Newark to Gainsborough road. Besthorpe village is 1.5 miles (2.4 km) north of Collingham village (on the A1133). Turn left (west) off the A1133 into Waddington Lane, a minor road at the south end of Besthorpe village, signed 'River Trent'. This is Trent Lane, which soon becomes a narrow track just beyond some obvious NP pylons. Park here and walk down a rough track to the right, between tall hawthorn hedges, to a closed gate. This track is very narrow and may be muddy in winter. Walk north along the track, through the gate, to view the settling lagoons, the first of which is now full and dry, while the second has beds of reed and reedmace with a small open water area in the southwest corner, on your right and the marshy area to the left.

For The Fleet continue north on the A1133 for 800 yds/m from the north side of Besthorpe village then turn left onto a minor road, Tinkers Lane, signed to Girton village. This minor road runs alongside the northern part of the Fleet and a public footpath runs off south down the eastern side of The Fleet. For the main Girton pits either continue along this minor road through Girton village and then turn left at the first fork, or from the A1133 turn left onto a minor road 1 mile (1.6 km) north of Besthorpe village, signed to Girton, and at the left bend after 100 yds/m

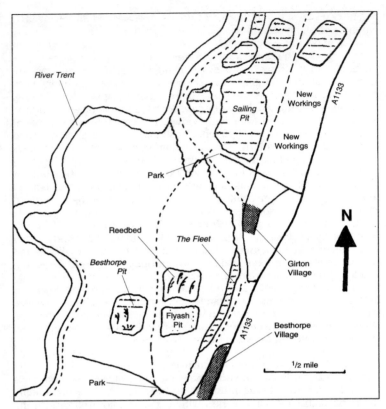

go straight on; the main sailing pit comes into view on the right after 600 yds/m. There is limited parking on the side of the pit and a public footpath runs off north on the eastern side of the pit, while a public footpath leads from Girton village northwest to the bank of the River Trent and thence follows the riverbank northwards. A further area of new workings, between the main pit and the A1133. can be viewed by turning right, along a driveable track, at the southeast corner of the main pit.

Calendar

Resident: Great Crested and Little Grebe, Greylag Goose, Canada Goose, Gadwall, Tufted Duck, Stock Dove, Reed Bunting, Corn Bunting.

October–March: Cormorant, Bewick's Swan, Pink-footed Goose (scarce), Shelduck, Wigeon, Teal, Shoveler, Pochard, Scaup and Long-tailed Duck (both rare), Goldeneye, Goosander, Smew (scarce), Merlin (rare), Water Rail, Golden Plover, Lapwing, Redshank, Dunlin, Ruff, Snipe, Jack Snipe, gull roost, Short-eared Owl (rare), Fieldfare, Redwing.

April–September: Shelduck, Oystercatcher, Little Ringed Plover, Ringed Plover, Redshank, Greenshank (scarce), Ruff, Green Sandpiper, Common Sandpiper, rarer waders, Common, Arctic and Black Tern, Turtle Dove, Cuckoo, Swift, Sand Martin, House Martin, Swallow, Yellow Wagtail, Grasshopper Warbler, Sedge Warbler.

Habitat

Immediately to the north of Newark the series of flooded gravel and sand workings at South Muskham are bounded on the west by the old Great North Road and in the east by the upgraded version, the A1(T). The busy main east coast rail line bisects the series of pits, which are part of an extensive series of such workings stretching along the River Trent valley right through Nottinghamshire into south Derbyshire. The largest pit is used for sailing and fishing, while most of the smaller pits, to the east of the railway line, the largest being immediately north of the River Trent, are also used for fishing. The largest pit has grazed banks on all sides, and where cattle and sheep go down to drink this creates muddy edges which prove attractive to a variety of birds.

Species

Winter wildfowl, passage terns and to a lesser extent, waders are the main species of interest at the pits. Typical wintering wildfowl include good numbers of Wigeon (up to 500 birds having been regular in recent winters), Teal (up to 400), Tufted Duck (700), with a maximum of 1046 having occurred in December 1994), Pochard (maximum 430, March 1994), and Goosander, which have reached peaks of 150 birds in some winters. These birds do commute between other gravel pit complexes in the Trent Valley and also feed on the river itself when the pits are frozen, but South Muskham seems to be the most favoured site for the species at present. A flock of Greylag Geese may number 100 birds but again there may well be interchange with sites like Girton and Besthorpe further north.

The pits are exceptional, however, for Great Crested Grebes, which have topped 120 during some midwinter counts, and are being used increasingly by Cormorants, which have built up with counts in excess of 60 birds in midwinter. Black-necked, Slavonian and Red-necked Grebes and all three divers have also appeared from time to time, with Black-throated Diver being almost annual. Other species of duck also occur, with Gadwall, Goldeneye (up to 35), Scaup and Pintail the most regular, but there are also infrequent records of Red-breasted Merganser, Common and Velvet Scoters, Smew, and even Ferruginous Duck. A truly exceptional inland record was of a flock of 28 Eider on 31 October 1993, the only record of this species ever! Whooper and Bewick's Swans occur in some years but seldom stay for long. There are also a few records of Shags, which again are exceptional inland.

Good numbers of gulls are usually present, with a small roost typically containing 1,500 Black-headed, 200 Common, up to 200 each of Lesser and Great Black-backed and Herring Gulls. Inevitably, odd rarer species have been located, which include Glaucous, Iceland and Mediterranean Gulls. The surrounding farmland holds flocks of Golden Plover and Lapwing, which come down to the water to bathe and preen. Short-eared Owls are rare winter visitors and there may be a wintering Stonechat present in some years.

The spring migration period is an exciting time as it offers the chance of encountering flocks of terns, wagtails, hirundines and other migrants, passing along the Trent Valley (during March–June). Particularly in cool or inclement weather, large flocks of Sand and House Martins,

Swallows and Swifts will be forced down feeding low over the water surface in search of emergent insects. The pit banks may well hold good numbers of Yellow and Pied Wagtails, with the chance of odd White Wagtails during April and early May. Scrubby areas may host the odd Redstart or Black Redstart, the latter usually in the early spring from late March.

Passage waders are likely at this time, with species such as Common and Green Sandpiper, Dunlin, Redshank and Greenshank and Ruff being regular, and exceptionally there may be a Wood Sandpiper, Turnstone, Sanderling, either of the godwits or Curlew Sandpiper present in their breeding finery. Flocks of Kittiwakes make occasional visits in the early spring and sometimes autumn. It is, however, the flocks of terns which hold a real fascination for the birdwatchers as South Muskham pits have proved one of the better complexes in the valley for pulling in good numbers of terns in the spring. Common Terns are probably the most regular species, but the visits of flocks of Arctic Terns, in all their full, tail streamered summer dress, and the exquisite grey-and-black Black Terns, all dipping to the water surface picking up insects, are the essence of inland spring birdwatching at its best. Arctic Terns have peaked at 65 birds on some May days, and Blacks at 77 on 2 May 1990. Little and Sandwich Terns are also rare visitors at this time, completing the 'set' of regular tern species, and even a Caspian Tern has been recorded on one occasion.

In addition to the terns there may well be small parties of Little Gulls, again often with adults in breeding plumage, accompanying the feeding flocks of terns, their visits being unfortunately all too transitory. Rarer species at this season have included Twite, Water Pipit and Osprey, while there is a summer record of Fulmar and also one of Ring-necked Duck.

Breeding birds include Reed, Grasshopper and Sedge Warbler, with a sprinkling of other warblers, Willow Warbler and Whitethroat the most numerous, in the surrounding scrub. Ringed and Little Ringed Plovers, Redshank, Mallard and Tufted Duck all nest but Common Terns have not done so in recent years.

Autumn migration brings much the same mix of species as the spring passage but with better chances for Little Stint, Curlew Sandpiper and Wood Sandpiper. Numbers of the commoner species such as Dunlin, Common Sandpiper, Redshank, Greenshank, Ringed Plover and Ruff are usually higher, and birds tend to stay for longer periods. Rarities have included Pomarine Skua and Red-necked Phalarope, while the elegant Hobby is quite a regular sight from July to September.

Timing

The pits are at their best during the winter when wildfowl and grebes dominate the species mix and, in the spring, from late March to early June, for passage terns, waders, hirundines and wagtails.

Access

South Muskham pits are 1.5 miles (2.4 km) north of Newark, to the south and east of the village of South Muskham.

Leaving Newark north on the A616 towards North Muskham, 1 mile (1.6 km) north of the roundabout on the A46(T), the road crosses the River Trent, the largest pit appears on the right of the road. Park sensibly in a pull-in off the roadside at the northwestern end of the pit and

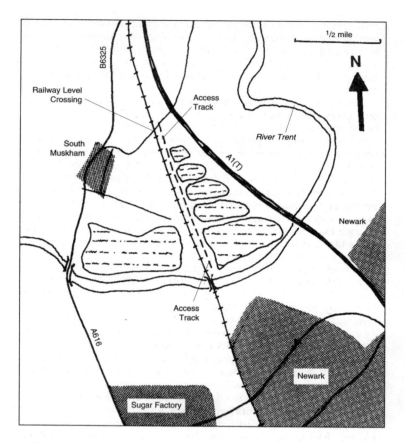

walk down the track along the northern edge of the pit to view the whole of this pit.

To access the other pits carry on north on the A616 into South Muskham village and take the second turn on the right, which then passes the church and goes over a railway crossing. Park immediately over the railway crossing in pull-ins on either side of the road then walk south down the track, to the east of the railway line, to view the series of pits between the A1(T) and the railway line. Note that further pits south of the river by the sugar factory are all private with no open access.

Calendar

Resident: Great Crested Grebe, Cormorant, Greylag Goose, Tufted Duck.

October–March: Red-necked and Slavonian Grebe (both rare) Bewick's and Whooper Swan (scarce), Wigeon, Teal, Gadwall, Pochard, Goldeneye, Goosander, Golden Plover, gull roost, Mediterranean Gull (rare), Stonechat.

April–September: Hobby, Dunlin, Ringed and Little Ringed Plovers, Curlew Sandpiper and Little Stint (rare), Green, Common and Wood

Sandpiper, Greenshank, Redshank, Ruff, Kittiwake, Common, Arctic and Black Terns, Little Gull, hirundines, Swift, Black Redstart, Redstart (both passage).

47 COLWICK/NETHERFIELD/ HOLME PIERREPONT   OS Sheet 129

These three sites, situated on the northeastern outskirts of the City of Nottingham, lie along both sides of the banks of the River Trent and, being in such close proximity, tend to attract some of the same flocks and individual birds. Each site, however, is different and has its own unique blend of habitats and species.

COLWICK COUNTRY PARK

Habitat

Colwick Country Park, which was opened in 1978, is based on some former gravel workings, which have been landscaped and planted with a variety of trees and shrubs, to form a recreational facility for the City of Nottingham, the whole park lying within the city boundary. Prior to the extraction of gravel the area was a natural rough island, flanked by the Trent Cut, a man-made navigation canal, and the River Trent itself. The site has a history going back to the Domesday Book, with several notable archaeological finds having been made in the area.

The park proper is dominated by two lakes, of 62 acres (25 ha) and 24 acres (10 ha) respectively; the southern boundary of which is the River Trent, which separates the park from Holme Pierrepont. To the north lies the Colwick Woods escarpment, a well wooded glacial ridge with extensive public access.

Within the park are a number of different habitats which prove attractive to birds. The nature reserve is dominated by sycamore with occasional oak and birch trees, in addition to which there is a small narrow lake and overgrown marsh area. Scattered throughout the park are numerous small, and relatively new plantations, with food trees such as alder, beech and hazel. There are several quiet woodland rides and some areas of damp grassland, although all areas are heavily used by the public.

The west lake, the smaller of the two lakes, is used for coarse fishing and windsurfing with consequent disturbance all year round. The larger Colwick Lake is a trout fishery with a running season from mid March to the end of November. Trout boats are often active on the lake, especially at weekends, and there is some sailing in summer, blue-green algae permitting.

Species

The park list stands at around 220 species, with an annual total of between 140 and 150 species being recorded. Because of its location on the Trent Valley migration corridor, passage movements of many species are often a feature of a visit, with winter thrushes, pipits and larks moving through in considerable numbers at times.

The large expanse of water draws a good mix of wildfowl including Pochard, Tufted Duck, Gadwall and Wigeon, and winter counts of Goldeneye can exceed 100 birds. All three species of diver and the rarer grebes have been recorded, with Black-necked Grebe being almost annual in spring. During March 1994 a drake Bufflehead was present for just over a week, attracting 4,500 observers during its stay, which in turn led to the discovery of several other county rarities such as Razorbill, Long-tailed Duck and Lapland Bunting, showing the potential for the discovery of unusual birds at the site.

Parties of terns pass through every year, with Black and Arctic Terns and Little Gulls often present after periods of easterly winds. Up to ten pairs of Common Terns have bred on specially built artificial platforms in the lakes, and during July and August up to 85 birds roost on the trout boats each night. Mediterranean Gulls are annual, some individuals remaining for several days, and the summer months produce several sightings of Yellow-legged Gulls.

In excess of 60 species breed within the 250-acre park annually, with Great Spotted Woodpecker and Kingfisher both being common. Eight species of warbler are present in summer, including Reed and Sedge Warblers, and Blackcap and Chiffchaff also regularly overwinter. From April to September Hobbies appear regularly, taking advantage of the large hirundine and Swift flocks feeding over the insect-rich area. Both Sparrowhawks and Kestrels breed and are a common sight in the park.

During the winter months a special feeding area attracts large numbers of small birds with Bramblings often being present. Siskins attracted to the alders frequently number in excess of 100 birds.

Rare birds in recent years have been almost prolific, with records of Night Heron, Bufflehead, Red-footed Falcon, Caspian Tern, White-winged Black Tern and Yellow-browed Warbler.

In addition to the ornithological value of the site, 23 species of butterfly and 17 species of Odonata have occurred.

There is an active wildlife group and a sightings log is kept in the Fishing Lodge, where the annual wildlife report, published since 1989, can also be bought.

Timing

Owing to disturbance, mainly by dog walkers and anglers, early morning visits are most productive. Weather conditions are also most important as Colwick is situated within a geographical funnel, which means that it is almost always windy to varying degrees. Birdwatchers' favourite conditions, easterly winds with drizzle, provide good watching (during April–May and August–October). Light northwesterly winds with clear skies usually guarantees some visible migration especially in autumn.

Access

The park is open at all times but visitors are asked to exercise care when on the footpaths. The area has three major parking areas which are free, in addition to which there is a lot of parking within the park for an exit fee of 50 pence. Sheltered car parks are best avoided as car crime does occur, the safest car parks being next to the fishing lodge and outside Colwick Hall. Buses for Colwick leave Nottingham City Centre fre-

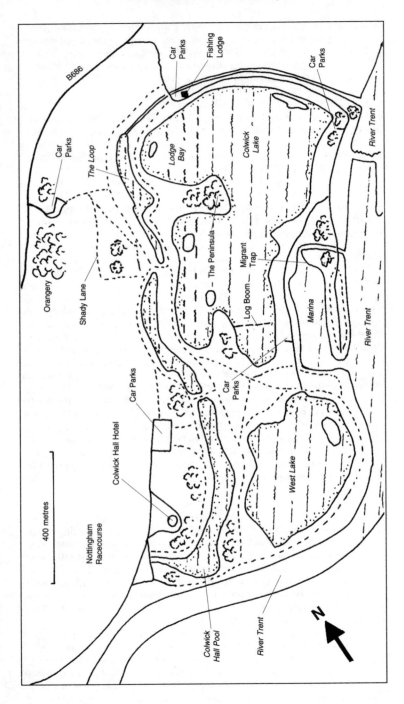

quently and Netherfield railway station is about 15 minutes walk away. Vehicular access to the park is off the B686, which passes Nottingham Racecourse; follow signs for water user entrance only, and turn off Mile End Road onto River Road. Disabled birdwatchers can view both lakes from their vehicles at several points.

Calendar

Resident: Great Crested and Little Grebes, wildfowl, Sparrowhawk, Kestrel, Great Spotted Woodpecker, Kingfisher, tits, woodland species.

April–July: Hobby (frequent), Common Tern, Reed and Sedge Warbler, Chiffchaff, Willow Warbler, Whitethroat and Lesser Whitethroat, Blackcap, Garden Warbler.

Annual rarities: Black and Arctic Terns, Mediterranean and Little Gulls, Water Rail, Lesser Spotted Woodpecker, Black-necked Grebe. Slavonian and Red-necked Grebes (rare).

NETHERFIELD

Habitat

The disused gravel pits at Netherfield have been partly used as a dump for coal slurry. The whole area is a part of the Trent floodplain and the two remaining gravel ponds are frequently used by anglers. The two slurry pits are separated by a raised causeway, which is elevated some 50 feet (15 m) above the pits, giving a commanding view of the area. The largest tank is virtually full but retains some water, with muddy edges attractive to waders and roosting gulls and terns. The smaller tank is mainly deep water, attracting good numbers of wildfowl, with smaller birds feeding and breeding around the tank edges. The whole area is undergoing change as the new owners of the site, a private mining company, seek to secure the locality after use. The Nottinghamshire birdwatchers and other interested parties are attempting to reach agreement with the landowners for the provision of a site for passage waders as part of the subsequent development.

Species

Because of the largely temporary nature of the main slurry lagoon sites, much of the avian interest is restricted to passage and wintering birds. A railway embankment, which forms the western boundary of the site, holds Turtle Doves and Lesser Whitethroat during the summer and occasionally Long-eared Owl in the winter. The scrubby banks of the gravel ponds are a frequent stopping-off point for small numbers of Whinchat and a regular wintering site for Stonechat. Cormorants roost on the electricity pylons and parties of wild swans sometimes feed on the extensive sewage farm fields to the east.

During the spring, pools created on the slurry attract most of the common species of wader, with Little Ringed Plovers being common from April to September. Regular species in autumn include Ruff, Dunlin, Greenshank, Redshank, Green and Common Sandpipers. In the late autumn up to 4,000 Golden Plover and 1,000 Lapwing use the pools as a roost site, along with several hundred Wigeon and smaller numbers of Teal, Shoveler and Pintail. The weedy banks and fields attract good

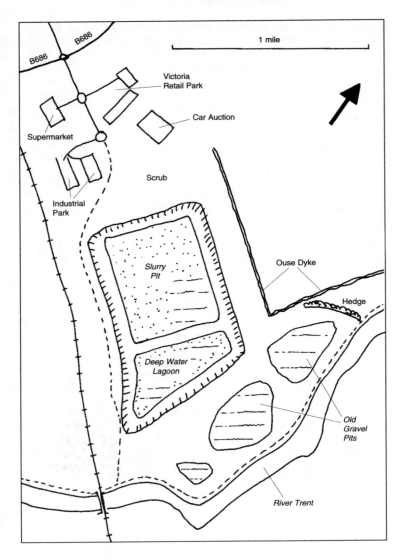

numbers of Skylarks and Meadow Pipits, with Yellow Wagtails being common in the summer.

A good selection of rare birds have been located at this site through regular checking of the migrant waders and wildfowl and have included American Wigeon, Pectoral, Buff-breasted and Broad-billed Sandpipers and White-winged Black Tern.

Timing

April to June is the best time for passage waders, with terns and gulls also moving through the area. In autumn, birds begin to arrive from early August onwards, with passage peaking in September and October. Winter produces good numbers of birds until the pools freeze over in harsh conditions. Mornings and evenings are the best times to visit, especially at weekends when motor-cycles can be a problem.

Access

There is unrestricted access at all times, although the slurry lagoons are, in theory at least, private. Netherfield railway station is 15 minutes walk away and buses arrive from Nottingham city centre on a regular basis. Vehicle access is directly off the B686; park in the large retail park (look for Morrisons), and then walk 300 yds/m to the first patch of scrub. It should be noted that this site is in a state of continual transition. The local wildlife groups are hoping that a reserve can be created at the end of the sites' working life.

Calendar

April–June: Rarer grebes, Hobby, passage waders, gulls, terns, hirundines, Grasshopper Warbler.

July–October: Wildfowl, Little Ringed and Ringed Plovers, Dunlin, Redshank, Greenshank, Green and Common Sandpiper, gulls, terns.

Whinchat

HOLME PIERREPONT

Habitat

This vast site comprises restored gravel pits, currently operative gravel workings and settling ponds, a water sports centre, meadows, grassland and scrub, with some small sections of woodland. Many of the best areas are private, although there is some access to view parts of these.

The site is dominated by two water areas, the 1000 m international rowing course and the 140-acre (56 ha), A52 pit. The rowing course has attracted a good number of county rarities over the years and once earned the name 'skua alley' after three of the four species of skua occurred there in one year. The A52 pit has also pulled in a remarkable

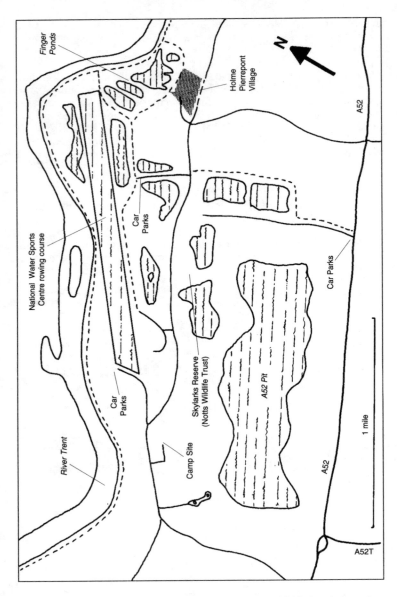

number of rarities since its formation in the early 1980s but it is unfortunately private and even local birdwatchers are finding it increasingly difficult to gain access. To the east of the A52 pit are the current works pits, which often prove attractive to waders, gulls and terns. Moving farther east towards the end of the rowing course are the old 'finger ponds', an area largely neglected by birdwatchers. There is also a small reserve of the local wildlife trust, which is mainly composed of an extensive willow holt with a pool and a tern platform.

The only woodland of note is around Holme Pierrepont Hall and its surrounding gardens. The main grassland areas are around the A52 pit, where they are grazed, at the eastern end of the rowing course, rough grassland, and adjacent to the finger ponds on a reclaimed tip.

Species

Winter wildfowl flocks usually hold all the regular species including Gadwall, Teal, Wigeon, Pochard, Tufted Duck, Goldeneye and Goosander, with the rowing course and A52 pit being favoured spots. The rarer grebes, Black-necked, Red-necked and Slavonian are virtually annual along with Smew, Red-breasted Merganser and, mainly in spring, Garganey. Waders favour the A52 pit and the works pits, with good flocks of Golden Plovers in autumn and winter and also regular Jack Snipe and Ruff. Passage species include the usual mix of Little Ringed and Ringed Plovers, Dunlin, Redshank, Greenshank, Green and Common Sandpipers, with occasional records of other species such as Sanderling, Little Stint and Curlew Sandpiper, Spotted Redshank and Wood Sandpiper.

During favourable conditions good numbers of migrant birds pass through the site, especially terns and Little Gulls. Hobbies are seen regularly both on passage and during the summer months. All three species of woodpecker occur and Long-eared Owls occasionally roost in scrub around the site. In total, 240 species have been recorded including many local and several national rarities.

The best of the rarer waders recorded have been Lesser Yellowlegs, Pectoral and Spotted Sandpipers, while Spotted Crake, White-winged Black Tern, Richard's Pipit, Golden Oriole and Lapland Bunting all show the wide variety of scarce species which may be located on an obvious migration route, even at inland localities.

Timing

For passage birds, as with most sites in inland Nottinghamshire, spring is the best period of the year (from April–June). Apart from the A52 pit, which is private, most areas are open to the public and therefore suffer from disturbance, particularly the rowing course. Early morning visits are therefore recommended, with most visible passage taking place during the first few hours of daylight. During high summer, birds are more elusive and the public more numerous! Avoid national water sports events at all costs!

Access

There is open access to the rowing course, the finger ponds, open fields with public footpaths and the bank of the River Trent. The Nottinghamshire Trust 'Skylarks' reserve is private but can be viewed from the periphery. Viewing of the A52 pit is difficult as the whole area is private farmland at the present time. The southwestern corner of the lake can be viewed directly from the A52. The southeastern section has a metalled road, which can be accessed from a pull-in 150 yds/m past the Happy Eater restaurant when driving east along the A52. This track will also give views over the works pits.

There is public transport available from Nottingham city centre to the water sports area and the whole site can be walked in three to four hours. Car parking is easy, although some parks charge a fee and, as usual, beware of car thieves in 'quiet' car parks.

Calendar

October–March: Great Crested and Little Grebe, Gadwall, Teal, Pintail, Pochard, Tufted Duck, Goldeneye, Goosander, Ruddy Duck, Golden Plover, Jack Snipe, gull roost, Long-eared and Short-eared Owls.

April–June: Little Ringed Plover, Ringed Plover, Sanderling (rare), Dunlin, Ruff, Green and Common Sandpiper, Common, Arctic and Black Terns, Swift, Sand Martin, Swallow, House Martin, Yellow Wagtail, Northern Wheatear, warblers and passage migrants.

July–October: Rarer grebes, Little Ringed Plover, Ringed Plover, Dunlin, Ruff, Green and Common Sandpiper, Common, Arctic and Black Terns, Swift, Sand Martin, Swallow, House Martin, Meadow Pipit, Yellow Wagtail, Northern Wheatear, Whinchat, warblers and passage migrants.

48 LOUND

OS Sheet 120

Habitat

In essence the site which birdwatchers refer to as Lound is a gravel and aggregate extraction complex in the northeast of Nottinghamshire but the site has a much greater variety of habitat than most such complexes and its extensive acreage means that it has developed into one of the foremost birdwatching localities in the county.

Formerly worked by North Notts and Hoveringham gravel company the site is now managed by Tarmac Roadstone who have extended the area of new workings dramatically. All the pits at present lie on the western side of the River Idle, from a position immediately adjacent to the river, running westwards. The complex now stretches from the northwestern outskirts of Retford, Belmoor Quarries, skirting the villages of Sutton-cum-Lound and Lound and extending almost north to the village of Mattersey. As the site is a working area, however, the local geography is constantly changing, and pits which are good for birds one month or year may have changed completely by the next visit, whereas new areas may have been created which may then be the best spots for certain species. These changing conditions are particularly important with regard specifically to the number of wildfowl and waders using the site.

The whole area to the west of the River Idle has a very sandy substrate with resultant sandy heathland vegetation, while that to the east of the river is composed of heavier clays and is mostly used for arable farming.

The area as a whole encompasses a wide variety of habitat types in addition to the working and disused sand and gravel workings. Some of the larger old disused pits were embanked and have been and are being filled with flyash, which is pumped from Cottam power station on the River Trent to the east. The oldest pits, now filled, have been topped with soil and grassed and are now grazed with sheep. These areas form interesting habitats for a variety of species such as pipits, wagtails and Skylarks, corvids and for hunting raptors. Once stabilised, these areas are, however, given back to agriculture.

The newly worked pits offer a variety of shallow and deeper water areas, with muddy margins and grass of varying heights growing around the edges and on any islands. The variable water levels and the extent of recent excavations have rapid effects on the the numbers of wildfowl and breeding gulls and terns which use the site. Apart from the older pits, which have been filled and returned to agricultural usage, others have been left for fishing, water-skiing, windsurfing and, in the centre of the complex, is a captive wildfowl reserve centre which has provided a number of escapees in the past! A small area of willow carr by the side of the River Idle is a reserve of the Nottinghamshire Wildlife Trust. Thus there are pits with deep water, newly worked areas with shallow water with colonising sedge, reed and reedmace around the edges, small sandy islands and extensive areas of willow and sallow carrs.

The River Idle itself winds around the eastern edge of the complex, and although fairly narrow, it offers running fresh water and is an important dragonfly habitat. The wide access tracks which run through the complex are bordered with large old hedgerows left over from times prior to the excavations. The hedgerows consist mainly of hawthorn but there are also a large number of old oaks and a wide variety of other tree species including ash, elm, old willows, alders and elder. There is a healthy understorey of bramble and, in more open areas, willow herb, gorse and broom dominate, with areas of long rough grassland, thistles and docks being found on colonised spoil heaps.

By the side of Neatholme Road, where it leaves Lound village, are grazed horse paddocks which offer a further area of interest for species like thrushes and wagtails. Towards the end of the lane newly worked open pits either side of the track are very attractive to wildfowl. At the end of Neatholme Road the track crosses the River Idle via a narrow bridge, and on the opposite bank is an interesting area of willow and sallow carr with a central area of rough grassland. Additional habitats include areas of set-aside fields, an old Scots pine plantation and a newer conifer plantation near Tiln, small riverside plantations of poplars again near Tiln and Belmoor Quarries and extensive areas of grazing fields around Sutton-cum-Lound village. The open arable fields to the east of the River Idle are a haunt of plover flocks, corvids and wintering raptors.

Species

With such a wide variety of habitats Lound has a long list of bird species, which includes several rarities and no less than two firsts for the county. The site also lies on a known visible migration route and is close enough to the Trent Valley migration corridor to attract passage migrants moving along that route. It is, however, difficult due to the largely even local topography to find a good vantage point from which to watch visible migration, as many of the birds involved seem to move on a wide front, being concentrated one day at one point and on others at differing locations. The site attracts significant totals of some normally coastal wader species for an inland locality and it is for the wildfowl and waders that the complex is best known. It must be stressed again, though, that the numbers of waders and wildfowl are greatly affected by the water levels and the state of development of various pits throughout the year.

Many species of wildfowl are present throughout the year, with some obviously reaching peak numbers in midwinter, while others such as

Shoveler (up to 70) and Pintail tend to peak earlier in the autumn, usually in August/September. Large flocks of Canada and Greylag Geese are usually in evidence, with over 200 of the latter usual and a several pairs breeding. Additionally, flocks of Pink-footed Geese and even parties of White-fronts are occasional on the arable fields across the River Idle. Mute Swans breed and reach totals of over 100 birds in the early autumn, while small numbers of both Bewick's and Whooper are also occasional in winter.

Principal wintering duck by weight of numbers are Gadwall, which have increased and now peak at about 125, Pochard (7–800), Tufted Duck (3–400), Teal (200–250) and Wigeon (2–300). Other species include regular Goosander (20–35) and Goldeneye (up to 35 birds). Rarer species have included fairly frequent Scaup, Red-crested Pochard, Ferruginous Duck, American Wigeon and Green-winged Teal. The first county Lesser Scaup was found here in May and there have been some exceptional records, such as the flock of 115 Common Scoter seen resting on the pits on 22 October 1990. Shelduck are recorded in small numbers through the year and pairs have bred, while Garganey are also regular in spring and have on rare occasions bred.

Good numbers of both Great Crested and Little Grebes breed and are to be found throughout the year, while Black-necked Grebes have been recorded with increasing frequency in recent years and have even been known to have bred. Red-necked and Slavonian Grebes have also occurred infrequently and the numbers of Cormorant using the site have increased rapidly in the last five years, with the establishment of a breeding colony on the River Trent. The area also supports a large winter population of Coot, with counts topping the 1,000 mark and large numbers being recorded in all months. Water Rails are possibly resident and may breed but are certainly evident in winter, while Bitterns are most probably annual, but with such an extensive area of suitable feeding habitat and cover they are very difficult to locate and usually only seen when making one of their infrequent flights from feeding to roosting sites.

Winter also sees large flocks of Golden Plovers (up to 6,000), and Lapwing (4,000) on the nearby fields, with the birds commuting to the shallow pits to bathe and preen. The same fields hold large flocks of Woodpigeon and Stock Doves, with up to 100 of the latter being a significant total. The hawthorn hedgerows attract feeding flocks of Redwing, Blackbird and Fieldfare from October onwards, with up to 1,000 birds present during peak periods, often in December. Other rarer winter passerines have included wintering Stonechats, the odd Snow Bunting and fly-by Lapland Bunting, and there is even a record of Shorelark.

Sparrowhawks and Kestrels are resident and often obvious, while Merlins are often present on the fields to the east of the Idle in winter, Marsh Harriers have become frequent passage migrants in spring, Osprey and Peregrine are just about annual and Hobbies have also increased, with regular summer records suggesting breeding nearby. The large numbers of dragonflies around the pits during the autumn period provide ideal hunting for the fledged young birds, which may provide excellent viewing as they hunt over the pits and adjacent hedges. Long-eared Owls breed and Short-eared Owls are fairly regular from autumn through to April, with usually 1–2 birds to be seen hunting the rough grass areas around the pits.

Long-eared Owl

A winter gull roost at the pits has varied with the state of filling of some of the larger pits but at times it has held large totals of four species, with peaks of 8,000 Black-headed, 600 Common, 500 Herring, 600 Great Black-backed Gulls in midwinter and up to 450 Lesser Black-backed Gulls in September–October. There have been regular records of Mediterranean and Yellow-legged Gull and odd Glaucous and Iceland Gulls. A breeding colony of Black-headed Gulls varies with the amount of suitable habitat but up to 150 pairs have nested, as have odd pairs of Lesser Black-backed Gull, and even a pair of Little Gulls attempted to nest one year.

All three woodpeckers occur, with Lesser Spotted usually being found in the old oaks but Green being by far the commonest species. Many other species also breed with good totals of Sand Martin in the newer worked areas, odd pairs of Kingfisher and a wide variety of passerines including Reed, Sedge and Grasshopper Warblers, Whitethroat, Lesser Whitethroat, Blackcap, Garden Warbler and Willow Warbler. Nightingale has bred in the past in plantations near Tiln, Turtle Doves nest and there are large numbers of Skylark and Meadow Pipit with attendant Cuckoos during the spring. Yellow Wagtails occur in their greatest numbers during passage periods, with up to 50 recorded in a day in May, but some pairs also nest, as do Pied Wagtails, with Grey Wagtails being noted regularly on passage in autumn and occasionally in winter.

The spring migration period also brings large flocks of hirundines and Swifts, up to 500 of the latter in May, which feed over the pits and, given suitable weather conditions, arrivals of parties of terns may be witnessed. Black Terns appeared in good numbers in May 1990 with a peak of 55 recorded but usually totals are lower, while Arctic Terns are regular with Little and Sandwich also having been noted. Common Terns breed, with about 20 pairs annual, as well as occurring as passage birds and, to complete the tern set, vagrant Caspian and White-winged Black Terns have also paid a visit. Often accompanying the passage

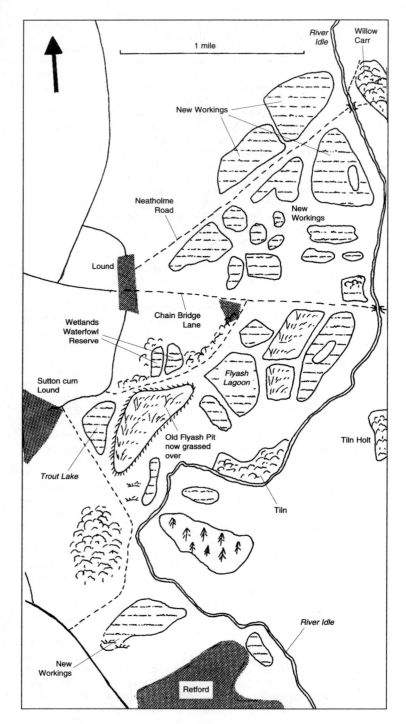

terns are small parties of Little Gulls and, on occasions, single or small flocks of Kittiwakes may appear in March–June.

Waders are a special feature of this locality, with species such as Grey Plover having been recorded in exceptional numbers for an inland locality, up to 30 birds on good autumn days for instance. Most species occur during the migration periods of April–June and late July–October but there are regular winter records of Green Sandpipers, Jack Snipe and Common Snipe, odd Dunlin and Ruff, and even Spotted Redshank has been noted. Little Ringed and Ringed Plovers, Oystercatcher and Redshank all breed in small numbers, with the latter reaching peak numbers in March/April (up to 30), while northern populations of Ringed Plovers pass through in late April and May. This is also the best period for spring records of Sanderling, Turnstone, Little Stint, Ruff, Whimbrel, Black and Bar-tailed Godwits, Common Sandpiper, Greenshank and Spotted Redshank, with odd Wood Sandpipers also being nearly annual. Autumn numbers are greater and birds often stay for longer periods of time so the chances of seeing them are greater at this season. Dunlin may peak at over 100 birds, and more regular species at this season include Little Stint and Curlew Sandpiper, Black-tailed Godwit and Common Sandpiper. Curlew may occur at any time, they have also been known to breed, but usually peak in autumn when Whimbrel are rare.

As different pits have been in prime wader condition over the years there has been a good selection of rare waders, with records of Pectoral Sandpiper, Buff-breasted Sandpiper, Grey and Red-necked Phalaropes.

The migration periods also produce a few records annually of species such as Northern Wheatear, Whinchat, Stonechat and Redstart, with less frequent Black Redstart and Ring Ouzel. Overhead flocks of Skylarks and Meadow Pipits may be in evidence during the late autumn passing westwards, with peak day counts of 150 of the latter noted. Rock Pipits are occasional in April and October and a vagrant Richard's Pipit was located on one of the grassed spoil heaps in late October 1990. Large flocks of finches, Goldfinch, Greenfinch and Linnet, 250–400 of the latter two species, gather in the autumn to feed on seeding weeds and grasses and, until recently, Corn Buntings were regular visitors from the surrounding fields.

Other rare birds located in recent years include the first county Ring-billed Gull, Spoonbill, Golden Oriole in the poplar plantations along the river, Bluethroat, Red-backed Shrike and, possibly the most bizarre of all, a Razorbill.

Timing
With its good list of species, this locality will repay a visit at any time of year. Spring and autumn are obviously favoured for the variety of passage waders and passerines recorded, but the winter is just as productive for wildfowl, and even summer has a good range of breeding birds.

Access
The centre of the Lound complex lies approximately 2 miles (3.2 km) north of Retford. From the A638 Retford to Blyth road turn right (north) 1 mile (1.6 km) outside Retford onto a minor road to Sutton. In Sutton village turn right onto another minor road signed to Lound. On leaving Sutton village, after 800 yds/m a public footpath runs right (south) to the east of a trout pond to Belmoor Quarries. At the point where the

minor road bends left, 800 yds/m before Lound village, a wide track runs right between old oaks to the wetlands wildfowl centre. It is possible to park 400 yds/m down this track and view the ash lagoon and reclaimed fields to the right or continue down the track to where it joins Chain Bridge Lane. Alternatively, Chain Bridge Lane can be accessed from Lound village centre and is driveable with care to the River Idle.

A footpath along the riverbank is not a designated public footpath but is widely used by the general public. It leads north to Neatholme bridge or south to Tiln, and thence to Belmoor Quarries. Neatholme Road is also accessed from Lound village where there is rather limited parking and a public footpath down Neatholme Road to the River Idle. All other tracks in the area are private.

The Nottinghamshire Wildlife Trust Reserve is adjacent to the track at the end of Chain Bridge Lane.

Calendar

Resident: Little Grebe, Great Crested Grebe, Cormorant, Greylag Goose, Mute Swan, Shelduck, Gadwall, Pochard, Tufted Duck, Coot, Sparrowhawk, Kestrel, Black-headed Gull, Stock Dove, Long-eared Owl, Kingfisher, Meadow Pipit, Green, Great Spotted and Lesser Spotted Woodpeckers.

April–September: Black-necked Grebe (scarce), Shoveler, Garganey (scarce), Marsh Harrier, Osprey (annual), Hobby, Oystercatcher, Little Ringed and Ringed Plover, Grey Plover, Sanderling, Little Stint, Curlew Sandpiper, Dunlin, Ruff, Snipe, Black-tailed Godwit, Bar-tailed Godwit, Whimbrel, Curlew, Spotted Redshank, Greenshank, Redshank, Green Sandpiper, Wood Sandpiper, Common Sandpiper, Turnstone, Little Gull, Common, Arctic and Black Terns, Turtle Dove, Swift, Sand Martin, House Martin, Swallow, Yellow Wagtail, Grey Wagtail, Reed, Sedge and Grasshopper Warbler.

October–March: Whooper and Bewick's Swan, Bittern (rare), Wigeon, Teal, Goldeneye, Goosander, Merlin, Water Rail, Golden Plover, Lapwing, Jack Snipe, Green Sandpiper, gulls, Fieldfare, Redwing, Grey Wagtail.

49 ATTENBOROUGH NATURE RESERVE/ATTENBOROUGH AND LONG EATON NEW WORKINGS

OS Map129

Habitat

The Attenborough Nature Reserve is situated on the southwestern edge of Nottingham and covers approximately 240 acres (97 ha) of disused gravel pits which lie along an important northeast to southwest, cross-country migration route. It is owned by Ready Mixed Concretes (Butterley Aggregates), and jointly managed with the Nottinghamshire Wildlife Trust. The Delta area has been designated as an SSSI.

One of the main assets of the reserve is the wide variety of habitats to be found in a condensed area, with eight or nine pits each at varying stages of maturity. The most established areas, such as the Delta, have already developed mature willow and alder woodland, with the fringes offering dense hawthorn scrub and thick aquatic vegetation. Both the Delta and Wetmarsh areas boast a good area of rapidly expanding *Phragmites*. The most recently worked pits offer more open habitat, with a mixture of shallow water, vegetated islands and exposed spits. The fields, with surrounding mature hedgerows, to the south of the River Trent are typical of the local rolling farmland and produce another range of bird species to be seen around the reserve boundaries.

The majority of the pits have, in the most part, shallow edges which then drop abruptly into deep water. The higher ridges of the undulating contours below the water's surface may, after extensive dry spells, usually in late summer and autumn, appear as exposed spits and islands, which may then attract waders, gulls and terns.

The River Trent does not provide any special habitat, but running southwest to northeast the Trent Valley acts as a migratory corridor and thus must be considered an important factor in attracting migratory birds to the area. The recent general improvement in the river's quality is a welcome sign, and the increase in invertebrates and fish stocks has provided an important food source for many waterbirds and, in particular, is probably responsible for the increased success of Kingfishers.

It is possible to see in excess of 50 bird species on the reserve at any time of year, and during the spring migration a total of 87 species has been recorded in a day on two occasions.

The New Workings is an important additional area, lying outside the Attenborough Reserve boundaries, but can easily be included in a visit. It is possible to walk from the reserve or alternatively to drive and park (see Access). This area consists of the most recently worked areas of the complex. It is possible to walk around the perimeter of the site, although the land is private and on no account should anyone walk onto the scrapes. Common sense and respect will enable the good understanding between the landowners and birders to continue. The area is made up of shallow gravel pools with little vegetation but some reed areas are starting to develop. The whole area is liable to change, however, as new pits are continually being dug and others filled in.

Species

During the winter months the main interest is in the wildfowl and waterbirds, but additionally winter thrushes, finches and tit flocks are normally well represented. Typical wintering waterfowl include Great Crested Grebe, Mallard, Tufted Duck, Pochard, Goldeneye and Ruddy Duck, the latter in flocks of up to 50 birds. Pintail, Gadwall, Wigeon Goosander and Shelduck all occur but in smaller numbers. The number of all species is often subjected to dramatic increases during spells of hard weather when it is worth looking out for odd Smew and Redbreasted Merganser. The most productive areas are generally Clifton and Coneries Pits. If all the pits freeze over the birds will move to the unfrozen River Trent, and it is often on these occasions that rarities are found and wild swans and geese are noted.

Cormorants roost on the islands off Barton Lane, with maximum counts in December exceeding 200 birds. The Delta and Wetmarsh play host to Teal and Water Rail, the latter often being seen at close range. In recent years these spots have occasionally held Bittern and an increasing area of reedbeds has seen individuals of this species present throughout the winter period. Black-headed and Common Gulls are fairly numerous, with Herring, Great and Lesser Black-backed Gulls being regular. All the gulls can be seen in highest numbers as they gather in the late afternoon before flying off to roost. At least one Yellow-legged Gull is usually present and tends to loaf around the silt on the works pond.

The alders around the Delta attract small flocks of Siskin and Redpoll and tit flocks are ever present, with Long-tailed and Willow Tits always in evidence. Sparrowhawks are resident but most obvious as they indulge in their territorial displays over the Delta area in late winter. All three woodpeckers occur but Lesser Spotted has recently become somewhat scarce. The sewage farm off Barton Lane is always worth checking as it is frequented by good numbers of Pied Wagtails and the flocks normally contain the odd Grey Wagtail.

The New Workings are of less interest during the winter but provide a site for Snipe, Jack Snipe, Green Sandpiper, Corn Bunting and Tree Sparrow. Stonechats have wintered regularly here and rarer winter species have included Merlin, Peregrine, Water Pipit and Great Grey Shrike.

Spring usually brings a reasonable passage of waders, the more regular being Ringed and Little Ringed Plover, Dunlin, Ruff, Curlew, Bar-tailed Godwit, Greenshank, Green and Common Sandpipers. Scarcer species which are recorded occasionally include Black-tailed Godwit, Whimbrel, Wood Sandpiper and Turnstone. The principal areas for these species are the New Workings, with the largest area of shallow water and suitable exposed margins, which support breeding Ringed and Little Ringed Plovers, and the Delta front and River Flash. The latter two areas are less consistent, however, being more dependent upon varying water levels but usually the River Flash holds water until May.

The rough grassland around the New Workings and the fields south of the Trent attract passage Northern Wheatear, Whinchat, Yellow and White Wagtails and Meadow Pipit during April, with freshly worked fields sometimes holding gatherings of ten or more Northern Wheatears. April and May also offer the best chance of a sighting of a passage Marsh Harrier or Osprey, both of which are annual, but invariably do not linger.

Common Terns begin to arrive by mid April and two rafts now support a thriving breeding population. Arctic and Black Terns are also annual in spring but the timing and number of birds involved are governed by the prevailing weather conditions. Main Pond is generally the best place to look as they tend to mix with the breeding Common Terns. Kittiwake, Little Gull, Sandwich Tern, Garganey and Black-necked Grebe are all scarce but occasional visitors during April–May. Kingfishers are particularly noisy and therefore more noticeable during the spring, the river outflow near the Bund being a generally guaranteed spot for bumping into this flashing blue streaker.

A wide variety of summer visitors and resident birds breed on the reserve, from Great Crested Grebe through wildfowl to Sparrowhawk, Cuckoo, Tawny Owl, Sand Martin, the three wetland warblers, Sedge,

Great Grey Shrike

Reed and Grasshopper, the six scrub warblers, Blackcap, Garden Warbler, Chiffchaff, Willow Warbler, Whitethroat and Lesser Whitethroat to various tits, Tree Sparrow and Reed Bunting. Additional species breed at the New Workings, with Little Grebe, Ringed and Little Ringed Plover (3–4 pairs), Meadow Pipit and Corn Bunting. Grey Herons from the nearby heronry, on the south side of the Trent (30 pairs in 1994) also make regular fishing trips to the pits. Common Terns breed on rafts in Main Pond and Church Pond and also occasionally on islands at Clifton Pit.

The best area for seeing and hearing the warblers is along the pathways surrounding the Delta and the thick hedgerows along Barton Lane which normally have Whitethroat, Lesser Whitethroat and Sedge Warbler. Spring rarities have included Bluethroat, Little Egret and Avocet.

Autumn migration begins in July with the first returning Common and Green Sandpipers, Greenshank and Dunlin. More waders occur in autumn than in spring and birds tend to linger for longer periods. Favourable weather conditions normally produce small numbers of Oystercatcher, Ruff, Black-tailed Godwit, Redshank, Spotted Redshank and Wood Sandpiper. The best areas are along the Delta front, Clifton Pit and the Wetmarsh areas where water levels should be low, particularly in dry spells, providing food-rich muddy margins. The New Workings are also worth checking.

One of the notable events of September and October is the build-up of Mallard and Shoveler, with up to 250 of the latter and 500 of the former. Large flocks of Swifts and hirundines feed over the pits, sometimes bringing in a hunting Hobby. The numbers of Common Terns are swollen with flying juveniles and passage birds. Although not a great time for migrant passerines on the reserve, the autumn may always come up with some oddity such as the Penduline Tit in 1994. Other recent rarities have included Little and Great White Egrets, Bluethroat and Great Grey Shrike.

Timing

The whole area is at its best during the migration periods of spring and autumn but but there is always something of interest throughout the year. The New Workings are best visited early morning or evenings in midweek and on Saturday afternoon and Sundays to avoid the working times of the gravel company.

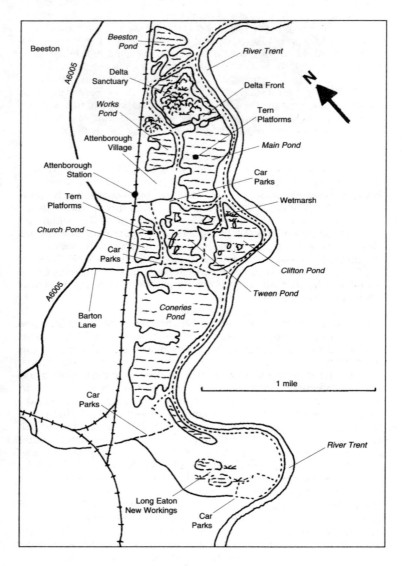

Access

Attenborough Nature Reserve is situated between Beeston and Long Eaton, 5 miles (8 km) southwest of Nottingham, off the A6005. From junction 25 of the M1 take the A52, signposted to Nottingham; after 1.5 miles (2.4 km) turn right at the roundabout on the A6003, signposted to Long Eaton, and Toton. A further 1.25 miles (2 km) on turn left at traffic lights on the A6005. After half a mile (0.8 km) turn right at the traffic lights through Chilwell Retail Park, continue straight on at the round-about onto Barton Lane and after 800 yds/m park in the obvious car park. All areas are easily accessible from here.

The New Workings can either be reached by: (1) continuing on foot to the end of Barton Lane and taking the footpath south along the banks of the Trent, the pits eventually being reached after approximately 2 miles (3.2 km) behind the windsurfing pit; (2) by taking the A6005 towards Long Eaton, straight on at the traffic lights, signposted Long Eaton and Derby, then after 400 yds/m take the left fork down Station Street, continue for approximately 1 mile (1.6 km) and turn left immediately after the petrol station down New Tythe street. Follow this road to its end, after crossing the railway line the road bends to the right and becomes a single-track lane; go to the end of the lane and the New Workings are obvious to the left of the lane.

Calendar

Resident: Great Crested Grebe, Cormorant, Grey Heron, Tufted Duck, Sparrowhawk, Kingfisher, Tawny Owl, Great Spotted Woodpecker, Pied Wagtail, Long-tailed Tit, Willow Tit, Tree Sparrow, Bullfinch, Reed Bunting, Corn Bunting.

October–March: Little Grebe, Bittern (scarce), geese and wild swans (rare), Gadwall, Teal, Shoveler, Pochard, Goldeneye, Goosander, Red-breasted Merganser, Smew (all rare), Ruddy Duck, Water Rail, Snipe, Lapwing (flocks), Yellow-legged Gull, Long-eared Owl, Green Woodpecker, Lesser Spotted Woodpecker (scarce), Fieldfare, Redwing, Goldcrest, Siskin, Redpoll.

April–September: Black-necked Grebe (scarce), Garganey, Common Scoter (scarce), Osprey (regular, never lingers), Hobby, passage waders, Little Gull, Common, Arctic and Black Terns, Cuckoo, Yellow Wagtail, White Wagtail, Whinchat, Northern Wheatear, Grasshopper Warbler, Reed Warbler, Sedge Warbler, Garden Warbler, Whitethroat, Lesser Whitethroat.

ADDITIONAL SITES

Name	Hills and Holes.
Grid Reference	SK 556 681
Habitat	Grassland and hawthorn scrub set in a formerly quarried area in the valley of the River Meden.
Species	All three wagtails, Kingfisher, winter thrush flocks, Green Sandpiper, occasional Hawfinch.
Timing	All.
Access	Between Shirebrook and Market Warsop; public footpath off B6031; the area is used extensively by local people but footpaths are not well signed.

Name   Wollaton Park (central Nottingham).
Grid Reference SK 527 397
Habitat   Large park with mixed woodland and small lake.
Species   Waterfowl, common woodland species including Lesser Spotted Woodpecker, large corvid roost; Rook, Jackdaw and Carrion Crow.
Timing   All year.
Access   Open access dawn to dusk but gates locked at night.

Name   Bestwood Lodge Country Park (northern edge of Nottingham City).
Grid Reference SK 569 465
Habitat   Mixed deciduous woodland, open grassland, scrub, wet meadows, river and small lake.
Species   Typical deciduous woodland species including Marsh Tit and all three woodpeckers, breeding Snipe and Lapwing.
Timing   All year.
Access   Unrestricted in public areas.

Name   Thorndale Plantation.
Grid Reference SK 622 505
Habitat   Small mixed deciduous woodland.
Species   Typical woodland species including Green and Great Spotted Woodpecker, Nuthatch, Treecreeper, Marsh and Willow Tit.
Timing   All year.
Access   Only via footpath on Mansfield Lane, Calverton. No access from B6386. Woodland section to the north of the road strictly private.

Name   Rufford Country Park (southwest of Ollerton).
Grid Reference SK 641 645 or 646 657
Habitat   Small lake, open parkland, mixed deciduous woodland.
Species   Wildfowl, woodland species including Nuthatch and three species of woodpecker, occasional Hawfinch and owls.
Timing   All.
Access   Public access dawn to dusk with a charge for car parking.

Name   Stoke Bardolph, Burton Meadows, Gunthorpe (stretch of River Trent between Stoke Bardolph and Gunthorpe villages.
Grid Reference From SK 647 421 to 680 438
Habitat   River Trent, riverbanks, hedgerows, farmland, small fishing lakes and wet meadows, in autumn/winter, subject to flooding.
Species   Wildfowl, notably Goldeneye, Goosander, occasional Scaup, waders, typical birds of open farmland and hedgerows including Meadow Pipits, Reed Bunting, Yellowhammer, terns, gulls, geese flocks.
Timing   All year.
Access   Public road, footpath along riverbank and around lake.

Name	Huthwaite Refuse Tip.
Grid Reference	Approximately SK 460 580
Habitat	Waste disposal site.
Species	Large numbers of gulls in winter, with a good chance of Glaucous and Iceland.
Timing	Winter months of October–April.
Access	Strictly no access to the site, with viewing from public roads and footpaths.

Name	Moorgreen Reservoir (Mansfield Reservoir on southern outskirts of Mansfield).
Grid Reference	SK 515 596
Habitat	Small reservoir, sewage works, scrub.
Species	Good counts of Little Grebe, highest in county, Ruddy Ducks, other wildfowl, occasional waders.
Timing	All year.
Access	Off A38 or B6139 onto access path which runs all round reservoir.

Name	Cottam.
Grid Reference	SK 830790
Habitat	Series of two large lagoons and ponds, willow and hawthorn scrub, small reedbed, dykes, rough grassland, River Trent.
Species	Winter wildfowl, with good counts of Wigeon, Teal, Mallard, Tufted Duck, waders, occasional Bittern, Garganey, Reed and Sedge Warbler.
Timing	All year.
Access	Footpath along west bank of River Trent from Laneham.

USEFUL ADDRESSES AND PUBLICATIONS

Lincolnshire

County Recorder: Howard Bunn, 16 Vivian Avenue, Grimsby, North Lincolnshire, DN32 8QF.

Lincolnshire Bird Club: Secretary and Records to: John Mighell, 3 Church Walk, Metheringham, Lincoln, LN4 3HA.

Lincolnshire Trust for Nature Conservation: Banovallum House, Manor House Street, Horncastle, Lincolnshire, LN9 5HF.

Gibraltar Point Field Station: Gibraltar Road, Skegness, Lincolnshire, PE24 4SU.

Publications

The Birds of Lincolnshire and South Humberside Atkin, K and Lorand, S. 1989. Leading Edge.

Lincolnshire Bird Report (produced by LBC). Annual from 1979–1993. Available from: Rob Watson, c/o Herrick Watson Ltd, 8 High Street, Skegness, Lincs, PE25 3NW.

Northamptonshire

County Recorder: RW Bullock, 81 Cavendish Drive, Northampton, NN3 3HL.

Northants Bird Club: Secretary: Mrs Eleanor K McMahon, Oriole House, 5 The Croft, Hanging Houghton, Northants.

Banbury Ornithological Society (includes western part of Northants in their recording area): Secretary: Phil Douthwaite, Townsend Farm, Radway, Warwickshire.

Northamptonshire Wildlife Trust: Lings House, Billing Lings, Northampton, NN3 4BR.

Publications

No County Avifauna since *The Birds of Northamptonshire and Neighbourhood* by Lord Lilford (2 vols), published by RH Porter (1895).

Northants Bird Report back to 1972, available from RW Bullock as above. Prices on request.

Derbyshire

County Recorder: Rodney W Key, 3 Farningham Close, Spondon, Derby, DE2 7DZ.

Rare breeding bird records: Roy Frost, 66 St Lawrence Road, North Wingfield, Chesterfield, Derby, S42 5LL.

Derbyshire Wildlife Trust: Elvaston Castle Country Park, Derby, DE72 3EP.

Derbyshire Ornithological Society: Steve Shaw, 84 Moorland View Road, Walton, Chesterfield, Derby, S40 3DF.

Publications

Birds of Derbyshire. RA Frost. Moorland Publishing Company. 1978.

Birds of Sheffield Area including NE Peak District. (Eds) Jon Hornbuckle and David Herringshaw. 1985. Higham Press/Sheffield Libraries Publication. Sheffield Bird Study Group.

Leicestershire

County Recorder: Rob Fray, 5 New Park Road, Leicester, LE2 8AW.

Leicester and Rutland Ornithological Society: Miss C Nelson, 38 Field Close, Melton Mowbray, Leicester, LE13 1DS.

Leicester and Rutland Trust for Nature Conservation: 1 West Street, Leicester, LE1 6UU.

Rutland Natural History Society: Mrs L Worran, 6 Redland Close, Barrowden, Rutland, LE15 8ES.

Publications

Birds in Leicestershire and Rutland. Hickling, R. 1978. LROS.

Birdwatching walks in Leicester. LROS/Leicestershire Museums Service. 1991.

Leicestershire and Rutland Bird Reports. Leicestershire and Rutland Ornithological Society (from County Recorder).

Rutland Breeding Bird Atlas. Mitcham, T. 1992. Spiegl Press.

LRTNC Reserves Handbook. Bullock, JA and Tobin, RW (eds). 1987.

Wildlife Conservation in Charnwood Forest. Nicholson, PB *et al*. 1975. NCC.

Nottinghamshire

County Recorder: John Hopper, 4 Shipley Rise, Carlton, Nottingham, NG4 1BN.

Nottinghamshire Bird Watchers: David P Goddard, 30 Cliff Hill Ave, Stapleford, Nottingham, NG9 7HD.

Annual Bird Reports available from: Mr Gordon Ellis, 2 Tracey Close, Beeston, Nottingham.

Nottinghamshire Wildlife Trust: 310 Sneidon Dale, Nottingham, NG3 7DN

Publications

Birds of Nottinghamshire. Edited by Austen Dodds for Trent Valley Birdwatchers. 1975. David & Charles.

National

RSPB Central England Office: 46 The Green, South Bar, Banbury, Oxon, OX16 9AB.

English Nature (all except Derbyshire): Northminster House, Peterborough, PE1 1UA

Derbyshire (Peak): English Nature, Attingham Park, Shrewsbury, Shropshire, SY4 4TW.

Tide Tables

Annual tide tables with calculations for the whole of the British Isles are printed in the *Birdwatchers Yearbook*. Monthly tables appear in the two monthly magazines *Birdwatch* and *Birdwatching*. Additionally, tables may be obtained from Tourist Information offices at Cleethorpes, Mablethorpe and Skegness and various sea-angling shops.

SPECIES INCLUDED IN THIS GUIDE

Red-throated Diver	*Gavia stellata*
Black-throated Diver	*Gavia arctica*
Great Northern Diver	*Gavia immer*
White-billed Diver	*Gavia adamsii*
Little Grebe	*Tachybaptus ruficollis*
Great Crested Grebe	*Podiceps cristatus*
Red-necked Grebe	*Podiceps grisegena*
Slavonian Grebe	*Podiceps auritus*
Black-necked Grebe	*Podiceps nigricollis*
Fulmar	*Fulmarus glacialis*
Sooty Shearwater	*Puffinus griseus*
Manx Shearwater	*Puffinus puffinus*
Mediterranean Shearwater	*Puffinus yelkouan*
European Storm-petrel	*Hydrobates pelagicus*
Leach's Storm-petrel	*Oceanodroma leucorrhoa*
Northern Gannet	*Sula bassanus*
Cormorant	*Phalacrocorax carbo*
Shag	*Phalacrocorax aristotelis*
Bittern	*Botaurus stellaris*
Little Bittern	*Ixobrychus minutus*
Night Heron	*Nycticorax nycticorax*
Cattle Egret	*Bubulcus ibis*
Little Egret	*Egretta garzetta*
Great White Egret	*Egretta alba*
Grey Heron	*Ardea cinerea*
Purple Heron	*Ardea purpurea*
Black Stork	*Ciconia nigra*
White Stork	*Ciconia ciconia*
Spoonbill	*Platalea leucorodia*
Mute Swan	*Cygnus olor*
Bewick's Swan	*Cygnus columbianus*
Whooper Swan	*Cygnus cygnus*
Bean Goose	*Anser fabalis*
Pink-footed Goose	*Anser brachyrhynchus*
White-fronted Goose	*Anser albifrons*
Greylag Goose	*Anser anser*
Canada Goose	*Branta canadensis*
Barnacle Goose	*Branta leucopsis*
Brent Goose	*Branta bernicla*
Red-breasted Goose	*Branta ruficollis*
Egyptian Goose	*Alopochen aegyptiacus*
Ruddy Shelduck	*Tadorna ferruginea*
Shelduck	*Tadorna tadorna*
Mandarin	*Aix galericulata*
Eurasian Wigeon	*Anas penelope*
American Wigeon	*Anas americana*
Gadwall	*Anas strepera*
Teal	*Anas crecca*
Mallard	*Anas platyrhynchos*
Pintail	*Anas acuta*
Garganey	*Anas querquedula*
Shoveler	*Anas clypeata*
Red-crested Pochard	*Netta rufina*
Pochard	*Aythya ferina*
Ring-necked Duck	*Aythya collaris*
Ferruginous Duck	*Aythya nyroca*
Tufted Duck	*Aythya fuligula*
Scaup	*Aythya marila*
Lesser Scaup	*Aythya affinis*
Eider	*Somateria mollissima*
Long-tailed Duck	*Clangula hyemalis*
Common Scoter	*Melanitta nigra*
Velvet Scoter	*Melanitta fusca*

Species Included in this Guide

Bufflehead	*Bucephala albeola*
Goldeneye	*Bucephala clangula*
Smew	*Mergus albellus*
Red-breasted Merganser	*Mergus serrator*
Goosander	*Mergus merganser*
Ruddy Duck	*Oxyura jamaicensis*
Honey Buzzard	*Pernis apivorus*
Black Kite	*Milvus milvus*
Red Kite	*Milvus milvus*
White-tailed Eagle	*Haliaeetus albicilla*
Marsh Harrier	*Circus aeruginosus*
Hen Harrier	*Circus cyaneus*
Montagu's Harrier	*Circus pygargus*
Goshawk	*Accipiter gentilis*
Sparrowhawk	*Accipiter nisus*
Common Buzzard	*Buteo buteo*
Rough-legged Buzzard	*Buteo lagopus*
Osprey	*Pandion haliaetus*
Kestrel	*Falco tinnunculus*
Red-footed Falcon	*Falco vesperitinus*
Merlin	*Falco columbarius*
Hobby	*Falco subbuteo*
Peregrine	*Falco peregrinus*
Red Grouse	*Lagopus lagopus*
Red-legged Partridge	*Alectoris rufa*
Grey Partridge	*Perdix perdix*
Quail	*Coturnix coturnix*
Pheasant	*Phasianus colchicus*
Water Rail	*Rallus aquaticus*
Spotted Crake	*Porzana porzana*
Little Crake	*Porzana parva*
Corncrake	*Crex crex*
Moorhen	*Gallinula chloropus*
Coot	*Fulica atra*
Common Crane	*Grus grus*
Oystercatcher	*Haematopus ostralegus*
Black-winged Stilt	*Himantopus himantopus*
Avocet	*Recurvirostra avosetta*
Stone Curlew	*Burhinus oedicnemus*
Collared Pratincole	*Glareola pratincola*
Black-winged Pratincole	*Glareola nordmanni*
Little Ringed Plover	*Charadrius dubius*
Ringed Plover	*Charadrius hiaticula*
Killdeer	*Charadrius vociferus*
Kentish Plover	*Charadrius alexandrinus*
Greater Sand Plover	*Charadrius leschenaultii*
Dotterel	*Charadrius morinellus*
Pacific Golden Plover	*Pluvialis fulva*
American Golden Plover	*Pluvialis dominica*
Golden Plover	*Pluvialis apricaria*
Grey Plover	*Pluvialis squaarola*
Sociable Plover	*Chettusia gregaria*
Lapwing	*Vanellus vanellus*
Knot	*Calidris canutus*
Sanderling	*Calidris alba*
Little Stint	*Calidris minuta*
Temminck's Stint	*Calidris temminckii*
White-rumped Sandpiper	*Calidris fuscicollis*
Baird's Sandpiper	*Calidris bairdii*
Pectoral Sandpiper	*Calidris melanotos*
Sharp-tailed Sandpiper	*Calidris acuminata*
Curlew Sandpiper	*Calidris ferruginea*
Dunlin	*Calidris alpina*
Purple Sandpiper	*Calidris maritima*
Broad-billed Sandpiper	*Limicola falcinellus*
Buff-breasted Sandpiper	*Tryngites subruficollis*
Ruff	*Philomachus pugnax*
Jack Snipe	*Lymnocryptes minimus*

Species Included in this Guide

Common Snipe	*Gallinago gallinago*
Great Snipe	*Gallinago media*
Long-billed Dowitcher	*Limnodromus scolopaceus*
Woodcock	*Scolpax rusticola*
Black-tailed Godwit	*Limosa limosa*
Bar-tailed Godwit	*Limosa lapponica*
Whimbrel	*Numenius phaeopus*
Curlew	*Numenius arquata*
Spotted Redshank	*Tringa erythropus*
Redshank	*Tringa totanus*
Marsh Sandpiper	*Tringa stagnatilis*
Greenshank	*Tringa nebularia*
Lesser Yellowlegs	*Tringa flavipes*
Solitary Sandpiper	*Tringa solitaria*
Green Sandpiper	*Tringa ochropus*
Wood Sandpiper	*Tringa glareola*
Common Sandpiper	*Actitis hypoleucos*
Spotted Sandpiper	*Actitis macularia*
Turnstone	*Arenaria interpres*
Wilson's Phalarope	*Phalaropus tricolor*
Red-necked Phalarope	*Phalaropus lobatus*
Grey Phalarope	*Phalaropus fulicarius*
Pomarine Skua	*Strecorarius pomarinus*
Arctic Skua	*Strecorarius parasiticus*
Long-tailed Skua	*Strecorarius longicaudus*
Great Skua	*Strecorarius skua*
Mediterranean Gull	*Larus melanocephalus*
Laughing Gull	*Larus atricilla*
Little Gull	*Larus minutus*
Sabine's Gull	*Larus sabini*
Black-headed Gull	*Larus ridibundus*
Ring-billed Gull	*Larus delawarensis*
Common Gull	*Larus canus*
Lesser Black-backed Gull	*Larus fuscus*
Herring Gull	*Larus argentatus*
Yellow-legged Gull	*Larus cachinnans*
Iceland Gull	*Larus glaucoides*
Glaucous Gull	*Larus hyperboreus*
Great Black-backed Gull	*Larus marinus*
Kittiwake	*Rissa tridactyla*
Gull-billed Tern	*Gelochelidon nilotica*
Caspian Tern	*Sterna caspia*
Lesser Crested Tern	*Sterna bengalensis*
Sandwich Tern	*Sterna sandvicensis*
Roseate Tern	*Sterna dougalli*
Common Tern	*Sterna hirundo*
Arctic Tern	*Sterna paradisaea*
Bridled Tern	*Sterna anaethetus*
Sooty Tern	*Sterna fuscata*
Little Tern	*Sterna albifrons*
Whiskered Tern	*Chlidonias hybridus*
Black Tern	*Chlidonias niger*
White-winged Black Tern	*Chlidonias leucopterus*
Guillemot	*Uria aalge*
Razorbill	*Alca torda*
Black Guillemot	*Cepphus grylle*
Little Auk	*Alle alle*
Puffin	*Fratercula arctica*
Feral Pigeon	*Columba livia*
Stock Dove	*Columba oenas*
Woodpigeon	*Columba palumbus*
Collared Dove	*Streptopelia decaocto*
Turtle Dove	*Streptopelia turtur*
Great Spotted Cuckoo	*Clamator glandarius*
Cuckoo	*Cuculus canorus*
Barn Owl	*Tyto alba*
Snowy Owl	*Nyctea scandiaca*
Little Owl	*Athene noctua*

Species Included in this Guide

Tawny Owl	*Strix aluco*
Long-eared Owl	*Asio otus*
Short-eared Owl	*Asio flammeus*
Nightjar	*Caprimulgus europaeus*
Swift	*Apus apus*
Alpine Swift	*Apus melba*
Kingfisher	*Alcedo atthis*
Bee-eater	*Merops apiaster*
Hoopoe	*Upupa epops*
Wryneck	*Jynx torquilla*
Green Woodpecker	*Picus viridis*
Great Spotted Woodpecker	*Dendrocopos major*
Lesser Spotted Woodpecker	*Dendrocopos minor*
Short-toed Lark	*Calandrella brachydactyla*
Woodlark	*Lullula arborea*
Skylark	*Alauda arvensis*
Shore Lark	*Eremophila alpestris*
Sand Martin	*Riparia riparia*
Swallow	*Hirundo rustica*
Red-rumped Swallow	*Hirundo daurica*
House Martin	*Delichon urbica*
Richard's Pipit	*Anthus novaeseelandiae*
Tawny Pipit	*Anthus campestris*
Olive-backed Pipit	*Anthus hodgsoni*
Tree Pipit	*Anthus trivialis*
Meadow Pipit	*Anthus pratensis*
Red-throated Pipit	*Anthus cervinus*
Rock Pipit	*Anthus petrosus*
Water Pipit	*Anthus spinoletta*
Yellow Wagtail	*Montacilla flava*
Citrine Wagtail	*Montacilla citreola*
Grey Wagtail	*Montacilla cinerea*
Pied Wagtail	*Montacilla alba*
Waxwing	*Bombycilla garrulus*
Dipper	*Cinclus cinclus*
Wren	*Troglodytes troglodytes*
Dunnock	*Prunella modularis*
Alpine Accentor	*Prunella collaris*
Robin	*Erithacus rubecula*
Thrush Nightingale	*Luscinia luscinia*
Nightingale	*Luscinia megarhynchos*
Bluethroat	*Luscinia svecica*
Red-flanked Bluetail	*Tarsiger cyanurus*
Black Redstart	*Phoenicurus ochruros*
Redstart	*Phoenicurus phoenicurus*
Whinchat	*Saxicola rubetra*
Stonechat	*Saxicola torquata*
Northern Wheatear	*Oenanthe oenanthe*
Desert Wheatear	*Oenanthe deserti*
Ring Ouzel	*Turdus torquatus*
Blackbird	*Turdus merula*
Fieldfare	*Turdus pilaris*
Song Thrush	*Turdus philomelus*
Redwing	*Turdus iliacus*
Mistle Thrush	*Turdus viscivorus*
Lanceolated Warbler	*Locustella lanceolata*
Grasshopper Warbler	*Locustella naevia*
Savi's Warbler	*Locustella luscinioides*
Aquatic Warbler	*Acrocephalus paludicola*
Sedge Warbler	*Acrocephalus schoenobaenus*
Blyth's Reed Warbler	*Acrocephalus dumetorum*
Marsh Warbler	*Acrocephalus palustris*
Reed Warbler	*Acrocephalus scirpaceus*
Great Reed Warbler	*Acrocephalus arundinaceus*
Booted Warbler	*Hippolais caligata*
Icterine Warbler	*Hippolais icterina*
Dartford Warbler	*Sylvia undata*
Subalpine Warbler	*Sylvia cantillans*

Species Included in this Guide

Sardinian Warbler	*Sylvia melanocephala*
Barred Warbler	*Sylvia nisoria*
Lesser Whitethroat	*Sylvia curruca*
Whitethroat	*Sylvia communis*
Garden Warbler	*Sylvia borin*
Blackcap	*Sylvia atricapilla*
Greenish Warbler	*Phylloscopus trochiloides*
Arctic Warbler	*Phylloscopus borealis*
Pallas's Warbler	*Phylloscopus proregulus*
Yellow-browed Warbler	*Phylloscopus inornatus*
Radde's Warbler	*Phylloscopus schwarzi*
Dusky Warbler	*Phylloscopus fuscatus*
Wood Warbler	*Phylloscopus sibilatrix*
Chiffchaff	*Phylloscopus collybita*
Willow Warbler	*Phylloscopus trochilus*
Goldcrest	*Regulus regulus*
Firecrest	*Regulus ignicapillus*
Spotted Flycatcher	*Muscicapa striata*
Red-breasted Flycatcher	*Ficedula parva*
Pied Flycatcher	*Ficedula hypoleuca*
Bearded Tit	*Panurus biarmicus*
Long-tailed Tit	*Aegithalos caudatus*
Marsh Tit	*Parus palustris*
Willow Tit	*Parus montanus*
Coal Tit	*Parus ater*
Blue Tit	*Parus caeruleus*
Great Tit	*Parus major*
Nuthatch	*Sitta europaea*
Treecreeper	*Certhia familiaris*
Golden Oriole	*Oriolus oriolus*
Isabelline Shrike	*Lanius isabellinus*
Red-backed Shrike	*Lanius collurio*
Lesser Grey Shrike	*Lanius minor*
Great Grey Shrike	*Lanius excubitor*
Woodchat Shrike	*Lanius senator*
Jay	*Garrulus glandarius*
Magpie	*Pica pica*
Nutcracker	*Nucifraga caryocatactes*
Jackdaw	*Corvus monedula*
Rook	*Corvus frugilegus*
Carrion Crow	*Corvus corone*
Raven	*Corvus corax*
Starling	*Sturnus vulgaris*
Rose-coloured Starling	*Sturnus roseus*
House Sparrow	*Passer domesticus*
Tree Sparrow	*Passer montanus*
Chaffinch	*Fringilla coelebs*
Brambling	*Fringilla montifringilla*
Serin	*Serinus serinus*
Greenfinch	*Carduelis chloris*
Goldfinch	*Carduelis carduelis*
Siskin	*Carduelis spinus*
Linnet	*Carduelis cannabina*
Twite	*Carduelis flavirostris*
Redpoll	*Carduelis flammea*
Arctic Redpoll	*Carduelis hornemanni*
Two-barred Crossbill	*Loxia leucoptera*
Common Crossbill	*Loxia curvirostra*
Parrot Crossbill	*Loxia pytyopsittacus*
Common Rosefinch	*Carpodacus erythrinus*
Bullfinch	*Pyrrhula pyrrhula*
Hawfinch	*Coccothraustes coccothraustes*
American Redstart	*Setophaga riticilla*
Northern Waterthrush	*Seiurus noveboracensis*
White-throated Sparrow	*Zonotrichia albicollis*
Lapland Bunting	*Calcarius lapponicus*
Snow Bunting	*Plectrophenax nivalis*
Yellowhammer	*Emberiza citrinella*

Species Included in this Guide

Ortolan Bunting	*Emberiza hortulana*
Rustic Bunting	*Emberiza rustica*
Little Bunting	*Emberiza pusilla*
Yellow-breasted Bunting	*Emberiza aureola*
Reed Bunting	*Emberiza schoeniclus*
Black-headed Bunting	*Emberiza melanocephala*
Corn Bunting	*Miliaria calandra*

CODE OF CONDUCT FOR
BIRDWATCHERS

Today's birdwatchers are a powerful force for nature conservation. The number of those of us interested in birds rises continually and it is vital that we take seriously our responsibility to avoid any harm to birds.

We must also present a responsible image to non-birdwatchers who may be affected by our activities and particularly those on whose sympathy and support the future of birds may rest.

There are 10 points to bear in mind:
1. The welfare of birds must come first.
2. Habitat must be protected.
3. Keep disturbance to birds and their habitat to a minimum.
4. When you find a rare bird think carefully about whom you should tell.
5. Do not harass rare migrants.
6. Abide by the bird protection laws at all times.
7. Respect the rights of landowners.
8. Respect the rights of other people in the countryside.
9. Make your records available to the local bird recorder.
10. Behave abroad as you would when birdwatching at home.

Welfare of birds must come first
Whether your particular interest is photography, ringing, sound recording, scientific study or just birdwatching, remember that the welfare of the bird must always come first.

Habitat protection
Its habitat is vital to a bird and therefore we must ensure that our activities do not cause damage.

Keep disturbance to a minimum
Birds' tolerance of disturbance varies between species and seasons. Therefore, it is safer to keep all disturbance to a minimum. No birds should be disturbed from the nest in case opportunities for predators to take eggs or young are increased. In very cold weather disturbance to birds may cause them to use vital energy at a time when food is difficult to find. Wildfowlers already impose bans during cold weather: birdwatchers should exercise similar discretion.

Rare breeding birds
If you discover a rare bird breeding and feel that protection is necessary, inform the appropriate RSPB Regional Office, or the Species Protection Department at the Lodge. Otherwise it is best in almost all circumstances to keep the record strictly secret in order to avoid disturbance by other birdwatchers and attacks by egg-collectors. Never visit known sites of rare breeding birds unless they are adequately protected. Even your presence may give away the site to others and cause so many other visitors that the birds may fail to breed successfully.

Disturbance at or near the nest of species listed on the First Schedule of the Wildlife and Countryside Act 1981 is a criminal offence.

Copies of Wild Birds and the Law are obtainable from the RSPB, The Lodge, Sandy, Beds. SG19 2DL (send two 2nd class stamps).

Rare migrants

Rare migrants or vagrants must not be harassed. If you discover one, consider the circumstances carefully before telling anyone. Will an influx of birdwatchers disturb the bird or others in the area? Will the habitat be damaged? Will problems be caused with the landowner?

The Law

The bird protection laws (now embodied in the Wildlife and Countryside Act 1981) are the result of hard campaigning by previous generations of birdwatchers. As birdwatchers we must abide by them at all times and not allow them to fall into disrepute.

Respect the rights of landowners

The wishes of landowners and occupiers of land must be respected. Do not enter land without permission. Comply with permit schemes. If you are leading a group, do give advance notice of the visit, even if a formal permit scheme is not in operation. Always obey the Country Code.

Respect the rights of other people

Have proper consideration for other birdwatchers. Try not to disrupt their activities or scare the birds they are watching. There are many other people who also use the countryside. Do not interfere with their activities and, if it seems that what they are doing is causing unnecessary disturbance to birds, do try to take a balanced view. Flushing gulls when walking a dog on a beach may do little harm, while the same dog might be a serious disturbance at a tern colony. When pointing this out to a non-birdwatcher be courteous, but firm. The non-birdwatchers' goodwill towards birds must not be destroyed by the attitudes of birdwatchers.

Keeping records

Much of today's knowledge about birds is the result of meticulous record keeping by our predecessors. Make sure you help to add to tomorrow's knowledge by sending records to your county bird recorder.

Birdwatching abroad

Behave abroad as you would at home. This code should be firmly adhered to when abroad (whatever the local laws). Well behaved birdwatchers can be important ambassadors for bird protection.

This code has been drafted after consultation between The British Ornithologists' Union, British Trust for Ornithology, the Royal Society for the Protection of Birds, the Scottish Ornithologists' Club, the Wildfowl Trust and the Editors of *British Birds*.

Further copies may be obtained from The Royal Society for the Protection of Birds, The Lodge, Sandy, Beds. SG19 2DL.

INDEX OF SPECIES

Site number references are given here. Species mentioned in the Additional Sites sections are not included.